FORSAKE FEAR

The author's family photographs (*clockwise from top left*): mother Fanny Nekrich (1890–1975), father Moisei Isidorovich Nekrich (1884–1965), and brother Captain Vladimir Nekrich (1916–1943)

Forsake Fear

Memoirs of an Historian

Aleksandr Nekrich
Translated by Donald Lineburgh

Boston
UNWIN HYMAN
London   Sydney   Wellington

Unwin Hyman, Inc.
955 Massachusetts Avenue, Cambridge, MA 02139, USA

Published by the Academic Division of
Unwin Hyman Ltd
15/17 Broadwick Street, London W1V 1FP, UK

Allen & Unwin (Australia) Ltd
8 Napier Street, North Sydney, NSW 2060, Australia

Allen & Unwin (New Zealand) Ltd
in association with the Port Nicholson Press Ltd
Compusales Building, 75 Ghuznee Street, Wellington 1, New Zealand

First published in 1991

Cover photograph: Captain Aleksandr Nekrich in East Prussia, May 20, 1945. Provided by the author.

Library of Congress Cataloging-in-Publication Data

Nekrich, A. M. (Aleksandr Moiseevich)
  [Otreshis' ot strakha. English]
  Forsake fear : memoirs of an historian / Aleksandr Nekrich : translated by Donald Lineburgh.
        p   cm
  Translation of: Otreshis' ot strakha.
  Includes index.
  ISBN 0–04–445682–4   : $29.92
  1. Nekrich, A. M. (Aleksandr Moiseevich). 2. Historians—Russian S.F.S.R.—Biography. 3. Jews, Russian—Biography. I. Title.
  DK38.N36A3 1991
  947.084'092—dc20
  [B]   90–41182
                                                                    CIP

British Library Cataloguing in Publication Data

Nekrich, Aleksandr 1920–
  Forsake fear : memoirs of an historian.
  1. Historiography. Nekrich, Aleksandr, 1920–
  I. Title
  907.202

  ISBN 0–04–445682–4

Typset in Garamond 10 on 12 and printed by
The University Press, Cambridge

Contents

Preface

The time has now arrived for remembrances. I am fifty-two years of age. I can already feel the inexorable passage of time. It can be measured in smaller and smaller units: at first there was eternity; next there were decades, then years; and now the count goes by months, weeks, days, until eternity comes once again.

It has been five years since my official duties began to diminish. My study on the history of British foreign policy has been lying idle for three years now, approved by specialists, confirmed for publication by the academic council of the Institute of History and held up by the editorial publications board of the USSR Academy of Sciences. My protests have gone unheeded. I have no graduate students, since my superiors believe that I have nothing worthwhile to teach them.

Occasionally, once every year or two, they permit an article of mine to appear in the small-circulation publication of the institute, and all my colleagues congratulate me with the joyful enthusiasm usually reserved for a pupil who was kept back and has finally made it to the next grade.

I am thoroughly fed up with all of this.

So in order not to die of premature sclerosis, and also, of course, for the edification of those who may wish to read this manuscript, I have taken pen in hand—or, rather, I have sat down at the typewriter, after cleaning the keys and inserting a new ribbon. If I remain in good health, if the typewriter doesn't break, if typing paper is available at the store . . . well, then, I shall try to tell, as truthfully as possible, of events in which I have been a participant and to which I have been a witness over the past quarter-century, that is, since the end of the Second World War.

I am aware that I shall relate neither all events nor all their participants, since the majority of the latter live in the Soviet Union and I am afraid of harming them inadvertently. But I wish to mention warmly my friends and acquaintances, even without giving their names. May they not take my silence to be an offense.

Moscow, 1972

Preface to the English Language Edition

It is said in the Bible that to everything there is a season. This is, no doubt, the case. This book, *Forsake Fear*, now being introduced to the English-speaking reader, was written about fifteen years ago; it was first published in a Russian-language edition in London in 1979, three years after I had left Moscow. Only isolated copies of it reached the Soviet Union. In 1983 an edition was prepared in West Germany. And now is the time for an English-language edition. It is the height of paradox that, at this very moment, a Russian edition is being proposed for the Soviet Union, and a sizable edition at that. Well, as the French say, "Qui vivra, verra" ("Time will tell"). I have mixed feelings about this: I would like my fellow countrymen to read my work, of course, but I am pleased that the Western reader will have that opportunity as well.

I have made one addition to the original version: the story of a friend of mine who lived in Moscow at that time—Donald Maclean. For understandable reasons, I could not write about him in 1979. But since his death in March 1983, nothing more can harm him. I have also clarified some facts, but on the whole I have not tampered with the text, leaving it essentially as it appeared in the first edition. I think the translation itself has turned out rather well; the translator has preserved the nuances of the Russian and the ideas of the author.

It is my hope that the book will be of interest not only to those whose profession it is to deal with the history and culture of Russia, but also to a broader circle of readers, those whose curiosity has been aroused by perestroika and the Gorbachev phenomenon. I am convinced that readers will discover, on reading *Forsake Fear*, a surprising similarity between the events of the 1950s and 1960s and those taking place in the Soviet Union today, even though there certainly exists an enormous qualitative difference between them. I myself felt this while spending the winter of 1989–90 in Moscow.

February 1990
Cambridge, Massachusetts

If you are a man, then be one,
for you have no other choice.

Jerzy Lec

1
The Return

From East Prussia to Moscow — Maisky's graduate student — at the Institute of History — a cold war rages within the country — Yakov Kharon and Guillaume de Vauntray — Mandel' appears — poetry, poetry — We're drowning! — the Karaite Gokhan Khadzhi-Sarai Shapshal

In the first few days of August 1945, at the platform marked "Bezymyanka" at the Riga railway station, a troop train in from East Prussia disembarked. The field command of the Second Guards Army had arrived in Moscow. According to a high-level decision, staff officers and those in the political department of the army were to supplement the staff and political command of the Moscow military district. For now we were being sent to the Aleshinsky barracks, not far from the Stalin automobile factory.

The Muscovites were lucky, for we were returning home!

I spent a month in semibarracks status, passing the nights at home, wandering about Moscow, meeting with friends, and appearing at the barracks only for morning inspection. Gradually the barracks began to empty out: some men had already been assigned to new jobs, while others received leave and rushed back home. I submitted a report requesting demobilization. Finally, my wish to return to the hustle and bustle of the civilian world was fulfilled. By order of Glavpur; the political directorate of the Soviet army, on September 7, 1945, Guards Captain Aleksandr Moiseevich Nekrich was transferred to the reserves.

I was in my twenty-sixth year. Ever since the war had ended for our army—a few days after Königsberg was taken in mid-April 1945—I had been languishing at the East Prussian spa of Rauschen, where our army staff was stationed. In my mind I was already home. I dreamt of studying, for I wished to be a student. It seemed I could pore over books twenty-four hours a day without stopping.

Yet sometimes I felt a nostalgic sadness—for my older brother, Vova, killed in 1943; for fellow students from the university who had not returned from the war; for Run'ka Rozenberg and his brother Os'ka, or Misha Pollak and others. I remembered comrades in the political department who had been killed—Captain Sedov, Captain Lokhin, Lieutenant-Colonel Glinsky—the senseless death of Shura Averkieva (a stray bullet from a sudden pistol shot killed her instantly as she slept—that was in Lithuania in 1944), and the similar accidental death of the political department driver Tcheremisin.

I dreamt about the war. At night I would suddenly awake as if from the roar of dive-bombers and the explosion of bombs. I would jump up—but all around me there was silence, for the war was over, and I was home. For several years I had the same dream: I am walking in a village, when all of a sudden German attack planes are flying over me at low altitude. I roll head over heels into a ditch. I raise myself up a bit and see explosions of sand coming closer and closer . . . And then a sharp blow to the head. Everything is quiet. I get up and feel my head. There is a huge hole on the right side. I close my hand over it and wander along the street. I arrive at the medical unit and go in. Two doctors are having a lively conversation. On seeing me they rise, come closer, put me on a stretcher, and stick a rag soaking with chloroform under my nose. In a daze I hear the voice of one of the doctors: "He's going to die now." At that very second blood gushes from my throat and ears. In my dream I suffer the classic death. But suddenly a bright light begins to glow. I open my eyes. The same hut, the same two doctors, chatting calmly together. "So, doctor, I didn't die after all," I say joyfully. The doctors turn around and look at me in surprise. This dream would repeat itself over and over again. Then it disappeared, just as the drone of the planes and the explosion of bombs disappeared without a trace. And along with them, the war gradually receded and was no longer a part of the real world.

I did not feel like a hero out of Remarque or Hemingway. I did not believe that my youth was coming to an end. Indeed, it seemed to me that my years of being young would last for a long, long time to come. In short, I was enjoying life, and I entered what seemed an endless round of encounters, wild parties, and fun. From early youth I had loved the theater and cinema. Now I became a habitué of assorted premieres, dress rehearsals, previews, closed film screenings, and concerts. My circle of acquaintances, especially passing ones, expanded enormously. But my circle of close friends remained rather narrow, as it had been in my childhood and adolescence.

Social life, however, was not my major concern after returning from the war. Immediately after my release from the army, I decided to enter graduate school (at the beginning of the war I had graduated from Moscow State University with a degree in history). First, of course, I went to the history department at the university, but I didn't like the atmosphere there. Someone advised me to stop in at the Institute of History of the USSR Academy of Sciences on Volkhonka Street. It had been a dream of mine ever since childhood to become a diplomat, but by now I had gotten over it. I remembered that back in 1940 my older brother, a student in the geography department at Moscow State University, was thinking about enrolling in the Academy for Foreign Trade, but the secretary of the Komsomol organization from whom he had requested a recommendation explained to him in a comradely way that the academy accepted only party members—and, he emphasized, only ethnic Russians.

At the end of the war I had heard rumors that a political worker had been either demoted or not promoted because of his Jewish origins. But, I must confess, I did not want to think about it at the time, especially since I myself had never experienced any overt form of anti-Semitism. The Institute of History had two graduate-level vacancies in the department of modern history and current events, and I was received there quite cordially. (I suspect my military uniform and medals played some part in this.) Entry into graduate school at that time required two recommendations from professors with whom the candidate had studied. I asked professors S. V. Bakhrushin and V. M. Khvostov, both of whom willingly complied with my request.

When I arrived to get my recommendation from Khvostov (he had just been named director of the Higher Diplomatic School), I had to sit in the waiting room for an hour and a half, and this irritated me a great deal. I was the last to be called in, even though I had been the first to arrive! Professor Khvostov was guided by another principle other than first come, first served: the importance of either the matter or the person being kept waiting. Naturally, I was the last by both these criteria. I was to recall this episode frequently in the years to come when I saw how many employees at the Institute of History had to sit for hours on end in the waiting room of the director—Academician V. M. Khvostov. At last he received me warmly, made an excellent recommendation, and even told me he was sorry that he could not accept me as a student at the Higher Diplomatic School since "admissions were already closed." "Jews need not apply," I remember was the remark from the film *The Dream* by Mikhail Rohm. And they don't bother to apply, I thought to myself, borrowing another phrase from the same film, and sauntered out.

There was very little time left—only a month and a half—before the graduate entrance exams. Not only was I facing the prospect of an exam in my areas of specialization—that is, in modern history and current events in the West and German language—but also, in accordance with the rules at the time, it was necessary to pass a minimum entrance requirement in philosophy. About twenty days before the exams I realized that there was hardly any time left to study philosophy. Feeling desperate, I and went to the secretary of the social sciences division, Academician V. P. Volgin, to ask for permission to take the exam later. I gave my name to the secretary Debora Petrovna Rykovskaya, a pretty, pleasant woman who, sadly, died of cancer not long after. Soon there emerged from the office a stout, ruddy, cheerful man who asked me was I not the son of the journalist Moisei Isidorovich Nekrich, who in the 1930s had worked in the foreign department of the newspaper *Economic Life*. I confirmed this. "I worked with your father there. My name is Vladimir Vladimirovich Al'tman," said the cheerful man. "Why do you wish to see Vyacheslav Petrovich? I am his aide." I told him. Al'tman dissuaded me from making such a request and with a chuckle and a firm handshake, suggested that I make every effort to pass all my exams. Later on I would frequently remember V. V. Al'tman with gratitude.

I received a "4" in philosophy, having scored fourteen out of fifteen points, and was admitted to graduate school in the department of modern history and current events. I decided to specialize in current events in Great Britain. Sergei Vladimirovich Zakharov was named my academic adviser.

The winter of 1945–46 was a difficult one for me. I suddenly came down with various annoying minor ailments: apparently this was the body's delayed reaction to the stress of the war years. My ill health was compounded by family problems, leading, at the end of 1946, to a break with my wife. I went back to live with my parents in our one-room basement apartment at 26/1 Gorky Street at the corner of Staropimenovsky Lane (now called Medvedev Street), where we had lived since 1926. There had been four of us before the war; now there were only three.

My academic adviser, S. V. Zakharov, met with me only twice. He was a very busy man, since he worked in the party Central Committee apparatus and, in addition, taught in the Higher Party School. He struck me as a kindly and decent person. But when Sergei Vladimirovich died suddenly at a relatively young age, I was left without an adviser. After several months had gone by, the department head, Academician Abram Moiseevich Deborin, said to me, "Well, you're going to have a real Englishman as an adviser," but he refused to name him, only casting a playful glance at me from behind the lenses of his spectacles. A short time later a man in diplomatic uniform with a marshal's star on his shoulder boards, thickset, almost bald, with a small, black, pointed beard, came to a department meeting. Many recognized him from photographs. This was Ivan Mikhailovich Maisky, the well-known diplomat, our ambassador to London, who had just been elected to the Academy. Deborin presented him to the department staff as their new colleague. Then, after the meeting, Deborin introduced me to Maisky as his graduate student. This is how we began our acquaintance, which gradually developed into a friendly relationship that continued up until his death in August 1975.

The department of modern history and current events, where I was a graduate student until May 1949, comprised a group of scholars—both Western and Asian specialists—many of whom in the postwar years published basic studies which were to become a permanent part of Soviet historiography and world scholarship. But the atmosphere in the department was tense; the collective was torn by group interests and squabbling. As its head, Deborin was undoubtedly an outstanding scholar but an exceptionally weak individual, incapable of controlling obstinate staff members, each of whom was firmly individualistic. Furthermore, he had lost out in more than one dispute and this experience had led him to show caution and even inertia when decisive and imaginative action was required. Deborin was also burdened in those years with many academic duties: he served as deputy chairman of the editorial and publishing board of the USSR Academy of Sciences, editor of the *Academy of Sciences Herald,* and in other similar capacities. But since 1931, this man, who had been denounced as a "Menshevistic idealist," had been barred from the field he loved, and in which he was most gifted.

Deborin was one of the most erudite Russian Marxists. His real name was Abram Moiseevich Ioffe; Deborin, at first his pseudonym, later became part of his family name. He was born in 1881 in Kaunas, Lithuania, of a poor Jewish family. In his youth Deborin trained to be a metalworker. In 1897, at the age of sixteen, he became a fixture in illegal Marxist circles. Persecuted by the tsarist police, he left Russia in 1930. During his years in exile in Switzerland, he graduated from Bern University, where he became a close friend of G. V. Plekhanov, the father of Russian Marxism, and shared many of his views. Deborin returned to Russia in 1908 and took an active part in the struggle against tsarism. During the 1917 Revolution he served for a short time as chairman of the city soviet in the Ukrainian town of Poltava.

Deborin, who was a Menshevik in his political views, joined the Communist party (Bolsheviks) in the 1920s at the suggestion of S. Ordzhonikidze, who gave him a recommendation. *Introduction to the Philosophy of Dialectical Materialism,* Deborin's best-known work, which went through many editions and was translated into several languages, was written in 1916, just before the Revolution. From 1922 into the 1930s he edited the central theoretical organ of the Communist party, *Under the Banner of Marxism.* These were halcyon days for Deborin. He taught at the Sverdlov Communist University in Moscow, at the Institute of Red Professorship, and in the Communist Academy and worked as deputy director of the Marx and Engels Institute. He was becoming the most authoritative figure in Marxist philosophy. Deborin the orthodox Marxist helped to crush various "heretical" trends in Soviet Marxist philosophy, such as the Mechanist movement and others. He fought them quite ruthlessly on the theoretical front, perhaps not even realizing that accusations of heresy might have tragic consequences for the personal fate of those who held Mechanist views.

In 1929 Deborin, together with a group of other Communist social scientists, including D. B. Ryazanov, was elected a member of the Academy of Sciences. Henceforth, the Academy would quickly come under the influence of the party, to which it was completely subordinate. Subsequently Deborin would occupy high-ranking positions in the academic hierarchy, even after his work had been ostracized.

The next generation of philosophers—M. B. Mitin, P. F. Yudin, Ralzevich, I. K. Luppol, Ia. E. Sten—were all Deborin's pupils. The first two became close ideological supporters of Stalin, while the remaining three disappeared in the purges. In fact, Sten used to teach Marxist dialectics to Stalin and word had it that he was not very satisfied with his pupil's progress.

The decisive turning point in Deborin's fate was his refusal in 1930 to proclaim Stalin the master of philosophical science and leader of the philosophical front. Deborin related this story to me himself during our many confidential talks.

In the summer of 1930, he told me, his pupils Yudin, Mitin, and Ralzevich came to him and complained that some of his pupils (I. K. Luppol, for example, by now an academician) were linked to the Trotskyites, and that Deborin should vigorously dissociate himself from them. The term *dissociate* was quite popular in the party lexicon at the time and has not lost its significance to this day. In short, Deborin was being urged to betray his pupils. Abram Moiseevich was astounded, since he was certain that Luppol was no Trotskyite. He replied that he had no grounds for repudiating or denouncing Luppol or his other pupils.

But this was not the main point of the conversation. Yudin, Mitin, and Ralzevich then tried to convince Deborin that Stalin was not only the leader in all practical party activities but also a major theorist of Marxist philosophy. "Who better than you, a universally respected Marxist philosopher, to state this openly and proclaim Comrade Stalin leader of the philosophical front?" they asked. "But," Deborin answered naively, "Stalin has not written any work on philosophy."

The confrontation went on for nearly three hours. As they left, Yudin, Mitin, and Ralzevich once again asked Deborin to think about what they had advised him to do: renounce his Trotskyite pupils and proclaim Stalin head of the philosophical front. "Then, Abram Moiseevich, you will always remain our beloved and respected teacher."

Deborin was puzzled. Very soon afterwards, at a regular meeting with the head of the agitation department of the party Central Committee A. I. Stetsky, Deborin was to hear something that recalled what he had been told by Yudin, Mitin, and Ralzevich. "Things here have reached the point," Stetsky told him frankly, "where we will have only one leader, one chief in both practice and theory. There cannot be two chiefs in the party."

Later I heard more of this story, which seemed to me reasonably truthful, although of course I have never, either then or now, been absolutely certain. According to this account Deborin, who thought highly of Stalin as a man of action, unintentionally compared him with Friedrich Engels. Deborin sent Stalin a letter in which, recalling the great collaboration between Engels and Marx, he proposed to Stalin the same kind of collaboration with himself. It was said that Stalin, on reading this, snorted, "Again I'm being compared to Engels!" Stalin was not one to reject comparisons with Marx, but he would not agree to play Engels to anyone. This half-joke is meant as a psychological insight into the man Stalin and the thinking of Deborin himself.

Whatever the case may be, Deborin refused to proclaim Stalin a genius of Marxist philosophy, and he was to pay dearly for it. Stetsky's prediction soon came true. Deborin's former pupils, Yudin, Mitin, and Ralzevich, issued a strongly worded article in which they called for a campaign against any deviation from the party line. Soon Deborin was being declared a "Menshevistic idealist." This term in itself was meaningless, since if Deborin was to be considered a Menshevik, he could hardly be an idealist in philosophical terms, since the Mensheviks were a Marxist party and had always based their beliefs on Marxist philosophy.

But here Stalin had devised a very clever scheme: he combined the two most hated concepts in the Communist party of the Soviet Union—idealism and Menshevism. No one could ever explain what the epithet meant, but after 1931 articles began to appear denouncing Deborin and his "school." In one of the latest editions of the *Philosophical Dictionary* the term *Menshevistic idealist* is not even to be found, but it does state about A. M. Deborin that he and his group "underestimated the Leninist stage in the development of Marxist philosophy, and insufficiently emphasized the basic opposition of Marxist and Hegelian dialectics." Rather inoffensive words, in sharp contrast to the condemnations leveled at "Menshevistic idealism" in Stalinist times.

After Deborin was declared a "Menshevistic idealist," he was completely barred from philosophy. Although he was to retain his position as academician, on which he depended entirely as a means of support, he was deprived of the opportunity to pursue the study of philosophy. Publication of his books was banned. Many of his pupils perished in the terror of the 1930s, among them such talented people as the academician and philosopher I. K. Luppol, the well-known biologist and one of the leaders of the Bavarian Soviet Republic Max Levin, and the physicist E. M. Gessen.

In Deborin's office I used to see piles of his unpublished manuscripts, accumulated over twenty-five years of ostracism. Abram Moiseevich, however, did not lose hope. His sharp, scholarly mind was eager for action. In the years before the Second World War he wrote a number of articles on the history of German Fascist ideology. But after the war, when he attempted to publish a large work on the same subject, it went no further than the proofreader. The book never saw the light of day. During the war Deborin helped set up the program of the Academy of Sciences, and afterwards he held a number of posts in the Academy. Gradually, however, he declined in importance and finally was made an ordinary senior scholar at the Academy's Institute of History.

Organizational matters in the department were actually handled by the academic secretary, a woman with strong personal preferences who not only did not oppose petty squabbling but was actually behind one of the quarreling groups. It so happened that during elections for department party organizer, the conflicting parties agreed on me as a candidate. My status as a graduate student suited them since I was dependent on them and I was an outsider to all disputes. Each of the parties hoped to subject me to its influence. It took a great deal of effort to stop the bickering. Finally, Abram Moiseevich suggested that I serve as academic secretary, even though I was still a graduate student. So it was that I found myself unexpectedly in the thick of institute affairs.

At that time (1946–47) the Institute of History was small (not more than 150 people), but it had a highly qualified staff. At the head of the institute was Academician B. D. Grekov, an acknowledged authority on the history of Russian feudalism and Slavic studies, a field represented by such outstanding scholars as S. V. Bakhrushin, S. K. Bogoyavlensky, N. M. Druzhinin, M. V. Nechkina, and V. I. Picheta. Under the guidance of these scholars there emerged a whole constellation of able historians who were graduate students or doctoral candidates in the Institute of History at the time. It was here that the staff of the future Institute for Slavic Studies was formed, headed by Academician V. I. Picheta. A strong point in the activity of the Russian side of our academic staff was the publication of documents and source materials. Specialists on the West included academicians E. A. Kosminsky, C. D. Skaskin, A. S. Yerusalimsky, L. I. Zubok, A. Z. Manfred, S. B. Kahn, B. F. Porshnev, F. O. Notovich, V. M. Turok-Popov, and others. Specialists on the East were A. F. Miller, G. N. Voytinsky, V. B. Lutsky, and A. N. Kisilev. Many of the institute staff had just returned from the front, while others had come back from being evacuated. People had missed their usual work in the archives and libraries. Gradually everything was being restored, and life, it seemed, was settling into a normal routine. I say "it seemed," for the thunderous harbingers of ideological storms to come were gathering on the horizon.

A year after the end of the Second World War, the cold war was already at its height. Very quickly the cold war atmosphere began to spread to the ideological sphere as well. The campaign against bourgeois ideology and its infiltration among Soviet scholars was high on the agenda. The "turning of the screw" in the ideological sphere was due not only to the sharp aggravation in relations between the Soviet Union and its former partners in the anti-Hitler coalition, but also to the internal political situation. The devastating war, bringing with it the Fascist occupation of large areas in the European part of the country, untold human suffering, and huge material losses, had taken its toll. The hardships were enormous. While many, especially among the intelligentsia, were prepared to make sacrifices, they also hoped for change, for a democratization of society. The war had broken down borders and torn down barriers which had so reliably protected the soul of the Soviet people from "contamination" by capitalist infection.

The Soviet army had entered Europe, bringing liberation to its peoples enslaved by Hitler. Hitler's followers, the Fascists, were a clearly perceived enemy. They committed atrocities, they tortured, burned, and killed. The death camps of Treblinka, Auschwitz, Mauthausen, and Dachau lay before the liberating soldiers. Not just seeing but actually breathing in this hell was difficult. At last the soldiers of the anti-Nazi coalition returned home, rightly convinced that they had rid the world of barbarism, of the Fascist plague. But in addition to Fascist atrocities, many thousands and thousands of Soviet soldiers and officers saw something that they had never known of previously. Reality did not always coincide with their conception of this world which was so alien to them, about which they had known only from hearsay, from radio and newspapers, from school textbooks and films. This world had more variety. It was not painted just in shades of black and white. There were many colors, and even more nuances.

The Soviet troops, of course, had not just seen the death camps and the smoking ruins. They had fraternized with American soldiers on the Elbe, exchanged friendly embraces with the French and Belgians, and kissed and hugged their Slavic brothers the Bulgarians. Quite naturally they were inquisitive about how these people lived, and they took a careful look for themselves. The horizons of those who had taken part in the foreign campaigns at the end of the Second World War thus broadened immeasurably. And once they were back home, rightly proud of their victory, they recalled time and again those countries they had visited, and told their different stories. Their feelings were similar to those of the young officers who had returned to Russia after the foreign campaign of 1815.

Nineteen forty-seven also marked the end of the ten-year term in prison or in labor camp for many who had been sentenced in the purges of 1937, and they began to be released. The front door would open and in would walk fathers, brothers, wives, sisters, those for whom there had been little hope of returning, for they were "enemies of the people." Many kept silent about the horrible suffering they had endured: some were afraid; some simply did not wish to remember, hoping to put the memory behind them as quickly as possible and return to normal life. But stories of terrible places—about concentration camps in Kolyma, where thousands had died, overcome by backbreaking labor or executed for "sabotage" (that is, for being too weak to fulfill work requirements)—spread throughout the country. People whispered together, into one another's ears, their words muffled by music on the radio or water rushing from the faucet. But soon those who had served their sentence were being arrested again and sent back, this time forever. The "error" committed by the authorities in releasing them had been corrected.

In 1947 the father of Pavel Butyagin, a chemist whom I had met through my friend Zhora Fedorov after returning from the front, arrived from Kolyma. The elder Butyagin had been gone for ten years and was now back. He was an old Bolshevik, a member of the underground. During the Civil War Yury Butyagin commanded the Eleventh Army (party leader S. M. Kirov was a member of this army's Revolutionary Military Soviet, or Revvoensoviet). During peacetime he became prominent in economic affairs. A man of immaculate reputation, intelligent and cheerful, he had been transformed, as if by magic, like hundreds of thousands of others, into an enemy of the people. He received the longest sentence given those who were not executed outright: ten years. He had come back, unbroken. But then one night they came for him at his home, apartment 21, 25 Kolobovsky Lane, and they took him away. He died soon afterwards at the Kazan' prison hospital.

In that same year, 1947, I met Yasha Kharon, a scriptwriter, musician, and sound engineer who had served a ten-year term in Siberia. He was nineteen when he was arrested and accused of planning a terrorist act. He landed first in prison, then in camp, and then worked in a factory. Yury Vainer, a friend of his from prison, arrived along with him.

They were unusually talented people. They had composed in prison and brought with them a small volume of sonnets, refined, clever, and deeply poetic. They attributed these sonnets to a supposed Frenchman, Guillaume de Vauntray (who in fact had never existed), a Huguenot who had supposedly lived at the time of the League and Henry of Navarre. Kharon was planning to return to the Sverdlovsk Film Studios, where he was to work after his release. Vainer stayed on in Moscow. After a month or so we saw Kharon off on the platform at the Kazan' railroad station. It was a sad occasion. An unpleasant-looking middle-aged man was already sitting in the compartment. Kharon looked at him with some alarm, and all of us who were seeing him off had a premonition of misfortune. We hugged Yasha, embraced him, and parted company—until 1956. Before arriving in Sverdlovsk, Yasha was arrested once again.

It is important to relate what happened to him later. After being released a second time, he became a sound engineer for the Moscow Film Studio, Mosfilm, made many films, and showed himself to be an expert of exceptional professional skill. But he did not succeed in realizing the cherished dream of his youth—to make a film about Garibaldi based on his own script.

Yasha also started a family. He married Svetlana Korytnaya, whose fate was a tragic as Yasha's. The daughter of the secretary of the Central Committee of the Ukrainian Komsomol, who was arrested during those terrible years, and the niece of Commandant I. Yakir, shot in 1937, Svetlana was sent after her father's arrest to a special institution where children were inculcated with the idea that their parents were traitors, enemies of the people, and they were obliged to curse, condemn, and slander them.

The years went by. Svetlana met Kharon, and they were married. A son was born to them. Svetlana became a film critic and published an interesting book. The last time I saw her was at a show, *How Do You Like That?* presented by students at the Moscow State University some years ago.

Soon afterwards Svetlana put an end to her life. It was said that in the final months before her suicide she was depressed, talked about fearing a renewal of Stalinism, and said that prisons and camps were what lay ahead. Yasha had been ill with tuberculosis for many years. He did not survive long after Svetlana's death, and he died, leaving their twelve-year-old son. A few months earlier he had been awarded honors for cultural activities in the Russian Soviet Federated Socialist Republic. As he lay dying, he was tormented by nightmares, and in a feverish state would repeat, "Lavrenty Pavlovich"— that is, NKVD Chief Lavrenty Beria — "let me go, I beg you, let me go!"

It is hard to say what he was remembering in those final moments of delirium. Perhaps it was a distorted recollection of what the investigator had said to him, a nineteen-year-old prisoner: "I believe you are not guilty. Now your passport will be brought to you and you can go home. I've really grown to like you. My work is so hard. I'd like to be friends with someone intelligent. Perhaps you would let me come and visit you from time to time." And indeed, he was brought the passport and the pass for release from Lyubyanka. They went out together. "Here's the car," said the investigator. "May I ride with you? I'll see you home." So together they went up the stairs of the house where Yasha Kharon lived. Yasha put out his arm to ring, but the investigator held back his hand, saying, "Excuse me, I forgot. Simply a formality. You have to sign your name here," and held out a statement to Yasha which said that he, Yakov Kharon, admitted that he was guilty of planning an act of terrorism. This was precisely the confession that Yasha had refused to make at his interrogation. "I cannot sign that," he said in distress. "Oh, you can't? Turn around, you bastard! Straight to the car!" And off Yasha went, back to the camp.

Some time later I also learned of the tragic end of Yury Vainer and his wife. On his arrival in Moscow, he had married a woman he had loved from afar. He had dedicated his sonnets to her, calling her Countess L. Then, like Kharon, Vainer was sent into permanent exile. His wife, who was pregnant, hanged herself the day after his arrest. Vainer himself, when he heard of his wife's death, according to one story, died of a heart attack; according to another, he jumped down a mine shaft.

From among Kharon's and Vainer's one hundred sonnets there were some I was especially fond of. This is one of them:

The Execution of Chevalier Boniface de la Molle

Throngs packed the Place de la Greve
Riveted, motionless, with baited breath,
As La Molle's head, chopped off,
Comes, literally like a ball,
bouncing down the steps . . . .

The executioner had failed to wrest
the smile off that countenance!
I saw a cheerful Boniface,
whistling, light of step,
bidding farewell, casting one more
glance from a pair of sorrowful eyes!

There is but love—all else is illusion!
Friends?—nay, traitors! Where is honor,
Where is faith?
No—give me death
Rather than slavery or shame!

If only I could thus prevail—
jokingly striding out onto the scaffold
grandly waving off the Father Confessor
and proffering my head to the axe!

And here is another.

Smoldering Rubble

Unharvested, a field endures the rains.
Far off, a windmill, wings immobile,
A home burnt to the ground, eyes downcast,
A child, dead in an empty courtyard.

Silence reigns, not a breath stirs,
Only a solitary raven
Circles above the chimneys, with
A stray mongrel
Slinking like a thief through
Wet bricks strewn about.
Grass has overgrown a forgotten crossbow.
All is banished, emptied, stripped of life.
Whose path is it, thus adorned
with a hamlet's ruins?
Who passed through here—
Papists? Or our own?

> How fearful your succession of calamities,
> Oh France! You have been
> smashed and torched from end to end!
> Your very own sons have crucified you.

I have always thought it a shame that the sonnets of Yasha Kharon and Yury Vainer never became known. And while I am on the subject of poetry and poets, I should mention yet another "discovery" of mine of the late 1940s.

I cannot recall who brought the short, nearsighted young man home to the Fedorovs. The little fellow was apparently poverty-stricken, like so many talented poets. He was a second-year student at the Gorky Literary Institute. Now his name is well known not only to those who like to read in Russia but far beyond its borders as well. A few years ago he left Russia to settle in the United States. At the time I met him, though, he was not yet published. In his absent-mindedness he would leave bits of paper in various places with his verses written on them, and this earned him an unpleasant reputation. At any rate, the first time he entered the apartment, he muttered something like, "My name is Mandel'," or perhaps he merely said "Emka." I no longer recall. But I do remember clearly how impressed we were at the time by his early, youthful, barely mature poems. They had a deep feeling of patriotic pride and at the same time a lyricism.

In those years he wrote such poems as "The Jacobin," "The Decembrist's Fiancée," "The Return," and many others. I remember how astonished I was at the time by "A Poem of Childhood and Romance." Not only was it deeply lyrical, but there already burned the flame of civic pride so characteristic not only of Emka Mandel' himself but of the poetry of Naum Korzhavin (Mandel's pseudonym) as well.

> Strolling they were, kissing, just
> enjoying life . . .
> And all the while, snarling, with
> a nasal whine prowled cars shut tight
> as they roused night-watchmen from their
> nocturnal slumber.
>
> A finger, never hesitating, pressed the button.
> And as though through nerve cords,
> A wave leapt forward . . .
> The buzzer rang out. . . . And the children woke up
> With the women starting up out of their dreams.
>
> The city meanwhile slept on.
> And the lovers went their way,
> Not caring a bit about the harsh glare
> of headlights,

With the acacias and maples in bloom
And their aroma wafting its way along
the sidewalks.

I won't go on about myself:
We poets all share the same fate.
Everywhere I am taken for a vagrant
Though a window I have yet to break in my life. . . .

And I looked on, in anger and in fury
And I could not bring myself to believe it.
When people, insincere to their very core
Would speak to us of enemies. . . .

The Romance, they have trampled under foot,
The Banners, gathering dust all around. . . .
And I wandered among the acacias, as if in a fog.
So wanting to be an enemy.

Many friends and acquaintances would come to the Fedorovs' home to hear Mandel's poems. I am not sure that among Emka's colleagues at the Literary Institute there were not a few who wished him harm. His careless habit of losing or forgetting his poems, his candor in conversation with his friends, and, most important, the atmosphere of oppression, suspicion and fear, and the authorities' desire to remove those whose heads were held a bit higher than others', or who could potentially rise higher, led to Mandel's arrest in 1947. It is possible that the immediate reason for his arrest was the poem "October 16th."

After Stalin's death a poem such as that would have been considered something of an apology, especially the last quatrain. But at the time, the very reference to such a painful and inglorious day in the history of the defense of Moscow, a day of panic, flight, and withdrawal of thousands of the capital's inhabitants, was considered a crime. Even today a reference to October 16, 1941, would not be welcome. Zhora Fedorov's apartment was searched in connection with Mandel's arrest. Thanks to the resourcefulness of his wife, Maya, it was possible to save a notebook of Mandel's poetry. Emka went off to the Novosibirsk region for three years. He spent another three years in Karaganda. We did not forget or abandon him. We sent him packages of warm clothing and food and wished for his speedy return Fortunately, he did come back.

We're drowning! Not figuratively but literally. We—that is, Zhora Fedorov and I—are floundering in the waves of Lake Havel in Trokay and soon, exhausted, we will fall to the bottom of the sea. Then all the local inhabitants will come out to swim with a sigh of relief, for there exists a superstition that the lake will become safe for swimming only after someone has drowned.

The Most High is punishing us for our curiosity, for our outright insolence. Anya, an actress we know, has set out with one of the local men, Pavel, on his sailboat for an island in the middle of the lake, supposedly to gather walnuts. They have been gone for quite some time. And we, overcome by unhealthy curiosity, get into a canoe and begin to row out to the island. All of a sudden, a storm comes up. Our canoe fills quickly up with water, and we find ourselves out in the lake too far from shore. The theater costumes we are wearing are soaked. Only help can save us.

There is a commotion on the shore. Some girl has awakened Maya, who has been sleeping under a tree. She cries out cheerfully, "Aunt Maya, Aunt Maya, your husband is drowning!" There are no boats nearby, so someone sets out on a raft for the opposite shore to get a boat. All of a sudden, a miracle occurs. The sailboat has set off from the island (apparently Anya and Pavlik have eaten their fill of walnuts) and is heading right toward us in full sail. Just another split second and . . . yelps of joy and shouts of hurrah from the shore! But then, the sailboat turns abruptly and goes off to the side. From the shore come shouts, curses, swearing. The sailboat approaches us a second time and takes us aboard. It turns out that on hearing the joyful shouts, Pavel decided that he had come upon a picture being filmed and that we were only "drowning" according to the script. But the common Russian curses he heard caused him to have doubts and return. Providence has decided merely to frighten us this time. But so as to let us know clearly what His intentions are, an hour later, as we are returning on the same sailboat to the far shore of the lake, the sail suddenly collapses. My father, on learning of our adventure, says "Friends who drown together cannot be separated by water."

In that summer of 1947 Zhora and Maya, Maya's mother, the film director Vera Pavlovna Stroeva, and I found ourselves, for different reasons, in Lithuania. Zhora was on an archaeological dig; Vera Pavlovna was making a film, *Maria Melnikaite* (*Marite*); and I was on official leave in Geruliai, near Klaipeda. Then, unexpectedly, Zhora and I joined up with Vera Pavlovna at the Bristol Hotel in Vilnius, and she suggested that we do a few scenes in her film. I was thrilled at the proposal, for I needed money badly and the pay for a scene was seventy-five rubles a day—one-tenth of my monthly stipend as a graduate student. The glamour of being a film actor did not really entice me, for after the war and the front, such egotism had all but vanished. I really did earn my keep, though, and worked hard for the money. I was given the role of a farmhand who, during the action, while sitting on one horse and leading another by the reins, must ride off through the pouring rain. The rain was heavier than normal: I was soaked with ice-cold water from a fire pump at very high pressure. In addition, I mistakenly jumped onto the mare and held the reins of the stallion. The stallion continually tried to mount the mare. Eventually the downpour of water cooled his ardor somewhat—and froze me. Bitter is the actor's cup! Zhora, as always, did very well for himself: he played a farmhand who dragged bags of hay (weighing about five hundred grams each) and a wounded partisan. When the film was released, it was a success, but we weren't in it. Our scenes had been edited out.

During the filming in Lithuania we became friendly with Tanya Lennikova, the young actress who played the role of Maria Melnikaite. She was a sweet, pleasant girl who was dyingg to go on the stage. Although naturally gifted, Tanya was still learning to act. Later on her dream came true: she entered the Moscow Art Theater. She played many roles, becoming first an Honored Artist, then a People's Artist. She married Andrei Petrov, the artistic director, a wonderful fellow with gypsy eyes. We were friends for many years but gradually drew apart. We saw less and less of each other; then there were only phone calls, and finally they stopped as well. Life (or perhaps the Stanislavsky method) separated us. Sometimes when I go through old papers I come across a photograph of Tanya with the dedication "To a dear, beloved friend."

My other "discovery" from Lithuania was a Belorussian girl, Galya, who was also breaking into films and the theater. She studied in Moscow, then got married, left for Yerevan, gave birth to three children, and became a film critic. Her husband, Gurgen, a former student in the film-making department, became a popular photographer in the Armenian capital. During those years Gurgen kept trying to get an answer to a question that bothered him no end. "Listen, Sasha," he would say, "We like Negroes. So why isn't there any Negro jazz played here?" Why indeed? We became friends for many long years.

Sergei Markovich Shapshal, or Khadzhi-Sarai Shapshal, for that was his name in Karaite, was a discovery of Zhora's. They met in Vilnius in that same hot summer of 1947. It was simply amazing how Zhora, with absolutely no knowledge of the intertwining streets of the city, could come across the Karaite Museum. That evening he told me with excitement about the museum, but most of all about its curator. I must confess that I was skeptical about his story, since I remembered the joke from our student years that you always had to divide Zhora's stories by eleven: that was the ratio of reliability. But this time I was wrong. I will not describe Shapshal here in detail; Zhora has already done so in his story "Green Root," first published in *Novy mir* and then in the review *Dnevnaya poverkhnost'*.

Shapshal was a Karaite Gokhan—that is, a spiritual and lay leader of Karaites the world over. Since 1920 his official residence had been in Trokay. He was an outstanding Eastern scholar, a member of many academies and scientific societies. Sergei Markovich was a friend of our famous countrymen and Eastern scholars Ignaty Yulyanovich Krachkovsky and Vasily Mikhailovich Alekseev. He had gathered a unique collection of Karaite, Eastern, and Polish-Lithuanian artifacts, including weapons, utensils, manuscripts, coins, and much more. In 1940 he donated his collection to the Soviet state and was kept on as curator of his own museum at the paltry salary of 750 rubles a year. He managed to save his collection during the Occupation, and saved the lives of many of his countrymen as well. Shapshal was often visited by a certain scholarly German colonel who worked at the Ostland headquarters of Rozenberg. He warned Shapshal in time of the planned extermination of the Karaites and gave him some extremely useful advice. In order to save the Karaites from destruction (the Occupation had marked them for death, like the Jews), Shapshal, at the German's advice, wrote a memorandum about the origins and history of his people. The memorandum was skillfully drafted, and the extermination was called off. Shapshal, a man of great personal courage and impeccable honesty, could not refrain from expressing his condemnation of the anti-Semitic activities of Hitler's followers. In the same memorandum were these words: "Moses' Commandments remain to this day the basis for world civilization. No one will be able to forget or eradicate the historic service rendered by the Jewish people."

Sergei Markovich was able to save the entire museum collection during the Occupation. He fooled the German Command when, on receiving orders to evacuate the valuables to Germany, he filled the crates with bricks and sent them off. From 1944 onward he once again served as curator of the museum, at the same 750-ruble salary, on which he had to subsist together with his wife, the first woman in Russia to become an eye doctor. Were it not for the support of the Karaite community, Shapshal and his wife would have been left to die of hunger.

And how did the Soviet State show its gratitude? We met Shapshal at a difficult time for him, when, out of spite and ignorance, the local authorities had classified the Karaite church, along with the Catholic church, as an enemy of Soviet power. A decision was made to eliminate the Karaite Museum and transfer its contents to the Lithuanian Museum of History and Ethnography. It was necessary to act, and to act swiftly. Fortunately I had with me a party card. I went to the Central Committee of the Communist party of Lithuania. The instructor of the cultural department turned out to be bright and good-natured. I managed to persuade him not to go ahead too quickly with the elimination of the museum. Once in Moscow, Zhora and I went to see the vice president of the Academy of Sciences, Academician V. P. Volgin. He immediately took steps to halt the seemingly imminent destruction of the museum. At Volgin's insistence, Shapshal was put on the staff of the Lithuanian Institute of History. He was, however, given the post of a junior staff member without any scholarly rank, despite the fact that he was a member of the

Polish Academy of Sciences, professor at Petersburg University, and holder of an honorary doctorate from Lvov University! Even afterwards, following the intercession of academicians Krachkovsky and Alekseev, and with the support of the Lithuanian Academy of Sciences, an effort was made to grant Sergei Markovich the rank of doctor of history without dissertation, but someone denounced him as a cult member to the High Qualifications Commission. There the matter stopped. It took several years of obstinate struggle, with the active participation of Volgin, before the deserving scholar, who was by now over eighty, received the rank of doctor of sciences and finally became a senior scholar, with the appropriate salary.

Shapshal had no children, and when he lost his wife, the people closest to him were the Fedorov family. He came to Moscow after Vera, the eldest of the Fedorov offspring, was born, bringing with him an ancient Arabic book of fates, with which he cast Vera's horoscope, promising her a happy, fruitful life. (And indeed Vera, on completing her studies in art history in the history department at Moscow State University, went on to work in the Pushkin Fine Arts Museum and later emigrated with her husband to Israel.)

Incidentally, he also cast my horoscope. It promised that I would have many daughters, but alas, my fortune turned out to be mistaken.

Shapshal lived a long life. He died at the age of ninety-two, a tall, slender old man who seemed to incarnate all the wisdom and kindness in the world.

Sadly, before he died, the only museum of Karaite history in the world was liquidated after all, and its contents distributed to the Lithuanian Museum of History and Ethnography.

2

War on Cosmopolitans!

We shall say to the enemy: strike our Homeland no more! Or we shall
unleash destruction and war!
—song from the Stalinist artillery unit

Rootless cosmopolitans — the main danger — Grigory Rasputin and Trofim Lysenko — pogrom on the social sciences — characters from the Institute of History — the fourth element — the story of Professor Zil'berfarb

In the spring of 1948 the party bureau secretary for the Institute of History, Vasily Dmitrievich Mochalov, called me into his office.

"Well, how are things over there in your department? What is the mood like?"

"Everything seems okay," I replied.

After listening to my brief report on the work under way at the department, Mochalov asked, "How is Academician Deborin holding up?" The question gave me pause, for I felt there was some hidden, incomprehensible meaning behind it. "Has something happened?" I asked pointedly. "No, they were interested 'upstairs'" (that is, at the party central Committee) "There's something going on at home, some kind of family changes. You haven't heard anything about them?" "No," I answered quite sincerely, but I thought to myself, "All I need now is to have to look into other people's family matters." I knew that Abram Moiseevich's wife had died several years earlier.

Mochalov did not pursue this line of conversation, but he said to me, "Aleksandr Moiseevich, not everything is fine in your department. It is quite possible that there will be some changes. Try to stay out of it."

He rose. Our talk was over. The warning of the gods, I thought. But still, the advice of the party bureau secretary was good: "Stay out of it."

Over and over again, as I thought about our conversation, I came to the conclusion that there was no cause for alarm in our department, and that I had nothing to be blamed for. After that talk, my sympathy grew for the old man Deborin, since there seemed to hang over him some unspoken threat.

Since the middle of 1946, only ten months after the end of the war, the cold war at home had been in full swing. The press, the radio, the entire vast party propaganda machine were all mobilized for a new ideological offensive. A crusade was being launched against the so-called cosmopolitans.

The lists of Jewish surnames, with two or three Russian or Armenian names thrown in for good measure, left no doubt that *cosmopolitans* meant

Jews, and that the entire campaign was anti-Semitic in nature. But it went beyond that. It soon became apparent that the threat of persecution affected everyone who did not roll with the tide of ideological conformism.

The fire and brimstone of the new crusade were meant to intimidate, if not strike down, those who, even in their innermost thoughts, dared to doubt or deviate from the orthodox faith, or, conversely, those who studied Marxism too seriously and fervently wished to "improve" it for the good of socialism. This was, in fact, the more dangerous heresy. The scholarly journals were already filling up with bombastic articles in which nearly all inventions and discoveries were attributed to Russian craftsmen, Russian pioneers, Russian engineers. It was not for nothing that people later said jokingly, "Russia is the homeland of elephants," or "Russian clocks are the fastest in the world," and so on. Foreign words which had long since entered the Russian vocabulary were mercilessly expunged, and the search was on for antediluvian equivalents; archaisms were proof of patriotism and loyalty.

The first caricature of cosmopolitans appeared in the magazine *Crocodile*. It was drawn by one of the most talented caricaturists of the time, Boris Yefimov, the brother of the publicist Mikhail Kol'tstov, who had been executed in 1940. The brothers were of Jewish origin. Taking an entire page of the magazine, Yefimov contrived to include all those literary figures officially branded as cosmopolitans. For some reason I particularly remember the critic-saboteur D. S. Danin, who was aiming a bow and arrow at the very heart of our Russian literature! A real scoundrel, right? This supposed humor magazine also took pride in an article by Vasily Ardamatsky "Pinja from Zhmerinki," which was downright anti-Semitic. And all this was happening only two years after the Nuremberg trials of Hitler's henchmen, only two years after the whole world had discovered the shameful spectacle of the annihilation by Fascist murderers of six million Jews.

Anyone inclined to believe that the crusade against 'cosmopolitans' was something out of the ordinary or merely the last gasp of the Stalinist era is likely to be misled. The ideological windstorms aimed at "cleansing" Soviet society of "alien" and "hostile" views, as well as of those who held them, was, and remains, one of the central features of the existing social order in the Soviet Union. Ideological purges were as natural for our society from the outset of the October Revolution as was mass repression. Purges are but one of the forms of that repression.

The new ideological campaign continued with only the briefest interruption right up until Stalin's death, and gradually grew into a widespread policy of repression whose impact may have been greater than that of the purges of the 1930s. The campaign took place against the background of the so-called Leningrad affair. A hard blow was dealt not only to the Leningrad party organization and the state bodies but also to the creative intelligentsia and scholars. The secretary of the party Central Committee, A. A. Zhdanov, who was behind the campaign, publicly denounced Anna Akhmatova, that marvelous Russian poet, and Mikhail Zoshchenko, an original and profound writer. Meanwhile, some time after the execution of Politburo member N. Voznesensky, Central Committee Secretary A. Kuznetsov, and others, the repression was aimed at Leningrad Asian and Near Eastern scholars and historians.

In the social sciences the campaign began with the crusade against the creative intelligenstia in full swing, while in the field of history it came only after the 'suppression' of the philosophers and the elimination of genetic scholarship.

The atmosphere of the time was reminiscent of Rasputin's sway. But now, instead of Rasputin there was Trofim Lysenko, a peasant's son who had scaled the academic heights. Lysenko, of course, could not cast a spell, but he managed to destroy science as well as scientists in the field of biology and genetics.

Zhores Medvedev, in one of his books, has already carried out comprehensive research on this matter, demonstrating how Lysenko accomplished his rise. As a historian, I was more interested by the analogy between Lysenkoism and Rasputinism. Such a parallel may at first appear strange. Actually, though, despite the very different concrete historical situations, there are a number of strikingly similar features and circumstances.

Grigory Rasputin came on the historical scene at a time of profound moral crisis for the tsarist autocracy, and an age of decadence in the highest court circles and in the tsarist entourage. The crisis that engulfed tsarism was characterized, in particular, by the belief in and desire for some kind of miracle that would supposedly save Orthodox Russia. Onto this scene there appeared Rasputin, who was said to be able to cast a spell on blood. (The tsarevich, Aleksei, is known to have suffered from hemophilia.) He quickly gained enormous influence over the tsar's court as a miracle worker. Rasputin was soon surrounded by a group of shady characters who tried, through the influential monk, to get a bigger, richer piece of the pie.

Trofim Lysenko appeared precisely at a time when the Soviet state was experiencing a serious crisis, not only economically—particularly in terms of the food supply—but also and especially morally, for the expulsion from the land and mass deportation of peasants along class lines, often simply out of spite, had led to mass hunger and the deaths of millions of people. Later, all this was dismissed as a "deviation," and in recent years the eloquent word *voluntarism* (which, by the way, is not at all Russian in origin) has appeared, making it easy to explain away everything that happened, is happening, and no doubt will continue to happen in our country—all the errors, abuses, and crimes.

Incidentally, the seer Rasputin, who did not know this word, explained everything in terms of divine providence.

Lysenko promised to provide an abundance of food in a short time, to save the soil from exhaustion, and so on. Since agricultural policy was based on force—or, shall we say, on *voluntarism*—and not on science, even though it passed for such, only a miracle could be hoped for. And Lysenko guaranteed that it would happen. This is why he was welcomed with open arms in higher party circles.

Not such an easy conjuring trick, abundance, though of course it is neater than casting a spell on blood!

The belief in Lysenko's ability to 'perform a miracle' pointed to the profound moral crisis, not to mention the ignorance, of the top Soviet leaders. Lysenko succeeded in doing what Rasputin could not even dream of: he created a pseudoscience and annihilated a genuine science—genetics—along with its most talented representatives including Academician Nikolai Ivanovich Vavilov, who was "eliminated," and the academician and biologist Lina Shtern, who ended up in prison.

In practical terms, Lysenko's influence caused enormous harm, for government policy was based on it for many years, and Lysenkoism—that is, swindling and fraud, willful misrepresentation, and pseudoscience—spread throughout the vast territory of the country, wreaking tremendous havoc. Lysenko's followers and pupils filled the ranks not only of the scientific institutions of the Academy of Sciences and the All-Union Academy of Agricultural Science but also the party and state apparatus as well. Lysenkoism became a state policy, a common feature of the Soviet way of life. Then it began to penetrate historical scholarship as well.

In the everyday life of the state, the social sciences, despite the publicity they attracted from time to time, played a subordinate, nearly insignificant role, and with the swift development of physics and mathematics in the 1940s and 1950s they were relegated to the background altogether.

Perhaps that is why historians did not have their own Rasputin-Lysenko, although the philosophers almost did have theirs. I refer to the late G. F. Aleksandrov, director of agitprop of the Soviet Communist party's Central Committee. Later on, when he became minister of culture, Aleksandrov was involved in a whorehouse scandal. (The ladies involved, as in Grigory Rasputin's time, and especially under his associate Mitka Rubenshtein, used to swim in champagne.)

In January 1947, on Stalin's personal orders, the Institute of Philosophy of the Academy of Sciences held a discussion of Aleksandrov's book *The History of Western European Philosophy*. Since the editor of the book was head of the propaganda office of the Central Committee, that discussion, as we might expect, was a dry one and did not lead to the inflammatory conclusions anticipated by the Party bigwigs. On instructions from the Central Committee in June 1947, a second discussion was held, during which A. A. Zhdanov, dedicated as he was to an all-out campaign against "bourgeois objectivism," spoke. Zhdanov called for an equivalent to the agricultural institute session, which he described as "an example of how to campaign for progressive Soviet science." Zhdanov's words were repeated constantly at historians' discussions and conferences.

Aleksandrov finally transferred to the Institute of Philosophy as director, leaving his high-ranking post in the Central Committee. When not visiting the whorehouse, he spent his time teaching Marxism, Bolshevik ethics, and moral purity to sociologists.

The agricultural institute session and the philosophical discussion created murky waves of simpleminded patriotism, chauvinism, and ignorance, which began to spill over into other disciplines as well. They quickly reached the historians' shores. But, I repeat, to our good fortune, no Lysenko had yet arisen in historical scholarship; there wasn't even an Aleksandrov. It is not possible to describe in this book all the permutations of the campaign against cosmopolitanism in the field of history. I do so, at any rate, in my study *The Twilight of the Stalinist Era*. Therefore, the reader will forgive me if I speak only of the most important and flagrant episodes in those "great days of struggle" against the "rootless" ones.

Among the early events, undoubtedly the most important was the discussion in 1947 of the nineteenth–century Caucasian nationalist Shamil movement which finally led to an orgy of chauvinism. At a meeting of the Institute of History's department of the history of the Soviet peoples in the nineteenth and twentieth centuries (chaired by associate member N. M. Druzhinin, who was elected academician in 1953), a report was read, entitled "The Historical Essence of Caucasian Muridism." Despite the widely held view among Soviet historians that this had been a progressive liberation movement, the speaker, Kh. G. Adzhemyan, demanded that the movement henceforth be considered reactionary, and that the views of Marx and Engels on the Caucasian War as a colonial war of conquest be revised. Adzhemyan made opportunistic use of the deportation of the Chechens and Ingushes in February 1944 in order to slander the old Shamil movement and intimidate his own opponents as well. Adzhemyan's scholarly arguments were not very convincing, and no one supported him.

Druzhinin, in summarizing, said, "If we were to take the speaker's point of view, we would have to consider any national liberation movement in tsarist Russia to be reactionary, and that is totally inadmissible." Druzhinin turned out to be a prophet; this was precisely the viewpoint that was subsequently imposed from above on Soviet historians. But Druzhinin emphasized yet another aspect of the issue, namely, that one could not consider scholarly and correct the view that all action taken against tsarist Russia in the name of nationalism was necessarily progressive. In accordance with the Marxist view on tangible truth, he insisted on an aanalysis of the concrete historical situation in each and every case.

The discussion seemed dispassionate at the time, but in reality passions were already flaring beneath the surface. At Moscow State University, in the Academy of Social Sciences, the forces of darkest reaction were gathering strength and preparing for an attack on and reprisals against colleagues and rivals who occupied key posts in the field of Soviet history in Moscow's educational institutions and scientific establishments. These forces were led by Professor A. L. Sidorov, deputy rector of Moscow University. All of Sidorov's activities and those of other party chauvinists were, of course, approved by the Central Committee.

The campaign against cosmopolitans forced me to give serious and profound thought to what was happening in my country. For I knew personally many of the historians who were being persecuted, and no speeches or newspaper articles or even Central Committee decrees could convince me that these people were hostile to our state or had defected to the enemy. In fact, one's first thought was to wonder who these enemies were. There were so many of them by now: there were not only the "still-unbeaten" German revanchists and the former war allies—the Americans and the British—but also close friends of our country, comrades in arms such as Tito. And these, as it turned out, were not just enemies but enemy spies. None of this made any sense. There was Yasha Kharon and Yury Butyagin and so many others that we were all left to wonder where we were heading, who was leading us, and what we were doing in general on this earth. I recall the famous quote from Pushkin: "O wonderful vain gift of life, why are you given us?" And the response "Life is for living." True, man has a fervent desire to live, but this was no answer. All we could do was take action—action *against*. We talked among ourselves and discussed what was happening. We didn't just chat, but tried to resist the onslaught of the "Black Hundreds," tried to do something for those people who were being persecuted. What we did amounted to very little, but it still made things more bearable. My friend Zhora Fedorov, once a member of the party bureau of the Institute of Archaeology, was invited to a meeting of the institute's board of directors to discuss what to do about Mikhail Grigor'evich Rabinovich. The director of the institute, A. D. Udal'tsov, insisted on firing Rabinovich, who had long been director of archeological fieldwork in Moscow. The argument was crystal clear. Udal'tsov muttered in his typical fashion, "Here's Rabinovich and here's Moscow. And so what to do?" He said this and looked at everyone with his clear, pale blue eyes. They all remained silent. Then Udal'tsov added, "We must release Rabinovich from work." After that, each participant gave his opinion. Zhora's turn came. He said, "I thought that I had been invited to a meeting of the board of directors and party committee of the institute, and I find myself at a meeting of the Union of the Russian People." (This was in tsarist times an organization of Russian "Black Hundreds" whose message had a clearly anti-Semitic and antirevolutionary tinge.) He got up and left. Rabinovich was subsequently hired by the Institute of Ethnography, but he no longer led archeological digs in Moscow.

In the department where I was a graduate student I tried to stifle passions and tone down, as much as possible, mutual recriminations and attacks, which, as a rule, ended with political accusations. But I was not often successful at this. I openly supported those who were being persecuted, first A. F. Miller and L. I. Zubok, then later V. M. Turok-Popov. Then I myself became one of the targets of attack.

A number of meetings occurred just before the great rout at our institute. There was one that I remember very clearly. That was a closed party meeting. It took place in the meeting hall of the department of historical sciences at 14 Volkhonka Street. There was talk of cosmopolitanism. No personal accusations had yet been made, but it was already clear where future developments would lead. Yuzef Polevoi, a fine individual, took the floor to explain to the party gathering why Jews were so infected with petty bourgeois ideology. "Vasily Dmitrievich [Mochalov, the party organization secretary] has raised the issue here as to why Jews take cosmopolitan positions," he began. Then Polevoi went on to talk about the diaspora, the pale of settlement, and so on. His entire speech sounded like an apology. I thought with bitterness during those moments that Yuzef was not saying what he should, that he should have exposed the evil and falseness of the fabrications about cosmopolitanism rather than offering an explanation. I spoke to Polevoi about this during the break and he seemed a bit embarrassed. At that same meeting A. M. Deborin was attacked for problems in the work of the department. I had to respond rather sharply and defend Deborin. During the break a respectable-looking woman professor said to me, "Why did you defend Deborin? You shouldn't have done that."

"But what they said about him was untrue. It's not fair," I objected. "You shouldn't have defended him." she repeated. All I could do was shrug my shoulders.

One of our graduate students by the name of Kuzin, who had returned from the front with a serious head wound, was saying to someone excit-edly, . . . and so Gurvich [a well-known literary critic, one of the first to be branded a cosmopolitan] wrote a letter to the Central Committee saying 'Give me a job as a teacher.' And you know what they replied?" Kuzin cast a trium-phant glance at his listeners, anticipating the effect that what he had to say would have on them. "They said to him, 'We can't trust a wicked shepherd to take care of the flock!'"

Meanwhile, an incident occurred that became a sort of test for me. I. M. Maisky needed an assistant. As an academician he was entitled to one, and he found an assistant himself. She was a middle-aged woman Maisky had met while working in London by the name of Gransberg. She was told to file her papers through our personnel office. Foreseeing the obstacles that might arise during the excesses of the anticosmopolitan campaign, I asked Maisky to recommend Gransberg himself, which he did willingly. The recommendation went to the personnel office. The next day it was learned that the woman had been arrested. Aware of the high-level dislike at the time for Ivan Mikhailovich, I was concerned that the arrest might be used against him. I felt personally responsible, since on the eve of the arrest, at my own request, he had written a very flattering recommendation. The solution came to me in a flash. I went to the institute, obtained the Gransberg recommendation on some pretext, went to Ivan Mikhailovich, and, after explaining the matter, returned it to him. A few hours later I was called urgently to the personnel office and ordered to bring back the recommendation. I replied calmly that since Gransberg could not be hired as an assistant, and since Maisky had written the recommendation at my request, I had destroyed it. "No! Did you really do that?" asked the personnel manager in a hushed tone, hardly believing her ears. "I shall have to inform Viktor Ivanovich [V. I. Shunkov, deputy director of the Institute of History]." "Needless to say," I replied, "you are required to do so."

Viktor Ivanovich was a complex man. But I knew him to be intelligent and refined. I went to him and repeated the story. He looked at me carefully, as if to size me up. Then he said, "You're not getting your career off to a very good start." Again he looked at me, smiled and concluded, "Well, since this is the first time, you can be excused. But never do anything like that again. I hope it all works out." And, in fact, there were no consequences.

In connection with the celebration in early January 1949 of the 225th anniversary of the founding of the Academy of Sciences, a commemorative session of the general assembly and of the departments of the Academy of Sciences was held in Leningrad. President S. I. Vavilov urged us in his report to "restore the historical truth and to demonstrate the lofty place of our national scholarship in world culture, to restore and defend many of its neglected priorities."

Academician I. I. Mintz, who had come under attack back in 1947 and then had been left alone for a while, was eager to deliver a paper at the Leningrad anniversary session entitled "Lenin and the Development of Soviet Historical Scholarship." In vain did he praise Stalin's *Short Course on the*

History of the Communist Party of the Soviet Union and spoke enthusiastically of the "rout of bourgeois historiography, of Menshevist-Trotskyite concepts," disregarding, of course, the fact that every campaign had concluded with the physical destruction of many historians. Mintz, in his paper, called for an end to obsequiousness and sharply criticized those who supposedly held social-democratic ideas.

The content and style of Mintz's paper may be illustrated by the follow-ing sentence: "This error is especially inadmissible in light of the current treachery of the Schumachers, Blums, and others active in the despicable 'third force' party." This paper, which was the lead article in the New Year's edition of the 1949 *Voprosy istorii*, nonetheless played an extremely damaging role for Mintz himself, in that he had "raised his voice"—that is, he brought himself to the attention of his most resolute opponents. Shortly after he presented his paper, we began to hear indignant protests claiming to represent "scholarly public opinion." The paper was evaluated in the Central Committee as "erroneous and pretentious."

Finally, the order came down to hold a meeting of the entire institute on the issue of cosmopolitanism. The meeting was chaired by Sergei Lvovich Utchenko, who was executive secretary of the history and philosophy depart-ment at the time and had been elected in 1948 as secretary of the party organization at the institute.

Before the war Utchenko had begun to study chemistry, but then he transferred to the history department at Leningrad State University. His field was the history of ancient Rome, and he had done interesting work on the age of Cicero and Augustus.

At the time, Sergei Lvovich was in the prime of life and had a brilliant future ahead of him. He was a capable man and certainly a charming one. Furthermore, he liked—and knew how—to live as he pleased. He was not a bad person, but his best-intentioned relations with people were tempered by extreme caution, which in moments of crisis could be taken for cowardice. He was very popular in our collective, and his conformism was not aggressive, while his wit and resourcefulness gave him a reputation for being easygoing.

Utchenko was for many years secretary of the party organization and usually a member of the party bureau. At elections he always came out in the top five in the balloting. In his capacity as deputy director of the Institute of History, he did not abuse his administrative authority. An opportunist by nature, Utchenko wanted to please, and most of the time he was able to get along with the bosses. He held the theory, widely shared at that point in our Soviet time, that a decent person was one who did not do anything reprehensible on his own initiative. But if, in the final analysis, the higher-ups or party discipline so required, well, then there was nothing you could do. You just had to go along.

In short, Utchenko considered himself a thoroughly decent man, and the majority of his colleagues would have agreed. If you were to remind them today that it was the same Sergei Lvovich, that nice Sergei Lvovich, who conducted the campaign against cosmopolitanism in the Institute of History of the Academy of Sciences, they would look at you in disbelief and say, "Really? That can't be possible!"

It may be that the leading role he played in the "great days of struggle" was not to his liking, and that he would have declined it with the greatest of pleasure. But, then, his successful, promising career would have been jeopardized. And anyway, he was being forced to do it.

Everyone sooner or later pays for what he does in this life. Sergei Lvovich had to pay too—for his success, for the trust the bosses put in him at the time. And pay he did. He also had to pay another, invisible price: he considered himself Russian, but in fact he was half Jewish, and his wife a very beautiful, pleasant, and cultivated woman, was Jewish.

And so it happened that S. L. Utchenko had to chair a meeting on the campaign against cosmopolitanism in historical scholarship. The most active champion of the cause was Arkady Lavrovich Sidorov, a historian of the Soviet period who had studied at the Institute of Red Professorship, out of which emerged a host of party historians in the 1920s and 1930s. Sidorov had already had his share of troubles, fighting all those with whom, in the party's view, one had to fight, but at one second supporting the Trotskyites, an episode that had held back this undoubtedly able and dynamic individual. But now he was riding high.

Sidorov chose Mintz as the main target for his attack. Mintz, in the role of a cosmopolitan! This was truly surprising, since there was no more faithful party member than Academician Mintz. Every time the trumpet sounded another ideological crusade, Mintz recalled his past war experience (during the Civil War he had served in the First Cavalry under S. M. Budyenny), laced up his boots, and went off to battle the ideological enemies of the party. He headed the editorial group at *Istoria grazhdanskoi voiny* and was one of those historians who vied with each other in contributing to the falsification of the history of the Communist party and of our country in keeping with the constantly changing requirements of the party leadership. A. L. Sidorov, who had also worked for many years on the editorial board of *Istoria grazhdanskoi voiny*, apparently had a score to settle with Mintz.

The meeting took place at the end of March 1949, in the inadequate space of the department of historical sciences, which could hardly accommodate all those who wished to attend. With the help of a radio broadcast the matter was rectified.

At the same time, across the hall, a similar meeting of economists was taking place. Here they were holding forth against Academician E. S.

Varga, former director of the Institute of World Economy of the Academy of Sciences, former member of the executive political committee of the Communist International, member of the 1919 Hungarian commune, professional revolutionary, and generally selfless person. He was being raked over the coals by a well-known drunkard, a certain Colonel Antonov. He accused Varga of making an inaccurate assessment of Germany's oil resources at the beginning of the war, thereby causing thousands of Russians to be killed. "Varga has the blood of the Russian people on his hands," the intoxicated colonel shouted. And this about a man whose only son had been killed at the front during the Great Fatherland War!

I thought then, and still believe to this day, that the main instigators of the pogrom, such as A. L. Sidorov, associate member A. D. Udal'tstov, A. P. Kuchkin, and others like them, seasoned as they were in party battles, could not fail to understand that by deriding their fellow historians they were in fact providing ammunition for possible accusations of hostile activity against their own comrades. And I cannot believe that a person as experienced as Sidorov did not realize that it was a short step from accusations of cosmopolitanism and lack of patriotism to arrest.

Just think about his assertion that "Academician I. I. Mintz and his pupil, Professor I. M. Razgon, pretending to pose as founders of the history of Soviet society, have done serious harm to the development of Soviet historical science."

Sidorov compiled an entire file on Mintz. (Who would have thought to dredge up a statement made by Mintz to a congress of historians in Oslo back in 1928, except for use in memoirs?)

Sidorov's speech was modeled on the best examples of the indictments of A. Ya. Vyshinsky, the prosecutor during the notorious trials of the 1930s, in which totally disparate facts from a person's life, all purely coincidental and unrelated, were built into a systematic case for the prosecution and used to creat the impression that a public figure had been engaged in hostile activities or even espionage from the time he was in diapers.

Similar "pearls" were to be found in Sidorov's statement. For example: "Mintz, while a pupil of Pokrovsky back in 1928, had an admiration for German historiography. A bit later on, Academician Mintz expressed antiparty views on the history of our party." But one thing had absolutely nothing to do with the other! Of course the Western reader will find it difficult to understand why admiration for German historiography should be thought a crime, even if Mintz had displayed any such proclivity (which, in fact, he had not). Alas, it is virtually impossible to explain. The strength of such accusations lies in their absurdity. After all, accusations of witchcraft in the Middle Ages always led to conviction even if such witchcraft could not be proven but might be thought possible!

In actual fact, Sidorov's statement, like the prosecution's argument at a trial, had already assigned the blame. Here, in brief, is the case against Mintz, based on Sidorov's statement. Mintz was accused of monopolizing the history of Soviet society with the help of I. M. Razgon, B. G. Verkhoven', S. A. Shevkun, and, outside the Academy, Ye. N. Gorodetsky (who had worked within the Central Committee apparatus but was then expelled and sent to work at Moscow University). The opponents of the criticism of Mintz in the history of Soviet society department of the Institute of History were A. Ya. Gurevich and A. P. Sheliubsky.

Such were the lofty arguments of Sidorov, a technique that was not his alone. It was the typical Soviet style of discourse, whether it was used at the show trial where N. I. Bukharin and others were accused, in an ordinary ideological exercise, or in discussing plumbing repairs in some housing council. This type of accusation, however, became more harsh after 1948.

A great deal has been said in the USSR about "mistakes" in modern history. The future director of the Institute of History, and future academician, Aleksei Leont'evich Narochnitsky, was especially adept at this kind of criticism.

Young scholars who had come into the field after returning from the front took an active part in the new ideological crusade of the Communist party of the Soviet Union (CPSU). Some of them did this for purely careerist considerations, others on instructions from their party secretaries, and still others were caught up in the pogromlike atmosphere: they were like soldiers sent out in droves by their commanding officers to plunder a city recently taken from the enemy. A graduate student of A. L. Narochnitsky's by the name of Batueva wrote a criticism of a specialist in American studies, Professor Lev Izraelevich Zubok, accusing him of nothing less than being an "agent of American imperialism." Another graduate student, Yu. V. Borisov, chose as his target Professor Filip Osipovich Notovich, already advanced in years, who had just published a book on the diplomatic history of the First World War. Borisov went on to have a successful career, first in the Ministry of Foreign Affairs' Institute of International Relations and then as a professor and doctor of historical sciences working at the Soviet embassy in Paris as an adviser on cultural affairs. He may be an ambassador by now, for all I know.

During a break at that fateful meeting of the history department, the higher-ups in the department of science of the Party Central Committee were informed of progress in the inquiry into cosmopolitanism but were still not satisfied with its scope. When the meeting was resumed, Utchenko appealed to those present: "I see that the names Kahn, Molok, Notovich, and Zubok have been mentioned. We must speak out and name other names."

His heartfelt appeal was heeded. Other names were given. Such distinguished historians as L. V. Cherepnin and A. S. Nifontov once again attacked the author of a book on Soviet historiography, N. L. Rubinshtein. He had already been criticized in 1947, and the attack had been going on for two years now. At the same time it was announced that his views were supported by the Leningrad professors V. M. Stein and I. P. Yeremin. General Sukhomlin, head of the department of military history, gave yet another name—the Soviet historian K. V. Basilevich. Here, it seems, he was off target: no one supported him, for Basilevich was not a Jew!

The medievalists took the rostrum. They talked about the cosmopolitanite errors of the Leningrad professor O. L. Vainstein, about his effort to minimize the significance of Soviet medieval studies in the work of professors V. M. Lavrovsky and B. T. Goryanov. Even Academician E. A. Kosminsky was involved in this misconception.

Then it was the turn of the ancient historians. Professors M. N. Mashkin and K. N. Serbina pointed out the "flagrant cosmopolitanism" in the views of Professor S. Ya. Lur'e. It seems that along with "his group" (E. I. Solomonik, B. I. Nadel', Ya. N. Lubarsky), he was undermining the publication of ancient texts! See how far those cosmopolitans had gone!

Nowadays this all seems like some kind of horrible nonsense, some sort of hocus-pocus, but it all really did happen.

Cosmopolitans came under fire along the entire front of historical scholarship. At a meeting of the board of fellows of the Pacific Ocean Institute of the Academy of Sciences, its director, the young, elegant Professor Yevgeny Mikhailovich Zhukov (he would later become an academician and head all historical scholarship) stated that some scholars were still in thrall to harmful ideas, as if there were any such thing as worldwide Eastern scholarship. What a dangerous misconception! Zhukov exposed many Eastern specialists for harboring cosmopolitan errors, and demanded that Professor A. F. Miller's book *Essays on the History of Modern Turkey* be severly condemned. This appeal was heeded. Other speakers (T. A. Akopyan, A. M. Valuisky) condemned Miller's doctoral dissertation as well—a splendid study entitled "Bairaktar".

But Professor B. N. Zakhoder bore the brunt of the criticism. He was criticized for the very air he breathed. And then, suddenly, the rules of the game were violated. Zakhoder resisted. He fought with all the determination of a desperate man. He refused to confess his mistakes. He responded to his opponents with a ferocity and anger equal to his own.

Next came a new spectacle: a declaration from those students and graduate students who had attended Zakhoder's lectures reached the presidium. They announced their solidarity. With their teacher? No, God forbid. With his critics.

Then, as if some unseen trigger had been pulled, the firing began at the former Soviet ambassador to London and former deputy foreign minister of the USSR, Ivan Mikhailovich Maisky. He was not at all popular "upstairs." Neither, in fact, were those still in the diplomatic service dating from M. M. Litvinov's time. There was as yet no pretext for criticizing Maisky, since he had not written anything recently. So his critics dusted off and dragged out a book entitled *Mongolia Today*, which he had published in 1920!

The book's origins are rather curious. Ivan Mikhailovich told me about it himself. In 1920, on instructions from the Siberian Central Union (Tsentrosoyuz) he went on an expedition to Mongolia in order to investigate the possibility of establishing economic relations between Russia and Mongolia. Using the statistical methods of Professor Luyo Brentano, with whom Maisky had studied in Munich, he compiled the first statistical property census in the history of Mongolia, which in subsequent decades remained the sole source for studying the economic and social conditions there just before the Revolution. Naturally, the information had become out of date over the intervening thirty years. But what did Maisky have to do with that? Maisky was a cautious, compromising man by nature. He sent the presidium of the meeting a note in which he announced that he was preparing a new edition of the book and acknowledged the drawbacks of the previous one. In so doing he pulled the rug out from under his opponents. TThere was no further sniping. The new edition of Maisky's book came out in 1959.

The heated discussions continued. The Asianists did not leave alone such pillars of scholarship, men who had earned glory for their homeland, ass I. Yu. Krachkovsky (attacked for his "un-Marxist methodology") and Academician V. M. Alekseev. There can be no doubt that the treatment of these famous Leningrad Asianists was closely linked to the so-called Leningrad affair, when Leningrad came under fire from the party leadership in every respect.

But most flagrant of all was the campaign against cosmopolitanism in the history department of Moscow University. The meeting lasted three days (March 25, 26, and 28, 1949). The report of the dean of the faculty, Professor G. A. Novitsky, was discussed. A. L. Sidorov was the main speaker here as well. Once again the names of Mintz, Razgon and Gorodetsky, N. L. Rubinshtein, Zubok, I. S. Zvavich, A. I. Neusykhin, V. M. Lavrovsky, Kogan-Bernshtein, Miller, Galperin, Lur'e, Blumin, and V.M.Stein were on everyone's lips. Even the ninety-year-old Academician R. Iu. Vipper was not left in peace.

The archaeologists, too, were caught up in the fray. Professors A. V. Artsikhovsky and S. V. Kisilev accused V. I. Ravdonikas, the Leningrad alternate member of the Academy of Sciences, of cosmopolitanism. This was, so to speak, a counterpunch on Artsikhovsky's part, since Ravdonikas had earlier accused Artsikhovsky of cosmopolitanite errors in his textbook *Introduction to Archaeology*, but Artsikhovsky, with some foresight, engaged in severe self-criticism, thus striking a balance, one might say.

What a pitiful sight! Artemy Vladimirovich Artsikhovsky, the man who had taught hundreds of students, who had discovered Novgorod as a site of Russian culture, beating his chest and settling scores with other prominent scholars, and this all at the whim of the party bosses.

In addition to Sidorov, an active part in this bacchanalia was played by the young historian A. D. Nikonov (son-in-law of Molotov), by the historian of ancient studies A. G. Bokshchanin, and by the ancient Asian studies professor V. I. Avdiev, the French specialist Bendrikov and the graduate students Belinsky and Semyonov. The storm engulfed an ever-greater number of scholars, people well known in their fields, with considerable moral authority. Professor B. F. Porshnev, unfortunately, did not resist. He was to accuse his colleague in the same field (the history of the Thirty Years' War), O. L. Vainstein, of taking a scornful view of the real significance of Russia in world history: "Rubinshtein and Vainstein have the same cosmopolitan viewpoint." Having declared war on Vainstein, Porshnev found himself unable to call a truce and would continue to wage it for many years. He once confessed in an outburst of candor, "How pleasant it is to take the enemy by the throat."

Let us now look at how the so called cosmopolitans conducted themselves. I have already mentioned B. N. Zakhoder, who firmly rebuffed the accusations made against him. Ye. N. Gorodetsky attempted to defend himself before the history department of Moscow University, but it was impossible. The journal *Voprosy istorii* remarked with regard to Gorodetsky's speech that "this one refutation was interpreted by the audience as an attempt to shed responsibility for unpatriotic activity by Academician Mintz's group." He acknowledged mistakes in his own work "of an objectively cosmopolitan nature."

Once again (how many times!) did N. L. Rubinshtein repent. Another defendant, B. G. Verkhoven', on criticizing Mintz, agreed to the accusation that he had failed to expose Mintz. Professor I. S. Zvavich went farthest of all, in confessing not only to errors of a cosmopolitan nature but also to having whitewashed British imperialism and the Labourites in his works.

A confession of errors was also made by the head of the medieval studies section of the history department, Academician E. A. Kosminsky, followed by two other medievalists, professors V. M. Lavrovsky and A. Neusykhin. But at the Institute of History, Professor L. I. Zubok virtually refused to repent.

After a few days rumors began to spread that Deborin, along with a number of other colleagues, was to be fired from the institute. And indeed this is what actually happened. Deborin, however, was quickly reinstated, not as a department head this time but merely as a senior researcher. A number of individuals were removed from the academic council of the institute. These included Nikolai Leonidovich Rubinshtein, who had worked at the Higher Party School and in the Academy of Social Sciences. I had known Nikolai Leonidovich from our military service together in the political section of the Second Guards Army. In 1943–44 he had been the deputy director for agitation in the political department.

I met him going up the stairs at Volkhonka Street and warned him of the decision to expel him from the board of fellows at the institute. Then we exchanged a few words about what was going on. Rubinshtein was a very cautious and experienced man. At one time he had worked in the central apparatus of the People's Commissariat of Internal Affairs, or NKVD, and God only knows how he managed to get out of there alive and with his reputation intact. "Naturally," he said to me, "there may be mistakes. But you do understand, I hope, that the campaign currently under way in the party is a necessary one." Luckily for the two of us somebody else attracted his attention, and his question went unanswered.

At about the same time a similar episode occurred. S. L. Utchenko came up to me before a party meeting and suggested that I express support for the bosses' firing of several historians, promising me that after this "operation" he would take me on at the institute. I became furious and firmly rejected this proposal. Utchenko was embarrassed and asked me not to tell anyone about this incident. Nina Aleksandrovna Sidorova, the party organization secretary, with whose knowledge the proposal had been made, upon hearing my indignant account blushed profusely, became upset, and kept repeating, "I told him, I did, not to do this. Oh, how awful, how awful!" She and Utchenko, as I later learned, were very much afraid that I would reveal the proposal made to me at a meeting.

Toward the middle of 1949 the war against the cosmopolitans began to subside. At the conclusion of the campaign against cosmopolitanism in historical scholarship, a few articles appeared in the journal *Voprosy istorii* devoted to the outcome of the "struggle." A final "screening" was conducted: the cosmopolitans had been identified by the higher authorities, and they were to be granted this title in much the same way as were Honored or People's Artists in science or the arts. Of course, the difference was a rather significant one.

As one of these articles explained, cosmopolitanism had infiltrated our holy land from three sources: from M. N. Pokrovsky (who was not forgotten here either), from Russian historiography of the nobility and the bourgeoisie, and, naturally, from Wall Street.

In order to show what fairly sophisticated Soviets thought of Wall Street (and some historians as well), I shall relate a remark made by one man who had been to New York: "And so one evening," he said, "I go out along that grim Wall Street, in whose basements American billionaires are weaving their golden web to entangle the whole world . . ."

It seems that these same "rootless" ones had come up out of those basements . . . and turned up in Moscow!

A lead article in *Voprosy istorii* (no. 2, 1949) clearly formulated the concept of cosmopolitanism as it applied to historical science: "The rootless cosmopolitans are today distorting the history of the Russian people's heroic struggle against their oppressors and foreign invaders; are diminishing the leading role of the Russian proletariat in the history of the revolutionary struggle for our homeland, and for the whole world as well; are stifling the socialist nature and international significance of the Great October Socialist Revolution; are falsifying and distorting the worldwide historical role of the Russian people in building a socialist society and in the victory over the enemy of mankind—German fascism—in the Great Fatherland War."

What was involved here was exclusively the history of the *Russian* people, not the *Soviet* people. This was an overt manifestation of Great Russian chauvinism, not even camouflaged for the sake of appearances by talk of internationalist principles and the Soviet state.

The list of cosmopolitans as finally drafted and approved by the higher bodies included Academician I. I. Mintz and professor I. M. Razgon, N. L. Rubinshtein, O. L. Vainstein, V. Lan, L. I. Zubok, I. S. Zvavich, and G. A. Deborin (the eldest son of Academician A. M. Deborin).

What did fate have in store for them?

Mintz was forced to leave the Institute of History and the department at the Academy of Social Sciences for several years, but he retained his chair in Soviet history at the Pedagogical Institute. Razgon left to work on the fringe of academia. Vainstein was harassed for many years in Leningrad. The American studies scholar Lan was soon arrested. Zubok was forced to leave the Institute of History and all other institutions of higher learning where he had worked, including the history department at the university, and was able to remain at the Institute of International Relations of the Foreign Ministry thanks only, according to him, to the personal intervention of V. M. Molotov, whose daughter had at one time been one of Zubok's students.

G. A. Deborin left the department at the Military–Political Academy and went to work first at the Higher Diplomatic School, and then at the Institute of Marxism-Leninism of the Central Committee. He still had many accomplishments to his credit within the party, for he was one of the authors of the historic pamphlet *Falsifiers of History*, which gave a new interpretation of the outbreak of the Second World War and an analysis of the Soviet-German pact of August 23, 1939, which has remained virtually unchanged to this day. Deborin's inclusion on the list of cosmopolitans could have occurred at someone's personal initiative, a sort of settling of scores, and perhaps because, for all his dedication, he was still a Jew and had to be put in his place. His situation showed once again how precarious was the position of professors of Jewish origin, even those who would zealously perform any task for the bosses. In the ghettoes of Hitler, after all, there existed the so-called Jewish police, who helped herd their compatriots into the death camps and then sent them off to the crematoria.

The English specialist I. S. Zvavich, an outstanding orator and publicist, was expelled from the university. In the end his own bombast betrayed him. Zvavich, to his misfortune, while justifying his nonexistent cosmopolitan errors, stated at a university meeting: "We have our own mutual admiration society," and listed several names. Naturally, Zvavich meant this only in a figurative sense, but the champions of anticosmopolitanism interpreted his words as they saw fit. Zvavich said farewell to Moscow and went off to Tashkent. But he had a weak heart, and the Central Asian climate proved too harsh for him.

Shortly before Zvavich's departure, I met him by chance in the Metro. Isaak Semyonovich said to me with a smile, "I had always been taught that there were three elements in this world: Water, Wind and Fire. Now I see there is a fourth one." On saying this, he grinned at me slightly, waiting for my response. "Which is that?" I asked out of curiosity. "Shit!" answered Zvavich enthusiastically, and we both chuckled.

Only a very short time later Professor Zvavich was no more.

Colonel Antonov's speech against Varga had demonstrated the danger of pent-up passions. The physicists had rebuffed attempts to rout them on the pretext of a campaign against cosmopolitanism, and it was only with great difficulty that they were gathered for the meeting. But here one of the founders of Soviet nuclear physics, Academician A. F. Ioffe, took the floor and said, in essence: "Either we sit at meetings, wasting valuable time on listening to endless palaver about how we physicists should deal with physics, or we get to work. If we are to hold meetings, then let those who intend to teach us what to do take our places in our work." Ioffe's statement caused embarrassment and confusion. A recess was called, and the meeting was postponed and never resumed. For the physicists, the need to create a nuclear weapon still took precedence over the ideological struggle. There is one very important conclusion to be drawn from this lesson: whenever there is a clash between the interests of ideological struggle and those of government priorities, it is as a rule the government interests that prevail.

The campaign against cosmopolitanism began to abate in connection with a forthcoming national holiday—the celebration of Stalin's seventieth birthday. Peacemaking was called for, at least for a while. We were occupied with holding discussions about Stalin's life, preparing exhibits, and planning gifts, among other things.

A meeting was called in the Central Committee, and the signal was given to retreat. Immediately there was talk about excesses. A very prominent comrade, condemning these excesses, was reported to have said, "We here in the party Central Committee gave a warning of "Look out!" but in the field it was heard as "Strike out!" and contritely shook his head. These words were transmitted eagerly by those who had been beaten, as well as those who had done the beating.

So, the campaign against cosmopolitans had been a success: many talented people were thrown out of scientific and cultural institutions, and some of them even died. Subsequently, statements against cosmopolitanism and other deviations from the true teachings of Marxism-Leninism would be used to serve the practical purpose of ousting people of Jewish background everywhere this was considered desirable and possible.

I have before me a small book. It was published by the "Nauka" ("Science") publishers in Moscow in 1971 under the imprint of the Institute of World History of the Academy of Sciences. It is entitled *Ideas and Traditions of the French Revolution in the Struggle between the Forces of Democracy and Fascism.* The author of the book is Yioganson Isaakovich Zil'berfarb. Professor V. M. Dalin wrote the preface.

I remember Professor Zil'berfarb. I can see him still—tall, with graying hair and strong features. Very polite, very mild-mannered and cultivated, and a passionate tourist.

Professor Zil'berfarb devoted many years to the study of socialist ideas, their history, and their impact on the development of social thought. He became a history professor at the age of twenty-nine, not a common occurrence. In 1940 Professor Zil'berfarb, at the suggestion of Academician V. P. Volgin, became his assistant in the commission on the history of social ideas of the Institute of History.

When I was a graduate student in 1947, Professor Zil'berfarb brilliantly defended his doctoral dissertation, "The Socialist Philosophy of Charles Fourier and His Place in the History of Socialist Thought in the First Half of the nineteenth Century."

It was Zil'berfarb's misfortune that his dissertation, when presented for approval to the Higher Qualifications Commission, came to the attention of P. N. Pospelov, a party historian, director of the Institute of Marxism-Leninism, editor of *Pravda*, at one time alternate member of the Presidium of the Central Committee, and Central Committee secretary, and so on and so forth. Pospelov did not like the dissertation, and he gave instructions for it to be rejected, calling it bourgeois-objectivist in a lead article in *Pravda*. At that time this was tantamount to handing down a death sentence. Zil'berfarb tried, in vain, to refute with scholarly arguments the accusations made against him. But attempts by both Zil'berfarb and his colleagues to mollify and persuade Pospelov were useless. After all, how could Pospelov, who had taught Lenin's wife, N. K. Krupskaya, how to write her memoirs and, most important, what to recall about Lenin, be expected to change his opinion of a work written by someone called Zil'berfarb?

Dalin writes in his foreword to Zil'berfarb's book: "For a number of reasons the major monograph by Yi. I. Zil'berfarb on the social philosophy of Fourier came out only in 1964." What a tragedy is concealed between these lines! Seventeen years of struggle were necessary before the Higher Qualifications Commission finally approved the dissertation.

Throughout the entire seventeen years Professor Zil'berfarb remained without employment. Nor did he obtain work after the publication of his monograph and his certification as a doctor of historical science. Another major monograph of his, "The Ideological Preparation of German Imperialism for the Second World War," has never been published.

Professor Zil'berfarb died in June 1968. He passed away a modest, refined, cultured man, a genuine scholar who for twenty years went without a job. But against the background of the passions that flared during those years, the tragedy of Yioganson Isaakovich Zil'berfarb went unnoticed.

I often wonder what might have happened to Karl Marx if he had lived in our time. For he so liked to repeat, as he paced across his room "I am a cosmopolitan, I am a cosmopolitan . . ."

3
Worse to Come

A break in my dissertation defense — I finally defend it — Academician Deborin's assistant — tragedy of the talented — the arrest of Yuzefovich and Gural'sky — party slackers — the flowering of Russian chauvinism in historical scholarship — another purge of the ranks

The title of my doctoral dissertation was "British Policy of the Eve of the Second World War." Those historians who had been chastened by experience, such as Vladimir Mikhailovich Turok-Popov, with whom I had been on friendly terms since 1946, warned me about dealing with recent subjects which were not yet considered history, such as the Second World War. Professor L. I. Zubok also spoke to me about this, advising me in a friendly way to concentrate on the nineteenth century. But I disregarded their warnings.

Our family was profoundly 'political.' My father, one of the oldest Soviet international journalists, was always well informed. He spoke several foreign languages fluently (he had studied before the First World War in the history and geography department at the Sorbonne in Paris with Professor Ernest Lavisse). At home, my father still had a burning interest in politics and history, and especially in current events.

My own experience as a participant in the Second World War also played a substantial role in my choice of a topic. During the first years following the end of the conflict, there were very few who had dealt seriously with the history of the war. While I was at work on my dissertation, a sharp political dispute arose, caused by the revelation at the Nuremberg trials of a good deal of material pertaining to the secret annexes to the Soviet-German treaty of August 23, 1939 (the House testimony). In 1947 a series of documents entitled *Nazi-Soviet Relations 1939-1941* was published in the United States, in response to which the historical reference *Falsifiers of History* was issued in the USSR in 1948. That study was for many years the basic reference work on the origins of the Second World War. Its authors were G. A. Deborin, B. Ye. Shtein and V. M. Khvostov. The text was vetted by Stalin. Also published at this time was a two-volume collection of German diplomatic documents from the period of the Anschluss and the seizure of Czechoslovakia, including notes from talks with the British on the conclusion of the Munich agreement. As it turned out, my dissertation was very much needed at the time.

In the autumn of 1947 my first publication appeared, devoted to British policy on the Czechoslovak question. The following year yet another article of mine was published, on the British policy of nonintervention in Spanish affairs.

The deadline for my graduate studies was the end of 1948, but owing to difficulties in obtaining foreign materials, I had to go through a lengthy procedure for secret clearance, and my graduate work was prolonged until May 1949.

Finally a day was scheduled for my defense: May 19, 1949. I recalled this recently while looking for my synopsis. In my search I unexpectedly came across the synopsis of another graduate student, who was defending a dissertation at the same meeting of the academic council. I now have this synopsis before me: "The National–Political Struggle in Bohemia in 1848 and F. Palacky." On the title page is a dedication: "To Sasha Nekrich—good luck to us both" and a signature, Udal'tsov. This was Ivan Ivanovich Udal'tsov. We had known each other since college days (he was two years ahead of me in the history department at Moscow State University). During the war Udal'tsov served in the Czechoslovak corps. He was Academician Picheta's graduate student, and after the Institute for Slavic Studies was formed, he went there. For many years he worked in the party Central Committee apparatus, and then he came back to the Institute for Slavic Studies, this time as its director. Some time afterwards Udal'tsov was again hired at the Central Committee. He had often been to Czechoslovakia and finally became an adviser to our embassy in Prague. In the memorable year 1968 he was among those who called for the harshest, most decisive measures against the recalcitrant Czechs. He had been a nice, sympathetic sort of fellow, but he turned into an ardent Stalinist. After my book *June 22, 1941* came out (Udal'tsov tried in vain to prevent a Czech translation; the book was published in Prague in 1967), Ivan, speaking in confidence to several Slavic historians, declared: "Nekrich must be expelled from the party immediately. The book must be banned." I believe he wrote to the authorities in Moscow in the same spirit. (During the investigation of my case by the party Control Committee, G. A. Deborin stated: "Czech historians have told me we need books like Nekrich's.") Udal'tsov also told his fellow historians, who had come to Prague full of malice and spite for the Czech intelligentsia (this was in 1967, in the presence of Czech president Antonin Novotny), that arrests should be carried out immediately, and if necessary, some of the Czechs should be "put up against the wall." This from a man who firmly considered himself an intellectual, the son of a professor, the nephew of a professor! Czech acquaintances of mine told me after 1968 that Udal'tsov came to be widely hated in Czechoslovakia. For his "services" he was made a member of the Central Committee apparatus, then was appointed director of the Novosti press agency, and then became ambassador to Greece. But all this happened much later, long after Ivan Udal'tsov and I were scheduled to defend our doctoral dissertations before the academic council of the institute on the same day.

Around the time of our dissertation defense, the situation in the contemporary history department had undergone a radical change. Appointed as department head was Fedor Vasilevich Potemkin, a historian of France in the first half of the nineteenth century. He was head of the world history department at the Higher Party School, and, although not a party member, enjoyed the favor and trust of the Central Committee. Potemkin was far removed from the problems of current history, but he learned very quickly. Before him the department had been run by A. M. Deborin, and consequently its output was faulty. At one of the first meetings of the department after his arrival, Potemkin made it clear that he would follow an ideological hard line. As regarded graduate students and their dissertations, already recommended for defense, the new department head announced that it would not be possible for the department to hire them after their period of graduate work was over. Therefore, I saw before me the unpleasant prospect of either being unemployed or else setting out for a provincial pedagogical institute, where research work would be out of the question for years.

But not hiring me was not enough for F. V. Potemkin. He did not at all like my friendly relations with Deborin and Maisky, the authority I enjoyed among my co-workers, and especially my independent manner. Potemkin changed the composition of my already appointed panel of examiners and arranged with Higher Party School Professor I. F. Ivashin to give a negative review. (I learned all this later, of course.) Ivashin took a long time over his review; I received it on Saturday, and my defense was scheduled for Monday. The review was devastating (unlike the very good review I had received from one official examiner, Professor N. L. Rubinshtein). It was easy to see that the review was made up of flagrant distortions and even outright falsification of the text. This was the first time I had directly experienced this particular form of the ideological struggle.

Over the few days remaining before my defense, I had to do the enormous job of collating texts and preparing a reply to Ivashin's critique. Were it not for the friendly assistance of Lydia Vasil'evna Pozdeyeva, I would hardly have managed in time. On Monday morning, the day of my dissertation defense, I learned that the authorities were inclined to postpone the session in light of the unfavorable review. But I was ready for battle; I was straining for action. The dissertation defense procedure allowed for a defense even in the case of negative reviews. It seemed to me that Ivashin's distortions were so glaring that I would be able to convince the members of the academic council that I was correct. The readers could not possibly think that my dissertation was somehow "seditious" in its understanding of events or its interpretation of

British policy in those years before the war. The work was in the mainstream of the official viewpoint on this issue and was based, in particular, on the historical reference work *Falsifiers of History*. The dissertation paid due tribute to Stalin's wisdom in anticipating and thwarting the plans of the imperialists by concluding the treaty with Hitler on August 23, 1939. But the work was also based on a great deal of factual material gleaned from foreign "bourgeois sources"; it dealt with a broad range of problems in British policy and with Britain's relations with other states. Finally, I attempted to analyze the prewar situation by using not only the usual two colors—black for imperialism and white for the Soviet Union—but others as well. Furthermore, I dared to recall the merits of M. M. Litvinov and other Soviet diplomats, in particular I. M. Maisky, in fighting for collective security. But both of them were now out of favor, and even a reference to their names was cause for annoyance, not just then, in the late 1940s and early 1950s, but as much as twenty-five years later as well.

At the institute I heard yet another piece of news: Ivashin did not intend to appear at the session. His plan to ruin my defense was obvious. I had a sharp exchange about this with Potemkin. Present at this conversation was my academic adviser, Maisky, who tried hard to calm me down and demonstrate the need, under the circumstances, to refrain from presenting my defense, to acknowledge some of Ivashin's comments, and to request a postponement until the fall. I categorically refused saying that to do so would be amoral and that I would not accept any deals. Potemkin responded, "So, in your opinion our morality is lower than yours?" I did not reply, for my answer was already perfectly clear.

Maisky took me aside. "Aleksandr Moiseevich, don't be a fool. There are times when it's better to wait things out, withdraw, and gather your strength." Since I had cooled off a bit, I realized myself that the conditions for defending my dissertation were unfavorable; the negative review and then the nonappearance of the man who had submitted it would deprive me of the opportunity to mount an effective defense. The members of the academic council would think: Well, the arguments given by the author seem convincing, but without Ivashin, we don't know what counterarguments he might have given. Moreover, it was far from clear how the Higher Qualifications Commission would view such a defense.

I was forced to swallow my pride and submit a statement to the chairman of the academic council: "In view of the fact that the official opponent I. F. Ivashin has given a negative review of my work, and himself did not appear for its defense, thereby depriving me of the opportunity to debate him, I request that the academic council postpone my dissertation defense and see to it that I. F. Ivashin is present at it." The deputy director of the institute, V. I. Shunkov, read out my statement to the council. From the back row I could hear a voice: "Strange!"—and that was all. The defense was postponed until autumn. I submitted the dissertation to the heads of the academic council so that no one could think later that I had made any changes in the text.

In the meantime I had no work. I had to think about earning my daily bread. I was rescued by the historian Aleksandr Yakovlevich Manusevich, then head editor for world history of the *Great Soviet Encyclopedia*. He proposed that I write articles for the first volumes and also serve as a consulting editor. The pay at the beginning was very high, and I earned a sufficient living.

My dissertation defense finally took place in September of that year. The previous spring the academic council had appointed a third examiner at my request, just in case Ivashin once again failed to appear. And that is exactly what happened. On the eve of my defense Ivashin sent the academic council a letter in which he asked that the defense procedure not be linked to his presence or absence. The statement was read out at the beginning of the meeting and was met with a buzz of comment and laughter. The dissertation defense went off successfully, and I became a candidate of historical sciences.

That autumn A. M. Deborin proposed that I work with him privately as his assistant. With joy and gratitude I accepted his proposal. My job consisted of researching and compiling brief reviews of foreign literature in the field of current political studies. Working with Deborin was extremely useful to me, as it broadened my horizons. What is more, Abram Moiseevich told me many interesting stories about his past life. Then, at the beginning of 1950, Deborin received from the presidium of the Academy of Sciences a stipend for half-pay at the junior researcher level for his assistant. As of March 1 that year I was appointed to that position as a staff member of the Institute of History. A year later I was put on staff full time, and I began to do independent research. I was no longer Deborin's assistant, but we remained close friends for many years until his death on March 8, 1963.

Meanwhile, things had quieted down a bit on the ideological front. The tension caused by the campaign against cosmopolitans abated somewhat but did not disappear altogether. In the depths of the history and philosophy departments there was still a personal power struggle going on. As far as the researchers were concerned, however, most were thrilled to return to the archives and libraries. Those who had come to the field not by some quirk of fate or as the result of an unsuccessful political career but by vocation—and they were in the majority—continued working relentlessly, even during the hardest, darkest times, so when the light was turned on, they were able to come out with many new studies. Such was the case, for example, with L. I.Zubok, who had worked during his years in disgrace on a number of serious studies of U.S. history and the American labor movement; this was also the case with A. Z. Manfred, A. S. Yerusalimsky. V. M. Turok-Popov and others.

My friend G. B. Fedorov had been studying the archaeology of Moldavia for many years, and even began excavations in the midst of those grim years. In the 1950s and 1960s he established a school of Moldavian archaeology, which remained in embryonic form until the Prutsko-Dnestrovsky expedition.

Other people, of course, had other solutions. After the persecution he underwent from 1947 to 1949, A. F. Miller, a man of outstanding ability and intellect, preferred not to publish his books, but rather devoted himself entirely to a ten-volume collective work entitled *World History*. I believe he made a great mistake in this—unfortunately an irreversible one, for the years go by quickly. He died in 1970 without having published even one new book.

Life goes on, regardless. But the quality of research in the field of history was much poorer than it would have been without the self-censorship, without the severe state censorship, without the ideological criticism of those years. A significant part of many careers was spent on nothing, on overcoming various obstacles. The machinery of life continued to function, of course, in spite of everything, but frequently to no avail.

Upon finishing graduate school, I immediately began to prepare my dissertation for publication. Excerpts appeared in *Izvestii istorii i filosofii* and in *Voprosy istorii* from 1947 to 1950. The article in *Voprosy istorii*, "The Double Game of the Chamberlain Government and Its Failure," was also noticed abroad, translated, and published in a number of countries. In 1950 and 1951 several of my articles on British prewar policy appeared. I worked hard and enjoyed it. And the deeper I delved into sources, facts, and events, the more questions I had, and the more often I was overcome by doubt.

The lethargic title of my doctoral dissertation, "British Policy on the Eve of the Second World War," alarmed some and annoyed others. That title, in accordance with the terms in vogue at the time, smacked of "objectivism." The wording had to be changed. I hoped that, in making a concession on this point, I would be able to preserve the basic contents of the book to come.

Meanwhile a great misfortune had occurred in the department: the arrest, and later the execution on the accusation of Jewish nationalism (as part of the Jewish Antifascist Committee affair), of Iosif Sigismundovich Yuzefovich, an old communist. Yuzefovich, a friend of the old party functionary S. A. Lozovsky, worked in the Sovinformburo (Soviet Information Bureau) as well as in the Institute of History. Our family knew Yuzefovich and his wife well, since during the war and in the years immediately afterwards my father had done a great deal of writing for the Sovinformburo, especially for the world labor movement department, which was headed by Yuzefovich. Iosif Sigismundovich had been a communist since the time of the Revolution and the Civil War. He had been through it all. He actively campaigned against all the oppositionists, smashing the "workers' opposition," the Trotskyites, the Bukharinites, and everyone else there was to be smashed. Then his turn came. He was rehabilitated posthumously. In 1957 I was invited by his widow, Maria Solomonovna, to an evening memorial for him in the Museum of the Revolution. There people spoke of Yuzefovich's life, and one of his friends, who had spent seventeen years in a camp and lost his eyesight there, recalled joyfully how in the leatherworker's union led by Yuzefovich they had, well, smashed the oppositionists.

With Yuzefovich's arrest, the atmosphere in the department became gloomier. Now, in addition to the errors already committed by the department staff, lack of vigilance was alleged. It has often occurred to me how kind fate has been to the organizers of all these criticism campaigns, or rather how skillfully they handled them. Indeed, the secretary of the institute's party bureau, V. D. Mochalov, had good reason to warn me. After Yuzefovich, yet another department staff member was arrested: Abram Yakovlevich Gural'sky. He had been a professional revolutionary, having embarked on this path as a youth. Abram Yakovlevich had fought in the Ukraine during the Civil War. In the years after the wwar he became a Comintern functionary; he worked in France, in Germany, in Latin America. During the party disputes Gural'sky supported the opposition for a while, and signed some sort of platform document, but he soon broke with the opposition altogether. Nonetheless, henceforth he was under suspicion. The year 1937 went well for him. He was one of the few who, once arrested, were released soon after. For some reason Gural'sky took pride in this fact.

Abram Yakovlevich was a specialist in French history, but I believe that with his knowledge he would have been a good historian of the modern period in almost any country. He was a man of lively, sharp intellect, in his heart extremely far from dogmatic theories; but in his work and his statements he always relied on the decisions of the appropriate party congresses and plenums and the congresses of the Comintern. He was never given a chance to publish his major works. The authorities printed only his individual articles, and they were not very even generous with that. His basic study on the history of modern France was never published.

Some of the details of Gural'sky's life in the concentration camp subsequently became known from the book by the Leningrader Dyakov. Gural'sky was released in 1955, five years after his arrest, already fatally ill. He died several months later. His funeral was attended by only four colleagues from the institute, including V. M. Turok-Popov. But before his own death he was fated to endure the sudden death of his daughter, a young, charming woman, unfortunately with a weak heart. Abram Yakovlevich's wife, a Spanish scholar named Tul'chinskaya, did not live long after her husband's death.

Gural'sky's arrest further intensified the atmosphere of suspicion and hatred in our department. F. V. Potemkin soon left, and in his departure earned neither glory nor sympathy. Vladimir Vladimirovich Biryukovich, a medievalist by training and a doctor of history, was appointed department head. Professor Biryukovich was on active military duty, held the rank of colonel, and was head of the world history department of the V. I. Lenin Military-Political Academy. He was a kind man, but he was ill with a heart problem. I do not understand to this day why on earth he was sent to head our department. Apparently he wished to move eventually into the Academy of Sciences, where he was a part-time senior researcher in the medieval history department. Vladimir Vladimirovich was an extremely meticulous, honest man, and he expected the same attitude toward work both in his office at the academy and in our section. From May 1950 until October 1951 I served as academic secretary of our section. He and I established good businesslike relations very quickly, and these soon developed into a friendship. I would visit him at his home. He visited mine. Vladimir Vladimirovich was married but had no children. He and his wife lived with his elderly mother, a woman of about ninety. Her son Vlad was the only one of her children still living, and she loved him dearly. Vladimir Vladimirovich, in turn, was very kind and gentle with her.

We were brought together by our similar approach to work in the department and our common views. What also tied me to Vladimir Vladimirovich was the fact that he was on friendly terms with Nina Aleksandrovna Sidorova, who was a friend of mine.

With Biryukovich's arrival in the department, work began to return to normal. The department was enlarged with young people such as Zina Belousova, Nina Smirnova, Jóse Garcia, Viktor Chada, and Volodya Salov, all from Moscow State University. Then there appeared Yura Arutyunyan, with his passionate neophyte eyes. There were others. At Moscow State they had received a basic education and had some research skills. They all became, in the final analysis, good specialists. A sad fate awaited Viktor Chada, however, who, at the age of forty, died of an incurable disease.

Reinforcements came from another educational institution as well: the Academy of Social Sciences of the party Central Committee. As a rule, the academy trained ideological cadres for the party. Those who graduated normally received appointments as party regional committee secretaries for propaganda, senior agitators, discussion group leaders, and so on. But by 1951 times had changed; there were fewer and fewer vacancies in the party apparatus, and the competition was greater. It was necessary to find other employment for those who had finished the academy—that "treasure trove of our party," in the words of Georgy Malenkov. And it was found—in the social sciences. There really was a need here for highly qualified staff.

But the most capable graduate students the Academy of Social Sciences kept for its own departments. The first swallow to fly our way from the academy was S. A. Ovanesyan, already a middle-aged woman. Her speciality was the American labor movement, and she had been a graduate student under L. I. Zubok. After she became party organizer for the department, she was constantly "raising vigilance." At one time Ovanesyan had worked in the Cheka, the state security police, "under Beria's guidance," as she proudly used to put it before June 1953; after that she stopped talking about it altogether. Sofia Artemevna Ovanesyan was an unhappy woman. Her husband had been arrested in 1937, and one can imagine how hard she had had to try to regain the party's confidence in the years that followed. One of our graduate students decided to consult her about his dissertation, since there were so many facts and he could not decide on the basis of what principle he should sort them out. "So do as I do," she replied. "One or two facts and an in-depth analysis." This immediately became a quotable quote. Ovanesyan did not produce any creative work. Finally, she received a pension—a special one, I believe—and left in peace.

In the summer of 1951 there arrived a group of graduates from the Academy of Social Sciences—about six people in all. One of them, Aleksei Nikolaevich Filippov, was a staff member of the party apparatus and, before studying at the academy, had been propaganda secretary for one of the party regional committees. He was not a person accustomed to research work, although not very young, but he was kind and good-natured, and he soon fell completely under the influence of Boris Nikolaevich Krylov. The latter was an entirely different sort of person—tough, vain, and ruthless in achieving his goals. Another member of this group was Ivan Nikiforovich Slobodyanyuk, an extremely lazy but sharp-witted man. He headed the Spanish editorial office of the Radio Committee, and since he had some free time (as he put it himself), he had decided to engage in scholarship—that is, to receive from the Institute of History another salary of 3000 rubles in addition to the one from the radio. It should be said that the introduction in 1947 of new salary scales for researchers greatly improved their living standards. But the research institutes also began increasingly to attract the attention of those who sought a not-too-burdensome (from their point of view) but comfortable life. Slobodyanyuk belonged to that category.

Gradually Krylov threw together a group of "true party members" into which he brought a few other colleagues. Their main activity consisted of constantly broadcasting to the higher authorities any troubles in the department and in the institute, thereby creating an atmosphere of suspicion and mistrust. There was nothing surprising in this, since our microcosm was simply part of a larger world where the same kind of things took place, only on a much larger scale. Krylov stated openly that a class struggle was under way in both the department and the institute. But if this was the case, it meant that there must be class enemies. The party bureau of the institute, headed in those years by Leonid Mikhailovich Ivanov, an independent man of principle, rejected that thesis. Krylov, however, was not deterred. Time seemed to be on his side and on that of people like him. This campaign began to catch on in various official bodies, first in the personnel office of the presidium of the Academy of Sciences, which was headed by Krylov's friend Kosikov, than ever higher and higher.

I sift through the documents of that period with some interest and surprise. Here are shorthand reports of discussions of my manuscripts from 1951 and 1952; critiques; minutes of department meetings, excerpts from the report of the director of the institute, A. L. Sidorov, my letters to the academic council of the institute and to Academician A. M. Pankratova; correspondence over the Academy of Sciences presidium decree of March 20,1953; a letter to the director of the department of sciences of the Central Committee, A. M. Rumyantsev, dated April 21, 1953, and so on.

Did all that really happen? Twenty years have gone by. So much is different. There have been so many changes in the life of our institute. But something very important has remained unchanged.

The documents enable me to redraw a picture of what was happening in 1951–52. The department of modern history was notorious throughout the institute for the fact that its staff had not published any books for some years. In 1949 *Locarno*, the one and only book by V. M. Turok-Popov, came out. Then there appeared works by L. I. Zubok and B. Ye. Shtein, which were officially declared to be flawed. The department was drifting without a helm and without a rudder, partly out of carelessness, partly out of the fear of being accused of distorting something or misrepresenting someone. This led to a situation in which, over the more than ten years of the department's existence (up to 1952), no attempts were made even to lay down basic guidelines for the study of modern history. The department was feverish with activity: as soon as one plan was drawn up calling only for individual monographs, it would be canceled and another drawn up calling for no monographs at all. The restructurings took place yearly, some in connection with the Nineteenth Party Congress (1959), some on the occasion of the appearance of *Problems of Linguistics* (1952) by Stalin. The institute, like all other scientific institutions, was required to react to every new word from the leader, and it took on more and more obligations. And so it went, on and on. Historical scholarship increasingly became a branch specialized in the compilation of illustrative material on the "utterances of genius" made by the country's leader. The fire and brimstone unleashed against "bourgeois falsifiers of history" was not accompanied in those years by any kind of serious attempts at understanding trends in Western historical thought. Matters reached the point where the obscurantist slogan "We do not argue with the bourgeois historians. We reject them" was openly proclaimed.

Under such circumstances, the prospects for ignorance were enormous, and the idlers who took advantage lived very well indeed. S. A. Ovanesyan had been "working" in the department since 1948 on a monograph devoted to problems in the U.S. labor movement. After three years, the monograph was deleted from the program without the department's ever having seen or discussed a single aspect of it. And here is another example: for about two years a certain Boretsky, a graduate of the Academy of Social Sciences, worked in the department as a senior researcher. During that entire period he did not write one line. Next he was transferred to the Institute of Eastern Studies, where he spent another year and a half. The result of his "activity": thirty typewritten pages, half of which were lifted from the work of Professor A. F. Miller, whom Boretsky furthermore had slandered mercilessly. Also gone from the institute without leaving behind any scholarly output were Krylov and Filippov.

The cold war situation inside and outside the country had a remarkable impact on historical scholarship. Capable and talented people, genuine scholars, were criticized, indeed abused, for any slip, for even the slightest error, or even simply for "cosmopolitanism." And this harassment was engaged in by those idlers, cheap demagogues living like parasites off the body of science. They were interested in one thing: how much longer they could thrive at the expense of the state. As I wrote to A. M. Pankratova on November 17, 1952, "these people are creating a situation characterized by unprincipled cliques and mutual assistance among idlers."

To the credit of the overwhelming majority of historians from our institute, they viewed these people with great, albeit often covert, antipathy, although it is true that some staff members tried to curry favor with them.

In October 1951 the manuscript of my thoroughly revised doctoral dissertation was recommended for publication and sent to the Academy of Sciences. Here is where my troubles began.

In the summer of 1951 the Academy had published a book by Professor Boris Yefimovich Shtein, *Bourgeois Falsifiers of History*. The book claimed to be an analysis of foreign documents and memoirs of events leading up to the Second World War. Boris Yefimovich was an old hand at the Ministry of Foreign Affairs, he occupied a number of senior posts and held the highest diplomatic rank, ambassador extraordinary and plenipotentiary. Shtein headed at one time or another various divisions of the foreign department, and he served as ambassador to Italy as well. He had been at work on the history of international relations and the history of foreign policy for a long time—almost since the beginning of the 1920s—had written a great deal, and had also taught, primarily at the Higher Diplomatic School. He was often invited to the institute, either as a thesis examiner or as a participant in a discussion. It was therefore quite natural that Boris Yefimovich should ask our department to discuss his latest manuscript and recommend it for publication under the imprint of the Institute of History. The book was discussed, recommended, and issued. But someone "upstairs" did not like it. In issue number 8 of *Bolshevik* for 1952 there appeared a scathing review. The book was called "harmful, flagrantly distorting the historical truth," and "flawed." Moreover, something unheard of in academy practice occurred: on May 30, 1952, the presidium of the Academy of Sciences handed down a special decree concerning the "errors" in B. Ye. Shtein's book.

It was proposed that the institute review all works in modern history, even those currently in progress. These included my own, which furthermore had already been set in type. The new bosses mobilized all possible forces in order to squelch the manuscript. In a discussion on July 8, 1952, which lasted many hours, I was accused of everything imaginable. But still this wreaking of scholarly destruction did not succeed. I acknowledged those comments I thought to be justified, and point by point (my statement lasted an hour and a half) refuted those arguments that were based on distortions, fantasies, and outright falsification of the text. Only three of the speakers (M. N. Mashkin, I. M. Maisky, and L. V. Pozdeyeva) gave an objective appraisal of the work. My own arguments apparently had some effect. A. N. Filippov, in summarizing the outcome of the discussion, proposed giving me until the end of the year for further work. (It is not without interest that Filippov had spoken as a reviewer of my book at the academic council of the Institute and had given a positive written and oral reaction.) The recommended publication date of 1951 was not rescinded. But the Academy members decided to take revenge through the usual administrative channels. At a party group meeting they branded the positive reactions as "unprincipled." An article to this effect appeared in the bulletin board newsletter of the institute. Three months later, at a department meeting devoted to an entirely different matter, a decision was adopted that virtually reversed the appraisal of the work given during the discussion.

At this stage the matter ended with the cancellation of the typesetting. In the final analysis this was extremely fortunate for me, for had this not happened, I would have had to make amendments to the text which would have made me ashamed afterwards. But at the time it was a terrible blow for me. My status in the department was greatly diminished.

As early as the time of the discussion of my work on July 8, 1952 I had pointed out to those present that I. N. Slobodyanyuk had copied part of his review from the review of another staff member. This had seemed amusing to me, but nothing more. Two months later, at a meeting of the joint authors and editors of the ninth volume of *World History* (Maisky was the editor in chief at the time), there was to be a discussion of the chapter by Slobodyanyuk on Italy from 1929 to 1939. As I began to read the text, I realized that something was wrong; I felt as if I had read it somewhere before. On consulting a few general textbooks on the subject, I easily discovered that out of fourteen pages of text, Slobodyanyuk had "borrowed" thirteen! I realized that desperate attempts would be made to hush up the matter. Therefore I made a point of speaking at an open meeting. After this the case, contrary to existing practice, was give widespread publicity. In spite of the desperate campaign of the "true patriots" from the Academy of Social Sciences, on October 9 A. L. Sidorov issued the order to dismiss Slobodyanyuk from the institute on the grounds of plagiarism. This was a truly revolutionary step, unheard of in the history of national scholarship. Since then I have never heard of a case in which someone was dismissed for plagiarism, even though there were more than enough instances of it. The department voted to censure Slobodyanyuk, and demanded that he be dismissed from the department. Slobodyanyuk had worked for eight months in the department as a full-time researcher while simultaneously receiving a full salary from the Radio Committee. This was a flagrant violation of the rules on holding more than one office, although it was not the only such case.

In accordance with the charter of the Academy of Sciences, the post of senior research member was to go to academicians, corresponding members, and doctors of science. Candidates for doctor of science were to be taken on at that level only if they presented exceptional qualifications. Now, virtually all graduates of the Academy of Social Sciences were assigned this post. Therefore, a policy was initiated to establish a privileged stratum among social science scholars, who were easily managed by the relevant bosses. In the 1920s, when the majority of historians were nonparty members and, in addition, came primarily from the bourgeois and noble intelligentsia, the Institute of Red Professorship was established. Its graduates then made up the basic party elite among historians and philosophers. But these scholars were distinguished from the new generation—that is, the graduates of the Academy of Social Sciences—by a thirst for knowledge. (Most of them had come to the Institute of Red Professorship with experience in the Civil War and the underground under their belts.) The Academy graduates who ended up in our department were also thirsty—not for knowledge, though, but for jobs, positions of privilege. They were interested little, if at all, in history as a field of study, seeing it merely as one way to achieve a comfortable existence. They made up for their lack of professional knowledge with arguments of an administrative nature. As true Stalinists, they, like the father of our nation, respected and valued only strength. And they were strong—strong in their lack of principles, their readiness to apply in their struggle for success any methods, even the kind that would dismay decent people. They were strong, too, in their corporate unity, in their helpful assistance and mutual guarantees. I have it on good authority that Slobodyanyuk, after being kicked out of the institute, was called to the central party offices by a friend, who told him: "High-tail it, Vanya, to Kiev." So Slobodyanyuk set out for the Ukrainian capital for a position as nothing less than head of the journalism department at Kiev State University!

After the stormy meetings and oratory, the campaign against cosmopolitans had entered a calm period of what passed for routine and became an integral part of life in our society. In smashing the cosmopolitans, the higher organs had drawn attention to the need for asserting the beneficial role the Russian empire had played in uniting with the peoples of Central Asia and the Caucasus. The campaign against so-called local nationalism, however, followed along the lines not of internationalism but rather of great power Russianism.

The starting signal was given by an article by the secretary of the Central Committee of the Communist party of Azerbaijan, M. Bagirov, entitled "On the Nature of the Muridism Movement and Shamil" (*Bolshevik* no.13, 1950). The pretext for the article was the decision by the USSR Council of Ministers in May 1950 to withdraw the award of the Stalin prize to the Azerbaijani historian G. Guseinov for his book *On the History of Social and Philosophical Thought in Azerbaijan.* (Soon after that decision, Guseinov committed suicide.) The article also criticized a book by the Dagestani historian R. M. Magomedov, *The Mountaineers' Struggle for Independence under the leadership of Shamil*, which had been published in 1939. The inspiration cited by Magomedov in the preface to his book was characteristic of the values of those times: he had been stimulated in writing it, he said, by the desire to restore the historical truth about Shamil, the nineteenth-century Caucasian rebel leader, since "enemies of the people, who had made their way to leadership positions, had portrayed Shamil as a reactionary" (p. 17). Next, in the journal *Voprosy istorii* there appeared a small article on the same subject by the secretary of the Dagestani regional party committee, A. Daniyalov, repeating and in some cases expanding upon the basic contents of Bagirov's article. In 1951 articles were published by A. Yakunin (*Voprosy istorii* no.4, 1951), and A. Fadeev (no.9, 1951), as well as the editorial in *Voprosy istorii,* number 4 and others, in which it was stated categorically that the unification of the peoples of Central Asia and the Caucasus with Russia was a progressive affair. The fact that the unification had been accomplished by force and was a manifestation of tsarism's aggressive expansionist policy did not overly trouble the Marxist messengers of this doctrine. They completely disregarded the view of Lenin on this issue and defended the thesis that the border states of Central Asia were in danger of being swallowed up by other states more backward than Russia (such as Persia and Turkey) or enslaved by British imperialism.

At the beginning of 1951 *Pravda* published an article by G. Shashibaev, Kh. Aidarova, and A. Yakunin entitled "For a Marxist-Leninist Clarification of Issues in the History of Kazakhstan," which demolished a book by the Kazakh scholar E. Bekmakhanov, *Kazakhstan, from the 1820s to the 1840s*. This work had been defended by the author as his doctoral dissertation. The official examiners were corresponding members of the Academy of Sciences N. M. Druzhinin, A. M. Pankratova, and Professor M. P. Vyatkin.

As might be expected, after the article appeared in *Pravda*, a meeting of the Institute of History's academic council was convened on February 21, 1951. Deputy Director Utchenko, who presided, called for severe criticism of Bekmakhanov's work and recalled that in 1947, during the previous discussion of Muridism and Shamil, such leading historians as Druzhinin, Pankratova, and M. V. Nechkina had supposedly misinterpreted that movement, describing it as progressive. In accordance with the canons of that time, Utchenko's speech abounded in such epithets as "flawed," "anti-Marxist," "bourgeois-nationalist distortions." In his conclusion he stated: "Therefore, Bekmakhanov praises to the skies the Sultan Kenesary. By creating his own Kazakh Shamil, Bekmakhanov interprets Kenesary from a bourgeois-nationalist standpoint." The speaker called for a reappraisal of interpretations of other nationalist movements as well, such as, for example, the Andizhan uprising of 1898, since it was religious by nature and supported by British agents. Utchenko saw the reactionary nature of the Andizhan uprising in the fact that its objective was the establishment of a separate, independent Muslim state in the struggle to "tear away from Russia a substantial part of Central Asia." These words show the quintessence of the official view of that time: any attempt to stay separate from tsarist Russia was to be considered reactionary and a severing from Russia of her own territory. Utchenko's idea was followed up on by Yakunin, who presented the policy of tsarist Russia at that time in Central Asia as *defensive*! Yakunin talked about the aggression of the Central Asian khanates in Kazakhstan and stated that "the tsarist government was forced to build fortifications in order to protect Russian and Kazakh settlements from pirate raids." Kenesary then "relied in his struggle, in fact, on the Central Asian khanates, and they were the ones who inspired him." In the style of that time, Yakunin recalled the espionage activities of British colonizers as well. This statement virtually justified the colonizing policy of Russian tsarism

Among those forced to acknowledge their error in evaluating the Kenesary movement, and likewise the error in some of Bekmakhanov's views, were Druzhinin, Pankratova, and Vyatkin (who had been the senior editor of

Bekmakhanov's book), although Druzhinin did so in a very cautious and purely academic manner. Aidarova, one of the authors of the *Pravda* article, was Druzhinin's graduate student. He was so indignant over her statement before the academic council that he stopped speaking to her.

But the matter was not confined to a discussion. At Utchenko's suggestion, the academic council recognized as incorrect its previous decision to grant Bekmakhanov the title of doctor of historical sciences and rescinded it. During the first ballot on this question Druzhinin and Pankratova voted against this proposal (their objection, of course, was not mentioned in the press). Utchenko tried in vain to persuade them to vote along with the rest. They refused to do so. Then a recess was announced. The next day, the academic council met once again. Shortly before, Pankratova was called in by the Central Committee for a chat. On the second ballot only the nonparty member Druzhinin maintained his position. Those who knew Druzhinin, an impeccably honest man, a "knight of historical scholarship," as he has been described, expected nothing less from him. At the time, Pankratova could hardly have behaved otherwise. After all, she was a party member. (That same year, at the Nineteenth Party Congress, she had been elected a member of the Central Committee).

Bekmakhanov was deprived of his doctoral title, dismissed from work, and soon arrested. He spent several years in prison, then was rehabilitated after the Twentieth Party Congress, and his academic title was restored. The assessment of his work as flawed was recognized as erroneous.

People tried not to recall this story in subsequent years at the institute. It was quite an embarrassment.

The dispute over the progressive nature of the border peoples' joining the Russian empire, which might have progressed on a purely scientific basis, very soon developed into a pogrom, with name-calling, public defamation, and the settling of personal scores. Quite typical in this regard was an article by Yakunin, "On Evaluating the Nature of the National Movement of the 1830s and 1840s in Kazakhstan (*Voprosy istorii* no.4, 1951), which looked like a denunciation, since, in addition to condemning outright the "bourgeois nationalist" Bekmakhanov, the author named individuals who shared Bekmakhanov's point of view and supported him, including Vyatkin, Pankratova, Kuchkin, Druzhinin, and Bakhrushin, as well as vice-president Kenespaev of the Kazakh Academy of Sciences, secretary Omarov of the Central Committee of the Communist party of Kazakhstan, and the reviewer K. Sharipov.

In April 1951 the Kazakhstan central committee condemned Bekmakhanov's errors, as well as the "errors" in the second edition of the collective work *Istoria Kazakhstana*. This question was also discussed at the Central committee plenum. The academic council of the Institute of History,

Archaeology, and Ethnography of the Academy of Sciences of the Kazakh SSR decreed that the Kenesary movement was to be deemed reactionary. There followed immediately a decision to deprive Bekmakhanov of his titles of doctor of sciences and candidate of sciences and his position as professor. Similar punishment was meted out at the same meeting to a candidate of historical sciences named E. Dil'mukhamedov, who supposedly had committed "the same bourgeois-nationalist errors" in his dissertation. In October 1951 Dil'mukhamedov was stripped of his title. In November 1951 the same academic council saw to it that yet another member of the institute was stripped of his academic title as candidate in literary criticism—A. Zhirengin, for his work *Abai and His Russian Friends.* Zhirengin's "crime" consisted in his stating in his thesis that the creative work of the famous Kazakh educator Abai Kunanbaev had been influenced by various members of the People's Movement ("Narodniki") who subsequently became social revolutionaries, and that Zhirengin depicted these social revolutionaries as (heaven forbid!) "propagators of the idea of progressive Russian democratic culture" (*Voprosy istorii*, no.2, 1952, p.148).

Apparently this issue greatly alarmed the Kazakh leadership, since at the nineteenth Party Congress, the first secretary of the Central Committee of the Communist party of Kazakhstan, Zh. Shayakhmetov, dwelled especially on the errors of the Institute of History in appraising Kenesary, and at the same meeting Bagirov roasted the journal *Voprosy istorii* for its discussion of the formula "the lesser evil"; now, it seemed, one should speak only of the advantages in the unification of the border peoples with the Russian empire. This phrase originated in a letter from M. V. Nechkina to *Voprosy istorii* (no.4, 1951): "Regarding the 'lesser evil' formula . . ." The point was that for the border peoples of Central Asia and the Caucasus, unification with Russia was the lesser evil compared with the threat of unification with the other empires of Turkey and Persia, or with the backward, warlike Central Asian khanates, where British agents enjoyed so much influence. Nechkina proposed in her letter that this formula be considered in light of the development of the economic and cultural life of the peoples of the Russian empire, regardless and in spite of the policy of tsarism. She emphasized the need to clarify the history of the union of working people from various nationalities in a common struggle against exploiters. Reaction to the letter demonstrated that many historians tended to regard the unification with the Russian empire of Armenia, Georgia, and areas of the Volga as a blessing for their inhabitants. The outcome of the discussion of this topic was resoundingly summed up a year and a half later in an article by L. Maksimov, "On the Journal 'Voprosy istorii'" (*Bolshevik* no.13, 1952), in which Nechkina's published articles were described as a gross error.

The campaign against cosmopolitans gave the green light to the invasion of scholarship by warmongering ignoramuses. I recall an article by S. I. Kozhukhov (director of the museum in Borodino) on Academician Ye. V. Tarle's so-called incorrect evaluation of some aspects of the Fatherland War of 1812 (*Bolshevik* no. 19, 1951). I shall not repeat here all of Kozhukhov's nonsense, for this case could be considered rather a clinical one. Still and all, a special meeting of the academic council of the Institute of History was called on this matter at the end of October 1951. But this time the attempt to organize yet another smashing defeat of an outstanding historian failed. The scholars were roused to anger and, furthermore, were tired of endless critical campaigns. Some historians entered into polemics with Kozhukhov. Others simply kept silent. *Voprosy istorii* observed indignantly in an editorial that the historians had acted badly, "instead of confessing their mistakes" (no. 11, 1951, p.26).

Despite the fact that historians in 1951–52 fought with all their might against those who had to be opposed, especially the Marrists, Moloch continued to demand further sacrifices.

In the summer of 1952 there appeared in *Bolshevik* a devastating article on the activities of *Voprosy istorii*. At that time the July issue of the journal had already been impounded. Once again the desire to reaffirm the usual readiness for confession of error and repentance was so great that to every copy of the journal was attached an eight-line insert, which the criticism in *Bolshevik* found to be "totally justified." The editors of *Voprosy istorii* promised that in the next issue, they would print a lengthy criticism of their errors. The editorial board kept its promise. Complete repentance was published in a lead article under the title "From the Editorial Board of *Voprosy istorii*," in which were listed all the errors pointed out by the *Bolshevik* critic Maksimov, citing first and foremost "a backlog of work on problems facing historical scholarship in connection with the appearance of the work of genius by I. V. Stalin, *Marxism and Problems of Linguistics*" (no. 8, 1952, p.3). At the same time, the article roundly criticized its former and current editors in chief, A. D. Udal'tsov and P. N. Tretyakov, for following the linguistic theories of E. Marr in the past and not criticizing their own mistakes.

So it was that by the autumn of 1952 the circumstances were ripe for a complete purge in historical scholarship of "alien views," and of their proponents as well. At that time A. L. Sidorov was deputy director of the Institute (Utchenko had remained head of the department of ancient history). No matter how hard the editorial board of *Voprosy istorii* tried to beg for mercy from the bosses, it was all in vain. On October 17, 1952, the presidium of the Academy of Sciences recognized the work done by the journal as unsatisfactory.

But here history intervened. Within five months Stalin was dead. A new editorial board was formed soon after his death. Beginning with issue number 6 of 1953, it had almost an entirely new membership. Only B. D. Grekov and N. M. Druzhinin remained from the previous board. A. M. Pankratova was named editor in chief. Her deputy was E. N. Burdzhalov.

But thus far events continued to develop tragically for historians. Ten days after the presidium's decision, on October 27, 1952, an expanded meeting of the academic council was called in our institute. Sidorov had decided to organize a "gala" to commemorate the beginning of a new era in historical science. In addition to the academic council members, the leading historians in Moscow were invited to the meeting. Officially the paper Sidorov was to deliver in honor of the event was on historical scholarship in light of the new work by Stalin and the decisions of the nineteenth Party Congress. But the heart of his paper was directed against the staff members at the Institute of History.

The major aspect of Sidorov's report was the accusation that the institute pursued the "flawed practice of being conciliatory toward bourgeois concepts." By way of example, Sidorov once again referred to the evaluation of Muridism and the movement of Kenesary Kasimov. S. B. Veselovsky, I. I. Mintz, L. I. Zubok, and B. Ye Shtein were once again named propagators of cosmopolitan ideas.

New names appeared too: Z. Sh. Radzhabov, a former doctoral candidate who had written a dissertation on the history of social thought in Uzbekistan in the colonial period, G. I. Basharin, who had written a work on the history of Yakutia. The Higher Qualification Commission stripped them both of their doctoral credentials. The speaker then poured scorn upon those works that had supposedly been infiltrated with bourgeois ideas.

Following Sidorov's example, others began to attack unpublished manuscripts. They made mention of the mistakes in unpublished studies by Nekrich, Turok-Popov, Maisky, and P. A. Lisovsky, and spoke extensively of the errors of B. F. Porshnev. In the early 1950s Porshnev had published a series of articles on the nature of feudal society, in which he proposed the theory of the primacy of the class struggle. This point gave rise to polemics both in the institute and in the press.

In this discussion, in my view, it was not differences in interpreting the feudal nature of the means of production that prevailed, even though the discussion began on this point, but various passions of a purely personal nature. In this regard both sides would stop at nothing in dragging their opponents through the mud and humiliating them. This was the impression I had then, and the passage of time has not changed it.

Nechkina was attacked for the letter she had written to the editors of *Voprosy istorii*, and *Voprosy istorii* got its share of criticism too. Later the record pointed to unself-critical statements made by Mintz, Maisky, and Nechkina ("she did not understand her errors"). Even Utchenko was blasted for not being sufficiently self-critical in his own statement. And in a lead article in *Voprosy istorii* S. Trapeznikov was criticized because in his book *The Campaign of the Bolshevik Party for Collectivization in Agriculture during the First Five-Year Plan* "he does not show collectivization of agriculture to be an objectively natural process" (no. 12, 1952, p.7). What was involved were the "errors" of the current highest academic officers in the party Central Committee.

But who could have foreseen that the former director of the party school in Kishinev would become a member of the Central Committee and head the department of science? Yes, a great deal might have been done or not done had one foreseen what would happen—or so the leaders of our institute would sigh to themselves. But for now they tirelessly had to fight each and every deviation, every distortion. And in this struggle, "open," "honest," "principled" recognition of one's own errors, and a genuine heartfelt repentance, played a substantial role. At the end of 1952 repentance was required of the Marrists, and *Voprosy istorii* in its last lead article for 1952 called for repentance from those archaeologists whose works contained Marrist errors. And who among the archaeologists had not committed the sin of Marrism? The guilty included just about all the major scholars: P. P. Yefimenko, P. I. Boriskovsky, T. S. Passek, A. P. Okladnikov, and especially V. I. Ravdonikas (already branded a cosmopolitan) as well as M. I. Artamonov, P. N. Tretyakov, and A. D. Udal'tsov. Also under the strong influence of the Marrists, it seemed, were S. P. Tolstov, S. I. Rudenko, and especially the Jew A. N. Bernshtam. But archaeologists for some reason were not inclined to repent, and the most stubborn was correspondent member of the Academy of Sciences V. I. Ravdonikas.

It is interesting to see from the example of S. P. Tolstov that during this frightening twilight period of the Stalinist epoch not one scholar could be guaranteed that he would not be accused of errors. Everything was simply a matter of degree. A successful archaeologist and ethnographer who had excavated ancient Khorezm, the ambitious Sergei Pavlovich Tolstov was made in 1950 one of the seven "apostles." The Academy of Sciences presidium for some reason established seven new posts for academic secretaries of the Academy, and over them was placed a senior academic secretary. The academic secretaries were something like commissars, individuals who, on behalf of the presidium, monitored the activities of the Academy's divisions. Among the academic secretaries were two archaeologists, Tolstov and the extrovert S. V. Kiselev. Tolstov was given an unpleasant mission after the "Leningrad Affair" (the destruction of the social science scholars in Leningrad). To him went the "honor" of closing up the Institute of Eastern

Studies in Leningrad. I believe that the untimely death of Academician I. Yu. Krachkovsky was a result of the bitterness he felt on the closing of this institute. And yet, in spite of such valuable services rendered, Tolstov was still subjected to criticism. The story of the closing of the institute was never forgotten or forgiven. On several occasions Tolstov presented his candidacy for election to the Academy (he was counting on entering it directly, bypassing the post of correspondent member). And each and every time the elderly academicians voted amicably against him. Finally, in desperation, he decided to opt for a vote as correspondent member and was duly elected. He never got any farther, though. The post of academic secretary was abolished soon after the death of Stalin.

The appearance of Stalin's book and the grandiose campaign to apply the views expressed in it to historical scholarship, as well as to all other fields, were like the death throes of the Stalinist regime. But these convulsions overwhelmed some of the historians. For a long time during these discussions and campaigns of criticism Porshnev had stuck stubbornly to his work. But after a reference to his "errors" in the February issue of *Kommunist* in 1953, he sent to *Voprosy istorii* a lengthy letter of repentance, in which he subjected himself to sharp self-criticism, or rather self-flagellation (no. 4, 1953, pp.139–142). One can only imagine how much he regretted this when he learned soon after that Stalin was dead.

This was, in brief, the situation. Once again, the storm clouds were beginning to gather over my head as well.

4

Death Throes of the Stalinist Regime

The call of hatred: clanging the alarm out at sea
Snow coming down ... how cold it is!
The world is all drowned in fog
Life itself, all a-tremble, is racing toward familiar shores.
Away from the frenetic clanging out at sea.
—Paul Verlaine

On the *Diplomatic Dictionary* editorial board — V. S. Solov'yova's suicide attempt — district committee Secretary — anti-Semite and common criminal — I am accused of bourgeois objectivism — the manuscript is withdrawn from the printer's — "Savior of the Homeland," Lydia Timashuk — the arrest of Academician Maisky — when they started to clear out the roots — we mourn Stalin — everything flows, sometimes even backwards.

In the last twenty years a great deal has been said and written the world over about the mass crimes committed in the Soviet Union under Stalin's dictatorship. After the appearance of Aleksandr Solzhenitsyn's *Gulag Archipelago*, people remembered the violence committed in the years during the Soviet state's establishment under Lenin. There are no mass repressions at present in the Soviet Union, but persecution for political or religious reasons has continued to this day. It was in fact these persecutions—in addition to disappointment over a possible movement of Soviet society toward safeguarding human rights, democratization of all aspects of Soviet life, and, most of all, freedom of speech and of the press without fear of the consequences, as well as the openly complacent use of force demonstrated during the invasion of Czechoslovakia by Soviet forces in August 1968—that gave rise to the dissident movement.

There has been a great deal of debate as to whether violence and abuse of power are merely the undesirable consequence of revolutionary fervor or a flaw inherent in a society that itself arose through the use of force. Violence is therefore interpreted as a constant element of that society, and only the forms it takes are subject to change.

A resolution to this debate can be found only through painstaking, dispassionate (insofar as is possible, of course, since completely dispassionate judgment is itself unachievable) research into all aspects of Soviet life and history.

61

In this connection I recall one particular episode from the final years of Stalin's life, which perhaps best reflects the special features of the Soviet regime.

In Moscow on Stanislavsky Street (formerly Leontiev Lane) is located the building housing the Office for Diplomatic Corps Affairs. In the late 1940s and early 1950s, the editorial board of the *Diplomatic Dictionary* would meet in a few small rooms on the first floor of that building. This editorial board was part of the Office of State Political Literature Publications (Gospolitizdat), but it led its own, somewhat separate life. There was not one professional historian or jurist of renown who had not taken part to some extent in the compilation of the *Diplomatic Dictionary*. The first and even the second edition of the dictionary could claim a high degree of scholarliness. The substantive content was gradually reduced in subsequent editions, and the personnel section began to grow quickly, so that the *Diplomatic Dictionary* gradually became a dry, purely formal directory.

I wrote for the *Diplomatic Dictionary* and liked to visit its editorial offices, where a friendly, relaxed atmosphere always prevailed, something that did not prevent, but rather encouraged, a businesslike ambience.

The editorial board of the dictionary was first headed by the chairman of the Soviet Information Bureau, S. A. Losovsky, and next by the former attorney general of the USSR, then first deputy minister for foreign affairs, A. Ya. Vyshinsky. Its membership also included the former deputy minister for foreign affairs and former ambassador to London, I. M. Maisky. The waves of the latest purge, unleashed by Stalin on a grandiose scale, soon reached the shores of the *Diplomatic Dictionary*. The first victim was Lozovsky, arrested in January or February of 1948 as part of the Antifascist Jewish Committee affair. Then the head editor, Teumyan, was arrested. Losovsky's arrest did not generally affect the editorial staff, in that the reins of power were held by Vyshinsky, and, at least for the time being, no one dared touch the institution he headed. The leaders of Gospolitizdat (director Chernov, party organization secretary Boldyrev, chief editor Matyushkin), shortly after the beginning of the anticosmopolitan campaign, a manifestation of anti-Semitism at the top, began to verify the work of the editors, for which purpose a special commission was established.

Denunciations began to spread among members of the editorial board. The first victim was the Eastern studies specialist A. B. Belen'kii, whose father had been a purge victim in 1937. I knew Aleksandr Borisovich well; he had been a year ahead of me in in the history department of Moscow University. I had the greatest respect for him, since he was, to my knowledge, the only one of the students in the department whose parents had been arrested who refused to denounce his father as an enemy of the people. This required a great deal of courage at that time.

Someone had spread the rumor that Belen'kii's father was Grigory Belen'kii, at one time a famous Trotskyite. Belen'kii was called in for talks on this subject with the leaders of Gospolitizdat, including the acting director of the publication house S. M. Kovalyov, no doubt the same Kovalyov who, twenty years later, would publish an article in *Izvestiya*, expounding the theoretical basis for the right of the Soviet Union to send troops into Czechoslovakia (the so-called Brezhnev doctrine). The suspicions made little sense, since Belen'kii's name was Aleksandr Borisovich, not Aleksandr Grigorevich. Belen'kii pointed out to the director of personnel that he could not be the son of a man named Grigory unless he had forged his documents. The matter was settled.

The year 1950 was a good one for members of the editorial board. The second volume of the *Diplomatic Dictionary* came out. The edition was complete, and it received good reviews. There was talk of a second edition. But for now, the editors were instructed to produce a political dictionary. Meanwhile, the political situation was clearly worsening. Early in 1951 V. V. Al'tman, editor and an active participant in the dictionary, was arrested and after him one of its authors, the nephew and namesake of a legendary commissar in the 1919 Hungarian Commune, Tibor Samueli.

The anti-Semitic elements in Gospolitizdat began to speak in the corridors, and then openly at meetings, of "Jewish predominance" on the editorial board of the *Political Dictionary*. Here two more unfortunate incidents occurred in rapid succession. The editors commissioned an article on the problems of Soviet economic development from the well-known economist A. B. Notkin. Soon afterwards, Stalin criticized Notkin severely, and this blame reflected on the staff at the dictionary.

In 1952 the authorities arrested one of the most senior officials of the publishing house, the deputy director, Verite. Although the editorial board of the *Diplomatic Dictionary* had nothing to do with Verite, the party bureau secretary, Boldyrev, with the support of the well-known Gospolitizdat troublemaker Kudryavtseva, and with the cooperation of the editor Patros and deputy chief editor Maiorov and others, began an anti-Semitic campaign, demanding purges of the publishing house staff and, first and foremost, a dispersal of the editors of the *Political Dictionary*. Malicious accusations were concocted and advanced: that the editors had chosen authors because of their Jewish background, that they had let down their vigilance, that they had organized drinking bouts (that is, that they were guilty of moral degeneracy). There was not a grain of truth to any of this. Even in the case of the "drinking bouts" (the most harmless of the accusations), what was involved was a few bottles of wine, drunk to celebrate the completion of the *Diplomatic Dictionary*. By the end of 1952 several members of the editorial board (Zalkind, Belen'kii, M. Persits, and I. S. Kremer) had been fired.

Belen'kii was let go with the depressing formula "as a son of an enemy of the people."

With such a résumé it was simply impossible to find another job. Belen'kii made inquiries at thirty-seven institutions, schools, and educational establishments where there were vacancies and came up against refusals everywhere.

At the end of 1952 the party bureau of the Gospolitizdat issued Belen'kii a reprimand, gave a severe reprimand to the head of the editorial board, Vera Semyonova Solov'yova, a woman of impeccable honesty, and expelled Kremer and Persits from the Communist party. Solov'yova could escape punishment only if she shifted the entire "blame" to her Jewish colleagues. In spite of the broad hints made to her, however, she rejected this course of action.

After the death of Stalin, party matters were referred to the Communist party railway district committee of the city of Moscow. The second secretary of the regional committee reassured the party's victims that their punishment would be reduced. The level of punishment determined to a significant extent the possibility of obtaining employment. That is, someone who had been excluded from the Communist party or had received severe punishment would find it extremely difficult to get work, especially in the ideological sphere. But the party bureau secretary for Gospolitizdat, who was deeply implicated in this matter, for reasons of personal prestige continued to insist on the harshest judgements.

On April 2, 1953, a month after Stalin's death, the railway district committee (the bureau's meeting was chaired by the regional committee's first secretary, Galushko) expelled the board members from the party, except for Belen'kii, who received a severe reprimand with a warning. He was spared only thanks to the intercession of S. M. Kovalyov, who, during the vote, had said a few words in defense of Belen'kii.

On April 3, Vera Semyonovna Solov'yova slashed her wrists; thanks only to a fortunate coincidence did she manage to survive. The next day, the newspapers published the announcement of the rehabilitation of the members of the "Doctors' Plot" (in which several physicians, predominantly of Jewish ancestry, had been falsely accused of plotting to kill certain Soviet leaders). Vera Semyonovna later confessed to her close friends that she had sought death out of desperation, since she saw everywhere in the party organization nothing but Fascists.

Those who had been excluded from the party were harassed in the party commission of the Moscow City Committee for a long time. Not until many months had passed were their punishments withdrawn, and they were once again entitled to membership in the party. But they all had a long way to go before returning to scholarly work.

Galushko, the district committee secretary, who had conducted the entire affair, insisted on the expulsion from the Party of the staff members of the *Diplomatic Dictionary*, and demanded that the party ranks be "cleansed" of them, was involved several years later in a major criminal case (he had accepted bribes from trade organizations to cover up the activities of thieves and protect them from punishment). He was sentenced to ten years' imprisonment in a correctional labor camp. This was in 1953. It was said, though, that even in the camp, Galushko prospered: he found himself work in the warehouse.

So this was the atmosphere in which my manuscript was withdrawn from the printer's and I was publicly accused of every imaginable sin: bourgeois objectivism, underestimating the role of American imperialism in the outbreak of the Second World War, and so on. The deputy director of the institute, Arkady Lavrovich Sidorov, also accused me at a meeting of the academic council of rejecting all the reviewers' comments. I then submitted a document to the academic council in which I refuted his allegations.

A few days later Sidorov called me in and proposed that I correct my "mistakes." He suggested I go to study in the evenings at the University of Marxism-Leninism. I almost burst out laughing: Sidorov regarded the University of Marxism-Leninism as punishment! Well, perhaps he was right. After all, isn't it true that in China not long ago all kinds of intellectuals were forced to learn quotations from Mao by heart? Sidorov was simply anticipating Chinese methods of instruction by just a bit. Of course I told the deputy director that I found his proposal absurd. And we parted on that note.

Issue number 10 of *Voprosy istorii* for 1952 published in abridged form Sidorov's report to the academic council. The accusation against me of "political errors" was toned down and replaced by the formula "methodological flaws." In those days that was a relatively mild choice of words. Nonetheless, the appearance in print of criticism of my unpublished work, in itself an exceptional incident, had an immediate effect on my prospects for publishing my articles in scholarly journals. For the next year and a half I succeeded in getting nothing into print. Sidorov's report forced me to adopt an aggressive defense, so to speak.

I was aware of the fact that a campaign was being waged by the heads of our department and decided not to delay any further. In November 1952 I sent a letter to Academician Anna Mikhailovna Pankratova, who had just been elected at the Nineteenth Party Congress to the party's Central Committee. This seven-page document, a copy of which I still have, contained an analysis of the status of modern history studies in our institute. I also dealt with more general problems, including the matter of new staff historians. I wrote that after the increase in salary levels for scholars in 1947, "people have been rushing into the field of history recently whose only interest is their own comfort. It is no accident that the majority of those who have defended their dissertations prefer not to publish them." In this regard I proposed that salaries be lowered and that as compensation there be an honorarium for work completed, along with stricter criteria for appointment to the position of senior scholar. These measures, in my view, "would rid historical scholarship of parasites, idlers, and hangers-on."

I later realized that my proposal for reform in payment for work was a bad idea, for this would mean increasing the opportunities for administrative arbitrariness in receiving, evaluating, and publishing works, thereby also increasing the dependence of each and every staff member on his or her administrative superior. The situation would be very different were there incentives for work or ability, This was the goal underlying my proposal, not the wish to encourage conformism or the readiness, as our famous satirists Il'f and Petrov once wrote, to "do everything that will have to be done henceforth."

Some time later Anna Mikhailovna met with me. The two of us sat together in an empty conference room on the second floor of the social sciences building at 14 Volkhonka Street and chatted quietly. She told me that my letter had been transmitted to the science section of the Central Committee, verified there and found to be in accordance with the facts. Then, all of a sudden she looked at me and asked: "Tell me, Comrade Nekrich, are you a Yugoslav?" I must confess that this was unexpected. Could the dispute with Tito have affected me by coincidence? (My Yugoslavian-sounding surname misled many people. The misunderstandings sometimes reached comic proportions. A fellow student once assured my own father that he was in the same class as a certain Yugoslav by the name of Nekrich.) Upon learning that I was Jewish, she said, with some embarrassment, "And we thought that you were being persecuted for being a Yugoslav." This was a statement fraught with significance, for in 1952 we did not know which was worse for someone living in the Soviet Union: being taken for a Yugoslav or being Jewish!

Anna Mikhailovna was a kindly, conscientious person and extremely decent by nature. Nevertheless, for the sake of her career and her prominent position she, like so many others, went against her conscience. But as soon as she saw the slightest opportunity to help someone, Pankratova did her utmost. I have it on good authority that she found it hard to endure Bekmakhanov's condemnation and the humilation she had to endure in the academic council. In the final years of her life, at the head of the journal *Voprosy istorii*, she did much to restore at least partial historical truth, thereby earning the hatred of the Stalinists and dogmatists.

Pankratova's intercession in my fate slowed the course of events some-what, but not for long. Denunciations against me poured one after another into the personnel department of the presidium of the Academy of Sciences, which was headed by two rather grim figures, Kosikov and B. A. Vinogradov. Kosikov has long since died, but Vinogradov had a brilliant administrative career, and on the basis of that a "scholarly" one as well, becoming a corresponding member of the Academy of Sciences and director of the Institute of Scientific Information on the Social Sciences (INION). In those difficult years Vinogradov was one of the major thugs in the Academy of Sciences.

At the end of 1952, in his statement to the presidium, Kosikov made a number of accusations against me. The leadership at the institute and the party bureau, from which I requested clarification, told me that the information, or rather disinformation, did not come from them and that they did not support the accusations. Kosikov's report appeared in the journal *Vestnik akademii nauk SSSR* (no. 2, 1953).

The final months of 1952 were alarming, not just for me but for the entire intelligentsia. Ominous rumors of forthcoming repression spread throughout Moscow. And in fact there were arrests, although not yet on a massive scale. The beginning of the new year 1953 turned out to be even grimmer. Reports were published on the "Doctors' Plot."

I had to face my problems in an entirely unexpected way. During the elections to public bodies, staff members at our institute performed agitation work on Marx and Engels Street, between Frunze Street and Volkhonka. The agitators' duties consisted of acquainting voters with the background of candidates, and of ensuring attendance at the polls on election day. The agitators often vied with one another to see whose voters would vote earliest. The institute's party organization was keen on completing the voting process for party district committee early, even though the voting continued formally until midnight. The district committee, in turn, urged local institutions to send the election returns to the city party committee, and as a result, everywhere at all levels there were attempts to gain approval from higher officials or organizations. Every voter was assigned a number on a list, and in a room set aside for the agitators an X was placed next to the name of each person who had voted. Those voters who were "late" — that is, who had not arrived at the polling place by between 11 a.m. and noon, were approached by an agitator and reminded that it was time to vote. The voters themselves were perfectly aware of how things were, and they tried not to let down the agitators, who could not go home until all those entrusted to them had voted.

It so happened that among those I was responsible for was Lydia Timashuk— the same Lydia Timashuk who had sent in a denunciation of the accused in the "Doctors' Plot" and was renowned for her vigilance throughout the country. On January 10, 1953, a report was published on the arrest of those involved in the Doctors' plot. And on January 21, anniversary of Lenin's death, the newspapers contained a decree of the Presidium of the Supreme Soviet granting Timashuk the highest award of the Soviet state, the Order of Lenin. This was deeply symbolic: the front pages of the newspapers carried a photograph of the founder of the Soviet state, and just below a blessing in his name of a stool pigeon for the Soviet state!

I have often thought about those times, and about the spiritual crisis our society was experiencing then. And that award on Lenin's anniversary demonstrated that the leadership of the party had apparently lost all sense of proportion, of reality, not to speak of good taste.

I remember very well the enormous multiroom apartment where Timashuk lived. As a matter of fact, an entire clan inhabited that apartment, which is probably why I remember it. All of them bore the same family name, except for Timashuk, who lived with her husband in one room. As part of my duties as an agitator, I would visit them there. Her husband appeared to be cultivated, and may also have been a doctor (Timashuk was a radiologist). He was getting on in years, and even Timashuk herself no longer looked like a young girl. I remember her husband's story of how they had lived in a mud hut in Velikie Luki right after the war. Their living conditions even now were quite modest. And Timashuk and her husband gave the impression of being modest people as well. How could one imagine even for a minute that this slightly plump, dark-haired woman, on instructions from the organs of state security, had actively participated in one of the most infamous provocations in all the years of Soviet power!

In the middle of February 1953 there were elections to the Supreme Soviet. Timashuk came to vote at the polling place, located in our institute building at 14 Volkhonka Street. At about that time Olga Chechetkina's article "Lydia Timashuk's Mail" had been published in *Pravda*, in which Timashuk was portrayed almost as a Susanin in a skirt. (Ivan Susanin was the legendary seventeenth-century peasant who sacrificed his life to save the tsar.) The article was unabashedly anti-Semitic. At the polls Timashuk was accosted by Polina Naumovna Sharova, a simple woman, almost neurotic, a former weaver who had reached the level of doctor of historical sciences. Sharova embraced Timashuk with great enthusiasm, thanked her, and kissed her in an outbreak of hysterics. Not only I but others who were present at this scene were embarrassed.

That was an exhausting day. It must have been the next day, after the elections, that one of the staff members at the institute came up to me and, looking around, asked me in a low tone of voice, "have you heard anything about Maisky?"

"What do you mean?" I asked in concern. "I saw him only a few days ago."

"You see," continued the comrade, "they say that Maisky was arrested yesterday."

Maisky arrested!

I left the institute and rushed to a phone booth. I dialed his number. No one answered.

The next day at the institute news of Academician Maisky's arrest had already become official. Immediately there were people—quite a few to my surprise—who claimed that Maisky had been a British spy. This was in fact what he was officially charged with later on.

I was the first graduate student of Ivan Mikhailovich's to defend a dissertation. Our friendly relations were common knowledge. In fact, it had never occurred to us to conceal them.

Once in the summer of 1952 I was on my way to the institute with Nina Aleksandrovna Sidorova, who had several times been elected secretary of the institute party organization. A medievalist by specialty, she took pride in the fact that she dealt with "real history" and not with the present day. We were on friendly terms. Nina Aleksandrovna would often urge me to abandon my study of modern history for medievalism. I am still not sure I was right in failing to heed her advice. Nina Aleksandrovna, normally rather reserved, was sometimes frank with me and was not afraid to talk with me about various "dangerous" subjects. She was a complex and contradictory person, and when I think of her untimely and somewhat mysterious death, I get a clear sense of how hard things were for her at times.

On that day, as we were on our way to the institute, talking about this and that, I joked a bit, but Nina Aleksandrovna answered lethargically, her thoughts elsewhere. We were about to reach the institute, when she glanced at me and asked point blank: "Tell me, Sasha, what is your relationship with Deborin and Maisky?"

"Very friendly."

"But there's such a difference in age, what could you possibly have in common?"

"Well, you see, these old men like me very much, and I owe them a lot. But most important, they know a lot that I don't know. I find it very interesting to be with them. And somehow they aren't bored with me."

My answer apparently seemed frivolous to Sidorova. She looked at me very seriously. It seemed that for a moment a warning gleamed in her eyes, but then it disappeared. Or was it just my imagination?

"Sasha," she began slowly, as if thinking to herself, and thereby drawing my attention to the significance of what she was about to say, "Sasha," she repeated, "some comrades find your friendship with Abram Moiseevich and Ivan Mikhailovich strange. I myself am on good terms with them, especially with Abram Moiseevich, but he, like Maisky, has a past and . . . " Here she stopped short, searching for words with which to express clearly what she wanted to tell me but perhaps should not. She ended unexpectedly abruptly: "When they start to clear out the roots, make sure things are not too bad for you either." The conversation was cut short. We went into the institute.

That expression "clear out the roots" is one I think I'll always remember. I can even hear and reproduce the intonation with which it was uttered. There was a kind of cruelty in it.

The next two weeks were days of uneasiness and anxiety for me. The heads of the institute received instructions to draw up lists of people to be fired. I found out about this from a friend who was a member of the party bureau. We agreed that I would phone him after the meeting at which these lists were to be approved.

That evening my wife, Lena (I had married a second time in the spring of 1952), and I were at the conservatory attending a concert by Mravinsky. During intermission I phoned my friend. His answer was brief: "It's happened."

"I'm on the list?"

"Yes."

A bell rang out. Intermission had ended.

Maisky's arrest raised the spirits of the former graduates of the Central Committee Academy of Social Sciences. A number of officials who previously had been maneuvering openly joined this group. It was learned that soon the presidium of the Academy of Sciences would hear a report from our leadership and that the destructive decision had already been made.

Meanwhile, our party group met to "react," as was usually the case, to Maisky's arrest. Despite the fact that no one knew exactly what Maisky had been accused of, he was declared, in accordance with established custom, an "enemy of the people," and each member of our party organization was expected to address this point—that is, publicly condemn the person arrested. I shall not hide the fact that I did so too. I had to speak twice, since my first statement did not satisfy the meeting because of its vagueness. I had no other choice if I didn't wish to challenge the state, with all the consequences that implied. But I was not yet prepared for the outcome.

The absurd lengths to which the meeting went are evident from the fact that one of the speakers stated that Maisky used a trip to Leningrad in order to engage in espionage in Kronstadt! Another boasted that while working in the department of history and philosophy, he had prevented

Maisky from traveling anywhere on business and sent him only to preside over the funeral services of academicians.

All sound and fury, signifying nothing.

Everything that took place during that nightmarish time showed that my fate, too, was predestined. Nothing, it seemed, could avert the logical conclusion any longer. But chance is a great helper. While in the higher echelons the issue of what to do with people who should be on the proscribed list was being cleared up, and a decree of the presidium of the Academy of Sciences was being prepared which was to lend some semblance of legality to the entire affair, there occurred an event that suddenly altered the entire situation.

On March 5, 1953, Stalin died.

In the commotion of mourning, panic, and funeral proceedings, the officials temporarily forgot about those people they had wanted to kick out of the institute and hand over to the authorities for reprisals. And then it became too late for that: history had taken a different turn.

In accordance with hallowed tradition, party members, in such tragic circumstances, come to the party bureau in order to demonstrate their common grief and unity. I had to come as well. We sat in silence, a few dozen people, among us the sobbing Nina Aleksandrovna Sidorova. Together with her I then went to the Hall of Columns for our last farewell to Stalin.

We were heading down Sretenka toward Trubnaya Square, when all of a sudden we found ourselves caught in a terrible crush. We were being crumpled, squeezed, pushed around, carried off. Someone fell at the street barrier. I grabbed Nina Aleksandrovna and threw her over to the other side of the barrier. With us was Zina Belousova, a French specialist. Someone, or perhaps something, lay in a terrifying lump on the ground.

"Is that Sonya?" Nina Aleksandrovna cried out in horror. She meant Sophia Iosifovna Yakubovskaya (a well-known historian of Soviet society) who had been right beside us. Fortunately, it was not. We decided not to try to reach the Hall of Columns. Instead we went along the boulevard, turned on the Sadovoye Kol'tso, and accompanied Nina Aleksandrovna to her home on Chkalov Street next to the Kursky railway station.

The man who for thirty years had held total sway over the bodies and souls of 200 million people was no more. His final path, like his entire life, was lined with corpses: five-hundred people were killed during those days in the crush of the crowd on the streets of Moscow. Twenty years later the poet Smirnov would recall with rapture in his poem "I Myself Bear Witness": "The souls of hundreds of trampled fellow citizens formed a funereal wreath."

Everything flows, sometimes even backwards.

It is not such a simple matter to bring to a standstill a machine that has been operating at full power. The long-planned decree of the presidium of the Academy of Sciences saw the light of day two weeks after the death of the leader, and it appeared in the same form in which it had been prepared in the final weeks of his life.

A substantial part of the decree of March 20, 1953, "On the Scientific Activity and Status of Staff at the USSR Academy of Sciences Institute of History," was taken up with a list of mistakes, flaws, and drawbacks in the institute's activities and those of its individual members. The decree did not emerge from out of the blue. It had been prepared painstakingly over a period of several months, and the draft had been discussed in the presence of many historians. Nevertheless, the final version, signed by the president of the Academy of Sciences, A. N. Nesmeyanov, contained a number of false allegations. The most striking was a paragraph devoted to Abram Moiseevich Deborin which said that Deborin had been tried for anti-Soviet activity. But in fact Deborin had never been brought to trial, even though he had been a victim of discrimination for many years. In the discussion of the draft decree someone pointed out this error, but the allegation was retained. The decree contained dozens of names, among them those of widely known historians. They were all charged with methodological, theoretical, and political mistakes. I too was accused. The decree demanded a review of the staff at the institute.

For their "services" in preparing the rout of the institute, the graduates of the Academy of Social Sciences were rewarded. B. N. Krylov, for example, who had not one scholarly work to his credit, was made head of the section on U.S. history. Once he got the position he wanted, he mellowed and made it possible for members of the section to work in peace, for times were changing quickly, and he understood this. A few years later he found himself a more congenial job, one involving foreign travel, and was even at one time cultural adviser at the Soviet embassy in Washington. But he wisely stayed away from scholarship. Many other graduates of the Academy of Social Sciences were to leave the institute, but a few remained, especially in the department of the history of Soviet society. But now few of them tried to teach us their views and called instead for raising historical scholarship to ever greater heights.

The decree was discussed at a general meeting of institute staff on April 13, 1953, ten days after the issuance of the famous communique announcing that the "Doctors' Plot" had been a fabrication by "the former leadership of the state security organs." Thus, the significance of the decree as a direct threat of dismissal for those staff members who had received negative mention was greatly diminished. A dramatic moment during the meeting was provided by the statement made by the old man Deborin. Neither before nor since have I heard such an emotional and embittered speech from Abram Moiseevich. He seemed to have been transformed. Deborin stood at the rostrum looking upset—no, rather, angry—and swept away, one after another, all the accusations that had been leveled at him in the decree. "All this is nothing but lies!" he shouted indignantly, and, leaving the rostrum, staggering, he made his way along the wall of the auditorium toward the exit. I was afraid that his heart would give out or that he would have a stroke, but fortunately neither happened. Many colleagues referred to in the decree protested in the presidium of the Academy, where a special appeals commission was established—another sign of the times. In the Stalinist era, just a month or so before, there would have been no such commission.

I protested too, although I received no attention. But this was of little practical significance, since the accusations made against me were already being investigated, in accordance with my request to A. M. Rumyantsev, the head of the science department of the Central Committee. In my letter to the committee I rejected all the political accusations, but I had to agree that my work contained "essential methodological drawbacks." This was more acceptable to me than confessing political errors. My appeal to Rumyantsev ended with the following words: "For more than a year and a half now, instead of devoting myself entirely to scholarship, which for me is my life's work, I have had to expend my efforts, nerves, and time in order to counter many attempts to slander me. I can no longer tolerate such a situation."

In mid-May I was invited in for a talk with the instructor of the science division, A. S. Chernyaev, an English specialist by profession, and a teacher in the history faculty at Moscow State University. He told me that the past should be laid to rest and that it was the view of the leadership that "Nekrich should work in the Institute of History." So, at last this episode was over.

On March 3, 1953, I turned thirty-three years old. Fortunately, my enemies had not succeeded in crucifying me, but neither had I read out any Sermon on the Mount. I did feel, however, as if I had just been taken down from the cross.

My father did not hide his joy over the death of Stalin. The old journalist for foreign affairs knew a great deal that was unknown to me, and not just to me, about the leader's activities. In the 1920s my father had worked in Baku and in Tbilisi. As he told it, the old workers on more than one occasion recalled Stalin's participation in expropriation raids. My father also used to tell how at a trial of police officials in Baku soon after the restoration of Soviet power, one of the accused demanded that Iosif Dzhugashvili be called to court as a witness for the defense. Some ugly pages from the life of Stalin began to come to light.

My reaction was different from my father's. I was so accustomed to Stalin as an omnipresent and eternal force, that when I read the announcement of his illness, I was stunned. Then came the suspicion that he had already died, and that the communiqué regarding his illness had been issued to prepare the public for word of his death, and perhaps to gain time for the leadership to recover from its confusion. I understood that Stalin's death might change our lives radically. But who would replace him? I was not the only one to wonder about this; indeed, it was on the minds of millions of people. My father and I agreed that another Georgian, such as Beria, could not head a state in which the majority was Russian—not a second time. And naturally we understood that for us, for our friends, for many people we knew and did not know, Stalin's death was tantamount to salvation.

While we wondered about a successor, a new leader, there were very few among us to whom it occurred that there could be another way, a way without a leader, without a dictatorship.

In late 1952 and early 1953 there had been persistent, ominous rumors about the construction of barracks on the banks of the Yenisei River for a forthcoming deportation of Jews. Supposedly some major cultural and scientific figures of Jewish origin had even signed an appeal to the government "requesting" that Jews be resettled from industrial centers to remote Eastern regions, so as to enable them to "adapt to useful physical labor, to the land." I shall not give their names here, inasmuch as I have not seen the document myself. But I know for certain that a high-ranking philosopher at that time, D. Chesnokov, who was made a member of the Central Committee Presidium at the Nineteenth Party Congress, wrote a brochure in which he "explained" the need for deporting the Jews. The brochure had been printed and was awaiting the green light for distribution.

Then in early 1953 Academician Deborin phoned and said that it was urgent that he see me. Abram Moiseevich's voice seemed somehow unusual to me, and I could sense a nervousness in it. Indeed, the old man was very upset. He told me that a closed party meeting of the Academy of Sciences presidium had just been concluded (at that time, all academicians, regardless of where they worked, were registered with the party in the Academy of Sciences presidium). At that meeting the academicians had demanded the death sentence for those accused in the "Doctors' Plot."

"I had never heard anything like it before," said Abram Moiseevich, "but what shocked me most was the statement made by Isaak Izraelevich." He meant I. I. Mintz. "It was disgusting. After all, no one was twisting his arm. He spoke on his own initiative," concluded Deborin.

But it turned out that it was not to tell me about the party meeting that Abram Moiseevich had summoned me. He had had a phone call from the *Pravda* editorial offices asking if he would agree to sign a document condemning the accused in the "Doctors' Plot." How Abram Moiseevich had replied remained unclear to me, since he was somewhat vague. I could tell that he was suffering from doubts, and I couldn't bring myself to wring the truth from him. But since Abram Moiseevich was asking for my advice, I told him that under no circumstances should he put his signature on a document he had never seen. "When they phone you again," I encouraged Deborin, "ask them to send you the text." Deborin agreed with me, and apparently that is what he did. Yet he never received any text. Soon after, Stalin died, and Abram Moiseevich lived on.

The institute called a meeting of solemn remembrance. Anna Mikhailovna Pankratova spoke very movingly. Many had tears in their eyes. It was almost as though we really had suffered an irreparable loss. Fortunately, there were enough false notes struck in the statements to have a sobering effect, somehow neutralizing the heightened emotion. The following words, for example, rang unbearably false: "This morning my daughter woke up and asked me, 'Papa, how are we going to live now that Comrade Stalin is gone? He was a best friend to all children!'" One could tell from the speaker's face that his daughter had said nothing of the sort and that this was merely a common device of demagoguery. The fact that this middle-aged man, a father of three children, a professional party official, had to resort to such cheap histrionics, showed that in many cases, grief for the deceased was forced.

> As Russia was forcing its way
> Into the old world,
> All its baggage seemed designed to make him fail
> Yet while all that was crumpled up . . . one thing remained:
> His
>   boundless power.
> Indeed he felt,
>   the path to truth was arduous,
> And that his power
>   through lying
>   To it would lead
> And now he is dead.
>   As for the truth, he didn't make it,
> And lies, like quicksand round us,
>   Suck us down.
> With fanfare and just a bit of haste
> they bury him,
> His fellow-comrades,
>   Eyes straining to fix the bier,
> As though from darkest nether gloom
>   He just might
> Rise again,
>   Seize everything and lower the boom.
> Cold is the grieving,
>   lofty the eulogies in tone.
> He made life miserable for all of them,
>   had not a friend to call his own . . .

Myself I do not even know
   was he for so many years
For our times
   A bane or boon.
The people alone did not forsake him,
   did not desert
Those who with him endured so much,
   suffered such hurt.
The people
   laid the revolution with him
in the ground,
Though, perhaps for that no real merit
   could be found.
In all he did,
   lies
Everywhere did abound
yet his palace guard
did shroud him with smoke screens all around,
So that just plain people
   could not sort it out
and closed their eyes,
blindly putting their faith in him.
O, Mother Russia!
   Is it true that while your wits were dulled,
All the fight
left you, went out of you!
Does Malenkov's look,
cross-tempered, short of vision,
   hold your whole fate?
Yet, perhaps, through
   hellish pain you will grasp
Along the way of all your hellish trials
That blind faith
   shouldn't be placed
In anyone,
And that truth is something
   to which lies cannot lead.

It seems to me that this poem by Emka Mandel' (Naum Korzhavin) most accurately reflects the contradictory feelings and ideas which were characteristic of those first days after Stalin's death. I do not know one poet, prose writer, or historian who could have grasped so accurately or so faithfully that moment in time, filtered it through his own perception, and expressed it.

I listened to the broadcast from Red Square on the day of the funeral. When the cannon rang out in final tribute, I got up from my desk. I stood there and thought that right then, at that moment, the old world was past and gone forever. I so wanted to believe that this was true.

5

Years of Hope

Now—behold the depths of our nation!—
And there you will discover a lavish source,
The means to live again.
Read its soulful tale,
And there you will see in its high-mindedness
The beacon for times of morality.
—Johann Wolfgang von Goethe

The beginning of spiritual emancipation — the first book — the return of I. M. Maisky — Estonian archives — captured documents — Twentieth Communist Party Congress — the truth, not the whole truth, and not nothing but the truth — The E. N. Burdzhalov affair — events in Hungary and Poland — in the microcosm of the historians — V. M. Turok-Popov — military historians — not according to one's labor and not according to one's ability — mind control — historian and reader — the All-Union Congress of Historians.

The whole atmosphere of Soviet life changed swiftly immediately after Stalin's death. An enormous role in this change was played by the Ministry of Internal Affairs communiqué of April 4, 1953, announcing that the accusations against those involved in the "Doctors' Plot" had been fabricated by officials of the former Ministry of State Security. This news caused a breach in the entire structure of power, opening up the floodgates.

In June 1953 our country rid itself of a dangerous pretender to dictatorship, Lavrenty Beria. I do not exclude the fact that aside from being the most seasoned of Stalin's companions in political intrigue, he was the only one who had a clear agenda in the event of Stalin's death.

The process of Beria's removal is now well known, not only from the oral accounts of Khrushchev, Marshal Zhukov, and Anastas Mikoyan, but also from a number of written testimonies.

At about this time commissions were already at work rehabilitating the victims of Stalinist terror. But only after the Twentieth Party Congress in February 1956, the most important congress in the history of the CPSU and of the Soviet state, did this rehabilitation become broader in scope.

With joy, clouded by grief for those who were dead, and tempered by the feeling that all the horrors (thank God) were behind them, Soviet citizens learned in ever-increasing detail of the arbitrary power which had held sway in our country for decades. But now a new and difficult problem had arisen—the problem of responsibility, not only of the authorities but of each and every Soviet citizen. I did not doubt for a minute that the older generation knew all about the atrocities, for the repression had affected hundreds of thousands of people, and it was simply impossible to be ignorant of all this. The details of the brutal camp regime in Kolyma were not known, and if people had been aware, they would probably have remained silent or pretended to be surprised. This was exactly how the Germans and our fellow Slavs the Poles had acted, living near such annihilation camps as Auschwitz, Majdanek, and the others, even as the fumes from the crematoria reached them, settling in dirty flakes on the snow. This is one of the reasons why I believe that the appeal for repentance made by Aleksandr Isaevich Solzhenitsyn to our people is totally appropriate.

In 1953 not only were we officially informed of the high-handedness which had flourished for decades; but we learned as well of something no less startling: our achievements in agriculture turned out to be a sham. We also heard acknowledgment that Soviet industry, having survived the ordeal of war, was in need of immediate modernization, that our science in many fields and in many respects was behind world science (a concept which, as our party ideologists had constantly asserted, supposedly did not exist at all.)

At one government conference Academician P. L. Kapitsa (a pupil of the famous British physicist Ernest Rutherford), a man who was once in disgrace but, after Stalin's death, became one of the most influential figures in Soviet science, likened our industry to the prehistoric brontosaurus, an animal with a small head and an enormous body. By the head he meant science.

The time had come when people were suddenly required to think, and to think without being prompted, independently. This was an unimaginable task, completely at odds with the kind of life to which we had become accustomed. Moreover, the appeal to independent thinking was in contradiction to the spiritual organization of Soviet society, and after a while this became quite apparent. Reason, after all, is the first step toward treason The labor camp inmates knew this better than anyone else: a sideways step is considered an attempt to escape, and the guards shoot first and ask questions later. The entire Soviet Union had been like one enormous prison camp. Shots could be fired without warning at any citizen who suddenly believed that he was free, or simply to remind people not to take too many liberties. Of course, scarcely had the Soviet people been urged to think more independently than the pendulum began to swing the other way. Deviations from the orthodox-conformist line encompassed the entire scope of life in the country, but were especially noticeable in the spheres of science, culture, art, and literature.

As early as 1954 *The Thaw* by Ilya Ehrenburg and *Was Ivan Ivanovich Here?*, a play by Nazim Khikmet, a Turkish emigré poet dedicated to the ideas of communism, aroused enthusiasm and great expectations among the intelligentsia. The play, however, was banned after five performances. I was lucky enough to see it. It was a satire about cringing before a certain mystical force—"Ivan Ivanovich"—behind which lurked the menacing image of Stalin. Alas, Ivan Ivanovich was still alive. The banning of the show testified to that.

Yet the process of spiritual emancipation had begun all the same. It was not very simple; indeed, it was very complex, diverse, and contradictory. We began to hear slowly, piecemeal fashion, in measured pharmaceutical doses, grains of truth about the difficult situation in which our people and state had found ourselves during the years of Stalin's dictatorship. At this time he was still considered to be a great man; his works continued to be published, and authors continued to cite them in their books. But there was lacking the former enthusiasm, with a fair amount of careerism thrown in for good measure, which had marked praise of Stalin in his lifetime. The nightmare of fear seemed to be shrinking, diminishing, receding. Still, although it was receding, the fear had not disappeared altogether. It nestled somewhere in the subconscious, prepared to crawl out again.

I once saw a Japanese toy, a loathsome, shaggy, sticky, squeaking mechanical monster. It seemed to me to represent what fear was, and I pushed away in disgust that vile product of human fantasy.

The future was finally in our own hands—or, rather, almost in our hands—if only we could take hold of it. Just one more try, just one more. Now a great deal depended on us: our spiritual liberation, the democratization of our institutional foundations (which seemed impossible to democratize), the future itself—our own, our children's, and that of succeeding generations.

Disorder and hesitation among the bosses, who were required to liberalize the regime further, could and should have been used advantageously for making rapid and irreversible decisions. In order to do that, however, the foundations had to be replaced, not democratized. The "new" leadership was new only in relative terms; it was made up of the old Stalinist cohort, grown dull and flabby from a steady diet of power. Along with their leader, Stalin's comrades in arms, as they proudly called themselves, bore responsibility for everything that had been going on for decades. But for some reason no one felt like answering for this. It was simpler and more convenient to blame on Stalin, and Beria as well. And, in fact, both of them deserved it. Something else, though, was more important: who among the new leadership, was not afraid to take responsibility? Who was prepared to break with the past and undertake speedy democratization of state and society, not only from above but with support from below? The blessing of the USSR Constitution provided opportunity for such reform. The question was: Would we be able to live under the basic rule of law, as formally set out in the Constitution? Was it sufficient to abrogate the most savage, barbaric laws such as, for example, the ones laying criminal responsibility on family members of "traitors to the homeland," or prohibiting marriage with foreigners, both throwbacks to the sixteenth century?

Indeed, except for a short period between the end of the Civil War and the beginning of collectivization, a span of only about seven or eight years, our people had lived under extraordinary laws. But the extraordinary was normal and habitual in the Soviet Union. Even the introduction of the 1936 Constitution, on the one hand more democratic but, on the other, depriving the working class of its privileges, did not change the situation. Following the Constitution, the repressions came thick and fast, and we have not yet recovered from them. Much would depend on how dedicated we were to our conformist past, on whether we had the desire to live differently, and, finally, on what we believed in. Did we still have any ideals left, or had everything been washed away in the River of Blood?

Everyday life forced people to think not so much about reforming society as about housing, clothing, and jobs. I had to think about these things as well. In 1953–54 I thoroughly redrafted my manuscript, expanding it and supplementing it with new documents. The atmosphere for research work had taken a turn for the better, and although censorship, only slightly softened by the new regulations, was still in effect, and we were simply unable to rid ourselves of the self-censorship still ingrained in our subconscious, there had been a number of irreversible changes in our basic view of society and state, and we knew this, even though we concealed it from ourselves out of habit.

In the spring of 1954 I was called in by the new deputy director of the institute, L. S. Gaponenko, formerly an instructor in the science department of the Central Committee, and was asked when I planned to submit my manuscript for publication.

The book was ready by that time. In June of that year the publishing house resumed its work on it, and in March 1955 my first major work, *The Policy of British Imperialism in Europe, October 1938—September 1939*, finally appeared in print. The critics both inside the Soviet Union and abroad gave the book favorable reviews. In comparison with what had already been written about the pre-Second World War period, this was a step forward. Still, this first book of mine paid substantial tribute to the orthodox understanding and interpretation of events. The academic council of the Institute of History entered the monograph for a prize from the presidium of the Academy of Sciences, but the award was granted to Academician M. V. Nechkina for her outstanding work on the Decembrists. I had a feeling of satisfaction all the same. My book was dedicated to the memory of my older brother, Vladimir, who had been killed on the Kursk Bulge in August 1943.

At about that time a rather curious thing happened to me. The journal *Voprosy istorii* published my article on British-German colonial contradictions during the Second World War. In the article I referred to the adventures of the chief of staff of the Egyptian army, El-Misri, who, during the Italian attack on North Africa, attempted to join up with the Italian side, but without success, for he was in an airplane accident. A few days after this issue of the journal came out, an official in the editorial office phoned me, extremely upset, and asked me to come over immediately. It turned out that this same General El-Misri was now the Egyptian ambassador to Moscow!

A certain American journalist, on reading my article, had sent his newspaper a report headlined: "Moscow Repudiates the Egyptian Ambassador." The account of El-Misri's story in my article caused an uproar. I received demands for documented proof of the episode, which I provided. Then I was asked whether I had known that El-Misri was ambassador to Moscow, and if I had not known, then why not. (Why on earth should I have known?) And so on and so forth. The matter ended with the Nazi minion's departure from Moscow a short time later, but his recall, I believe, was related not so much to my article as to political turmoil in Egypt. If such an incident had occurred in Stalinist times, I would have ended up in a labor camp, or been expelled from work at best, whereas here I had just caused a bit of commotion. Truly, times had changed.

The truth of this observation was borne out further by Maisky's return from imprisonment. As I mentioned, Ivan Mikhailovich had been arrested at the end of February 1953, two weeks before Stalin's death.

Maisky (Lyakhovetsky) was well known in the West. He had begun his revolutionary activity in Russia at the turn of the century, was arrested by the tsarist authorities, lived in exile, and then as an émigré in Germany and Britain. After the 1917 Revolution he returned to Russia, joined the Mensheviks, and became one of the few members of that party to take part in the struggle against Soviet power, for which he was expelled from the Central Committee and from party ranks. He was a member of the government of the Committee of the Constituent Assembly and held the post of comrade minister of labor. After the government of the "Uchredilka" (as the Bolsheviks contemptuously called the Constituent Assembly) moved from Samara to Ufa, and in Omsk Admiral Kolchak declared himself Supreme Ruler of Russia, Maisky's political career ended abruptly. Disappointed in his political ambitions, he turned to the Bolsheviks, wrote the dramatic poem "Vershiny" ("The Heights"), and sent it to the People's Commissar for Enlightenment, A. V. Lunacharsky, along with a letter in which he asked for help in embarking upon the true path. Soon afterwards, with the support of Yemelyan Yaroslavsky, then editor of

Soviet Siberia, Maisky was sent to work in the Siberian Economic Planning Commission. The chairman of the Siberian Revolutionary Committee, whose office included the economic commission, was a noteworthy individual, I. N. Smirnov, who was known as "the Siberian Lenin."

After a public repentance, first in a letter to *Pravda* and then in the book *Democratic Counterrevolution*, Maisky was forgiven and accepted into the Bolshevik Communist party. At the suggestion of his good friend M. M. Litvinov, he was sent to work at the People's Commissariat for Foreign Affairs.

Like Litvinov, Maisky was a proponent of the policy of collective security. After Litvinov's dismissal in 1939 as People's Commissar for Foreign Affairs, Maisky still remained ambassador to Britain. During the war he played a substantial role in strengthening Anglo-Soviet relations, in organizing Lend-Lease, and in opening up a second front.

Maisky was one of those few Soviet diplomats of the older generation who had escaped the repression of the 1930s. At one time he, like all other Soviet diplomats abroad, was forbidden to meet with officials of the country to which he had been accredited without being accompanied by an embassy adviser (in Maisky's case this was Kiril Novikov). One-on-one meetings with the minister for foreign affairs of another country were strictly forbidden. Later on, as Maisky told me, the Politburo made an exception for the Soviet ambassadors to London and Washington, allowing them to meet with British and American officials unaccompanied. For other Soviet ambassadors, however, this ban remained in effect for a number of years.

Many historians and others as well have expressed surprise at how people managed to survive when their past had been quite dubious from the orthodox Soviet point of view. The explanation, as I see it, is simple: Stalin always kept on hand a few representatives from the past, and he retained several former ideological enemies who subsequently had come over to his side. They were the people most dedicated to the regime. Maisky was not the only one. A. Ya. Vyshinsky, one of the most active Mensheviks, rose to an extremely high position and gained notoriety during the trials of the 1930s as the "procurator of death." The former active Menshevik publicist D. Zaslavsky also went very far. There were others as well. Maisky was sufficiently flexible, and his cultured, refined manner made him an extremely acceptable figure for contact with the West. He was especially well received in Britain. Among his English friends were the Webbs, George Bernard Shaw, H. G. Wells and others.

Maisky, like Litvinov, was called back to Moscow in 1943, and he served as deputy minister for foreign affairs until 1946, when Maisky and Litvinov were dismissed from the ministry. Stalin, caught up in the cold war, no longer needed their services. But Maisky was made a full member of the Academy of Sciences, which guaranteed him a decent living and a dignified position until the end of his days.

It is a matter of interest that Litvinov, one of the most popular figures in the party, was dismissed with a pension of one thousand rubles a month (one hundres rubles in today's terms). His pension was one-ninth that of Maisky. "Smiling Maisky," as he was usually called in Britain, could count his blessings.

Litvinov died in 1951. His death was announced in a small notice in *Izvestiya* published on the day of his funeral. Maisky was destined to live a long life, but he was to endure a grim ordeal. At the age of sixty-nine he was arrested and imprisoned in solitary confinement, where he spent two and a half years. Later he told me that he himself had requested to be kept separate from the other prisoners, since he was afraid of provocateurs and did not want anyone to break his train of thought. And he had a lot to think about.

Even in prison Maisky was lucky. The interrogations had hardly begun when Stalin died. Therefore Maisky escaped trial "by ordeal"—beatings, torture, hunger. But for a person who had never been without a pen in his entire life, it was agonizingly difficult to go without writing paper and ink: they were distributed only for drafting petitions and statements.

But such is the strength of the human intellect that even in prison Maisky found mental diversion. He composed in his mind a tale of a group of Soviet adventurers abroad during the Second World War. (Three months after his liberation this tale, called *Near Is Far*, was written down and then published in two editions and translated abroad.)

Maisky was released from prison in the summer of 1955, and I saw him soon afterwards. He had hardly changed, was as inquisitive as before. He joked. At first he told me a little about his stay in prison, then a bit more over the course of time, until not long before his death in the summer of 1975. He died at the age of ninety-one.

Many were surprised, and are in fact still surprised, that Maisky spent such a long time in prison after the death of Stalin. I must confess that I wondered too. During my many talks with Maisky I often returned to this subject, but he did not like to recall anything that happened after 1943. He especially avoided talking about his years in prison. This was no doubt an expression of his instinct for self-preservation, but there were, perhaps, other reasons as well.

From everything that Ivan Mikhailovich told me, and from other sources, I have good reason to believe that his lengthy stay in prison after Stalin's death was the result of an unfortunate set of circumstances, both objective and personal. Maisky was a kind person by nature. He got along very well with his students and graduate scholars. In the almost thirty years of our close acquaintance I do not know of one instance in which he did anyone any harm. He was incredibly good to me personally, and I always had feelings of friendship and affection for him.

Maisky was inclined to compromise. And this quality, very valuable under certain conditions, played a cruel joke on him during his stay in prison. The Lavrenty Beria affair unexpectedly intruded on his fate.

I would remind the reader that soon after Stalin's death, yet another act in the struggle for power was being played out among the new Soviet leadership. Beria was a member of the first "troika" (Malenkov, Molotov, and Beria) to head the state after Stalin's death. Beria occupied key positions in the area of state security.

Then, in July 1953, Beria was arrested. Soon afterwards, the Central Committee sent out a letter to all the party organizations in the Soviet Union, asserting that Beria had been attempting to overthrow the Soviet government in order to establish a one-man dictatorship. Among the facts adduced to support this accusation was his intention to release from imprisonment "the British spy" Maisky and even make him his own minister of foreign affairs. The letter even contained excerpts from Maisky's own testimony. Maisky supposedly confessed that having spent so many years working abroad, he had lost the feeling of belonging to his homeland and no longer knew whether England or the Soviet Union was his home. England seemed closer to him than the Soviet Union. Needless to say, such an acknowledgment had nothing to do with espionage.

Those who knew Ivan Mikhailovich well could easily imagine his being forced to say something like that. He may have supposed that by meeting the investigator halfway, he might mitigate matters, then the investigator would meet him halfway, and in the final analysis a compromise would be reached. Maisky, in solitary confinement, did not know that Stalin was no longer alive, although, as he told me, some imperceptible signs gave him the feeling that something momentous had occurred. Apparently Maisky had been too hasty in making his confessions and fell into a trap laid for him not so much by the investigator as by circumstances and his own tendency to compromise.

Meanwhile, Beria, even before he learned of the accusations against Maisky, did not doubt his innocence of either espionage or treason, or of anything else of that kind. According to information, Beria wanted to release Maisky but did not succeed since he was arrested himself. Events then developed quite simply: inasmuch as Beria had wished to release Maisky, Maisky was, consequently, a Beria sympathizer. The Central Committee letter on the Beria affair was written in a hurry, and, as Khrushchev later confessed, at that time it was very convenient to blame Beria for everything.

Maisky was not the only one named an agent in the letter. There were others. Not only were they not arrested however, but some even stayed on as party members.

Beria was a criminal, of course, but there was hardly one member of the Politburo at the time who was not up to his elbows in blood. This was absolutely clear in the documents published in the Soviet press in connection with the Twenty-Second Party Congress in 1961.

Since Maisky's name had been mentioned in the Beria affair, the new Soviet leadership found it inconvenient to release him immediately, especially since the investigation materials contained his own "confession." Strangely, the return to "normal" legal procedure also struck a blow at Maisky. The decision was made to put him on trial.

But Maisky was not the only diplomat arrested at that time. Zinchenko, Korzh, and other former officials at the Soviet embassy in London during the war met the same fate. Among those arrested as well was the former editor of *Soviet War News*, S. N. Rostovsky, a specialist in literature, also known under the pseudonyms Ernst Henry and N. Leonidov. Each one of those arrested was accused of espionage, while some, in accordance with established tradition, were accused of being agents for several foreign intelligence networks at the same time.

Maisky's arrest should not have come as a surprise, given his past and Stalin's personal dislike of him. The fact, however, that other officials of the London embassy were arrested at the same time demonstrates the special nature of this matter and shows that what was involved were some of the events from the war years. There are grounds for such an assumption. In May 1942 the Soviet minister of foreign affairs, Vyacheslav Mikhailovich Molotov, arrived in London to conclude negotiations and sign the Anglo-Soviet military alliance. Next, Molotov left for the United States, where he was received with great ceremony by President Roosevelt. He then returned to London and from there flew to Moscow.

It is only natural to assume that every step Molotov took, both in Britain and in America, was being carefully observed by intelligence and counterintelligence bodies of the USSR, and their findings were being reported at the highest level.

A man (let us call him "Ivanov", or X) who was somehow involved in the whole matter, told me that the investigator questioned those accused about Molotov's trip to England and the United States. The following picture gradually emerged. Stalin, on examining the materials pertaining to Molotov's stay abroad, drew attention to the fact that in America, Molotov had spent part of his trip in a private railway car. A suspicion entered Stalin's mind, and was harbored there until the end of his days, that Molotov was not traveling in the private car by chance: this was the most convenient way to come to agreement with the Americans behind Stalin's back.

So Stalin's faith in Molotov was shaken. Toward the end of his life this suspicion which had long been his obsession—for such is the sickness of tyrants—became even stronger. Stalin ordered that all the circumstances of Molotov's trip be carefully examined. The results of the inquiry, although favorable to Molotov, did not completely dispel Stalin's doubts.

I asked Maisky about this episode and was told that his investigator had never asked him personally about It. Other people, however, arrested before Maisky, were questioned about the details of Molotov's trip. One might suppose that in accordance with a scenario set up before Stalin's death, the trial of Maisky and other London embassy officials was to be the prelude to more important court proceedings against Molotov.

Maisky went on trial in the summer of 1955. The proceedings were closed. He was accused of treason and of anti-Soviet activities. The major witness for the prosecution was the doctor of economic science, professor, and retired colonel Grigory Abramovich Deborin, eldest son of the famous philosopher and "Menshevist-leaning idealist" Abram Moiseevich Deborin.

As to why the prosecutors came to choose Grigory Deborin, Maisky explained to me that he, Maisky, had once been chairman of a council in the academic town of Mozzhinka near Zvenigorod some seventy kilometers from Moscow. Deborin, who lived year round at his father's dacha, was Maisky's deputy on that council. Both of them were interested in political problems and would often go for walks together, chatting about different political topics. At the trial Deborin testified that these conversations on Maisky's part were anti–Soviet in nature. (That Deborin was lying is blatantly obvious to me. Knowing Maisky as I did for three decades, I am firmly convinced that he was constitutionally incapable of such talk.)

Maisky declined the services of a lawyer and took up his own defense. "During the trial," Maisky told me, "I morally demolished Deborin and demonstrated that he was lying."

The accusations against Maisky of espionage and treason were withdrawn. But Maisky had been under investigation for two and a half years, and, from the standpoint of the authorities, it was undesirable simply to pronounce him not guilty and release him. They had to justify his being kept under surveillance for such a long time. Therefore, after the accusations of state treason and espionage were withdrawn, Maisky was charged with violations and omissions in his official duties supposedly committed during the time he spent in London as ambassador. He received a rather heavy (by Western standards) sentence: a six-year prison term. But the entire procedure had been laid out beforehand. Maisky appealed to the Presidium of the Supreme Soviet for clemency and was pardoned. He was released shortly after the trial. But a very surprising thing happened later: Maisky was completely rehabilitated in civil court, and the sentence was rescinded—an outcome unique in Soviet party practice.

Maisky told me that Voroshilov and Bulganin had played a positive role in his case. Incidentally, the former was also considered by Stalin to be a British spy! Once I asked Maisky (this was in 1974, shortly before his ninetieth birthday, for which I was writing an anniversary article): "Tell me, Ivan Mikhailovich, several times in your life you were on the brink of catastrophe—during the Civil War, no doubt in 1937, and then in 1953. By what miracle did you manage to survive?"

The old man looked at me with his large and still lively dark brown eyes, smiled slightly, and said, "I always kept a cool head on my shoulders." And I thought: Had Stalin lived just a month or two longer, nothing would have helped either Ivan Mikhailovich—Maisky—or Vyacheslav Mikhailovich—Molotov—not even a cool head."

For decades researchers, especially in the field of modern history of the West and of the Soviet period, have suffered from "archival hunger." We, as a rule, were allowed into the archives only with the greatest of precautions, and just a few of us who were lucky managed at last to publish some truly important documents. In 1955 the rules for access to the archives were loosened, and the iron doors were opened up a bit here and there. Those who were quickest managed to slip through the crack. One staff member even succeeded in getting into the Ministry of Defense archives and obtained some reports of military attachés during the war. How we all envied him! The archives of other bureaus and ministries were opened. Some lucky individuals managed quite by chance to come upon important Politburo documents which had made their way into these archives. But that was pure good fortune, like winning an automobile in the lottery!

I racked my brains to figure which archives in the Soviet Union I might use for my work. A trip abroad for the purpose of doing research was something I did not even dream about at the time.

In 1957 Professor A. A. Guber, head of the National Committee of Soviet Historians, made a timid attempt to include me in a Soviet delegation going to London for a conference of British and Soviet historians, but nothing came of it. I felt that it was very important to work with the documents from the Nuremberg trials, specifically the minutes from the interrogations conducted by Soviet investigators, so I went to see L. P. Sheinin, the head of the investigatory department of the procurator's office. In addition to the specific purpose of my visit—to try to obtain materials on the trial—I was also eager to get a look at the man who, together with the general procurator, Andrei Vyshinsky, had prepared the notorious trials against Bukharin, Zinoviev and others in the 1930s. Sheinin was also the author of popular detective stories, some of which had been turned into successful plays. Later Sheinin would be assigned the "investigation" into the circumstances surrounding the death of the famous Jewish artist and chairman of the Antifascist Jewish Committee, S. M. Mikhoels. Sheinin was subsequently, relieved of his post and landed in prison, from which he managed to emerge safe and sound. According to one account, he misunderstood the higher-ups' instructions and conducted a serious investigation, which was not at all what they wanted.

In any event, I visited Sheinin in his office in the procurator's head-quarters on Pushkin Street in Moscow. Our talk was a brief one: I was not given permission. Fortunately, a multivolume edition of Nuremburg trial documents was published in Britain and the United States, and I was able to use this for my work. But Sheinin remembered me. Half a year later, while passing through the hall of the Moscow House of Cinema, I saw Sheinin and heard someone ask him while pointing me out: "Who is that?" Sheinin replied: "That is Maisky's graduate student, Nekrich." Sheinin's professional memory as an investigator was excellent.

Having failed to obtain access to the Nuremberg trial materials, I decided to investigate the archives of the Baltic republics, reasoning sensibly that in spite of the war, some materials might have survived.

This was back in 1951, a difficult and dangerous time. I still managed to learn that the archives in Latvia and Lithuania had been transported to the USSR Ministry of Foreign Affairs, while the Estonian archive was, for the time being, still in the Estonian capital, Tallinn. So it was that I went to that marvelous city for the first time and fell in love with it; I made some wonderful friends there and have gone back again and again.

I was very lucky. Despite the fact that I was working with a translator, I came across some extremely interesting documents on British policy in the Baltic. I virtually discovered this archive for Russian historians. After me historians from Moscow and Leningrad came pouring into Tallinn and Tartu. I returned once again to the Estonian archives in the early 1960s during work on my doctoral dissertation. I saw the Latvian and Lithuanian documents later in the foreign policy archive of the Ministry of Foreign Affairs in Moscow. Still, the Estonian documents were merely a palliative. I did not have available to me the major archive necessary for my work: the British one. It is true that in those years the British government archive for the Second World War period was closed to foreign scholars, but there were, of course, other possibilities: private archives; materials belonging to various public organizations, societies, and the like; and, finally, interviews with participants in the events. But at that time one could only dream about the possibility of a trip to England for research work. Alas, such a dream, modest and commonplace for any researcher living in the West, did not come true. But my thirst for archives was partly satisfied in another way.

In 1955—this was in the spring—the heads of the Institute of History put me in charge of a team of institute historians whose job was to sort out captured German documents which had been lying around in sacks and cartons for a good ten years. There were two major reasons for deciding, finally, to review these documents on a large scale. The first was that in the West, the governments of the United States, Britain, and France had begun the systematic publication of German documents. The second was that, with a view to the future return to the German Democratic Republic of those papers seized during the war, it was deemed advisable to microfilm any documents of interest. This work was going on in all the agencies to which captured German documents had been sent, in particular to the ministries of Foreign Affairs, Internal Affairs, and State Security. Our team worked in the so-called Special Archive of the Ministry of Internal Affairs.

Before us lay countless treasures—for the historian, of course. We virtually devoured the documents. How can one describe the feeling of the historian as he unexpectedly discovers for himself a needed document, when he sifts through the pages with trembling hands, not yet believing how lucky he is? I would compare the sensation most of all with the feeling of coming into contact with buried treasure, hidden from the eyes of the uninitiated, somewhere deep underground.

Among the many documents, my special attention was drawn, quite naturally, to those pertaining to the Second World War. Some of them I admit I used later in my work, without citation, since I did not have the right to refer to them. What luck! In my hands were the files of the British Expeditionary Corps in France in 1939–40—disparate documents, but very interesting all the same. One was the diary of a Canadian captain, taken prisoner during the raid on Dieppe in August 1942. Many years later I would write about this in an article published by one of the historical journals.

Look! What is this? Nothing less than the archive of Hermann Goering! And the imperial envoy's materials on the "four-year plan" (the German economic development plan, not unlike the Soviet five-year plans), as well as data on Soviet prisoners of war used in Reich enterprises in 1942 and 1943, on German investments outside Germany on the eve of the Second World War, and a great deal more. And the Gestapo archive! Files on communist underground groups under Fascist rule. But this matter was dealt with by officials from the Institute of Marxism-Leninism. Then suddenly the idea comes unexpectedly: What if all this "information" was concocted by the Gestapo and was false, just like that concocted by the NKVD in our own country against "plotters" and "terrorists"? Perhaps there really hadn't been communist activity in Germany on such a scale. After all, the Gestapo had to justify its own existence. I quickly stifle within myself this seditious idea.

During those days our team examined on a selective basis 150,000 files and did a complete review of 11,000. Never in my life, before or since, have I seen such a vast number of documents in one place. On our own initiative we conducted a survey of the records examined earlier by representatives of other organizations and revealed a substantial amount of valuable historical information. We were able to unearth all these materials, of course, because our team included highly qualified professional historians: M. S. Al'perovich, M. N. Mashkin, I. S. Kremer, L. V. Pozdeeva, L. V. Ponomaryova, V. M. Turok-Popov, K. Maidannik, and others. Many of their books are known outside the Soviet Union. In connection with our work in the Special Archive we developed a number of serious concerns of a practical nature, which I summarized and presented in a document sent October 24, 1955, to the leadership of the Academy of Sciences. We wished to draw attention to the unjust situation faced by researchers in modern Soviet history as compared with their colleagues abroad. Despite the distinctly irritating boastfulness about supposed Soviet victories over bourgeois historical scholarship, I wrote, "the serious lag in Soviet historical scholarship in the field of modern history behind bourgeois historical scholarship can be overcome [only] if Soviet historians are given the opportunity of working with archival documents." Urgent appeals to open up the archives became more frequent and persistent.

Soon after the Twentieth Party Congress I was included by the party Central Committee science department in a group appointed to study the situation regarding access to archives and prepare a draft decision for the Central Committee. But disagreement among the leadership and the staunch opposition of some agencies hindered our work and managed to stop us before we even began. We came up against the Ministry of Foreign Affairs, which wanted to manage its archives in accordance with its own rules (one of the tasks of our group was to establish uniform rules for work in all the country's archives, without exception).

At that time preparations began on a series of documents on the history of Soviet foreign policy, followed by the issuance of multivolume collections of documents on the history of the foreign policy of tsarist Russia. In addition, the systematic publication of state treaties with foreign governments was resumed. Academic institutions and their members were involved in this project. Yet, as anyone who has worked with the originals of these documents knows full well, there is a complex and lengthy procedure for each document before it is approved for publication. But most unfortunate of all is the fact that many documents, especially those on the history of Soviet foreign policy, were not published intact. Any "suspicious" phrases, and even entire paragraphs, had to be omitted from the documents and a diaeresis inserted. And this, as a rule, was done on the initiative of the editors of the volume, who were supposedly the leaders of historical scholarship in the Soviet Union.

It was a time of great expectations. In February 1956 the Twentieth Party Congress met, the first meeting since the death of Stalin. The era of rehabilitation—or the era of disorientation, as Aleksandr Zinoviev cleverly called it, was in full swing. Khrushchev's secret report was supported by the overwhelming majority of party members. While this report was not published in full in the Soviet Union, it was soon printed abroad. At meetings of communists, and separately among nonparty members, the report was read and the decisions of the congress hotly debated.

One cannot describe the inspiration with which hundreds of thousands of people, among them my friends and myself, reacted to what had happened at the congress: the exposure of crimes committed under Stalin and the new leadership's solemn assurances that no such thing would ever be repeated in the history of our country. Even the deliberately naive, but humanly understandable confession by Khrushchev, to the effect that the Politburo members knew about all the abuses but were afraid to act against Stalin for fear of their lives, was duly acknowledged. Khrushchev, while describing indignantly the crimes committed by Stalin against prominent party and government figures, remained silent, however, about the fact that the repressions had stricken all the people and not just the party elite. Later, many other claims were made about Khrushchev, many of them absolutely valid; but at the time, what the new party leader said and did was already such an enormous change for a nation that for decades had lived in an atmosphere of arbitrary rule that few could accept and digest even this limited dose of the truth. We now know of the struggle Khrushchev had to wage with others close to Stalin, such as Molotov, Voroshilov and Kaganovich, who berated him and told him that he had no idea what he was doing. Meanwhile, "down below" the mood was as if there had suddenly ended a kind of mystical cycle in which we were all born, lived, and died. The evil spell was broken, and the magician was dead. Now we didn't have to speak in half-truths and half-lies. Although, of course, Khrushchev himself had actually told a half-lie.

The Stalinists' barely restrained anger and hatred was the best indication that our country could still embark on the true historical path. It seemed at the time that socialism was not a mistake, that "the great experiment" had been a success, in spite of all the horrors, all the blood and grime. The party had told the people the truth, the whole truth.

The whole truth?

That was how it began. The truth was given in summary fashion. Yet people expected that tthe Gordian knot would not just be cut but untangled as well. But, we consoled ourselves, Khrushchev in his secret report had mentioned a number of crimes that were to be investigated—for example, the murder of Kirov—and this would lead in turn to the disclosure and condemnation of other crimes and the indictment of those who were guilty of them. It seemed that everything was proceeding as necessary.

At the institute, the party meeting on the results of the Twentieth Party Congress was held in the auditorium on the fourth floor of the building at 14 Volkhonka Street. After the report was read by A. M. Pankratova, the delegate to the congress, there were many other statements. The overwhelming majority of them amounted to reminiscences. From the professional standpoint, for the historians meeting there, these remembrances were not without interest. True, the speakers remembered primarily how historians had been forced to knuckle under, to write not only patent lies but even utter nonsense for the sake of the "cult of personality"—a convenient and not altogether understandable definition of the era of Stalin's dictatorship. There were personal attacks as well, for example, on the historian Vasily Mochalov, an ardent "cultist," and one of the authors of the official biography of Stalin. Needless to say, some had personal scores to settle here as well.

I clearly recall some of the statements in particular. The old Bolshevik Andrei Kuchkin spoke, one of the authors of the *History of the Communist Party of the Soviet Union*, who from time immemorial had been prepared to do the party's bidding. But even he had been affected, to the point that he called Stalin "a murderer of his own people." Coming from Kuchkin, these words made a strong impression—far more than if they had appeared, say, in some newspaper editorial. He was disputed by another man, not as old but still a Bolshevik, the head of the contemporary Western European history department, Nikolai Samorukov, who asserted that Stalin should never be called a murderer but could and should be labeled a tyrant. So things had reached the point where we could publicly debate what kind of criminal the leader of the people had been! But the most important thing, of course, was not the disputes themselves but the atmosphere of emancipation that reigned at the meeting. It would not be an exaggeration to say that there was a near-Christian readiness to repent, mixed with the traditional Russian tendency toward redemption.

Some, of course, made statements calling for restraint and caution. Some hinted that Khrushchev, perhaps, should not have said all that he had, and others had doubts about the security of Khrushchev's position. A colleague of mine, a very well educated historian but a hopeless careerist, said thoughtfully, "Well, now, for the next ten years it will be better not to publish anything." And he took his own advice. He wrote and defended his doctoral dissertation on the history of Soviet society, but published it only after Khrushchev's removal. He went on to become a corresponding member of the Academy of Sciences and head of one of the departments at the Institute of History. So, from a practical, everyday point of view, he turned out to be far-sighted. But how limited a point of view! How it crippled him morally! And not just him. For a small part of the so-called new man created during the years of Soviet power—*Homo sovieticus*—was to be found to some extent in each and every one of us. But *Homo sovieticus* was surprisingly capable of reincarnation and adaptation to any circumstances, and deep down was prepared to do anything required of him, as long as it could be said that he was doing it unwillingly, that he was being forced to it, since there was no other way. There is not one illusionist as capable of reaching such heights in the art of reincarnation while remaining in the same packaging as *Homo sovieticus.*

The new atmosphere had a favorable effect on scholarly work, on the approach to solving crucial problems of history. In the professional periodicals there appeared much interesting, fresh material. All this was taking place during a covert struggle, sometimes breaking out into the open, between the proponents of Khrushchev's policy (a relative term, of course) and the Stalinists.

A few articles appeared in the journal *Voprosy istorii* in which attempts were made to clarify Stalin's true role during the Revolution, and more genuinely highlight some key problems of Soviet history. This began as early as 1954, when A. M. Pankratova was named editor in chief and E. N. Burdzhalov became her deputy. He, in particular, was the moving force behind the journal.

Burdzhalov's life was a complex one. He had been one of the leading propagandists of the party Central Committee, heading its lecturers' group. Then he was named deputy editor of the newspaper *Kultura i zhizn'*, the organ of the propaganda and agitation division of the Central Committee, headed at the time by G. F. Aleksandrov. This newspaper was once the highest authority on ideology. The critical remarks published there often determined not only the fate of a given work but the fate of individuals as well. Once, annoyed by the constant railings, a friend and I decided to make fun of the illiterate articles published in that paper. We chose two of them for this purpose: one was an article by the literary expert and administrator V. R. Shcherbina on Boris Lavrenev's play *For Those at Sea*, the second an article by a certain Nestev, supposedly a music expert. We wrote a letter to *Pravda* in which we gave examples of poor writing and suggested that *Kultura i zhizn'* work more closely with its authors. I remember especially one sentence from Shcherbina's article that sounded like absolute nonsense: "Borovsky behaves in society just the way he does in private life: thus he abuses the trust of two women." We received no response to our letter, though, and Shcherbina has since become either an academician or a corresponding member of the Academy of Sciences. We then joked that Shcherbina became an academician by following our advice.

Burdzhalov played an important role in *Kultura i zhizn'*. But he, like any human being inculcated since childhood with a sense of decency, had pangs of conscience and felt the need to share his ideas, which, no doubt, he had been pondering for quite some time. Burdzhalov published an article on the February Revolution, in which he demonstrated that the Revolution had occurred spontaneously. This was in flagrant contradiction to the orthodox point of view on the significant contribution of the Bolshevik party in preparing for the Revolution. Then Burdzhalov, on the basis of documents, showed that after the Revolution, Stalin and Kamenev, among others, came out in support of the provisional government. Burdzhalov asserted that, even after the April 1917 conference, Stalin continued to maintain this view. Burdzhalov also produced information on elections to the Central Committee of the Russian Communist party (Bolsheviks) showing that Zinoviev actually came in second in the voting. But his main point was that virtually the only one in favor of an immediate uprising against the provisional government was Lenin, but at the time he was in hiding in Razliv, near Petrograd. This meant the destruction of a great myth, according to which the two leaders of the 1917 Revolution were Lenin and Stalin. This legend finally took hold after the physical annihilation of all the other prominent leaders of the October coup—Zinoviev, Kamenev, and the rest. Then the *Short Course* of the history of the Communist party was published, and went through many multimillion-copy editions, in which this falsification became firmly established. In his article Burdzhalov relied on the memoirs of Shlyapnikov, one of the three free members of the Russian bureau of the Central Committee in 1917 (the other two being Molotov and Zalutsky). Shlyapnikov wrote his memoirs right on the heels of the events, certainly no later than 1918-19.

But the article was not the last of it. Burdzhalov became very active in speaking out at public debates against the falsification of party history. In one instance he spoke at a discussion of Likholat's book *The Victory of the October Revolution in the Ukraine*. Likholat, a historian of Stalinist bent, was head of the history section in the party Central Committee and enjoyed a great deal of influence over historical scholarship. A meeting was called at the Institute of Marxism-Leninism to discuss Likholat's book. It was chaired by the deputy chief of the Stalin archive, a certain Pentkovskaya. At that meeting everyone apparently jumped on the bandwagon in praise of Likholat's book, with the exception of the well-known historian of national relations S. I. Yakubovskaya. Likholat in his book had listed many Ukrainian communists as revisionists, thereby justifying after the fact the repression later used against them. He also failed to mention the Great Russian chauvinism, which came into play when the Ukraine was, for a time, declared a part of Russia. The book gave rise to protests among a number of surviving old Bolsheviks. At the Twentieth Party Congress Anastas Mikoyan spoke out against this book. Likholat had to leave his post in the Central Committee and go work at the Ukrainian Institute of History in Kiev.

Soon after the events in Hungary in 1956, *Voprosy istorii* convened a conference for readers at the Public History Library in Moscow. At A. L. Sidorov's initiative, the leaders of the journal, Pankratova and Burdzhalov, were attacked at the discussion from a Stalinist perspective. The Stalinists were trying to take revenge. Unfortunately, they were assisted in this by some very able historians. One of them, whom I shall not mention by name, later, on realizing his mistake, fell seriously ill from nervous shock. The unsavory methods still resorted to by the party chameleons even after the exposure of Stalin's crimes can be illustrated by this campaign. The head of the Soviet social history section at the Institute of History sent one of his colleagues, Rostislav Dadykin, to Odessa (where Pankratova had once done some party work) in order to find documentation proving that Pankratova had been not a Bolshevik but a socialist revolutionary. Although Dadykin could discover nothing, for the simple reason that Pankratova had never been a socialist revolutionary, in return for his services he was awarded the position of section head. (Payment for dirty work at state expense is one of the inherent aspects of life in Soviet society.)

After the events in Hungary, and in connection with Burdzhalov's speech (to thunderous applause) at the Public History Library, he and Pankratova were summoned to the science department of the Central Committee, where they were accused of having deviated from party principles. The meeting was chaired by the head of the science department, V. A. Kirillin (at present chairman of the state committee of the USSR Council of Ministers on Science and Technology). The editors were charged with three accusations: of publishing a lead article in the journal in which bourgeois historiography was said to have been put "under protection"; of printing an article by Burdzhalov in which he supposedly diminished the role of the party and slandered the Central Committee; and of publishing an article on worker management. Pankratova confessed that there were a number of articles in the journal which she had not read. Burdzhalov refused to acknowledge any guilt and argued that he had acted purely from a party standpoint. The Central Committee secretariat decided to relieve Burdzhalov of his post as deputy editor, to censure Pankratova, and to fire the editorial worker, S. S. Khesin, who had been responsible for preparing the articles for publication (after two years without work Khesin was finally hired at the Institute of History). Pankratova then submitted a request to be released from her duties as editor of the journal. Burdzhalov was sent to work at the Institute of History. But the matter did not end there.

The institute's party bureau secretary, P. N. Sobolev, former propaganda secretary of the Leningrad city party committee, and notorious for his Stalinist views, invited Burdzhalov to the party bureau and asked him what he thought of the decisions made by the Central Committee secretariat. Burdzhalov answered frankly that he considered them wrong. And here began the final act of the drama. Sobolev called an urgent meeting of the party bureau and told of the conversation with Burdzhalov, who was then expelled from the party. For him this was tantamount to a death sentence. Nevertheless, when the party bureau's decision was adopted at the party meeting, Sonya Yakubovskaya opposed the expulsion and proposed that they limit themselves to a reprimand, a course which, in spite of the ardent protests of the Stalinists, was adopted by a majority. Soon afterwards the academic council of the institute, under great pressure, conducted a special review of Burdzhalov's credentials. Lacking two votes for election to the post of senior researcher, he was dismissed. By the time Burdzhalov's book on the February Revolution was published many years later, he was a sick old man.

Anna Mikhailovna Pankratova died a few years after this incident. Kaganovich and Molotov came to her funeral.

The rear-guard action of the Stalinists, while it succeeded in stifling Burdzhalov, did not turn into a counteroffensive, in spite of the Hungarian events. The Stalinists' clout had clearly diminished. The main thing was that they could no longer stir up popular hysteria and use it for purposes of solidifying their power. After Stalin's death this had become impossible.

The uprising in Hungary in the autumn of 1956, caused by the ultra-Stalinist policy of the Hungarian "little Stalin" Mátyás Rákosi, who had acted not only in accordance with instructions from Moscow but fully in harmony with the dogmatic thinking of a Comintern official, played directly into the hands of the Stalinists. The party leadership was already alarmed by the situation in Poland. Furthermore, Khrushchev and others were disheartened by the fact that in October 1956 it was the working class that took to the streets of Warsaw, demonstrating its determination to repel the Soviet divisions which Marshal Konev was prepared to send to that rebellious city. But what Khrushchev did not risk doing in Poland, he did do, and not without Tito's knowledge, in Hungary. The uprising was suppressed with the aid of tanks and cannons.

Events in Poland and Hungary showed that the atmosphere in the countries of Eastern and southeastern Europe had become extremely tense and that the people of those countries did not want that kind of socialism for themselves. Yet the psychological influence of the Twentieth Party Congress was still so great that in our microcosm, in the Institute of History, the Hungarian events were discussed freely in the corridors, the Soviet government's actions were openly criticized, and views were expressed which in Stalinist times might have cost one's life. Some time after the Hungarian events these views would be declared revisionist, and even later anti-Soviet. Our view of the movement in Hungary was no doubt influenced by the fact that blood had been shed: the Hungarians killed officials of the state security, infamous for their brutal torture of prisoners. Moreover, the indifference of the Hungarian peasantry to the movement in the city elicited caution: Did this movement really reflect accurately the mood of all the Hungarians? This concern gave Soviet propaganda the argument it needed to support its assertion that events in Hungary were counterrevolutionary in nature, that communists were being killed there. Therefore the bloody intervention of Soviet forces met with approval not only from the party elite but from a segment of the Soviet intelligentsia as well. The rest, at any rate, kept silent. Things remained calmer and more normal that way.

But still, I was not the only one shaken by the events in Hungary. People are inclined to focus on specifics, so there was special indignation not over the bloody repression used against the Hungarians in Budapest but over the trap set for the leadership of the uprising. The Soviet command, using the Yugoslavs as intermediaries, announced that if the struggle were to end, the leaders would be allowed to leave the country in a Yugoslav bus. But when these conditions were agreed to, and Pal Maleter and the other leaders came forward, they were immediately arrested, and later sentenced and executed. The head of the Hungarian government, Imre Nagy, also fell into the treacherous trap: he was sent to Romania and then hanged.

The Soviet leadership had to take what they viewed as a highly undesirable step: to agree to a new Hungarian government, which proclaimed itself "revolutionary," and which was headed by people imprisoned under Rakosy, repressed and then rehabilitated, so to speak.

The events in Poland and in Hungary were the result of a crisis—political, economic, and moral—in which the Soviet state and society had found itself because of the Stalinist-style dictatorship of the proletariat. But could this dictatorship be anything but?

Still, this was not the point. The fact was that only seven months had passed since the Twentieth Party Congress, and people simply were not psychologically prepared for what happened in Poland and Hungary. Thus, they had no definite reaction to them. I would add that the so-called moral and political unity of the Soviet nation in fact sowed deep distrust, suspicion, and division among people. Therefore the reaction to events in Hungary was varied.

Furthermore, the war in October 1956 in the Middle East enabled the Soviet leadership to shift the focus of attention of emerging public opinion in the Soviet Union to the Anglo-French intervention in Egypt, and combine the events in Hungary and in the Middle East as a unified imperialist plot against the USSR, socialism, and the national liberation movement.

The Stalinists were eager to exploit the situation, so as to recoup their losses. They forced Khrushchev to stain their own hands with blood. Alas, he did this more than once: during the uprising in Temirtau, and in Tbilisi, and in Novocherkassk. Khrushchev was forced to renounce, for the time being, his initial intention of purging the central party and government apparatus of Stalinists, an intention that had grown stronger after June 1956, when, under pressure from the Stalinist members of the Politburo, and relying on the same Stalinist apparatus, both central and local, he deviated from the decisions of the Twentieth Party Congress, toning them down with the famous Central Committee decree on the cult of personality of June 30, 1956. After the events in Hungary and in Poland, Khrushchev began to recall in his public statements that Stalin had been a Marxist and had rendered the Russian and international workers' movements a great service. "Let us all be the same kind of Marxists that Comrade Stalin was," stated Khrushchev, to the applause of the Stalinists, in 1957.

These zigzags in Khrushchev's policy had an immediate effect on ideology, which was reflected in the social sciences, forcing historians and social scientists to maneuver and return once again to the conformist axioms and oaths which—prematurely, as it turned out—we thought had been discarded forever.

Gradually, though, even the most conservative of fields—history—threw off the chains of Stalinism. An enormous role was played by the subdued criticism of the *Short Course* of the history of the Communist party, which had served since the repression of the 1930s as the sole textbook, reference work, and interpretation for the history of Russia, the Soviet Union, the revolutionary movement, and related movements everywhere. At least now historians were free from the obligation of propagandizing the "two leaders" theory of the October 1917 Revolution—Lenin and Stalin—for it had been revealed that the latter did not play a particularly significant role.

Those historians with the most progressive views were prepared to take a fresh approach to such fundamental problems as collectivization of agriculture in the USSR, industrialization, the building of socialism in a single country, and so on. Wide-ranging changes were noticed as well in the approach taken toward the history of the Second World War and the Great Fatherland War of 1941–1945. At the Institute of Marxism-Leninism of the party Central Committee, a department was established on the history of the war, which, over a short period of time, published a six-volume history. In that edition many of Stalin's wartime actions were subjected to criticism. And, in spite of the groveling attempts to lionize Khrushchev as a military figure (for some reason it has always seemed to me that this was being done to compromise him), and in spite of the obvious distortions and silence on a number of important issues (the Soviet-German pact of 1939, the Vlasovites, collaboration with the enemy in occupied territory, and so on), this publication attracted the interest of historians and the reading public. There were heated discussions at the institute, as scholarly views began to make headway against obstacles of opportunism.

We know that two-thirds of the earth's surface is covered with water. Oceans, seas, lakes, rivers, rivulets, and streams form the world's oceans. A drop in the ocean is still a part of the ocean. Our institute might be likened to a stream in the limitless Soviet waters, and the contemporary history section, in which I worked, could be compared to a drop in the ocean. And just as a drop in the ocean reflects the color, taste, and smell of the entire ocean, our section reflected everything that was happening on a broader scale in the country as a whole, in our field, history, and in our institute. As an émigré I still say "our," since half my life on this earth and the greater part of my conscious existence were closely linked to the institute, indeed devoted to it. I spent thirty-one years there with only a nine-month break between the completion of my graduate studies in May 1949 and my entry into work in March 1950. In 1945, still in military uniform, I began graduate study at the institute. I left it forever on May 24, 1976.

In 1954 there were changes once again in our section. A new head was assigned to us: Nikolai Ivanovich Samorukov. He could not have been farther removed from the study of modern Western European history. He had previously been at the Institute of Marxism-Leninism, and did nothing there for many years, but, an obliging soul, he got himself elected secretary of the party organization there. Still, his idleness finally began to annoy the heads of his institute, so they decided to get rid of Samorukov—in a pleasant, subtle way, one approved by the higher authorities—by sending him off to the Academy of Sciences' Institute of History; let him sit idle there. In the distant past, during the stormy revolutionary years, Nikolai Samorukov had served as a sailor (supposedly on board the *Ochakov*). In 1918 he supported some sort of anarchist resolution; therefore, in spite of his absolutely irreproachable party work, or nonwork, in various institutions, including the Comintern Lenin School, which trained officials for foreign communist parties, Samorukov did not receive promotions through party channels but was used instead in subsidiary roles. He was a candidate of historical science, and his dissertation, which never saw the light of day, was devoted to the activities of the Russian revolutionary Lopatin. One or, perhaps two published articles was all Samorukov had contributed to what passed for history. Actually, this was to his credit. He constantly went on about his grandiose plans, but fortunately for scholarship, he never carried them out, thereby sparing the field any additional hackwork. Naturally, people like Samorukov found themselves constantly dependent on the bosses, who could at any moment show them the door because of their thoroughgoing professional uselessness.

During the Soviet era there formed in all areas of the economy, culture, science, and art, without exception, a rather powerful stratum of professionally useless people, who were and remain one of the most important bulwarks of the Soviet regime. They are supported, and paid a good salary, with the full expectation that they will produce absolutely nothing, but that they can be expected to do anything for appearances' sake. This breed has brought a great deal of unhappiness to our country and our people, and was the reason for the death of many of our comrades. I had to deal with such people on many occasions. They would seem unassuming, but they were fortified by their party membership and the support they got from other idlers like themselves.

At the outset Nikolai Ivanovich seemed a moderate individual, even decent by Soviet standards. But his professional incompetence and his tendency to do nothing immediately manifested themselves. But soon another, far less ingratiating quality emerged: his vindictiveness. Whether Samorukov got the idea himself, or whether it was suggested to him from "upstairs" on his appointment to his new post, his first step in his new position was to attempt a purge of the section. Samorukov first tried to defame one of the most talented historians and original thinkers I have known in my entire life, Vladimir Mikhailovich Turok-Popov.

Many in the Soviet Union and far beyond its borders know Turok well as a historian of the Austro-Hungarian monarchy, of Austria, and as a specialist in the international workers' movement and in international relations. Vladimir Mikhailovich's name was originally Popov; he took the pseudonym "Turok" for his articles. The pseudonym stuck, and later became part of his surname. In his youth Turok studied at the university in Vienna. With his outstanding linguistic skills, he quickly mastered not only the major European languages (he was fluent in German) but also the rather difficult Balkan tongues and even Hungarian. In Vienna he met the future leader of the Comintern (Communist International) Georgy Dmitrov, and began working with him in the Balkan secretariat of the Comintern. This was during the grim days of the 1920s, when the Balkan communists were cruelly persecuted in their countries, imprisoned, and killed. Turok was not a communist, and it is possible that during the Stalinist repression of the 1930s this saved his life. Upon his return home, Turok became a staff member of the International Agrarian Institute, a Comintern institution. At one time he specialized in the agrarian movement in Latin America. Sometimes life was hard for him.

In 1935 his wife's mother was arrested—Sofia Mikhailovna Antonova, who worked in Zinoviev's office at the Comintern. Her daughter, Turok's wife, Koka, was instructed to leave Moscow, and Turok left with her for a Siberian city, where he obtained employment as a statistician for the local land office. He was given the humorous nickname the "Decembrist's wife."

Turok was one of those inquisitive people. He was constantly expanding the scope of his interests, and in the final analysis he was virtually a walking encyclopedia. Unlike many other historians of his generation (Turok was born in 1904), he was not ambitious about his academic status and long remained a junior researcher. This is how I found him when I enrolled at the institute. It was not just Turok's vast knowledge but also his sharp wit, alertness, keen analysis of events, frankness in scholarly discussions, easy manner, and inquisitiveness, combined with his often merciless criticism of scholarship, that attracted people to him. Turok had a gigantic number of friends, colleagues, and casual acquaintances everywhere, beginning with Moscow and extending to the far-flung corners of the Soviet Union, including the Caucasus, Central Asia, the Western Ukraine and Moldavia, even Siberia. God knows where in the remotest reaches of the USSR one might not find his former pupils, whom he taught for many years at the Institute of Asian Studies, or his former graduate students from the academic institutes and universities of Moscow, Leningrad, and the cities of central Russia. Foreign historians, when they came to Moscow, tried to visit Turok at home, hoping to see him, to chat with him. But visiting him in his home was not such a simple matter. The rooms in his apartment were filled to overflowing with books—shelves of them from floor to ceiling. It was much the same in the room of his wife, Koka Aleksandrovna Antonova, a specialist on India and its medieval history. There were piles of newspapers and magazines all over the floor. Manuscripts which Turok had promised to read lay in stacks. Their authors trembled when they saw the chaos. The sofa on which Turok slept was like an island in a sea of paper. But what surprised me most was that there was some method to all of Turok's apparent madness, for when a desperate graduate student, who had given Turok his manuscript to read, thought it to be irretrievably lost, Turok triumphantly produced it from a pile of papers. Turok collected postage stamps, but showed no one his collection. One could write about Turok endlessly, and he richly deserves it. But I shall have to stop here, trusting that I have given the reader some idea of this remarkable man.

At about the time of Samorukov's arrival, Turok had finally completed his *Notes on the History of Austria, 1918–1938*, a work now considered a classic. Samorukov received orders to raise a row over the book during a discussion of it in the section, and not to allow its publication or indeed its defense by Turok as a dissertation for a doctorate of historical science.

I shall not describe in detail the discussion of Turok's book. I shall only say that I very actively spoke out in support of him. Finally, we upheld Turok's work and his right to defend it as a dissertation.

Next there began a series of clashes with Samorukov over our graduate students' candidate dissertations. In an attempt to demonstrate that before his arrival everything in the section had been wrong, Samorukov took the old, tested party way: he accused one graduate student of "anarcho-syndicalism," another of "anti-Sovietism," and a third of "bourgeois objectivism." Once again I had to issue a stern rebuff to Samorukov. Our relationship was ruined for good, but all our graduate students (Chada, Oskolkov, and Kolker) successfully defended their dissertations.

The decade between 1956 and 1966 was a fruitful one for many scholars and for those working in the fields of culture and the arts. Those were years of searching, of liberation from the threat of the past, years of creative enthusiasm. How quickly they went by! But then everything was seen through the rose-colored glasses of expectation.

During those years I worked, wrote and published a great deal. After my first monograph, I published a number of books for general consumption (*The War They Called Phoney* and others). They were received with great interest by the reading public and were favorably reviewed both in the USSR and abroad. In 1958, at the suggestion of the director of the Institute of History, V. M. Khvostov, we coauthored a volume entitled *How the Second World War Began*, which came out on the twentieth anniversary of the War in a large edition. Even though this book was devoted to the outbreak of the Second World War, we continued to avoid discussion of one of the major issues: the role of the Soviet-German pact of 1939 in unleashing the war. This question was and remains a most sensitive one for Soviet historiography, and no Soviet historian, myself included, as yet dared step over the line of the permissible and go beyond the official interpretation of the pact as being favorable to Soviet preparations against an attack by Germany two years later. Even if someone had tried to do so, such a manuscript would never have seen the light of day.

During those years I also published for the *Great Soviet Encyclopedia*, the *Diplomatic Dictionary*, and several journals. But my major work after 1958 was as part of the group compiling the ten-volume edition of *World History*. Wherever and whenever I found it possible, I opposed dogmatic views of history and historical events which had become embedded in our consciousness. This was not at all easy to do, especially in my chosen field, the history of the Second World War, where the Stalinists' position was particularly firm and unshakable, and where each of us had at one time shared the conformist viewpoint. This could be explained by a number of factors, first and foremost the victory of the Soviet Union over Germany.

The well-known aphorism "Might makes right" was, it turned out, not just a saying about the psychology of the victors but a statement of their philosophy as well. This philosophy is the basic ideology that prevails in the USSR. It was not so important to ask about the price paid for victory as to ask why it was so high. For in Stalin's time (in 1946), and for quite a long time to come, the figure for loss of life in the Soviet Union during the war was given as 7 million. Later another figure—17 million—was advanced. And only in 1965, when the sixth and final volume of *A History of the Great Fatherland War* came out, was the figure given by Khrushchev in 1961 affirmed: 20 million people, the official number of lives lost by the Soviet Union during the war years 1941–1945. I myself have some doubts about this last figure, although it perhaps comes closest to the truth. The number of Soviets killed in the Second World War, then, was twelve times greater than that of tsarist Russia during the First World War.

What was behind this frightening figure of human loss? And how did the Nazis manage to get as far as Moscow itself, reach Stalingrad and the Caucasus, and lay siege to Leningrad for nine hundred days? The official explanation, based on Stalin's statements during the war and soon afterwards, found in a curious document—the historical pamphlet *Falsifiers of History*—does not give a clear answer to this question. But it was a matter of concern to many, not just to historians but to people in the Soviet Union far outside the field of history. Among those in search of the correct explanation were professional historians and, above all, the military. In 1956 the *War History Journal* began to come out, and a trend toward the critical assessment of the history of the Second World War and of the Great Fatherland War emerged and gradually gained ground. The journal was a publication of the USSR Ministry of Defense, but it served two masters. Through administrative channels it came under the military-scientific office of the General Staff, and through ideological ones the central political office of the Soviet army. Colonel (now General) Nikolai Grigorièvich Pavlenko was appointed editor in chief. I later had occasion to work with him on the editorial board of the tenth volume of *World History*. Pavlenko was no doubt the right person for the job. Educated, intelligent, and flexible, with a fair dose of culture, he steered his ship skillfully through waters where reefs and shoals might suddenly arise at every turn, threatening shipwreck.

Pavlenko's immediate superior was General Vladimir Vasilievich Kurasov, then head of the military-scientific office. The editorial board of the journal was diverse; progressive historians as well as staunch Stalinists coexisted there, as well as some who were ready to follow every change in political policy. It was said of them that they "rolled with the tide of party policy."

A great deal was contributed to the study of Second World War history by Colonel V. M. Kulish, head of the criticism and bibliography department, by Colonel V. D. Polikarpov, and by Colonel V. I. Dashichev, who prepared important publications of German General Staff materials. Our assessments coincided on many aspects of Second World War history (Dunkirk, the Hess mission, Operation "Sea Lion").

The journal's policy was fully in keeping with Communist party policy of the time, of course. Such policy could be interpreted and treated differently, however. This was made especially clear in connection with decisions of the Twentieth and Twenty-Second Party Congresses. The journal accomplished excellent work in rehabilitating and restoring the good names of military figures, victims of the Stalinist terror of the 1930s, and the Soviet military leaders of the 1918–1921 Civil War period who had been unjustly slandered and executed. The journal also did much to dispel the myths about the military genius of Stalin, which to this day remain in the minds of the older generation who took part in the war.

It came as a surprise to many that a large number of military historians had been engaged for years in a profound reassessment of the Civil War in the USSR. Others were doing very serious and objective research into problems in the history of the Great Fatherland War. To see this, one need only look at the issues of the *War History Journal*.

I have mentioned that opportunities for research work in the social sciences expanded significantly as compared with the period of Stalin's absolute dictatorship. But this did not mean that anyone could dare to go beyond the limits of required political considerations of the time, not to mention of Marxist ideology. (Stalinism had been succeeded by Soviet conformism.) The monitoring of instructors from the science division of the party Central Committee, which had abated somewhat at the beginning of the new era, soon began to resume the usual forms, and by the end of the 1960s and the beginning of the 1970s was no less strict than at the time of the Stalinist regime. Scissors again came into use at the libraries, where the censors once again clipped out journal articles which were considered to be anti-Soviet. There were, of course, significant differences: people were not sent to prison for mistakes; they were dismissed from work less frequently, and when they were fired, a legal basis was sought, and sometimes new employment was provided; and campaigns to attach labels such as "bourgeois objectivist," "cosmopolitan," and the like were no longer carried out, although essentially any deviation was subject to severe criticism and punishment in the form of public dishonor in the press, forced repentance, and so on.

The situation differed depending on the field, of course, and this in turn depended not least on the people who were at the head of the various institutes with ideological connections. A new generation was on its way to power in Academy of Sciences institutes, a group not devoted to dogmatic ideas of doctrine but with an excellent understanding of how to use ideology for personal gain. Believing neither in God nor in Satan, these claimants to the new leadership showed a remarkable ability to organize totally useless collective works, numbering thousands of pages and taking years to compile, and impossible to read, with a view to involving in the editorial boards of these editions a few influential people, including ministers and Central Committee secretaries. These officials had nothing against becoming fictitious senior editors or members of editorial boards of publications on the history of Marxist thought, philosophy, the history of international relations and USSR foreign policy, the United Nations, and so on. Participation in such activities became a matter of prestige even for those in high positions, such as secretary in the Central Committee or head of a department in the party or state apparatus, or even minister, deputy minister, regional party secretary, right down to the lower-ranked members of the editorial boards of journals, where simple instructors from the departments of the Central Committee would end up. A glance at the lists of names of the editorial boards of the journals is enough to see this. It was not merely a feeling of prestige or vainglory that attracted these people, but also such a supposedly banal detail as money. The party and government elite continues to receive the highest fees available in the Soviet Union. High fees are also paid by the major theoretical publication of the Communist party, the journal *Kommunist*. The pay for members of the editorial staff is not very high—it depends on the financial status of each individual journal—but still, making an extra fifty to one hundred rubles per month has never bothered even an instructor from the party Central Committee.

There started to spring up editorial committees and editorial boards made up of several dozen people who, as a rule, appeared only on the masthead of publications and did not do any real work. As it turned out, more than enough people were willing to serve as figureheads. Oh, what pleasure there was in showing your friends a page where your name appeared right next to that of this or that person. "Wow," your acquaintances would say, "Ivan Ivanovich has really come a long way!"

Just as demand generates supply, the desire of party and government officials to become subjects of public interest suggested all types of projects to the minds of clever careerists. This is how the social sciences in the USSR go ever forward toward the yawning heights (to borrow Aleksandr Zinoviev's expression); still, the process does ensure work for dozens of researchers. When the threat of reducing staff at an institute arose, it would always be useful to flaunt the name of someone important who was "directly" involved in work at the institute. But you had to be careful, as well as skillful, in pulling strings. For authors in such enterprises, important archival materials normally closed to researchers were opened, and on rare occasions work was allowed even in the "inner sanctum"—the political archives of the Central Committee.

The ranks of the historians were more varied in the 1950s than they are now, especially in the field of modern history (that is, after the 1917 Revolution). A substantial stratum consisted of people who had entered the field not by vocation but by a quirk of fate and the ensuing downfall of a bureaucratic career: release from duties in the party or government apparatus for incompetence or for other misdemeanors, such as drunkenness. The personnel offices often set up such people in the humanitarian institutes, in the apparent belief that anyone can work in history or philosophy. Moreover, the salary earned at the academic institutes was fairly high (350 to 400 rubles a month for a doctor of sciences senior researcher; 250 to 300 rubles for a candidate of sciences senior researcher; 175 to 200 rubles for a candidate of sciences junior researcher). The humanitarian institutes thus received a flow of retired officers, former diplomatic officials, and former state security officers. As a rule, they all immediately received a position at the acting senior researcher level (they could not claim full status, since they had little or no published work to their credit), and this automatically meant a salary of 300 rubles. They would plan to work for three to five years, thereby assuring themselves of a peaceful existence for a while. There were among them the unique cases, people who remained in the field, tried their hand at research work, and eventually became professional historians. The majority of them, though, sought a secure life for themselves for a few years, and then either found more suitable work, in a field that did not require a researcher's bent, such as teaching in one of the various party schools, or else went into administrative work.

Now the moment of reckoning had arrived for these people. As the scope for research work expanded, the gap between their meager abilities and the demands on professional historians was growing ever wider, and the contrast between the quality of their work and that of others ever clearer, and it was extremely dangerous for them to resign themselves to this situation. Therefore the instinct for self-preservation, the struggle for existence, compelled them to embark upon intrigues, squabbles, and plotting. This is why, during all those years immediately following Stalin's death, suspicion, informing, political accusations, blackmail, and intimidation continued to prosper—all those methods that had enabled these people not only to hold on to their parasitic existence for so many years but to manage it so well. A "theory" uniting party experience with knowledge was even put forth: an experienced but talentless party worker in the role of researcher would see to maintaining the "purity" of Marxist-Leninist thought in the work of his comrades, simple lay researchers, while conducting virtually no research himself. This is how the watershed had occurred that separated those who did scholarly work from those who subjected this work to party criticism.

Nonetheless the time had come when everyone was required to show some work—to "hoist coal," in miners' parlance. For this category of researchers the only way out was to take part in collective works which stretched out over many years. But here barriers appeared unexpectedly as well. In spite of the constant need to oblige their bosses, the heads of institutes still wished to ensure that works published under the imprint of their institute were of some quality. But this required capable workers. Thus, institute directors, as a rule, tried not to include former party workers in collective projects such as *World History*, the multivolume *History of the USSR*, and *History of Historical Scholarship in the USSR*, preferring to close their eyes to the idleness of a certain portion of the institute staff, to so-called idleness by right, rather than take risks where important work was involved. The directors were afraid of openly opposing the idlers, or simply firing them, since they knew how close-knit and vengeful the party mafia could be. As far back as the early 1950s, I had managed to earn the undying hatred of these people in connection with the Slobodyanyuk plagiarism affair, and their hostility followed me for many years afterwards.

The director of the Institute of History, A. L. Sidorov, was deprived of his post for criticizing the idleness of a number of former graduates of the Central Committee's Academy of Social Sciences, including a certain Yakovleva, at a closed party meeting. Yet Sidorov was an influential person, a man who had access to the Central Committee and who had rendered the party valuable services during the "great days" of the campaign against cosmopolitans.

His successor at the Institute of History, V. M. Khvostov, had more foresight. He looked the other way in the case of "deserving idlers," but he extracted some rather unusual benefits from this, receiving from them constant information about what was going on in the sections, who said what, and how he said it.

One of the means of self-defense for the idlers was to attack those of their colleagues who, in addition to carrying out their work according to plan and fulfilling their obligations to the institute, found time to write articles and books, and naturally received for this work additional remuneration from publishers and journals. They accused these colleagues of self-interest, referring to their own personal example. We, they would say, are barely able to complete our scheduled work, and yet these people manage to write outside the plan! Against this background, squabbling, conflict, and scandal constantly arose. Capable researchers were forced to write explanations as to how they had managed to earn outside fees while on the institute's payroll, and so on.

I had to express my opposition to such a dichotomy between "scheduled" and "unscheduled" work on more than one occasion. This issue, I said, was being created artificially by people who were barely able to cope with their academic programs and whose scholarly output (planned or not) was inconsequential and of extremely low quality. Therefore every work published by anyone else met with a hostile reception from them, since they regarded it as yet another threat to their parasitic existence in the field of scholarship. The campaign against unscheduled works, in the form in which it was conducted, was a campaign against the backbone of the research staff, against those who had entered the field not by coincidence but by vocation, and for whom research work was the central point of their lives. The fact remained that these were the people who, having done the lion's share of the work at the institute, were doing work outside the plan as well.

The party elite couched its campaign to preserve its own idle existence in the demagogic terms of a communist attitude toward work. The example was given of the doctors at Rostov-on-Don who, in 1960, appealed to all doctors throughout the country to use part of their own time to perform medical work free of charge, on a voluntary basis. At first this initiative was supported by public organizations, but the enthusiasm gradually waned soon afterward. Why? Because medicine in the Soviet Union was and remains one of the lowest-paid professions. In order at least to put food on the table for their families and themselves, doctors were compelled (and still are today) to take on additional work. When they were forced to perform this same additional work for free, they were naturally put in desperate straits.

The arguments of those opposed to "unscheduled" scholarly work virtually amounted to denying the distinction between capable and incapable workers. Work outside the plan, and any remuneration received for it, was nothing less than payment for one's qualifications, abilities, and additional effort. In essence the party elite was opposing the socialist principle of "from each according to his ability, to each according to his labor" with its own principle: "not according to one's labor and not according to one's ability."

We upheld the right to unscheduled work at the time. In recent years, however, this matter has taken on a totally different character as a violation of rights guaranteed in the USSR Constitution.

Concerned over the fact that books and articles by staff members of the institute were appearing in the press, a practice that deviated from the orthodox line, the management of our institute in the time of Khvostov (1966) issued a decree requiring that research staff not only inform the management of unscheduled work but also obtain permission for its publication. It was not hard to understand that such a requirement was nothing other than an attempt to establish a kind of thought control. Some researchers in their published work, especially in articles written for the literary journals, found a safety valve for expressing ideas and views in contradiction with the official conformist line, thereby arousing the "mental indignation" of readers and colleagues. Ye. Plimak's articles in *Novy mir* on the Jacobean dictatorship were an example of this. G. Lisichkin's series of articles on the economics of Soviet agriculture was another, not to mention that harmful book by A. Nekrich, *June 22, 1941*. The requirement that institute staff obtain permission to publish work completed outside of office hours was yet another attempt to intensify the serflike dependency of the researcher on the authorities. From the legal standpoint, this decree was in flagrant violation of the USSR Constitution, which proclaimed for Soviet citizens basic democratic freedoms, as well as with labor legislation, which does not give the administration of institutions any right to monitor the nonworking hours of employees.

The staff members grumbled loudly—in the corridors—but no one dared oppose this decree openly.

Soon after Stalin's death a surprising metamorphosis took place in readers' attitudes toward works of history. People wanted to know the truth about the recent past in their country, and the not-so-recent past as well. They went to the history books but did not find answers to their questions there. Virtually all works by historians bore the unmistakable imprint of the Stalinist regime. Thousands upon thousands of books in the humanities lay piled up on the shelves of the bookstores. No one wanted to buy them. Then the publishing houses began to destroy the books, to shred them and send them to paper factories for recycling. This was taking place at a time when in the Soviet Union there was a hunger not only for books but for paper as well. There was a paper shortage. The demand for books was such that people stood in line for days on end in order to fill out subscription forms for the collected works of Tolstoy, Chekhov, Balzac, Shakespeare, Hemingway, but there clearly was not enough paper to print them on. Nonetheless, at the same time, the political publishing houses continued to print Marxist didactic literature in the millions of copies, which put readers either to sleep or in a state of despair. The public was desperate for easily readable, clearly written books on the history of their own country. From time to time conferences were convened on the subject of how to help the reader purchase or obtain books by historians. Popular literature series were published, but the work continued to be of low quality.

One episode in the dialogue between writers and readers involved a discussion in *Literaturnaya gazeta*, published in an article by V. M. Turok entitled "The Historian and the Reader" (February 4, 1961). The purpose of the article was to draw the public's attention to the status of historical scholarship, and in particular to the obstacles erected by parasitic elements who compromised it and interfered in its development. But to advance such an idea for an article was virtually impossible. Normally, articles that discussed problems were signed by an academician or a group of academicians, and the article was approved beforehand by the "higher authorities." An analysis of the status of historical scholarship, coming from Turok, a private individual, an historian who was not a party member, had no chance of being published. There was nothing left to do but choose a more innocuous title for the article, such as the role of style in historical composition, although, of course, this was not the crux of the piece.

V. M. Turok's basic idea was formulated as follows: "Only the test of time and of the text and not the academic rank and title, can attest to the emergence of a new scholar. . . . We must pave the way for those who are capable of conceiving and developing new methods and new ideas in their work and replace those who are not in a position to produce anything of value." Turok named a number of staff members at the Institute of History as examples of people who did not really belong in the field. One of them—let's call him L.—had begun his career at the end of the 1930s in party surveillance units, worked for the counterespionage body SMERSH during the war, and then ended up in diplomacy. He had to leave this line of work, however, because of a drinking bout in which he had indulged while serving as consul general in a certain friendly coastal country. Then, no longer young, he began graduate study at the Institute of History, defended his candidate dissertation with difficulty, and was nevertheless retained on staff at the institute. Malicious gossip had it that he was kept on because he proclaimed loud and clear that for the salary of a junior researcher he was prepared to attack any work by any staff member. L.'s candor pleased the management of the institute: such people were always useful. So L. became a staff member at an academic institute. But he was, of course, not the only representative of the powerful lobby of idlers which presented a united front at the institute in those years.

The Western reader might find it hard to understand the reaction to the publication of Turok's article, since in Western countries the publication of critical articles is a natural, routine aspect of freedom of the press. In the Soviet Union, however, it is like a bomb exploding.

And, indeed, the bomb which Turok had set off aroused enormous commotion and turmoil in the institute. The director, V. M. Khvostov, who took any criticism of the institute as a personal affront, went immediately to the chief editor of *Literaturnaya gazeta* V. I. Kosolapov, and told him that publishing the article was an error, since its author was not at all an historian (!), had a very bad reputation, and was well known for his views against—something or other. The editor was upset, and somewhat frightened, and promised to look into the matter. First of all, he called in the editorial staff member responsible for publishing the article and gave him a good dressing down. Fortunately for this staff member, and for Turok as well, the latest issue of the journal *Modern and Current History* had just come out with an advertisement for the following year's issues. It named prominent historians whose articles were to be published, and among them were the names of V. M. Turok and V. M. Khvostov. By a stroke of fate, and also as a consequence of Russian alphabetical order, the two names followed each other: first Turok, then Khvostov. Kosolapov regained his composure, and the editorial staff members rejoiced and agreed to hold a public discussion of the article.

Khvostov wheeled out his big guns for the discussion, including historians of major stature such as A. Z. Manfred and L. V. Cherepnin. On the other side of the "barricades," as they say in my homeland, were, strangely enough, the world-famous physicists V. L. Ginzburg and V. Goldansky. Physicists, it turned out, also felt the need for good books on history. It was a sign of the times that many people came to the discussion. Tempers flared. The overwhelming majority of those who spoke supported Turok's basic idea, but others disputed it. Particularly aggressive in tone were certain representatives of the "idlers." Even the husband of one lady mentioned in the article took part. The chairman of the discussion, the editorial board member V. Bolkhovitinov (later senior editor of the journal *Nauka i zhizn'*) was somewhat bewildered. But the discussion did not end there. The journal began to publish reactions to the article, and this lasted for more than half a year. The most interesting article was written by Professor Manfred. A master of style, Manfred skillfully used Turok's pseudopretext for the article, style in historical research, in order to emphasize that the drawbacks in Soviet historical scholarship were mostly due to the choice of literary expression.

Then the boomerang came back. As is usual after a discussion in the Soviet Union, the offended party showered the higher authorities—the presidium of the Academy of Sciences and the Central Committee of the Communist party—with complaints. The matter reached the Central Committee secretary for ideological affairs, M. A. Suslov. But here the "offended parties" miscalculated. Suslov permitted publication of letters from readers as the outcome of the discussion, but he proposed in passing that the identities of those mentioned in the article be clarified in positive terms. The matter was concluded at the height of autumn 1961 during preparations for the Twenty-Second Party Congress. This most likely explains Suslov's unexpectedly liberal position, for the congress dealt a sharp blow to the Stalinists when it decided to remove Stalin's body from the mausoleum in Red Square.

Nonetheless, Academician Khvostov, the most influential and powerful individual in the field of history in the years since the war, could not forgive

Turok for his statements in *Literaturnaya gazeta*. Soon Turok was forced to leave the Institute of History and transfer to the Institute of Slavic and Balkan Studies.

Turok's article and the polemics it provoked were of considerable significance for that time, since they focused public attention on the unsatisfactory state of historical scholarship. The article was, in a way, a prelude to the All-Union Conference of Historians, which met in 1962.

The convening of the All-Union Conference of Historians was the logical result of the decision made by the Twentieth and Twenty-Second Communist Party Congresses to eliminate the harmful consequences resulting from the dictatorial regime of the so-called Stalinist cult of personality. This was decided by the Central Committee and the Council of Ministers and therefore was completely official. All the major reports delivered at the conference, of course, were agreed on beforehand in the higher-level party bodies and were approved by them.

After the Twenty-Second Congress the conservative elements in the party, the Stalinists, although they had been overshadowed for some time, still had not laid down their arms. They were gradually preparing for revenge. I have it on good authority from participants in the congress that in the corridors, especially after the decision was adopted to remove Stalin's remains from the mausoleum, a number of prominent officials from the party apparatus were prepared to condemn openly the decisions of the congress and actually began to put together an opposition. Unfortunately, Khrushchev was not shrewd enough to outguess these maneuvers, nor was he sufficiently powerful to complete the work begun at the Twentieth Party Congress. He found himself increasingly isolated, for the government-building measures he had proposed were being sabotaged by those who were supposed to be carrying them out in the field. It would appear that he was intentionally being encouraged to take unpopular and unbalanced actions, thereby undermining his own authority and the popularity he had gained among the broad masses of the people during the early years of the post-Stalinist era. By the time the All-Union Conference was convened, the internal party struggle was at its height. This is why that conference, which might have opened up a new era for historians, was a practical failure.

Yet in spite of the fact that there was an ashamed silence about the conference very soon after its conclusion, it did play a positive role. For the first time in decades, the state of affairs in history and in the other social sciences resulting from the years of Stalin's absolute dictatorship was examined.

The very fact that the main report was delivered by B. N. Ponomarev, Communist party Central Committee secretary and head of the international department, and that the conference was opened by the Academy of Sciences president, M. V. Keldysh, increased the importance of this gathering of Soviet historians.

The conference was well attended. The enormous auditorium of Moscow State University could hardly hold all the participants at plenary meetings. The firm trend in opposition to the personality cult at the conference was emphasized from the very beginning by Keldysh. In particular, he stated: "The bold revolutionary measures carried out by our party in recent years in all areas of political, economic, and cultural life in our country have had an exceptionally favorable effect on the development of Soviet historical scholarship. As a result of our overcoming the harmful consequences of the Stalinist cult of personality, our historians have been given every opportunity for successful work." These words reflected not so much the real state of affairs as the possibility of creating one like it.

Ponomarev's summary report set out all aspects of the situation quite accurately. The speaker analyzed the status of historical scholarship over the preceding three decades, first and foremost the significant progress that had been made, especially in accumulating a gigantic body of factual material and establishing "working concepts" for studying the history of groups, national movements, sociopolitical thought, and so on. Considerable attention was given in his report, as well as in a number of other reports, to an analysis of the errors in historical evaluation from the time of the dictatorship. Most important, this established a clearly defined landmark: the year 1931, when Stalin's letter to the editors of *Proletarian Revolution* appeared. Stalin, in Ponomarev's view, subjected the study of history to his own, often mistaken views of the historical process and his concern for self-aggrandizement. "If we were to summarize the negative effects of the cult of personality on the field of history," the report stated, "they could be reduced to three main points: first, diminishing the role of Lenin, of the masses, and of the party in the history of our country and the exaltation of Stalin's role which distorted the truth; second, the application of a non-Marxist approach to the study of the historical process, and subjectivism and arbitrariness in evaluating historical events and personalities; third, and finally, administrative abuse, unfair criticism in academic collectives, and attaching various types of labels." To summarize the harm done to historical scholarship during the Stalinist dictatorship, according to the reports of Ponomarev, Zhukov, Khvostov, and others, it amounted to the following:

1. The vulgar contrast between the party spirit of historical scholarship and objectivity, whereas party spirit is the highest form of objectivity.
2. Dogmatism and intolerance.

3. Arbitrary evaluation of events, facts, and individuals, related to the violation of law, and the repression of many party and state officials, which automatically led to a distortion of their role in the struggle for revolution and socialism.

4. Oversimplification in dealing with the historical process, forcing it to fit in with Stalin's chosen schemes, resulting in flagrant violations of historical truth.

5. Voluntarism in dealing with the post–October 1917 period. Obsession with Stalin's guidelines and statements. Portraying opinion as fact.

6. The false theory of "two leaders" of the Revolution.

7. The false version of the supposedly decisive role of Stalin in the Civil War. Declaring prominent comrades of Lenin to be enemies of the people. Falsification of the activities of local party and government bodies.

8. Covering up Leninist criticism of Stalin's errors.

9. Covering up the gross blunders of Stalin, Molotov, and Kaganovich in pursuing the policy of collectivization.

10 Despite the obvious facts, and in spite of the major mistakes committed by Stalin before and during the Great Fatherland War, he was attributed a decisive role in the victory of the Soviet people.

11. The ideology of the cult of personality undermined Marxist-Leninist principles of historicism.

12. Distortion of the history of the past (Ivan the Terrible) in order to exalt Stalin. Galvanization of the theory of "the crowd and the heroes."

13. The spread throughout academic collectives of defamations of honest scholars. The expulsion of those considered objectionable. The physical extinction of some of them (Lukin, Piontkovsky).

14. The scholarly value of sources, of archival materials, was subjected to doubt. Archival materials, as a rule, had begun to be used merely to illustrate already well known theories. There was a loss of respect for fact, without which history as a scholarly endeavor was unthinkable. The new ranks of party historians and historians of Soviet society were poorly instructed in the methods of scholarly use of archival sources.

15. Archival research methodology was not developed.

16. The achievements of Soviet historical scholarship in the late 1920s and early 1930s in the history of the party and of Soviet society were wiped out. Many useful works (by Yaroslavsky, Nevsky, Bubnov, Popov, and so on) were withdrawn.

17. There was widespread dissemination of apologetic "works" (falsifications) of Beria.

18. Historians were inculcated with the belief that all evaluations in principle of the historical process either had already been made or could

be made only by Stalin. Mere mortals were not to strive for "higher" theory. The result: overuse of quotations and the like.

"The cult of personality," stated Ponomarev, "like chains, shackled the legs of Soviet historical science, but it nevertheless continued to go forward."

One can easily imagine the gait of someone going forward with chains on his legs! Academician Ye. M. Zhukov, repeating the comparison of the cult of Stalin with leg shackles, went even further than Ponomarev, saying that permitting criticism and forswearing the erroneous aspects of the Stalinist era did not mean "the complete elimination of all the harmful consequences of the cult of personality in historical scholarship." Zhukov drew attention to the psychological trauma experienced by scholars as a result of the systematic claims that only Stalin could write theoretically valid works, and that any new ideas and profound thoughts could come only from him. Everyone else could merely "in the best of cases comment on Stalin, without philosophizing or clever theorizing." The conclusion drawn by Zhukov was irrefutable: "For almost twenty years—a time when an entire generation of our people was being brought up—independent creative thought in the area of theory was subjected to doubt among 'mere mortals.' People lost the habit of thinking independently, and essentially were inculcated with the idea of their theoretical inferiority. This was in fact the source of the timidity of thought that was so harmful to scholarship."

Zhukov was right about everything he said, with one minor exception: this period did not last "almost twenty years" but nearly forty years. Yet this was not simply a mathematical error but a deliberate evasion. The situation was such that whatever field of historical knowledge one took, one found nothing but falsification, lies, and, at best, evasion and truth stretching. The head of the main political directorate of the Soviet army, General A. A. Yepishev, accused Stalin of decimating the ranks of the military and charged him with gross errors just before and during the Great Fatherland War, which, Yepishev said, "cost the Soviet people dearly." (A very short time would pass before Yepishev would make another official statement in which he would ask that his remarks made in a "time of troubles" be considered null and void.

The reports and statements of high-ranking speakers were supported by other historians, among whom were Academician I. I. Mintz, director Kasimenko of the Ukrainian Institute of History, and Academician M. V. Nechkina. She said, in particular, in referring to the atmosphere of the recent past: "A comrade could not talk with another comrade, you could not share your ideas or doubts even with close friends; and not because your friend would betray you the next day, but out of consideration for your friend, for fear that you would put him in a difficult situation by discussing some controversial issue." Nechkina found the appropriate wording in order to remind those present that life under Stalin had been fraught with fear and treachery, poisoned by mutual distrust, alienation, and isolation.

Although the majority of those who spoke, in one way or another, either sincerely or against their will, supported eliminating the consequences of the cult of personality, one could detect in a number of statements some dissatisfaction with the policy of the Twentieth and Twenty-Second Congresses. The director of the Institute of Archeology, Academician B. A. Rybakov, known for his ultraconservative views, a staunch Stalinist and Great Russian nationalist, began his speech with an extremely ambiguous phrase which indirectly condemned the anti-Stalinist policy line. "Recently," he stated, "it has begun to seem to us at times that the waves on the sea of everyday life have been rocking our ship too strongly, breaking its riggings and threatening the very course it should follow." The contradictions inherent in the proceedings of the All-Union Conference of Historians were clearly demonstrated by the fact that all the key reports were delivered by historians who for decades had praised Stalin and had engaged in outright falsification of history. Some of them, in fact, were at the forefront in the "great days" of struggle with the cosmopolitans. There was no doubt that these same people were capable of turning around and saying tomorrow the direct opposite of what they were saying at the conference today.

Hints that the tide was beginning to turn in the direction of Stalinism, even though it continued to seem on the surface that the struggle against the cult of personality was just gaining momentum, were evident even at that conference. P. N. Pospelov, in response to a question about Burdzhalov, reaffirmed a Central Committee decision of March 9, 1957, condemning an article by Burdzhalov published in *Voprosy istorii*. That Central Committee decree had been adopted at the time of the latest swing toward Stalinism, immediately following the events in Hungary. The continued force of that decree showed that the Central Committee was not inclined to reconsider any of its decisions made in the aftermath of 1956, even though some of them were in conflict with the anticult decisions of the Twentieth and Twenty-Second Party Congresses.

Hardly had the conference of historians adjourned when a tenacious struggle began over whether or not to publish conference materials, and if so, whether in full or in summary edited version. Finally it was decided not to print everything said there, but to publish a shortened version of the records, from which were edited out many examples of historical falsification that flourished during Stalin's absolute rule. It is curious to note that, since it had been decided to consider Stalin's direct interference in the social sciences to have begun with his letter to the journal *Proletarian Revolution* (1931), this meant that the ideological preparation for the repressions began, by official acknowledgment, three years before the murder of Kirov, four years before the arrest of Zinoviev and Kamenev, and six years before the show trials in Moscow.

In actual fact the falsification of history in the USSR began from the very moment that a single view of the historical process came to prevail in Soviet scholarship. Wherever there exists one point of view that is recognized to be the only correct one, falsification is inevitable, and it will be found in historical research regardless of the eras or the events under study.

Only a year later, in December 1963, after much hesitation and fighting, were the materials from the All-Union Conference of Historians submitted for publication, and the book itself came out largely thanks to the perseverance of the editors at the "Nauka" publishing house, V. I. Zuyev and A. I. Yukht. That book, published in an edition of five thousand copies (rather an insignificant figure in terms of both the norm for Soviet publications and its importance), sold out immediately and long ago became a bibliographical rarity.

During these years the two most senior staff members returned to the Institute of History—the French specialist and historian of socialist thought Viktor Moiseevich Dalin and the Soviet historian Sergei Mitrofanovich Dubrovsky. They had been arrested during the terror of the 1930s, had spent about twenty years in the camps, and had miraculously survived. How many historians never did return!

There were some sad events as well. On March 8, 1963, Abram Moiseevich Deborin died. In the final years of his life, his situation had improved somewhat. But this final chapter deserves to be recounted in greater detail.

In 1956, after the Twentieth Party Congress, Deborin requested that the Central Committee review its decree of 1931 on "Menshevist-leaning idealism." The Politburo instructed A. I. Mikoyan to look into the matter.

I remember well all those days of uneasiness before Abram Moiseevich was to go to meet with Mikoyan in the Kremlin. He was very nervous; what was at stake was his entire life as a scholar. Deborin lived in the Academy of Sciences building at 13 Lenin Prospekt. Driving to the Kremlin meant going through October Square and then along Dimitrov Street. Passing through the square, the car suddenly broke down. Only seven or eight minutes remained before the appointed time for the meeting. The militia came to the rescue, and Abram Moiseevich arrived at his appointment with Mikoyan on time.

He came back extremely excited, but pleased. He said that Mikoyan had been friendly and asked questions about what "Menshevist-leaning idealism" was. "I," said Deborin laughing, "said to Anastas Ivanovich that for twenty-five years now I had been trying to understand what it was, and still didn't know."

Mikoyan shook his head, laughed, and promised to support Deborin's request to withdraw this absurd accusation made against him. Deborin was walking on air. But the matter took a turn that was not at all as expected. When Mikoyan proposed abrogating the Central Committee decree on "Menshevist-leaning idealism," he was sharply opposed by P. N. Pospelov, the still influential party ideologue, who was both secretary of the Central Committee and director of the Institute of Marxism-Leninism. Some people said that at a meeting of the Central Committee, Pospelov came out against the political rehabilitation of Deborin and the abrogation of the 1931 decree, arguing that this would lead to erosion of the ideological foundation of the Party. In this regard Pospelov relied on a rather influential cohort of Stalinist social scientists, who had risen to attack Deborin and his "disciples." Among them were Pavel Yudin and Mark Mitin, both academicians, both members of the Central Committee, with a reputation as party intellectuals. In addition, they both had been connected at different times with the main theoretical publication of the international communist movement, issued first in Belgrade and then in Prague, *Problemy mira i sotsializma*. Yudin had been Soviet ambassador to Belgrade and Peking. After returning from Peking, he set up a sort of Chinese museum at his dacha in the academic village of Mozhinka (70 kilometers from Moscow), where a portrait of Mao was displayed. Yudin died a few years ago. Mark Mitin continues to prosper to this day, in spite of the serious accusations made against him by the families of several executed philosophers. The widow of Academician Luppol accused him not only of aiding in the destruction of her husband but also of appending his own name, after Luppol's arrest, to an article written by Luppol for the *Great Soviet Encyclopedia*, although his contribution to the text was just one sentence—to the effect that Luppol was an exposed enemy of the people!

As for Deborin, shortly before he died, the ban was finally lifted on the publication of his works. I assisted Abram Moiseevich in drawing up a plan for publishing his collected works in several volumes. In the final analysis only three of his books were published: in 1961 *Philosophy and Politics*, a collection of his articles from various periods; in 1958 the first volume of his *Sociopolitical Studies in Modern and Recent History*, and after his death, in 1967, the second volume.

I happened to head the commission on the posthumous edition of Deborin's works and took an active part in the preparation of the second volume for publication. When the ban on Deborin's books was finally lifted, he was already quite old, and found it difficult to work. Furthermore, time had gone by, new trends had appeared in world philosophical studies, and it was hard for him to catch up. His life as a philosopher and scholar had been cruelly destroyed when he was in his intellectual prime. Deborin was a mild-mannered and sympathetic person, and this brought him much affection from others. In the final years of his life he became interested in the movement of rhythms and, as he once told me in confidence, was on the verge of a most important physical-philosophical discovery: a universal law of rhythms.

I was at the hospital the day he died. He lay on his back, his tired eyes half open. When I entered, something like a smile of greeting passed his lips. I asked him how he felt. He shook his head as if to say that he was all right, was bearing up. He closed his eyes and drifted into a half-sleep.

The memorial ceremony took place in the conference hall at the Academy of Sciences. Deborin and I had been friends, and I was very fond of the old man. His death saddened me greatly. I thought regretfully of how there would be present at the funeral those who had tormented him for decades, ruined his life by slamming in his face the doors to the field to which he had devoted all his thoughts—philosophy. And they did indeed come. Those murderers of philosophers and pillagers, the academicians Yudin, Mitin, and others, they all came to the funeral of their teacher, whom they had not only betrayed but also slandered for decades. And I suddenly understood that I had to speak at these funeral proceedings and confront these people with the fact that their crimes would not be forgotten. One woman from the historical sciences department tried to discourage me: "Aleksandr Moiseevich, don't do this. You will make yourself some very dangerous enemies. They will never forgive you for what you do." There was some commotion. The deputy academic secretary of the department of historical sciences, Viktor Shunkov, came up to me and said in a friendly manner: "Let us speak together, but not here; at Novodevichy Cemetery." I refused, in spite of his insistence. Under the circumstances at the time, denying me the floor was impossible. This was at the beginning of 1963, when the anti-Stalinist mood among scholars was running high.

My words fell on a silence that was deafening. Yes, there is such a thing as a silence that fills the air. I spoke in aphorisms of the teacher who loved his pupils and never left them. I also spoke about how some of his pupils had abandoned him. And I spoke as well of the work and of torture of the scholar who was kept from his favorite endeavors.

After concluding, I glanced at Yudin. He had turned crimson and, pointing at me, was asking someone standing nearby: "Who is that?" My statement had apparently impressed the audience greatly. Many people came up to me, thanked me, or simply gave me a firm handshake.

Abram Moiseevich Deborin was buried in Novodevichy Cemetery in Moscow. Four years after his death, thanks to our joint efforts, the second volume of his *Sociopolitical Studies in Modern and Recent History* came out. This book sits on my shelf, in my study in Belmont, Massachusetts, where I am now writing. And the book bears an inscription from Deborin's widow, Irina: "In fond, and, I hope, long memory of the author."

I have more than once had occasion to read manuscripts not destined for publication. These were primarily poetry, epigrams, reprints of articles (more rarely books) published abroad. This was long before the appearance of samizdat, back in the 1940s. Strange as it may seem, the tradition of "anonymous letters" and of the Russian free press was carried on by none other than the Telegraphic Agency of the Soviet Union (TASS), which issued special press releases intended only for a narrow circle of official readers. These releases contained translations of articles and books with blatant anti-Soviet content. Then, with the establishment of the Progress publishing house, entire series of books and articles appeared in translation. They were likewise intended for a narrow circle of readers. Although each copy had a number assigned to it, these books were read not just by those to whom they had been sent directly but also by people far from Soviet officialdom through mysterious means. True, these people were pitifully few in number, but the information obtained in this manner nevertheless was disseminated through repetition, in the form of handwritten excerpts, and so on. People who had been abroad, especially those who traveled on diplomatic passports, sometimes brought back books, even though this could get them a long prison term, or at the very lease cause potential harm to their careers. After the war, many books were brought in from vanquished Germany. Not only such purely Nazi literature as *Mein Kampf*, *The Myth of the Twentieth Century*, and others ended up in private hands, but also a fair number of books written by Russian émigrés in Berlin in the 1920s. Publications categorically forbidden in the Soviet Union, books, and iillustrated editions were brought in after the war from Poland and Czechoslovakia as well and, in spite of all obstacles, were distributed throughout the Soviet Union. This is how Orwell's *1984* and *Animal Farm* appeared, were soon translated unofficially into Russian, and made the rounds. Later, thanks to the activities of foreign religious organizations, the Bible, especially the New Testament, was introduced into the Soviet Union, and foreign tourists, students, and businessmen who were not afraid smuggled in with them from abroad books that told the truth about the society and state in which we lived.

Very soon after Stalin's death and the beginning of the "era of delayed rehabilitation," as this period in history was jokingly referred to in the Soviet Union, there appeared the manuscripts of those who had been in Kolyma and in the Stalinist prisons. I was no doubt one of the first into whose hands fell V. Shalamov's *Kolyma Stories* and Yevgeniya Semyonovna Ginzburg's *Journey into the Whirlwind*. These stories had a devastating effect. Horror, indignation, shame—these briefly describe the feelings aroused by reading these manuscripts. I met Ye.S.Ginzburg soon afterward and was one of the first to hear readings from the second part of *Journey into the Whirlwind*. She gave the reading herself. She had an amazing memory and an exceptional reading technique, simple yet deeply affecting. I know people for whom reading *Journey into the Whirlwind* marked a turning point in their world view, a break with the past and the beginning of a new, consuming struggle and anxiety. For others, the discovery of the works of Solzhenitzyn represented such a turning point.

In 1962 *One Day in the Life of Ivan Denisovich* appeared. Long before I met the author of that book, I knew of the legend surrounding him. *Novy mir* made Solzhenitsyn accessible to the Soviet reader, and what the *Novy mir* editor, A. T. Tvardovsky, did—not just for Solzhenitsyn himself but for all of thinking and reading Russia—can rightly be considered a historic landmark in the world of second-rate imitations in which we lived.

All those whom I have just mentioned were very different kinds of people; but what they all had in common as a matter of principle was their attitude toward moral decency. In historical terms they were fulfilling a mission which the Communist party had been unable to carry out after the Twentieth Congress: embarking on the path of historical truth. I would include among them the fearless General Pyotr Grigorevich Grigorenko, who at a regional party conference in Moscow in 1962 openly warned against the danger of a return to Stalinist dictatorship.

Yes, those were years of hope—hope for a moral rebirth in our society. How soon they were over!

6
Abroad!

Abroad — Serov and Penkovsky — trip to England — incident in Copenhagen — with Stasik in Poland — unpleasant news — the aborted trip — the attempt to go to Hungary — ban on travel — murder in Kharkov

Abroad! How attractive the word sounds, what secrets it exudes, what dangers it harbors, what joys, disappointments, fears, and, yes, intrigues!

For many long years Soviets could not even dream of a trip abroad. Before the war only a few isolated individuals went on official business, to international congresses and so on. The fact that tourism existed probably did not even occur to most Soviets. After the war, when "the window on Europe" was carefully sealed up, foreign travel never even entered our minds. Moreover, even those who were sent on official business set out most unwillingly, for they understood full well that on their return they might be accused of God knows what. This had been borne out by the infamous trials of the 1930s.

In the second half of the 1950s the situation changed rather drastically. First, foreign tourists began to appear in the Soviet Union in relatively large numbers, and then Soviet citizens began to be allowed to go abroad. Many worked in the various People's Democratic Republics and were permitted to take their families with them. Next, tour groups started to travel to the socialist countries, and then groups appeared for trips to capitalist countries. Such trips were always in connection with some kind of international event, for example, Soviet exhibitions or sports competitions.

In 1961 an exhibition of Soviet achievements opened in Britain. This was a time of warming in Soviet-British relations. It was decided to send to Britain a rather large number of Soviet tourists. It so happened that I had received a call from the Union of Friendship Societies proposing that I be included in one of the tour groups for a trip to England. I didn't really believe anything would come of it. The fact was that I had once been listed for a delegation of Soviet historians to an Anglo-Soviet conference, but some authority intervened. The chairman of the National Committee of Soviet Historians, Aleksandr Andreevich Guber, with whom I had long worked in the world history section and with whom I was on friendly terms, told me confidentially and with some embarrassment, "You see, Sasha, when it involves people in your category, it's a very complicated matter" (tactfully substituting the word category for "ethnic origin"). On another occasion the institute sought to send me to Romania, and again I was excluded somewhere along the line. Therefore I filled out the forms without any great hope of going and went off to Tallinn to work in the archive. To my surprise, about two weeks later I received a letter informing me that I had to be in Moscow in early June in connection with the forthcoming trip to England.

Our group consisted of five men and eighteen women. The majority of the women were English teachers and doctors. Also traveling with us were the wife and daughter of the former KGB head, I. A. Serov. (At the time he was deputy chief of the General Staff.) Serov actively saw to it that we received our passports in time. At the last moment it turned out that the plane on which we were to fly could not accommodate us all for lack of seats. It was proposed that five people from our group take a different flight, leaving at four o'clock in the morning. A nearly empty plane was flying to London in order to bring back the Bolshoi Ballet troupe, on tour in England. The Serovs and myself and two more women agreed to take this flight. At my request, Serov sent his official car to pick me up at home, after which I stopped for the two women and in that way the problem of getting to the airport, located 50 kilometers from Moscow, was solved. Serov drove his own family to Sheremet'evo Airport himself.

As we walked out onto the airstrip in order to board the TU-104, we were accompanied by a young man, about thirty or thirty-five, wearing a gray tweed jacket and carrying a briefcase. He gave Serov a friendly hello. Once on board the plane, Varvara Ivanovna Serova introduced us, presenting the young man as a journalist. He gave his name in a somewhat muffled voice, and I could only catch the ending "–*ovsky*." Besides us, there were two or three Englishmen in the plane. One wore a pin from the Moscow Film Festival on his jacket lapel. When we reached London, for some reason he took off the pin and put it in his pocket. The other Englishman, a middle-aged, fragile-looking man, did not feel well during the flight, and, smiling helplessly, would rush to the back of the plane every once in a while. The journalist was telling the Serov ladies what they might buy in London—for example, a swing for the dacha, or some such thing. Then he took out his wallet and withdrew from it a pile of British banknotes to show them.

A few years later, one day, on opening the newspaper, I noticed a report from the prosecutor's office about the trial of a man named Penkovsky, who was accused of treason. There was a photograph of him. I thought his face looked familiar. I began to read the indictment and stopped short at the phrase "on July 18, 1961, Penkovsky flew to London." My God, that was the same day I flew to London! And suddenly I remembered the "journalist" and the mumbled surname ending in "—*ovsky.*" Of course. *That* had been Penkovsky!

We spent three hours at the London airport waiting for our group. I wandered around that enormous building and observed with great interest the human anthill in that gigantic international air terminal. This was the first time in my life that I had ever seen so many people from all over the world in one place. I didn't even notice the time go by.

We stayed in London for six days, seeing everything we could. As a sort of extracurricular activity, I managed to go at dawn to the Covent Garden wholesale market. I was astounded most of all by the flowers from France: each individual flower was packed in a separate cardboard container. During my free time I enjoyed wandering around the streets of that wonderful city. One evening I managed to catch a film, Fellini's *La Dolce Vita*. There is no sense in writing here about the essential points of interest in London; these are already well known. Everything was of interest to me, but most of all the Londoners themselves. I saw friendly people, neatly but modestly dressed and wearing shoes with a brilliant shine to them. They answered my questions quite willingly (how to get to such and such a place), were pleasant and well-mannered, but they were hardly interested in us at all, nor were they particularly inclined to talk about themselves. There was not an ounce of the stiffness or haughtiness about which we had been told so much all our lives. Naturally, a great deal had changed since the war. I was pleased to see London and the English almost as I had imagined them. I felt relaxed and free in that enormous city. London seemed to me the ideal city to live in.

I arranged to meet with Professor Andrew Rothstein in my hotel, the Stephen Court. I arrived punctually. We talked about the situation in England during the war, and I was astounded at how deep-seated were his conformism and dogmatism, for he was a highly educated man. I simply lost the desire to discuss the problems of the war with him. I left with him and accompanied him to the Waterloo Bridge. Along the way, we dropped into the Conservative party book store, where I hoped to find some wartime party materials, but it turned out that they had long ago been disposed of as superfluous. I entered the Underground in order to return to the hotel, which was located not far from Paddington Station. But not knowing the peculiarities of the London Underground, where a lighted panel indicates the direction in which the train is going, I went the opposite way. In the car I asked a question of a middle-aged man sitting across from me. He answered, and asked me in turn, "Are you Polish?" "No, I'm Russian," I replied. The old man smiled wanly and said, "My son was in your Murmansk. He was a pilot and was killed." I began to feel somewhat uncomfortable, as if I were guilty for having survived, and said, "I was at Stalingrad." Then, quite suddenly, the old man stood up and said in a solemn tone, "No stepping back!" (the slogan of the soldiers defending Stalingrad). We exchanged a firm handshake, and both of us, extremely moved, returned to our seats. The passengers sitting around us smiled benignly.

Meanwhile, the train came up from underground and ran along past some green areas. Almost no one was left in the car. I finally realized that I was going in the wrong direction, looked at my watch, and saw that within ten minutes lunch was to begin. I got goose bumps imagining the fuss that would be raised over my absence. I exited at the next stop, went up to the attendant—a strapping, short fellow with a friendly face—and explained to him my problem. He broke out laughing and said cheerfully: "Oh, you're Russian. I like Russians. Ga-ga-rin!" (I was in England just two months after the first manned space flight, and Yury Gagarin's name was on everyone's lips there.) Then he gave me a map of the London Underground, explained where to transfer, put me on the train, and waved good-bye with his massive hand. Naturally, I was late for lunch; naturally, there was an unpleasant exchange. But things were soon set right, for I had returned, and I had not requested political asylum!

Together with Rimma Naryshkina, a lawyer, I went to the Central Criminal Court, the "Old Bailey," where we followed with interest the proceedings of a rather dull case—involving theft on a beach. The defendant received a suspended sentence. When, after returning to the hotel, I told my comrades in the lobby about the trial, a young stranger with a beard, who was sitting next to us, asked me in rather good Russian, "Well, what is your opinion of English justice?" I wanted to reply, but here our group leader Viktor Sergeevich intervened and said nervously, "We don't have time; we're in a hurry to get to lunch," and pulled me by the sleeve. "Oh, so you're in a hurry," said the young man mockingly. I was furious with Viktor Sergeevich and replied, "Yes, we don't have time, but I'll still tell you my impression." And I explained to him why I had a favorable impression of both English justice and of the proceedings themselves.

After London we moved on to Cambridge, and then Stratford-upon-Avon. Next came Scotland—Glasgow, Edinburgh, the homeland of Burns. Glasgow seemed to me a rather grim city, and even the new public housing projects for workers built by the local municipality did not impress me. There was something poor about Glasgow. And although we were very well received there, and even went to a variety show where the cloakroom attendant was from Russia, I could not rid myself of what was, perhaps, a feeling of nervousness. In Glasgow we stayed at an old hotel, built of wood, where the window frames rattled and the floorboards squeaked. I slept in an enormous, very high bed, which must have dated from the seventeenth century. The chambermaid, to whom I had offered a souvenir upon arrival, showed me how to use the electric heater without throwing shillings into it, and when I got soaking wet in a rainstorm, she took my suit and pressed it, categorically refusing any payment.

On the way to Edinburgh we agreed among ourselves, at the initiative of our guide, Nina, not to ask endless questions about Mary Stuart, not to show our "erudition" in this matter, since that subject set the Scots' teeth on edge. (Shortly before our trip to Britain, a Russian translation of Stephen Zweig's book on the Scottish queen had come out, and we had all read it.) But scarcely had we entered Mary's sleeping chamber than the agreement was shamelessly broken, and we all vied with one another to tell everything we had learned about Mary Stuart and David Riccio from the book.

In Edinburgh Castle we were shown the treasure of the Scottish king Robert the Bruce, which had long lain hidden. It was discovered thanks to Sir Walter Scott, who found instructions in the castle library.

I was enormously impressed by the memorial museum dedicated to the Scottish soldiers who had been killed in the First and Second World Wars. The bas-reliefs, done in excellent taste, the books bound in red morocco, which contained the names of the dead Scots, the simplicity of the grief depicted—all this created an atmosphere of exalted purity.

I was turning the pages of one of the books when our guide, Nina, asked, "Tell me, is there anti-Semitism in Russia?"

"The fact is that our Communist party is discussing the matter," I replied evasively, adding something to the effect that I had never felt any anti-Semitism personally, and muttered something about the times having changed. I was ashamed and did not know what else to do. I told one of my more trustworthy colleagues about this conversation. He sighed: "Why did you do that? You should have told the truth." Later that day I looked for Nina by the television set and told her what things were really like. She smiled and answered, "I know that." It was as if a weight had been lifted from my shoulders.

At a reception given by the Anglo-Soviet Society, a young teacher by the name of Ike Asher came up to me. We began a conversation on the problems of the workers' movement in Europe. This led to correspondence between us, and an exchange of phonograph records and books. Asher came to Moscow twice. We met once again after I left the Soviet Union for good in 1976.

A farewell dinner at Victoria Station, then off to Tilbury, where we board our steamship, the *Mikhail Kalinin*. We have five days' sailing ahead of us to Leningrad. I am blissfully happy, for I have my own first-class cabin. I got it by chance: the cabin was intended for the wife of the Central Committee secretary, Kuusinen Amiragova, but she decided not to sail for some reason, and since the others were reluctant to pay for it, the stateroom was assigned to me.

All of us are pleased, for our Intourist coupons are accepted on board along with hard currency, so we are able to go to the bars and the like. The women pounce on the Danish chocolate with walnuts (seven kopecks a bar). Then along comes the purser who asks that the ladies be informed that they have bought up a month's supply of chocolate! We men have a chat with them, trying to make them listen to reason. Oh, this poverty of ours! It is the root of everything.

Rimma is also traveling first class. This means that we have our meals at a different time from the others (except for two couples and the Serovs, everyone else is traveling second class). Viktor Sergeevvich and Sasha—an engineer from Mosgorsovnarkhoz, if he is not lying—often come up to me. Viktor is pleased; everything is fine, and he can play chess in the salon. I go aft and play shuffleboard (a game halfway between hockey and hopscotch). I make a deal with my partners, one of whom is Indian, the other an English student: if they win, I'll shout "Long live Great Britain!" and if I win, they'll shout "Long live the USSR!" I win. My partners faithfully fulfill the conditions. Then, at the invitation of some French passengers, I play with them. Madame Mercedes, a tall brunette, cries out in admiration at my playing: "Oh, monsieur, what a stroke!" A little gold cross on her chest sways back and forth. Confound it, it's an omen, but is it a good-luck charm or a sign from Satan?

There are four of us at our table: Rimma, myself, and a very nice English couple—tourists who are traveling to Leningrad and Moscow—Fanny and Michael Lynes. Both are chemists. Michael works for Phillips Petroleum. We have become friends; now we get together before meals. Michael suffers from seasickness and has to lie down a lot.

One early morning I go up on deck. It is bright and clear all around. We are sailing along not far from the Danish coast. All of a sudden I hear Fanny's voice: "Look! You see that white castle with the green roof? That's Elsinore!" Even though I only got to see it from far away, how lucky I was not to have slept through it!

Our steamship stopped for a few hours each in Stockholm, Copenhagen, and Helsinki. Stockholm is very beautiful, very rich, very bourgeois. "When I look at that prosperous city, I feel the pirate in me," I said to Michael and Fanny. "I have the urge to jump on shore with a sword in hand and cut open featherbeds and pillows." We chuckled.

In Copenhagen there are canals, extremely beautiful quays and a seaside park. Here, too, there was an incident. We were being driven in the same tour bus as a group of tourists from Gorki who were also returning from England. Their group leader was a rather unpleasant-looking woman from Intourist. The Gorkiites complained to us that she had been mistreating them, not letting them out of her sight for a moment.

After visiting the monument to the mother-goddess of Denmark—who is seated in a chariot to which are hitched her sons, whom she has transformed into bulls, and in which she rides around inspecting the country—we went on foot to the harborside park to have a look at the famous Little Mermaid. The tour bus, empty, also headed there. Finally it was time to return to the ship, which was due to sail in less than half an hour. We boarded the bus only to discover that one of the women in our party was missing—a middle-aged English teacher. We all tried to remember where we had last seen her. It seemed that it had been by the monument to the Mother of Denmark. Viktor Sergeevich sent another English teacher, Elya, out to look for her. Then he began to get nervous and went out himself in search of her. I could understand his concern: if anything happened he would be in serious trouble with the KGB.

Viktor Sergeevich had just left, when the leader of the Gorki group, through the Danish interpreter, instructed the driver to proceed to the ship. "And what about our comrades?" I asked.

"We are not obligated to wait for them. Let them find their way themselves," the Intourist woman replied with annoyance. "But if they arrive here and don't find us, they'll get lost and will miss the ship. Without the two groups"—there were forty of us—"the ship won't sail. But it won't bother to wait for only three people." I tried to persuade her with common sense. All the other tourists remained silent, and that began to irritate me.

"We're going," the Gorki group leader said firmly. "I'm staying," I also said firmly, "and I'm going to wait for our comrades." With those words I got up and made my way toward the exit. All the others remained silent. Some looked out the window, as if none of this was any of their business.

"What is your last name?" the woman from Intourist demanded, almost shouting.

I told her my name and got off. As a gesture of solidarity, the old man who was our translator left the bus as well. He was beside himself with indignation, but controlled himself and merely said, "Not a very collegial spirit," meaning not very comradely. "I've never seen anything like it. But don't worry. I've stayed behind with you in order to show you the shortest way to the pier."

The bus pulled away. Not one of the comrades had followed my example, and this grieved me terribly. I felt as though, in the space of just a few short minutes, I had been rethinking my whole life. A few minutes later all three of our missing companions showed up, chattering away. "But where are the others?" asked Viktor Sergeevich in surprise.

"I'll tell you on the way," I answered. "Let's hurry now. We have only seven minutes left before sailing." Under the guidance of the Dane we walked quickly. Suddenly, around the corner, we saw standing at the pier our beloved five-thousand-ton *Mikhail Kalinin*. We gave the old Dane a friendly farewell and went on board. Everything seemed fine.

After dinner Viktor Sergeevich and Sasha came to my cabin to discuss what had happened. Strange as it may seem, Sasha did not share Viktor's and my indignation. I was furious, especially when I learned that the Intourist guide had already been to Copenhagen seven times and was fully aware that the pier was only a stone's throw from where we were waiting, and only a two-minute bus ride. Viktor Sergeevich spouted curses in powerful Russian. Sasha fell silent. I shouted: "Where is the solidarity among Soviets abroad that we were told about at briefings before our trip?" Sasha looked at me with interest. That night I couldn't fall asleep for a long time. I kept thinking about solidarity and about the silence. I wanted to know why no one had spoken. Were they all afraid that they would not be allowed to go abroad anymore? 'Tis a sad thing to live on this earth, as the proverb goes.

Back in Moscow, the Lyneses were waiting for me by their hotel. I borrowed a Volga automobile from a neighbor and, along with Rimma, drove over to pick them up. We rode along the Uspensky highway, went for a stroll there, and then back to my place for dinner. We drank to eternal friendship. Later on I received a card of thanks from England.

Ten years later, for New Year's 1971, I sent the Lyneses a greeting card. I received a reply a year later, for New Year's 1972. It seems that my card took a whole year to reach them, since the Lyneses had built themselves a new house and moved. Indeed, the photo on the card showed a new house with Fanny and Michael sitting on the lawn.

In the autumn of 1964 I left the USSR again, this time in a tour group of staff members from our institute for a nine-day trip to Finland. It was a wonderful, happy junket, and I still have fond memories of it. It was my second trip abroad. The third and last time was two years later, in the autumn of 1966, when I went to Poland.

This is how that trip happened.

Long before, in the winter of 1946, I was sitting studying by the window of our basement apartment at 26 Gorki Street. Suddenly a shadow cut off the daylight: a stranger was standing at the window with his forehead pressed up against the glass apparently peering in to see if anyone was at home. I rushed out to the street. My heart nearly stopped: My God, it was Stasik! I dragged him into the apartment. My parents embraced him; my mother was sobbing.

Stasik Liudkiewicz had been a classmate of my brother's and a very close friend. After leaving school in 1935, they both intended to enroll in the history faculty at Moscow State University. Stasik was accepted, but my brother failed the entrance exam. A year later my brother enrolled in the geography faculty. Stasik was the only son in a family of Polish revolutionaries who had emigrated to the USSR. His father was the executive secretary of the International Confederation of Revolutionary Writers. They lived in the House of Writers on Bolshoi Afanes'evsky Lane.

I adored Stasik and even imitated the way he walked until I almost became hunchbacked: Stasik was extremely stoop-shouldered. During those years my brother and Stasik treated me like a mascot. I greatly envied them what I thought of as their very important activities. An international section was established in our school, headed by my brother with Stasik's help. To this day I have stationery with the letterhead "International Section of Model School 25 of the Sverdlovsk District, Moscow." I too became involved in the work of the section: in my Pioneer unit I began a cell of the MOPR (International Organization to Aid Revolutionaries), collected money to aid the victims of capitalism, went to various meetings where former prisoners of imperialism spoke, and was even present at one of the meetings of the MOPR World Congress in the Hall of Columns at the trade union headquarters. At that time—I was twelve or fourteen—I was preparing to become a professional revolutionary in order to carry out the world revolution. At fourteen I wrote a letter to my cousin Wol'f Likhter, a Latvian communist who had been imprisoned in the Riga fortress. In my letter I informed him that "the day is not distant when the world proletariat will cast off the yoke of the bourgeoisie" and release him from the fortress. Later my aunt, Wollie's mother, told me that my letter nearly cost him a few more years in prison. In 1936 Wollie went to Spain on orders from the party to assist in the revolution there. He was killed in battle near Guadalajara in February 1937.

But let us return to the story of Stasik.

The year was 1937. Stasik's father, like many other Polish revolutionaries who had emigrated to the USSR, was arrested, accused of espionage, and executed. Soon afterwards Stasik, while a student at the university, was also arrested. Stasik spent five years in the camps and another three years in exile. He was released through the efforts of the of the Polish Communist party together with other Polish communist prisoners. He married a woman named Lida, the daughter of a work foreman. Now, along with her, their little boy Wladek, and Stasik's mother, he was returning to Poland. Stasik told us all this on that cold winter day. I remembered that after Stasik was arrested, my brother had taken Stasik's first wife, Lena, to the camp, but she was not allowed in to see him.

The years went by. Stasik became an important man: editor of the central youth paper, then department chief at the newspaper *Prawo Ludu*, and finally head of Polish television. He had visited Moscow several times. Then came the events of 1956. Stasik was among those who advocated greater democratization. But in 1957, when the signal was given for a "retreat," Stasik received a strong reprimand and a warning from the party about "giving the rostrum to revisionists." He was dismissed from his posts and became a secretary on the editorial staff of a Warsaw evening newspaper. A significant role in his fate was played by the fact that his mother's brother, a prominent party figure, had also fallen into disgrace. In the early 1960s Stasik and I began to correspond regularly. In 1966 he sent me an invitation, and in September of that year I set out for Warsaw. I spent seventeen days there. Then, together with Stasik, I went to Krakow and Zakopane. From there Stasik returned to work in Warsaw and I went on to Gdansk alone.

It was a marvelous trip in many respects. Thanks to the kindness of the director of the Polish Institute of Marxism-Leninism, Tadeusz Daniszewski, whom I had once met in Moscow, Stasik and I were able to stay in party hotels. This meant great savings in practical terms: we paid 10 to 20 zlotys per day instead of 150 to 200 zlotys in a regular hotel. Furthermore, in Warsaw I was able to attend the shows that were most in demand, such as *Namestnik* and *Tango*. Thanks to Daniszewski's assistance, I managed to work in the Polish archives and in the Institute of International Relations, from which I brought home photocopies and microfilms of unique documents for my work (the same work that would never be published).

Daniszewski was an intelligent and kind man. The events of 1968 did not spare him. He was dismissed from his job and given a pension. He died soon afterwards.

In Warsaw I lived at Stasik's: I was given his son Wladek's room, while Wladek went to stay with a friend. Everyone in their home worked: Stasik at the newspaper, Lida at the institute (she was an electrical engineer by profession), and Stasik's daughter Inka was taking an examination for admission to the philosophy faculty at Warsaw University. Stasik's mother, much advanced in age but still a very beautiful woman, lived separately with her aunt. Ludwiga Stanislavovna worked for Orbis, akin to our Intourist. They had a magnificent dog in the house, a beagle which woke everyone up in the morning in anticipation of going to get the newspaper (she had the privilege of carrying the paper from the newsstand to their home).

I shall not list here the Polish points of interest—just as I have refrained from doing so in my account of the trip to England—but only describe a few episodes. In Warsaw I paid a visit to the publishing house Book and Knowledge, which was putting out my book *June 22, 1941* at the time. At the publishers' request I wrote an introduction to the Polish edition, which came out with the book.

I went to Auschwitz with Stasik. It is so horrible that I do not feel like writing about it. Two things stunned me, though: first, the banality of the crimes committed there. Murder and torture were an everyday, routine matter at Auschwitz. They gave meaning and content to everything that was happening there. No wonder this factory of death ended up creating its own consumer goods workshop, where articles for daily use were produced from human skin. Second, I realized that the Nazis could not have performed their dark deeds here, if they had not been aided by some portion of the local population, however insignificant it may have been. Then I was told how, during the German occupation, a special profession arose—the so-called *szmalcowczy* (from the word *szmalec* for "fat"). The *szmalcowczy* sought out Jews in hiding and demanded payment in return for not denouncing them. That is, they "squeezed butter" from their victims. Those unfortunate people either paid them off or ended up in the hands of the Gestapo.

In Gdansk I lived at the hotel for the propaganda management office of the Communist party city committee. The representative of the committee suggested I join a Soviet party delegation that was staying there, in order to see the tourist spots. The delegation had a minibus which happened to have one free seat. The group was headed by the first secretary of the Grodno regional party committee, Vladimir Fedorovich Mickiewicz. Besides him (he was with his wife) there were three other couples with us. They were all very friendly to me. Vladimir Fedorovich and I talked about my book and about the events it dealt with.

Once in Gdansk I started out for the art museum but could not find my way. I went around in circles, returning to the place where I had started. Finally I decided to ask for directions from the first person I saw. This turned out to be a woman of indeterminate age in a stylish coat made of leather. She guided me to the museum, where we wandered around together. She did not speak Russian, so she explained things in German. We talked about religion (Beata was a practicing Catholic), and I recalled a marvelous sculpture I had seen in one of the Warsaw churches, the priest in a crown of thorns, in memory of the five thousand Polish Catholic priests tortured by the Nazis.

I shall always remember the trip to Poland with the warmest of feelings. Here I met and became friends (I hope for a lifetime) with Misha Heller, a friend of my Moscow friends. Misha was at one time, like myself, a student at the history faculty of Moscow University. His life had not been easy. In the end, fate took him and his wife, Zhenya, into Poland. At that time he was an editor at the Polish press agency. Misha, himself a passionate book lover, took me to the secondhand book store Atheneum, where, with his financial support, I obtained a lot of books. Among them was Orwell's *1984*, which was banned in the USSR. I managed to succeed in taking it back to Moscow. The Hellers now live in Paris, where Misha is a professor at the Sorbonne. He wrote a marvelous book, *The World of the Concentration Camp and Soviet Literature*, and many interesting articles on the works of Solzhenitsyn, Zinoviev, and Aldanov, as well as other writers and publishers. Now we are writing a history of the Soviet Union together. I hope will shall complete it. (Author's note: this book, *Utopia in Power*, was published in the 1980s in many countries.)

When I left Warsaw in the early days of October, there was nothing, it seemed, to indicate that I might never see Stasik again.

There were three of us in the train compartment: a young man from Minsk who had been staying with relatives, a Japanese woman, a librarian returning from an international conference on Esperanto in Paris, who had subsequently spent a few days in Warsaw at the invitation of the Esperanto organization there; and myself.

In Brest the Soviet border guards and customs agents entered our compartment. I helped the Japanese woman fill out her declaration. Three times during the night they came to inspect the documents and belongings of this poor, confused Japanese woman. Then yet another border guard appeared, awakened her once again and took her out to the frontier station. Meanwhile, we had to get out since our train was being transferred to a different track. Then the Japanese librarian told me how she had stood freezing on the platform for two hours. And over such a trifling matter: apparently the border guards were suspicious as to why a Japanese citizen was returning home through the territory of the USSR. She simply found it interesting to travel through our country, making a stop in Moscow, on her way home to Tokyo.

In the spring of 1967 I requested from the authorities an invitation to the USSR for Stasik's daughter, Inka. For a long time I received no response, and then was told that my request had been refused. By that time I had already been expelled from the party.

Stasik and I continued to keep in touch. His family suffered more reverses. After the student upheaval of March 1968 in Poland, there began an unbridled anti-Semitic campaign: people of Jewish origin were fired from their jobs and deprived of their livelihood.

After the war in Poland only thirty thousand Jews remained—the few who had survived or returned from other countries. This is an approximate figure, since after the mass annihilation of Jews by the Nazis, Polish passports no longer included a heading for ethnic group but indicated only citizenship. This was a wise precaution against a resurgence of anti-Semitism. But now Poland had begun a project reminiscent of the Nazis: a determination of people's family origins, their ethnic background, and the ethnic background of preceding generations as well. And this was happening at the end of the 1960s in socialist Poland, a country where only twenty-five years earlier the Nazis had destroyed millions of Jews.

The anti-Semitic campaign affected Stasik as well. He was warned that he would be fired from work. His mother was put on a pension. Inka took part in student demonstrations; like all the other students, she was expelled and, upon application for readmission, was not accepted. Stasik's family, like other Jewish families, was forced to leave their homeland. Deprived of his livelihood, Stasik, one of the pioneer builders of the new socialist Poland, had to emigrate. At first Stasik, Lidka, and Ludwiga Stanislavovna lived in Jerusalem. Lida found work in her profession, but Stasik did not have a full-time position, since it was not possible for him, as a talented journalist, to find suitable employment. Inka was living with a distant relative in Brussels, where she was studying at the university in the Slavic department. Wladek succeeded, along with his Polish wife, in obtaining a visa to Sweden, where they worked and studied at the polytechnic institute; there a daughter was born to them. Let us hope that Stasik's grandchildren will be spared the tortures of racial persecution and discrimination!

Stasik moved to Sweden to be closer to his son. Recently he sought me out. In 1969 an issue of *Literary Heritage* (no. 81), devoted to MOPR, was published in Moscow. It contained Stasik's reminiscences of his father, Clemens Liudkiewicz.

Staff members at our institute had begun traveling for study purposes beginning in the late 1950s. This gradually evolved from participation in scientific conferences to months-long trips for research work. Quite a few staff members, Americanists from the section of U.S. and Canadian history, were working in the archives at libraries in the United States, some having been there two or three times. Italian specialists went off to Italy, French scholars to France, and some of the Latin Americanists went to Mexico or Cuba. Others traveled constantly to the socialist countries of Eastern Europe, always the same people repeatedly. A person who had run the gauntlet of the authorities one time, including the highest—the exit commission of the party Central Committee—and had not compromised himself in any way subsequently, could count on further trips. It was very easy to become disqualified, however: by speaking with the wrong person, by saying the wrong thing, by stopping at a restaurant while abroad, by being suspected of running after women, or simply by quarreling with one of the higher-ups, and so on and so forth. But still, if you took a look at those staff members who had traveled abroad, you could see some pattern as to who got to travel and how often, and then it would become clear that it was not by any means the best, the most capable historians who were going abroad to study for long periods, but either those who occupied a certain bureaucratic position or those who were connected with institutions that had little to do with historical scholarship, or any scholarship at all for that matter.

I had worked in the Institute of History and in the Institute of World History for more than thirty years, and in that time had never once been sent on an academic trip abroad. I had been outside the country three times:

twice as a tourist—to England and Finland—and once by personal invitation to Poland. And only the last time, in Poland, was I able to work with archival materials in my field. I never participated in international conferences, either, not even those held in Moscow. Before 1965 this was because the speakers delivering papers at conferences tended to be, by and large, individuals who occupied certain sensitive posts, or people close to them. After 1965 the authorities did not send me to conferences, because they thought that I was too well known abroad as a historian in disgrace!

Three times they began to process my papers for a trip abroad: in the late 1950s for Romania, in 1964 for Kenya, and in 1964–1967 for England. And each time I ended up going nowhere. True, I was making steady progress. The first time my papers got only as far as the foreign division of the presidium of the Academy of Sciences; the second time I was summoned for a talk at the Central Committee, and the third time the foreign division of the presidium of the Academy of Sciences conducted an inquiry in connection with my obtaining an entry visa to England (this, at least, was what I was told in the foreign division). After my expulsion from the Communist party in June 1967, a ban was put not only on my taking any trips abroad but also on my even being present as a guest at international seminars and conferences in Moscow, on my meeting foreign colleagues, and so on.

I should like to dwell on the fate of my proposed trip to England in somewhat greater detail. There was talk of it beginning in 1962. In the middle of 1964, while I was beginning the last in a series of monographs entitled *British Foreign Policy before and during the Second World War*, I wrote a letter to the director of the institute, V. M. Khvostov, requesting permission for academic travel. Then, as I have mentioned, my relations with Khvostov deteriorated, and when I asked him about a trip to England, reminding him of the promise he had made, he answered me abruptly, saying: "Promises made earlier have now lost any value." Then I remarked in jest, "You know, Vladimir Mikhailovich, your answer reminds me a great deal of a popular saying these days: It was possible—I promise.'" He chuckled. Sometime later he did phone the foreign division, and things seemed to be moving again. I began to fill out forms and to talk with the people from the foreign division. One year later the institute drew up an "academic basis for travel" application, signed it, and sent it to the presidium of the Academy. My program for work in England was also drawn up and approved. Among the points in this program which had no direct bearing on my research work were the following:

> In case of proposals by British scholars for closer cooperation, state that such proposals will be transmitted to the heads of the Institute of History of the USSR Academy of Sciences on returning to Moscow.
> In case there is a need to conduct conversations on general political problems, explain the policy of the Soviet government based on the

decisions of the Twenty-Third Party Congress, the plenums of the Communist party Central Committee, and materials published in the Soviet press.
Strictly observe the rules of behavior for Soviet citizens abroad.

These three points were to be found in all programs for academic trips abroad, without exception. Every Soviet citizen who left for the dangerous world of capitalism was required to be a propagandist and purveyor of the policy of the Communist party and the Soviet state.

Hence, my exit file went from one desk to another, while the trip itself was postponed from one quarter to another, from 1965 to 1966, and then to the second half of 1967. And so, finally, when I had already filled out the forms for obtaining a British entry visa, the official who was in charge of my case informed me with sympathy that my exit file had been lost, and we had to start everything all over again! Here my patience was at an end. On arriving home, I quickly sent off a letter of protest to the head of the foreign division of the Academy of Sciences and to my director, V. M. Khvostov.

The letters had some effect. The foreign division understood that it had gone too far. Within three days the same official informed me, as if nothing unusual had happened, that my file had "been found."

But soon my party difficulties began, and in early June 1967 my file returned once again to the place where it had started—the Institute of History.

It is the nature of man to live in hope. No doubt, if no such conceivable possibility existed, mankind would long since have grown into a tribe of pragmatists, and intellectual and spiritual life would have become impossible. So it is plausible that people always hope for something, that they dream and live by hope in this world.

In spite of the fact that I was past fifty, my hopes had not abandoned me, for I could not reconcile myself to a life forever mapped out for me by someone higher up. So it was that five years after my expulsion from the party, in 1972, I decided on a change of scenery—a few weeks in Hungary, where I had an invitation to visit.

My Moscow friends discouraged me from such a scheme, fearing, not without reason, that I would not be allowed to take such a trip, and would suffer yet another disappointment. But the secret hope that perhaps the times had softened and changed the attitude toward me drove me to action. At worst, I told myself, I would at least know precisely where I stood.

In the Soviet Union, in order to apply to leave the country you need to obtain a recommendation (*kharakteristika*) from the institution where you work. I remembered the outstanding recommendations the institute had given me before I was expelled from the party. First I went to my section. They drafted a recommendation. Things didn't appeared to be going too badly: not only the trade union organization but even the deputy secretary of the party organization signed my *kharakteristika*. Only a third signature was lacking—that of the director of the Institute of World History, Academician Ye. M. Zhukov. When the *kharakteristika* was handed to him, he became outraged and said that this was an extraordinary occurrence and that he would not under any circumstance sign the document.

Then I went to the central telegraph office on Gorki Street and sent a telegram to Budapest announcing that I could not leave owing to the refusal of the institute to grant me a recommendation.

This was an open challenge to all the unwritten rules. Normally a person was supposed to think up a polite excuse for declining such an invitation—under the pretext, say, of illness, business, or family circumstances—but never was it permissible to name the real reason: denial of a recommendation.

That episode forced me to give serious thought to the situation in which I found myself. I believe that those who had refused to allow me to travel to Hungary were counting on just such a reaction on my part. But I am also sure they believed that thinking things over would lead me to capitulate. I came convinced of this three years later.

The simplemindedness of these people has always astounded me. Later on I came to the conclusion that this was one of the peculiarities of *Homo sovieticus* in power: the conviction that the realization that resistance is hopeless will sooner or later force a person to capitulate. Yet this possibility still seemed to me so simpleminded that I could not believe it totally. In actual fact, however, that was the case.

I referred at the beginning of this chapter to the intrigues involved in trips abroad. In my institute things reached the point where disputes arose among rival claimants to the same foreign trip. Dispute is a mild way of putting it: I mean denunciations in the international division of the presidium of the Academy, in the Central Committee, and, no doubt, in the KGB itself. Compromising the candidate, settling personal scores on the field of battle for a trip abroad, became a normal occurrence.

A foreign trip was both the carrot and the stick: if you behaved well, obeyed the bosses, and carried out all of their instructions, you would be awarded with a trip abroad; if you didn't obey, you didn't go. And people exerted themselves, did their utmost, intrigued, just to obtain permission for a business or even a pleasure trip, in order to spend two weeks in the capitalist hell!

There were cases where they did worse than that. One took place in the city of Kharkov, a major industrial and cultural center in the Ukraine. In one of the apartments of a multistory building, located on Krasnoshkol'naya Embankment, there lived two families of engineers by the names of Belinsky and Muratov, both members of the Communist party. Belinsky, aged thirty-six, a candidate of technical sciences, worked as director of the All-Union Scientific Institute. Before being promoted to this position, he had been division head and secretary of the party organization of his institute. The forty-seven-year-old Muratov worked as a laboratory chief in the same institute. Both Belinsky and Muratov were family men and had the reputation for being irreproachable in every respect.

Both scientific workers were to go to an international exhibition in the United States for a demonstration of an environmental anti-pollution device built by their institute. But, as often happens in Soviet practice, just before the departure date it became clear that only one of them could go; instead of the other, a representative of the ministry would be sent. Muratov, on learning of this, and wishing to eliminate his rival for the trip to America, submitted a statement about Belinsky, accusing him of concealing his Jewish origins. With state-sponsored anti-Semitism flourishing in the Soviet Union, and especially in the Ukraine, this was a serious accusation.

Belinsky, indignant not so much at Muratov's treachery as at the assertion that his father was a Jew, whereas he was in fact Russian, decided to settle the score with his rival. The former friends met in Belinsky's apartment to clear up the disagreement between them. A fight broke out between them, and the younger and stronger Belinsky, armed with a knife, killed Muratov, thereby not only eliminating his sole rival for a trip to the United States, but also taking revenge for "the insulted honor of a Russian." Belinsky dismembered Muratov's body in the bathroom, but since he could not manage alone, he sent an urgent telegram to his wife in Kiev. The two of them finished off this "work" together. They took the pieces of Muratov's body and buried them in various spots around the city. Then Belinsky went to the institute of which he was the head to hold a regular meeting with the other officials. His subordinates were somewhat surprised to see obvious traces of a fight on their boss's face and neck. Moreover, Belinsky in his haste had not succeeded in destroying all evidence of the murder. He was arrested and sentenced to be executed.

The Belinsky case is, apparently, a qualitative step forward in the history of international scientific relations.

7

June 22, 1941

Something shall be sculpted from clay,
Something shall be hewn from stone,
Something shall be written from the heart,
It shall be as it shall be!
Hurry not!
—David Samoilov

Manuscript on the beginning of the war — the testimony of Marshal F. I. Golikov — the KGB's objections — the riddle of the "Red Choir" — debut of June 22, 1941 — public reaction — discussion at the Institute of Marxism-Leninism — Is it possible to improve Marxism? — the Oleg Puzyrev affair — in the party committee of the Institute of History.

At the end of the war, while still on active duty, I often dreamed that, once back in Moscow, I would resume my history studies.

The war marked me for life, as it did all those who, willingly or not, took part in it. It would be many years before the physical and spiritual wounds of war were healed. When these years had finally gone by, youths found, to their amazement, that they had become mature adults, if not old men. You could try to change or redo things, but there was nothing you could do about the passage of time.

During the war I was able to see a great deal and understand even more. I hope to write a separate book about the war one day. For now I shall say only the following: it occurred to me to write a book on the start of the war in June 1941 while I was returning from East Prussia in an army van. But I was not able to carry out my idea until much later. Almost twenty years of studying history passed before I was ready to undertake such a book. After 1956 I gradually began to gather materials. I had many other plans and schemes, and *June 22, 1941*'s turn was still far off. The compilation of materials was completed in 1963; in the following year, after conducting a number of interviews with those who had participated in certain events, I wrote the text of the book. In the spring of 1964 the "Nauka" publishing house agreed to publish the book as part of a general educational series.

I wrote *June 22, 1941* in one sitting, so to speak, freely and easily, without concern for possible consequences and with a minimum of the habitual self-censorship. From the moment I began writing, I attempted to disregard outside considerations and write only that which cried out to be put down on paper. I decided to make the book compact, so that any individual, regardless of profession, might find it easy to read.

In October 1964 Khrushchev was sent into retirement.

The overall situation in the country, especially in the ideological sphere, began to change quickly after the October Central Committee plenum of 1964. Although there was not yet any clear swing toward neo-Stalinism, there did arise a kind of reverse reaction to the anti-Stalinist policy of the previous leadership. This swing was especially noticeable in the ideological sphere. I would soon feel its effects personally.

The journal *Mezhdunarodnaya zhizn'*, in which I had taken a rather active part in the second half of the 1950s and in the early 1960s, suggested that I write an article for the twentieth anniversary of the victory over Hitler's Germany. I gladly accepted the suggestion and wrote the article. At first the article seemed to be well received. But then began the proposals to "improve" it, which would be tantamount to softening its anti-Stalinist tone. This was a sign of the times. These were years when I had to withstand strong pressure from the head of the world history section, A. F. Miller, and one of the section members, M. Poltavsky, who were trying to eliminate from the tenth volume of *World History*, the compilation of which I was heading, elements critical of Stalin and of other leaders with regard to their unpreparedness for war with Nazi Germany. I managed to fend off such attacks. Now, I would have to fight for my book, which was with the "Nauka" publishers. The same demands were put forward there as well. This led me to the logical conclusion that the guidelines for treating problems in the history of the Great Fatherland War were being revised in the Central Committee, and that we were apparently heading toward a deviation from the Twentieth Party Congress line. Occupied as I was with *World History* and with my own book, and fearing that the burgeoning conflict with *Mezhdunarodnaya zhizn'* might backfire with regard to my book, I decided not to make any compromises with the journal, but not to fight for publication of my article either. I therefore sent the following letter to the journal:

May 9, 1965

To the editorial board of *Mezhdunarodnaya zhizn'*:

I am sending you a proof of the article "Great Deed." I submitted it for publication on condition that the text on the errors committed by Stalin and the People's Commissariat of Defense before the German attack be restored. In this connection I have written a new text for the fourth typed page, which is to be attached to the printed copy.

Without this insert I cannot agree to publication of the article. I see no grounds for excluding the issue of the cult of personality from the article. The terrible losses we suffered in the war with the Nazi invaders, especially during the initial period, are to a significant extent the result of Stalin's gross miscalculations and errors. This is the least one can say in this regard. Silence over these serious mistakes, condemned by the Twentieth and Twenty-Second Party Congresses, as well as by a decree of the party Central Committee of June 30, 1956, would distort the nature of events and would be a falsification of history.

I most earnestly request that you agree to the changes I have submitted.

If it is decided otherwise (at any stage of the article's preparation for publication) I ask that my article not be published.

A. M. Nekrich

The categorical nature of my letter was also a result of my fears that the editors might make arbitrary modifications and present me with a fait accompli. Such things had been done on more than one occasion in the history of Soviet publications. And just try and explain afterwards that you had nothing to do with it!

The article was not published.

It was at precisely this time that the fate of my book was being decided.

The difficulties began after Khrushchev's retirement. The first pages of the manuscript for *June 22, 1941* had already made my editor, Ye. Volodina somewhat nervous. The text ran as follows:

"The world as we knew it with its usual joys and sorrows unexpectedly fell apart. The war swept in and caught up in its whirlwind millions of human lives. Hitler's Germany had suddenly, treacherously attacked the Soviet Union.

SUDDENLY!
    SUDDENLY?
        SUDDENLY?!"

So, on the very first page doubts were expressed about the truthfulness of the official Soviet stance on the suddenness of Germany's attack on the Soviet Union. These doubts were made absolutely clear, and consequently the reader was meant to ask himself the question: So what did happen? And then another question: Who was responsible for the surprise nature of the attack; or was it, perhaps, not really such a surprise after all?

This wording survived until the first editing; but then, at the editor's insistence, I deleted all the repetitions of *suddenly*, so the last sentence read as follows: "Hitler's Germany had treacherously attacked the Soviet Union."

So began the "purging" of the text for anything that might appear suspicious to the censor.

My manuscript subsequently was reviewed by five sets of censors: the routine state censorship of Glavlit, military censorship to verify whether any secret information had slipped in, special military censorship by the Central Intelligence Directorate, the censors for the Committee for State Security (KGB) and for the Ministry of Foreign Affairs, and, finally, part of the book had to obtain the approval of the science division of the Central Committee. At times it seemed that after such a "once-over," there would be nothing left of the book. Actually, since the book was written in one stretch, while it may have been possible to cripple it, the ideas it contained could not be eliminated altogether. If you have a bad accident, the surgeon might amputate your arm or your leg, but you still have your head. So it was with the book. It had one main theme. So it might be edited, its various parts amputated, but as long as it had not been chopped to pieces, it was still alive.

The reader may, perhaps, wonder exactly what the censors did to the text of my book.

The Glavlit censor was both the first and the last to go over it. The evaluations were based primarily on the views of the other censors. On instructions from Glavlit, the manuscript and corrections were sent for review to the Ministry of Defense, the KGB, and the Ministry of Foreign Affairs.

The special censor of the Central Intelligence Directorate (GRU) deleted some very important passages from my interview with the former head of the directorate, Marshal F. I. Golikov. But this should be explained in greater detail.

The elevator takes me to the third floor. I enter a rather long hallway, with doors bearing nameplates both left and right. On these nameplates I am suddenly confronted with familiar names: Marshal of the Soviet Union X, Army General Y. So this is the "little corner of heaven"? (This was how military personnel jokingly referred among themselves to the inspectorate division of the Ministry of Defense, where deserving warriors, on being appointed inspector of the Soviet army, could more or less live out the rest of their days in peace. They lived as if they were in heaven. Hence the name.)

Here is the office I need. The door bears a nameplate reading: Marshal of the Soviet Union F. I. Golikov. I knock on the door. "Come in, come in," a voice rings out, whereupon the voice's owner rises to meet me. He is short, with a polished pate, gray-blue eyes, a marshal's uniform, and many rows of beribboned medals. This is Filipp Ivanovich Golikov. He invites me to sit down, across a wide desk. At another, smaller desk sits a lieutenant colonel, the marshal's adjutant. He rustles a few papers and then goes away.

I explain to the marshal the purpose of my visit. I tell him my idea for *June 22, 1941*, a book in which I shall attempt to give an objective account of the events that led directly to the attack by Hitler's Germany on that date.

"You, Filipp Ivanovich," I say, "can help me clarify a number of issues. In the course of my work"—my study of the history of the Second World War—"I have encountered some ambiguities in the history of the Great Fatherland War, especially its beginning. I need to clear them up both as the deputy senior editor of the tenth volume of *World History*, on the history of the Second World War, and as the author of a popular history book, being prepared for publication by the 'Nauka' publishers."

Long before I received Marshal Golikov's agreement for our talk, I had familiarized myself with his biography. It was unique. He was the only person to have occupied consecutively all the highest administrative positions in the Soviet Ministry of Defense: head of the Central Personnel Directorate, head of the Central Intelligence Directorate, head of the Central Political Directorate. During the war he was main coordinator for intelligence services, then deputy commander and commander at the front. Golikov was repeatedly elected deputy to the Supreme Soviet of the Russian Soviet Federated Socialist Republic and of the USSR, and was a member of the Communist party Central Committee. He had also carried out military-diplomatic instructions during the war. He had headed a military mission to Britain. And he had written several books and articles—memoirs of the Civil War and the Great Fatherland War.

I look at Filipp Ivanovich and I think, "Here he is going up to Stalin." But it is time to begin our talk.

From June 1940 onward the marshal was head of the Central Intelligence Directorate. This means that he must have been aware of any warnings that Germany was preparing for an attack on the Soviet Union.

I say to him: "There is much talk abroad about warnings received by the Soviet Union through various channels on preparations for an attack. One gets the impression that the first warning was around March 1941. What I have in mind is the report of U.S. Undersecretary of State Sumner Welles to Soviet Ambassador Konstantin Umansky. Is this the case?"

Filipp Ivanovich answers firmly and with conviction, "No, it is not. The first warnings came through Soviet military intelligence much earlier than March 1941. The Intelligence Directorate did enormous work in gathering and analyzing information received through various channels on the intentions of Nazi Germany, first and foremost against the Soviet Union. Along with compiling and analyzing voluminous data from agents, the directorate carefully studied international information, the world press, public opinion, military-political and technical information from Germany and other countries, and so on. Soviet military intelligence had reliable and verifiable sources for obtaining secret information in a number of countries, including Germany itself. Therefore the American report was not, or at any rate must not have been, news to the political and military leadership of the country, beginning with I. V. Stalin."

(Aha! This is indeed a most important statement. It seems that there *was* information. So, what was the problem then? I hasten to ask the marshal my next question: "What was Stalin's reaction to the intelligence information?"

Once again the marshal replies calmly: "My answer, more or less documented, can be given only as regards Soviet military intelligence." (Filipp Ivanovich is a very cautious person. What would entitle him to get involved in intelligence from the KGB, the Comintern, and other sources of information? But still, he would surely emphasize that the leader's opinion of information from any source was, apparently, the same as his own. But here is Golikov again.)

"Both the effectiveness and the final results of the work done by Soviet military intelligence (and apparently other types of intelligence as well), despite the seriousness and timeliness of the data submitted, were greatly compromised, first, by Stalin's conviction that all the assertions and data on preparations by the leadership of Nazi Germany for an attack on the USSR and on the imminence of such an attack were the expression and result of a well-planned and actively implemented political and military disinformation campaign carried out by British imperialists, personified by Churchill and British intelligence, so as to pit the USSR and Germany against each other in a major war for their own purposes; and second, a cautious attitude toward all intelligence data and acknowledgment only of those elements which to some extent or other might strengthen Stalin's erroneous assessments of the international military and political situation, along with a denial of anything that might not coincide with his concepts, especially as regards the reality of the German military threat and the growing possibility of invasion by the German army."

It was obvious that the marshal was well prepared for our talk. His phrasing was concise and extremely smooth. I would think back on that talk many times. I would also think about Soviet espionage agents—about

Ressler, Manevich, Rado, and Zorge. Were all their labors really an utter failure? Just the thought alone made me shudder.

As it turns out, Filipp Ivanovich has not yet finished answering this question. He gives a third reason: "the arbitrariness of the period of the Stalinist personality cult, and the groundless mistrust and massive destruction of the ranks of the party, government, and armed forces, including military intelligence." The marshal asserts that those imprisoned or killed were the "most valuable workers in military intelligence both from among the leading individuals at Center, and those abroad. Furthermore, it was a setback that many secret service agents were slandered, removed from intelligence work, and thrown out of intelligence agencies."

Golikov emphasizes that the work of military intelligence agents was greatly complicated by suspicion on the part of Stalin and his entourage. But the marshal does not clarify whom he has in mind specifically. For a moment I weigh the possibility of asking for clarification. But no, it's not worth it. I need to hear him out.

"This attitude," the marshal goes on, "was especially felt by those who had returned from abroad, particularly after performing intelligence work. They were met with suspicion. Obviously they were followed"—Obviously! But, Filipp Ivanovich, wasn't it you who . . . But these thoughts I keep to myself—"and frequently arrested without cause. Often they tried to slander good intelligence agents while still abroad. These conditions greatly hindered Soviet military intelligence."

Filipp Ivanovich sighs and looks at me expectantly.

I have another question. "A number of foreign books report the following incident: The GRU heads reported to Stalin information they had received giving a precise date for the supposed German attack on the Soviet Union. On reading this report, Stalin is said to have given orders more or less as follows: 'This is a provocation and disinformation. The person guilty is to be found and punished.' "

"I am not aware," Golikov responds, "of any such specific incident. Anyway the question you raise, as I see it, does not address the issue. The heart of the matter is Stalin's overall view of the reports from Soviet military intelligence, and I have told you about this. The question of whether a date was indicated for an attack of Nazi Germany on the Soviet Union is of essential interest from the following standpoint.

"As was discovered after the war, Hitler was repeatedly forced to change the dates we had learned of and which were reported by the higher authorities. He postponed them three times up until June 22.

"This greatly strengthened Stalin's position against intelligence reports and encouraged him to believe that he was right. It was not enough, as you said, that intelligence was giving disinformation and thereby adding grist to

Churchill's mill. It should be acknowledged by way of self-criticism that these postponements of the timetable for Germany's attack on the Soviet Union, Stalin's great self-assurance, and the force of his exclusive influence affected us and filled us with doubts, compelling us at times to interpret as British intrigues completely accurate data and information."

Later, several months would go by and someone, returning edited copy for *June 22, 1941*, would say, shaking his head mockingly: "Filipp Ivanovich is being clever. Oh, is he being clever. He himself, in fact, on submitting an intelligence report to Stalin on March 30, 1941, after giving most important information on Germany's forthcoming attack, wrote: 'It is not to be ruled out that all this information is disinformation and provocation on the part of British intelligence.' That's how things really went."

So that's what Golikov meant by Stalin's impact on the intelligence heads! They, like other high-ranking bureaucrats of the Soviet state, simply submitted to Stalin's moods and reasoning and presented matters to him in the way in which he preferred to see them.

It means that they sacrificed state interests to suit Stalin and to retain their own status. This idea troubled me for a long time and continues to do so to this very day. I can see the mountains of corpses, millions of them, soldiers who were killed in the Great Fatherland War, and I can hear Golikov's voice: "It should be acknowledged by way of self-criticism that . . ." and the voice of that other individual: "Filipp Ivanovich is being clever."

But then another idea occurs to me. What about now? Could it be that things are still the same? The system has not really changed, and consequently it could happen again. Information is screened, it goes through many filters, and then it is reported to the highest-ranking person in the country, the one whose voice will be decisive.

Hungary, 1956! Cuba, 1962! What was it like then? It seems clear that something was wrong with the information, or rather the manner in which and by whom it was reported—or perhaps both.

All these ideas disturb me even now.

But, let us return to that day at the end of September 1964. I am sitting in Marshal Golikov's office. In just twenty days, Khrushchev will be overthrown.

"Could it be said," I ask, "that Stalin simply disregarded intelligence data which did not fit in with the military-political scheme he had drawn up?"

"Yes, as far as I am concerned that was the case," Golikov replies. "Stalin held, as I have already said, that Britain was trying to provoke a war between Germany and the Soviet Union, wishing to use it [the war] for its own purposes. Considering himself to be an extremely skillful and clever politician, Stalin believed that, thanks to these talents of his, he would foil Britain's plans in August 1939 and thereby avoid war with Germany. Indeed, the Soviet Union's agreement with Germany in August 1939 was in our interests, and it upset the anti-Soviet plans of the governments of Britain, France, and the United States. However, Stalin continued later as well—in 1940 and 1941—to see the international situation through the same eyes. He clearly underestimated Nazi Germany as the main and decisive opponent of the USSR at the time, and overestimated in this regard the significance of the agreement reached with it in 1939.

"Before the Great Fatherland War," continues the marshal, "when the British government was headed by Churchill, a clever and very experienced politician, and an old enemy of the Soviet Union, Stalin, not realizing the new situation, regarded all warnings about preparations for an attack by Nazi Germany as nothing but British provocation. Believing that Churchill was trying to outsmart him, Stalin tried to outsmart Churchill. And it turned out that Stalin had outsmarted himself, thereby doing harm to the Soviet people, the state, and the Communist party of the Soviet Union."

"One gets the impression, I ask, "that toward the beginning of May 1941 Stalin's mood had changed somewhat. This is borne out in particular by his speech to graduates of the military academies on May 5, 1941, which, apparently, you heard yourself." Golikov nods in acknowledgment. "It also seems to me," I go on, "that Stalin's viewpoint was influenced significantly by Hess's flight to England. Is this your opinion?"

"It is possible that after that event Stalin began to take a more careful view of intelligence information, but this did not alter the essence of his position. It is enough to recall the contents of the TASS statement made a week before the invasion of the Soviet Union by Nazi Germany and the harm done by this statement from Stalin to the Soviet people."

I ask the marshal a number of other questions for clarification. Golikov points out that the plans for the strategic emplacement of Nazi Germany's armed forces were submitted by him to the political and military leadership of the Soviet Union no later than March 1941—almost three months before the attack. I try over and over to clarify this most important issue.

"What was Stalin's reaction to the first reports of preparations for an attack?"

"Negative. He did not believe it."

"At about what time did you, as GRU chief, no longer have any doubts that the Germans were preparing to attack?"

"I should think as far back as before the end of 1940.

I return home and pace fretfully and somewhat aimlessly around the apartment. There is one idea that I can't get out of my mind: If Golikov is telling the truth about having no doubts about a German attack as far back as 1940, then how could he not dare insist on this, not shout, yell, knock at every door? And suddenly another chilling thought: What difference would it have made? Who was there to complain to? What could anyone expect? The totalitarian system is merciless and destructive, even of itself. Like Uranus, it devours its sons, even the best of them, suppresses wonderful ideas, kills noble impulses, stifles initiative. Stalin and Golikov and the rest—all of them were slaves to this terrible system. They could not exist without it nor it without them, for they were part and parcel of it. And we are all elements of this system and serve it daily, each of us at our respective posts and in our own way. Someone will play at Stalin on a lesser scale; someone else will be a Golikov. Only soldiers in the field of battle are not playing; they fight and defeat the enemy or are themselves defeated, and then they die, or they are captured, only to die out there, in POW camps, or upon their return home, somewhere in Kolyma.

Eventually I get hold of myself and sit down at my desk. I need to draw up an account of the talk as soon as possible, send it to Filipp Ivanovich for review, and then summon up my patience and wait. And wait I do, until March 12, 1965, when Golikov signs the interview in my presence and his adjutant authenticates it with a stamp. At last this document belongs not to Golikov or myself but to history and will lead a life of its own.

But the life of that document begins with the special censor eliminating it almost entirely from my book, which finally comes out in September 1965. Despite the efforts of five censors, there are still a few bits and pieces left from the Golikov interview. Now, eleven years later, I still believe that the document will come to life again and see the light of day. I know it.

After my meeting with Golikov the manuscript was sent to the KGB. Fortunately I still have their reaction in my possession, and I can be extremely accurate in describing their comments. I still have my letter to the publisher in connection with the KGB comments as well. The KGB reaction states: "In our opinion, the author has not been able to give a correct analysis of some of the most important events of that period, inasmuch as they are considered and evaluated subjectively in a number of cases."

The KGB's overall argument was extremely weak, and therefore they resorted to the tried-and-true method of accusing the author of disregarding Soviet sources while using bourgeois ones extensively. The review states:

> In portraying the foreign and domestic policy of our country during the period after V. I. Lenin's death, the author has not made a single reference to decisions of the relevant Communist party congresses or to decrees of the Soviet government, but has meanwhile filled many pages with statements made by Hitler, Mussolini, Horthy, Antonescu, Ribbentrop, Hess, Matsuoka, the former German ambassador in Moscow Schulenburg, and others, as well as [*caveat* reader!] with excerpts from books by Soviet authors, basically from

the period when a subjective approach to the history of the Soviet people had become fashionable among some.

In this way, the first thing the KGB reviewer tried to do was to delete everything accomplished by Soviet historical scholarship, literature, and memoirs over the post-Stalinist decade. Fortunately, facts can't be erased from history. The KGB rejected information reported to the author by Marshal Golikov and others, on the grounds that "these are subjective impressions and cannot serve as a basis for scientific conclusions." The KGB would have been right, had the interviews been my sole source of information; but in actual fact (and the KGB was silent on this) the interviews were only one of many sources.

The KGB's specific comments should be of great interest to the reader, as they are to me.

But first I should explain—and this is an extremely curious story—that during the Second World War in Germany, there existed a Soviet intelligence organization closely linked to the German resistance movement. The activities of this organization, known as the "Red Choir," have been described in many books. Its leader, Garro Schultze-Boisen, and most of the members of the group were finally seized by the Gestapo and executed. At about the time my manuscript was sent for KGB censorship, accounts of Red Choir activities were highly valued in official Soviet publications. I should add that over the past ten years the Red Choir had become a textbook case in subversive activities against the Hitler regime. A month before my manuscript went to the KGB, in May 1965, the journal *Novoye vremya* had published an interview with a surviving member of the Red Choir, Greta Kunhof. In the German Democratic Republic, members of the Red Choir were included among the national heroes of the German people. At any rate, in the KGB review I was surprised to read the following: "On pp. 123–127 the author states that the anti-Fascist organization known as 'Red Choir' transmitted some important information to Moscow revealing the schemes of Hitler's Germany. *Since the activities of this organization involve much that is unclear and doubtful, it is hardly appropriate to refer to it, especially as a source of important information.*"(emphasis added).

On reading these lines, I was astounded and puzzled. If the KGB held such an opinion of Red Choir activities, then why was the Red Choir glorified in all the Soviet and Eastern European publications on the resistance movement and the activities of the Soviet spy network in Europe during the war? What really did happen?

Later on I learned one version of the story of the Red Choir. I cannot attest to its veracity, but the KGB's demand that I delete any reference to that organization disturbed me, and to this day I would not venture to give a definitive answer to those questions that arose. It was claimed (and I am told that this was precisely the basis for the KGB reviewer's comment) that the Red Choir possessed a low-power radio transmitter that was nonetheless powerful enough so that the coded information sent out by Schultze-Boisen and others at the risk of their lives might reach and be gathered by the USSR's special German interception service, located in East Prussia. But the signals were not strong enough for this information to be received by Moscow Center. If this version is authentic, then we are faced with one of the greatest tragedies involving an underground organization during the Second World War.

So what really did happen? This question is still waiting to be answered.

In any event, the KGB demanded the deletion from the text of my book of a statement that "an analysis unit of the border forces' Main Command drew up a diagram of enemy agent movements on the eve of the war based on border reports," and that a comparison of that diagram with other data inevitably leads one to discover the main route for the supposed German army strike.

The KGB review concluded: "In view of the above, we believe that it would not be advisable to publish A. M. Nekrich's *June 22, 1941* in its current form."

Previously such a reaction from the Committee for State Security would have meant a death sentence for the book. But times had changed a great deal since Stalin's death. Tremendous domestic evolution had taken place over the intervening twelve years. The KGB had lost to a significant extent the influence it had enjoyed in days gone by. The committee's view was no longer binding on publishers. In this case it could be disputed. Theirs was merely one of several views. But it was not impossible that this freedom was a temporary phenomenon.

After reading the KGB report, I decided to counter it immediately. In a letter to the "Nauka" publishers dated July 5, 1965, I discussed all the KGB's specific comments in detail, and showed them to be invalid and in contradiction with the opinions of other competent reviewers.

At approximately that time I was summoned to the Central Intelligence Directorate of the Soviet army, where I received a number of concrete criticisms. I heaved a sigh of relief: the comments were not on essential points. As a result, I was highly indignant when the corrected version returned from the GRU with entire pages from my interview with Marshal Golikov crossed out in red pencil. There was nothing to be done. I had to agree to the changes quickly in order to speed up the book's publication as much as possible. I had the feeling, especially after the solemn celebration of the twentieth anniversary of the end of the war, that the situation was taking a turn for the worse, even though existing guidelines had not yet been changed officially. Furthermore, my experience with the article in *Mezhdunarodnaya zhizn'* suggested that a race against time had begun, and that I could easily lose the contest.

Therefore, a few days later I sent another letter to the "Nauka" publishers, in which I reported that I had made corrections and additions following the comments made by the military censor and the Committee for State Security.

The moment of truth had arrived. Would the KGB want to look at the manuscript again, or would it be satisfied with a report from the publisher to the effect that the comments had been acknowledged and the manuscript corrected? A phone call was made to the committee. I was in luck. The KGB would not demand to see the manuscript for a second review (in other words, it did not wish to take responsibility); it found the publisher's report satisfactory. But then another set of proofs came back from the Ministry of Foreign Affairs. Something else had to be deleted. I agreed unconditionally: time won't wait! Then a final phone call, just to make sure, to the science division of the Communist party Central Committee, and the manuscript was sent off to Glavlit for final approval. At last it was ready for printing. I left for the Crimea to wait for the book to come out.

While work was still under way on the manuscript at the publisher's, however, another purely technical difficulty arose unexpectedly: all the printing presses at "Nauka" were working at full capacity, and the manuscript could go to press only toward the end of the year. I broke out in a cold sweat. What if some political changes should take place by then? You can just imagine what that would have meant. I came to an agreement with the production division that I should find another printer. And I knew just where to look. My very good friend from the front Aron Ainbinder was director of printing facilities for the Committee of Labor Force Reserves. I knew that they worked on a self-financing basis and took outside orders. Aron agreed to take on my manuscript, and this, in the final analysis, saved the book. I bombarded Aron with telephone calls from the Crimea: "When? When? Faster! Faster!" I could not explain to him all the difficulties involved, nor did I wish to. Time was of the essence.

At last, the book came out. I received the first fifty copies directly from the printer and handed them out as gifts. Then I bought more and more, while ot was still possible to do so, before the book was sent to the warehouse for distribution and sale.

Finally, in October 1965, the book appeared in the stores. In three days fifty thousand copies were bought up. Initially "Nauka" wanted to print eighty thousand copies, but then the publishing house decided to reduce the number, just in case. Letters and telephone calls started to come in from Moscow, Leningrad, Kiev, from the remote provinces, from the Arctic Circle, all begging, pleading for the book to be sent, for it could not otherwise be obtained. I bought some myself and sent them to a few very kind strangers. I handed out and mailed out six hundred copies, leaving myself with only fifteen. I began to hide them in various treasure troves around the apartment so that friends might not take copies away by mistake.

The initial reaction to the book was an enthusiastic one. I was congratulated. Friends and strangers came up to me in the corridors of the institute, shook my hand, asked me to autograph the book. The foreign media broadcast reports about the book abroad. Translations were begun in Poland, Czechoslovakia, and Hungary. In Yugoslavia *Borba* printed excerpts from the book in a few of its issues. *June 22, 1941* was sent out into the world to begin its life apart from the author. But the life of its author was getting a bit complicated. The book was receiving praise, but not one professional journal was willing to publish a review of it. Only *Novy mir* responded to the call. The editor in chief,. A. T. Tvardovsky, had read the book and liked it very much. A long review by G. B. Fedorov appeared in the January 1966 issue of the journal. Then, quite unexpectedly, the newspaper *Komsomolets tadzhikistana* somewhere in Dushanbe ran a full-column article by A. Vakhrameev entitled "Facing the Truth." And that was the end of it. The newspapers and magazines in the Soviet Union maintained a friendly silence about the book. But it still was making headway. I was invited to speak at the M. V. Frunze Military Academy. This is what the newspaper *Frunzevets*, the official journal of the military academy, had to say in its issue of January 22, 1966:

> A regular meeting of the academy's military history and military science department was devoted to a discussion of the book by Doctor of Historical Sciences Comrade A. Nekrich entitled *June 22, 1941* and led to a lively discussion of Fascist Germany's preparations for and unleashing of war against the Soviet Union.
>
> The author of the book spoke at the meeting. He told those present about the plans for Hitler's aggression against the USSR and our country's preparations for repelling the enemy.
>
> The audience gave its views on the issues under discussion . . . All the statements were in the nature of a debate. This exercise aroused great interest among members of the Military Studies Society and, no doubt, was useful to them.

My statement at the academy caused a commotion in the main political directorate of the Soviet army, whose leadership, especially the deputy head, Colonel General M. Kalashnik, was extremely hostile to my book. But among the military there were others who reacted differently. My long-time friend Alyosha Radus-Zenkovich, a lieutenant general in the engineering corps, and chairman of the tank research committee of the Ministry of Defense, told me:

"You know, your book was a great help to me. I thought about my plan of action and decided to make some changes."

I did not ask Alyosha about the details, of course. It would not have been proper, and it was none of my business. But I did have a feeling of satisfaction: my book was of practical use to the military. By and large, when I talked with military men on a one-on-one basis, with no one else present and without fear of being overheard, some of them were extremely critical of the way things were being done, especially for purposes of show; they offered various details on the preparations for war in 1941 and cursed the incompetence of the leadership.

Ah, Alyosha, Alyosha. Two years ago he died suddenly of a heart attack: he sank into a chair, let out a sigh, and was gone. He had recently retired and was working at the time as a deputy director for one of the military institutes.

Soon after my expulsion from the party, Alyosha stopped seeing me or taking my phone calls. I understood that he wished to end our relationship. I heard nothing about him for several years, and then I learned that he had died. Shortly after I was expelled from the party, he had been called in by the bosses and warned to stop associating with me. It is said that he was very upset about it, but of course he complied.

In the meantime, a full-scale attack on my book was being prepared. Once I happened to get hold of a document, from which I learned that the publications committee of the USSR Council of Ministers had asked a number of organizations and individuals their views on the book. The responses the committee received were positive. But this did not suit the committee: it needed negative responses. They asked for the opinion of the division of the history of the Great Fatherland War of the Institute of Marxism-Leninism as well. This was the answer:

January 2, 1966

Chief Editor for Socio-Political Literature
Publications Committee
USSR Council of Ministers

Comrade A. S. Makhov:

At your request A. M. Nekrich's book *June 22, 1941* ("Nauka" publishers, 1965) was discussed by a group of research staff from volume 1 of *A History of the Great Fatherland War* (headed by Doctor of Economic Sciences Professor G. A. Deborin). Below is a summary of the main comments made by our comrades. . . .

The confidential reaction to the book was, on the whole, a positive one. . . .

In conclusion I should state that, bearing in mind the exceptional interest in A. M. Nekrich's book, we agreed with the author to conduct a discussion of it in the division of the history of the Great Fatherland War, which we propose to hold in February of this year.

Division Head
Ye. Boltin

In December 1965 the head of that division, Major General Boltin, with whom I had worked on the tenth volume of *World History*, told me when we met at the Institute of History: "Aleksandr Moiseevich, we wish to discuss your book in our division. Do you have any objections?" Naturally I agreed. The discussion was scheduled for February 16, 1966.

The widespread reaction to the book was borne out by an invitation I received from the social sciences section of the presidium of the Academy of Sciences to deliver a paper in connection with the twenty-fifth anniversary of the attack by Nazi Germany on the Soviet Union. In that paper I repeated the basic theses of my book and emphasized the fact that the difficulties our country experienced as a result of the German invasion were largely due to Stalin's unlimited dictatorship.

I said: "The main reasons for the difficult situation prevailing just before the war, its root causes, were that all decisions were made by one person. It would be justifiable to say that unlimited power leads to unlimited mistakes."

Every ruler of the USSR, and not only Stalin, has strived for unlimited power: this was finally the case with Khrushchev not long before his overthrow, and this may be the case with Brezhnev. Evidently, it is a trait not only of the individual but also, primarily, of the system which constantly gives birth to Stalins large and small.

On February 16, 1966, at the Central Committee Institute of Marxism-Leninism, a discussion of my book took place. In January I had already heard rumors that a major attack was being mounted against my book: Stalinist-minded historians, with the support of the Soviet army's central political office, the publications committee of the Council of Ministers, and the science department and propaganda department of the Central Committee, were preparing a broad campaign to destroy my book. Quite naturally I was concerned. It seemed to me that an objective discussion of the book could be conducted only if the largest possible number of people were in attendance. The most important thing, I kept repeating to myself, to my friends, and to my colleagues at the institute, was openness. Evil deeds are carried out in silence, in darkness, or with half-suppressed publicity. Openness, the clear light of day, even simple light, while it may not kill evil, intrigues, and other abominations, may at least put a stop to them or at the very worst mitigate them.

Therefore I asked everyone to spread the word as much as possible about the upcoming discussion of the book and invited all those who wanted to participate in it, or just wantd to be there. Then I phoned the Institute of Marxism-Leninism and obtained their agreement to the presence of those of my colleagues who might wish to attend.

The discussion began in a small room, but so many would-be participants arrived that it became necessary to transfer the meeting to a conference hall. About 200 to 250 people attended. It was a large and representative gathering. In addition to officials from the Institute of Marxism-Leninism and the Institute of History, there were officials from other academic institutes, a large group of military, old Bolsheviks, a few participants in the democratic movement, including Ilya Gabay and Lenya Petrovsky, as well as mere curiosity seekers.

The presiding officer, Major General Boltin, began his introductory remarks: "Quite frankly, we did not think that this discussion would become such a broad public event. News of the scheduled discussion reached the Institute of History and other academic institutions in Moscow. We, of course, did not wish to prevent anyone from coming here."

Boltin stated from the outset that the organizers of the meeting had not intended to set up a "rout" of the book. This was an important statement which paved the way for a free discussion. Moreover, the need for such a statement was obvious and testified to the fact that such intentions were not far from the minds of some of the participants in the meeting. But a certain mood in the audience forced them to change tactics and withdraw.

The main report was delivered by Professor G. A. Deborin. Deborin aimed his critical fire at the third chapter of the book. He semed to feel a particular annoyance over the title of the chapter "The Warnings Which Were Ignored." Indeed, such wording was, to put it mildly, unusual. The very title stated outright that the Soviet leadership had disregarded timely information it had received on the forthcoming attack by Germany. Deborin attempted to shift responsibility to the Central Intelligence Directorate of the General Staff and on its head, Marshal Golikov, personally, and blamed the inaccurate evaluation of Germany's military-economic potential made by the Institute for World Economy and World Policy. Deborin's appeal to delve more deeply into a criticism of the personality cult virtually amounted to diverting attention from the leadership and shifting responsibility to lower-ranking individuals.

The usual official Soviet interpretation of the German-Soviet pact of August 23, 1939, was that it had been a very clever maneuver, given the specific historical circumstances. But in my book I pointed out for the first time in Soviet literature that the treaty primarily worked to the advantage of Nazi Germany. Deborin remarked in this regard: "The reason for Germany's proposing a nonaggression treaty to the USSR is presented in such a way that an aspersion is cast on the subsequent conclusion of this treaty by the Soviet Union."

Such a statement, under the circumstances, would have seemed a very serious political accusation with regard to a most acute and sensitive issue in the eyes of the Soviet leadership.

Deborin's criticism of the way in which I interpreted Stalin's annihilation of the most talented military figures—Tukhachevsky, Yakir, and others—in 1937 caused an outburst of indignation in the hall.

Let us turn to the verbatim record:

> *Deborin*: The author claims that "those who gave the order for their arrest must have known that the accusations were groundless and the documents a fabrication." The text as it stands contains an accusation of *deliberate* condemnation of innocent people, leveled at the judicial board. Yet it included the most upright people, known for their forthrightness and integrity. They had been misled.
>
> [*A voice from the audience: "The board was guided by statements prepared in advance."*]
>
> *Deborin*: . . . The objection just given here is incorrect. It should never be thought that participants in a trial . . .
>
> [*From the audience: "They knew, they knew!"*]
>
> *Deborin*: . . . that supposedly they knew that the accusations were groundless and the documents fabricated.
>
> [*From the audience: "Who gave the orders?"*]
>
> *Deborin*: . . . I mention this because it involves the honor of Blucher, and of Budyenny, who were part of the judicial board, as well as of its other members: Shaposhnikov, Belov, Dybenko, Kashirin, and Goryachev.
>
> [*From the audience: "They're all hangmen!"*]

Deborin's report, and especially this final comment, immediately created tension in the hall, and the presiding officer, Boltin, asked that the discussion not be turned into a shouting match.

The next speaker was Colonel Anfilov. In response to Deborin, who had defended "the honor of Voroshilov and Budyenny," he said of Voroshilov, " I feel my heart bleeding when he stands on the dais of Lenin's mausoleum."

Twenty-two people spoke at the discussion in all, and twenty-one of them gave *June 22, 1941* a generally positive evaluation. Many insisted on a more comprehensive analysis, and brought in some very interesting and important facts, while they corrected and supplemented my own.

But it was not simply an occasion for discussing the book. This was virtually an analysis of Soviet policy, and of the military unpreparedness of the Soviet Union on the eve of the attack by Nazi Germany. This was a critique of the functioning of the Soviet system in both normal and exceptional circumstances, and of its political and military leaders.

There were dramatic confrontations during the discussion, including one between Deborin and A. V. Snegov, an old communist who had spent twenty years of his life in Stalin's prisons. Deborin advised Snegov to think about "which camp" he was in (meaning whose side he was on), and Snegov retorted: "I am from the Kolyma camp!" Voices from the audience cried out: "This is a disgrace! This is a disgrace!"

At noontime a break was announced, during which events occurred that further oppressed the atmosphere of the discussion, making it even more tense. This was partly due to Snegov's reaction and the sharp tone used by Deborin and Boltin at the end of the meeting.

Among those present at the discussion was Colonel Andrei Sverdlov, a staff researcher at the Institute of Marxism-Leninism. Who was this Sverdlov? He was the son of Yakov Mikhailovich Sverdlov, a companion of Lenin's and chairman of the All-Union Central Executive Committee of the RSFSR. Practically from nearly the age of twenty, the younger Sverdlov had worked in the state security organs and had been guilty of torturing and killing innocent people. He had been a member of Beria's entourage. After the death of Stalin and the ouster of Beria, Sverdlov, instead of being brought to trial for his crimes, was sent by the Central Committee to the Institute of Marxism-Leninism, where evidently his practical experience was to be put to some use.

And so this same Colonel Sverdlov was at the discussion. During the break he wrote a denunciation to the Central Committee, which began: "As I write this letter, an anti-Soviet mob is gathered at the Institute of Marxism-Leninism." Sverdlov further described in dramatic tones the discussion which had taken place—as he saw it, of course. After writing the denunciation, Sverdlov showed it to Boltin, who was, quite naturally, upset. When the meeting resumed, Boltin said to me (we were sitting side by side on the rostrum): "You should rebut Snegov's statement."

"Why? Everyone expresses his point of view freely here. And Snegov has done the same."

"Aleksandr Moiseevich, you must absolutely disassociate yourself from Snegov's statement. Say something like you don't need to be defended this way. It is in your interest, I can assure you."

"No, I will not do that."

Boltin did not reveal to me the intricacies of the matter, but I had the feeling that something unpleasant was about to happen. Therefore, in order to create a more relaxed atmosphere, and to prevent the Stalinists from taking advantage of the discussion, I began my statement on a conciliatory note (although some of my friends later criticized me mercilessly for this). But I was thinking not at all about myself but about those who had spoken in the discussion, for I had already made my choice.

I began my concluding remarks:

> First of all, I believe it my duty to say that the discussion organized by the department of the history of the Great Fatherland War of the Institute of Marxism-Leninism has been a truly scholarly one, whereby each and every one of us has been able to express his point of view. And the heated exchange which we saw at the end of the meeting, I believe, was not inevitable. Far be it from me to think that G. A. Deborin, who spoke on behalf of the editorial board of volume 1, has tried to repudiate my book. I hope that he had purely scholarly objectives. This is how the issue has been dealt with during the discussion.

With all its drawbacks, the discussion was surely a victory for the progressive movement in historical scholarship. And this victory demonstrated that the study of history in the USSR was making progress, in spite of all the obstacles, that historians were demanding to be given the opportunity of working with primary source materials, and that a broad exchange of views without fear of the consequences should accompany their work. But the most important point was that in spite of all the uncertainties and reservations and so on, historians were realizing that the main reason for our unpreparedness for the war was the system of unlimited arbitrary power.

A few days after the discussion at the institute a summary record began to circulate by hand, and some time later still that record was published abroad.

The discussion caused a commotion in the central political office of the Soviet army and in the science and propaganda departments of the Central Committee. The central political office was upset by the fact that high-ranking officers had taken part in the discussion, and that their statements had sounded so critical. Immediately afterwards there began a systematic persecution of them, which was to last several years.

The authorities also began to put pressure on me. Once again it was initiated by the publications committee, which tried to engage in reprisals against me through the presidium of the Academy of Sciences. In this connection I sent out the following letter:

June 21, 1966

Academician M. D. Millionshchikov
Chairman of the Editorial Executive Board

Presidium of the USSR Acadamy of Sciences

Most respected Mikhail Dmitrievich:

In a letter to the president of the Academy of Sciences, Academician M. V. Keldysh, written May 19 of this year, the chairman of the publications committee, N. Mikhailov, grossly distorted the facts as they pertain to my book *June 22, 1941*, published by the "Nauka" publishing house in 1965.

N. Mikhailov alleges that the "book aroused a protest from many officers and generals, as reported in the newspaper *Krasnaya zvezda*."

Actually the newspaper *Krasnaya zvezda* has never published any article about my book. N. N. Mikhailov was simply misleading Academician M. V. Keldysh. But by falsifying facts outright, he further demonstrated his biased view of my book, against which the publications committee, of which he is head, was waging an organized campaign of slander.

As far as the press and the public were concerned, their reaction was exactly the opposite of what Mikhailov wished to achieve.

A positive evaluation of my book was given in reviews published in the journal *Novy mir* (no.1, 1966: Doctor of Historical Sciences G. B. Fedorov, "The Measure of Responsibility") and in the newspaper *Komsomolets tadzhikistana* (January 9, 1966: A. Vakhrameev, "Facing the Truth"), and also at a public discussion sponsored by the publications committee at the Institute of Marxism-Leninism of the Communist party Central Committee on February 16, 1966. Twenty-two well-known Soviet civilian and military historians of the Great Fatherland War and the Second World War took part in the discussion. As many as two hundred people took part in all.

The book was also warmly received by the press in socialist countries, where reviews and lengthy excerpts have been published. Translations of *June 22, 1941* are currently under way in Poland, Czechoslovakia, and Hungary.

Finally, letters received by the author and by the "Nauka" publishing house from readers testify as well to the favorable public reaction to the appearance of *June 22, 1941*.

One could cite many examples of letters from readers, but I shall limit myself to just one: the writer K. Simonov sent his expression of gratitude to the author "for an important and honest book on a most difficult subject."

These are the facts.

As regards N. N. Mikhailov's statement about my book, I should like to draw your attention to the campaign senior officials of the publications committee have been waging against the book and its author for some months now. Moreover, the methods resorted to bring to mind the notorious times of the personality cult. Here are a few examples.

The committee ordered private reviews (that is, safeguarding their anonymity) from academic institutions and private individuals. The results were disappointing, however, to the "customer," since the majority of the reviews were positive, and therefore the attempt to subject the book to destruction "on behalf of public opinion" was undermined. The discussion of the book at the Institute of Marxism-Leninism also turned out to be unfavorable to those few individuals from the publications committee. Next, a campaign against the book was begun through administrative and propagandistic channels. Making use of its administrative status, the committee heads made statements at various meetings slandering the book and its author.

Here the committee staff achieved some "successes": a number of journals which had intended to publish favorable reviews of the book were forced to renounce their intentions (*Nauka i zhizn'*, *Novaya i noveishaya istoria*). There are other similar facts.

It is not impossible, of course, that the committee will manage finally to "obtain" a negative review somewhere. For the pressure is enormous. ...

In conclusion, I should also like to state the following: the recently published issue of the *Military History Journal* (no.6, 1966) contains an article by the first deputy minister of defense, Marshal Grechko, on the twenty-fifth anniversary of the German attack on the Soviet Union (it is published in a somewhat abridged version in the journal *Novoye vremya* no.25, June 17 of this year). The general contents and main conclusions in that article fully coincide with the interpretation of events and the conclusions of the author of the book *June 22, 1941*. Will the Publications Committee decide to accuse Marshal Grechko too of "tendentiousness and one-sidedness"?

Respectfully,
Doctor of Historical Sciences
Senior Research Fellow of the Institute of History
USSR Academy of Sciences

A. M. Nekrich

In February of 1966 two writers were put on trial in Moscow—A. D. Sinyavsky and Yu. Daniel. Both of them had published their works abroad under a pseudonym. They were accused of allegedly advocating the overthrow of Soviet power in their works. The word was out in Soviet jurisprudence that the men accused were to be identified by the court with the characters in their books. Thus, expressions and intentions of their fictional heroes were attributed to the accused. This is the level of justice in our country. A noteworthy feature of the trial was the fact that one witness for the prosecution was Z. Kedrina, who attempted to demonstrate the guilt of the defendants by reading excerpts from their literary works.

Many Moscow intellectuals were furious over the trial, but many were also furious with Sinyavsky and Daniel for writing under a pseudonym rather than in their own names. The pettiness and dishonesty of these views were immediately obvious: whether to publish under one's own name or under a pseudonym—is this not a writer's personal prerogative? Actually there had always been a tradition in Russia of writing under a pseudonym. No one, for example, would even dream of reproaching V. I. Ulyanov for choosing as his literary pseudonym "N. Lenin"! Scriabin chose "Molotov" as his pseudonym. Bronshtein became "Trotsky" and Dzhugashvili "Stalin." There are numerous cases of political figures from the opposition, and not only writers, who preferred not to speak out under their own names but use a pseudonym instead.

The trials of Sinyavsky and Daniel marked the transition from Khrushchev's anti-Stalinism to Brezhnev's conformism. Very soon, quite literally in the several months following the trial, we could feel a sudden deterioration in the political situation of the country. I was one of those who experienced this firsthand. But there were still a few months remaining before the next stage of my worries.

Meanwhile, Nadya, my future wife, and I went to Lithuania, to beautiful Lake Dubiangai and spent our unofficial honeymoon there. We were married half a year later at the height of the storm which had broken out around me.

Let us turn back, however, for the "Nekrich affair" is impossible to understand properly without knowing what was happening during those years at the Institute of History of the USSR Academy of Sciences.

On October 14, 1964, I went with a tour group from our institute to Finland for nine days. Khrushchev's ouster found us in Helsinki. A curious incident occurred there. A correspondent from a Helsinki newspaper asked one of my colleagues, "Have you heard about the removal of Khrushchev?"

"No," he replied.

"But what do you think about it?"

"It is none of our business!" snapped my colleague.

The reply was, of course, amazing, but it embodied the quintessence of the behavior of *Homo sovieticus*, who, more than anyone else in the world, is afraid of ending up on the pages of a foreign newspaper. At the very least, he could be forbidden to take any further trips abroad.

On returning from Finland, I found that I had been elected in absentia to the party committee of the institute, although I had been last or next to last in number of votes among those who won. Subsequently, I was reelected in 1965 and 1966. So it was that I served as a member of the party committee for three years—difficult ones both for the institute and for me personally. The 1964 party committee was elected just after the change in party leadership, and the instability of the overall situation had an impact on the committee's membership as well. It contained, like Noah's ark, every type of animal, two by two—progressives and Stalinists and those who belonged to their own party (that is, those who were simply using their status as committee member to further their careers). Elected secretary was Yelena Golubtsova, an obliging woman, ready to do the bidding of the higher ups and very dependent on the director of the institute, Vladimir Mikhailovich Khvostov. Khvostov was a very dry, authoritative man, but also intelligent, educated, and ambitious.

Late in 1964 and throughout 1965 we were still living in a Khrushchevian world, and the legacy we had inherited from the Twentieth and later the Twenty-Second Party Congress had not yet lost its force. The party organization, which consisted of approximately three hundred members, was overwhelmingly anti-Stalinist, but the division was gradually growing clearer. Those scholars who had tried to depart from dogmatism and conformism, and to rethink the history of our country from a more realistic and objective standpoint, enjoyed considerable influence at the time. More and more attention was being paid to problems of historical methodology, new research methods, and changing trends in historical scholarship. At the institute a regular study seminar began to meet, specializing in problems of methodology. Here reports were given and discussions held by what I would say were the most capable researchers in the social sciences, both in our institute and elsewhere. The section and the seminar were virtually run by an extremely original historian, a pupil of A. L. Sidorov, Mikhail Yakovlevich Gefter, whom some called, perhaps only half-jokingly, the "idea machine". He was a complex person, and his life had not been simple. But in the final analysis in the 1960s and 1970s he had shown himself to be not only a gifted historian but also a man with clear-cut anti-Stalinist views. Gefter was a confirmed Marxist, pensive and profound. He attempted to rediscover Lenin, to purify Leninism, or at any rate the methodological basis for understanding the historical process of the features and myths which were later vulgarized. Gefter and several other professionals in the social sciences who attended his seminar sincerely wished to improve Marxism, to reach a correct understanding of it, and to continue to develop Leninism as it applied to our time.

My own view of these improvers (as they were ironically called) was ambivalent. On the one hand, I was becoming increasingly firm in my conviction that there was no point in attempting to improve Marxism. It was tantamount to pouring new wine into old botles. In discussing this issue with friends from among the improvers, I based my point of view on the fact that Marxist theory's claim to universality had turned out to be historically invalid. I recognized Marxism to be one of the possible and even necessary methods for studying and analyzing historical phenomena, but only in conjunction with other methods.

The history of Soviet society, and the history of the establishment of similar societies in other countries where the Communist party had taken power, had shown that the liberation from exploitation by private enterprise proclaimed by Marxism had become in practice a still more brutal exploitation of the working classes by the state, which played the part of sole employer. This seems to me the essence of the problem of socialist society. The individual's dependence on the state for virtually everything—employment, ideas, education, a strictly regimented life-style, even matters of personal life—had become total. In this sense it was absolutely correct to call the Soviet Union a socialist-type totalitarian state. In theory a socialist society did indeed appear to be the ideal. It is therefore understandable that very many honest, selfless people joined the Russian revolutionary movement, fought for the Revolution, in its own name, while sometimes not even noticing that what was under way was a transformation not only of society and state but also of something that had begun as an unnoticeable but gradually became a more tangible transformation of the idea for which they were fighting, all that was left of the idea being an empty shell, slogans, camouflage. But most important, there had occurred a significant but alas irreversible change in themselves. Distracted by the idea of a revolutionary transformation of the world, they gradually lost natural and necessary human characteristics: tolerance, friendship, love, a feeling of human and not just proletarian generosity. The normal criteria for human interaction—forthrightness, sincerity, honesty—began to be seen only as they applied to class distinctions: one should be forthright, but only as regards the working class; honest, but only as regards the Communist party. Everything good for the party was good for you. Here you had to be sincere, honest, dedicated, prepared to carry out any—I emphasize *any*—party task. And we know about the River of Blood that flowed from this blind, zealous faith, this denial of the simple rules of human interaction practiced over centuries.

Anatole France, with his deeply penetrating instinct as an artist, was a genius at grasping the essence of the matter. In his novel *Les dieux ont soif,* he drew a very realistic psychological portrait of the prosecutor Evariste Gamelain, who turned from an idealist into a bloody monster, sending dozens and dozens of innocent people to the guillotine. The Russian Revolution engendered hundreds of such Evaristes, perhaps even thousands. They rose up, destroyed others, and then the River of Blood swept them away as well.

This is why, when I am told that it is possible to improve Marxism, possible to purify Leninism, I answer "No!"

No, because behind Marxism-Leninism lies a cult of violence, an acknowledgment of violence as the primary and necessary element for restructuring societty.

No, because in the Soviet Union, Marxism-Leninism in practice has led to the destruction of society as a self-regulating organism, subjected it to the state, and then dissolved society into the state.

No, because the basis of a socialist state-society is the recognition of only one single idea as right and just.

No, because recognition only of the communist idea as right and just is not the free choice of each individual but an obligation. Conformism in society is enshrined in the state constitution. Going beyond communist conformism is a crime.

No, because Soviet conformism gave rise to hypocrisy and cruelty in society, permeating it from top to bottom.

No, because the rights of the minority are not protected by law.

No, because those many millions of victims, created for the sake of the idea of Marxism-Leninism, cannot be justified by any idea whatsoever.

No, because all these victims serve in the final analysis the party and state elite for the sake of their own power and their petty personal interests.

This is why I considered, and continue to consider, that those who sincerely believe in the possibility of improving Marxism are simply fooling themselves.

In those post-Stalinist years there were quite a few young people who were extremely critical of the realities of our life and who expressed their anger with all the intensity of youth. Some of them established circles where they discussed vital social problems, while others tried to put their ideas down on paper, wrote pamphlets, new "histories of the Communist party." The majority of them later ended up in labor camps and returned cowed into submission. But this was not the case with all of them.

Soon after the election in the autumn of 1964 of a new party committee, the so-called Puzyrev affair arose.

Oleg Puzyrev was a complex man. In childhood he had survived two terrible diseases—polio and meningitis. He moved painfully slowly, on crutches, but his physical tortures apparently made his mind sharp. Those who were close to him said that Puzyrev was a man of exceptional intelligence and of impeccable honor. He had graduated from the Historical Archive

Institute in Moscow. His degree thesis was devoted to the partisans in the area around Moscow during the Great Fatherland War. This work was not only original but explosive. Puzyrev established that an individual who was normally thought to have been one of the leaders of the Moscow partisans was actually a provocateur collaborating with the Germans. Puzyrev's conclusions were irreproachable from the standpoint of logic but totally inconclusive from a legal point of view.

At a theoretical seminar in 1961 during the height of an anti-Semitic campaign, Puzyrev spoke out in defense of Stalin. On entering the Institute of History, Puzyrev immediately chose a dissertation topic. His academic adviser was one of the most gifted modern historians in the USSR, Yury Vartanovich Arutyunyan. Puzyrev became close with Pyotr Yakir, who was working at the Institute of History at the time, and with an able young historian by the name of Makarov, a friend of Yakir's, who later transferred from the institute to work at the Committee for State Security. To fill out my psychological portrait of Puzyrev, I should mention one curious incident: once he performed a parachute jump from the tower of the Central Park for Culture and Recreation in Moscow and broke his good leg. At that time he was working (through public channels) as an agitator at one of the Moscow factories where he was loved by the workers. When he suffered this latest injury, many workers came to visit him.

Puzyrev's father worked in the personnel department of one of the institutions (that is, given the nature of his work, he was either an official of the state security apparatus or closely connected to it). Puzyrev was accepted as a candidate for membership in the Communist party. Then, in the spring of 1965, there arose the "Puzyrev affair."

Oleg Puzyrev had written a short study of the socialist structure of Soviet society—virtually a study of the Soviet elite. It is difficult to say what more he intended to do with this paper, but first he tried to have it typed and could find no better solution than to give the manuscript to a typist from the Central Archive of the October Revolution. The typist, having barely begun to work on the manuscript, saw that it contained seditious material, and either out of fear, or, more likely, because she was linked to the state security services, she typed an extra copy and sent it off to some oficial destination. From there the manuscript was sent to the party committee of the institute and submitted for analysis. This is how the party committee came to be involved in the Puzyrev affair. This is also how I came to have the opportunity to read the manuscript. In it Puzyrev criticized our elite from the standpoint of a confirmed "pure" Leninist. But from the standpoint of the post-Khrushchev leadership, it was an act against the party.

It was extremely difficult to defend Puzyrev under such circumstances. The Puzyrev affair was initially dealt with at a meeting of the local party organization for the department of Soviet social history. Some people secretly sympathized with Puzyrev, while others simply regarded him as an unwitting victim of the post-Khrushchev era, and still others wanted to use this affair, which had so fortuitously arisen, as a way of organizing an attack on the progressive elements in the institute. Some made clamorous, heartrending statements reminiscent of Stalinist times. Others made moderate, well-considered statements. The majority seemed to favor expelling him from the party, a severe measure which threatened his dismissal from work. Yura Arutyunyan was unusually kind, stating that he shared in the responsibility and offering to take Puzyrev home and help him gain a correct understanding of the situation. "I shall live with Puzyrev like one brother with another," said Arutyunyan. Sonya Yakubovskaya proposed that we limit ourselves to disciplinary action, but the majority voted in favor of expulsion. Then the matter was sent to our party committee. It was decided to exclude Puzyrev from candidate membership in the Communist party. The director insisted on expelling him from the institute immediately. This was an unlawful demand. Yakubovskaya, the trade union representative for the department where Puzyrev worked, categorically refused to sign the document for dismissal. The whole matter ended after a long ordeal with Puzyrev finally being expelled and then set up at the library of the Mendeleev Chemical Institute.

Thus ended the Puzyrev affair. The bosses did not wish to exaggerate the matter, since they did not want to confer on Puzyrev, who was severely handicapped, an aura of martyrdom. Furthermore, Khvostov brought all his influence to bear in order to suppress the incident. At the party committee meeting Khvostov made an angry speech. "Where do such things come from?" he exclaimed, "They come from books by Solzhenitsyn. They come from books by Zalygin." Khvostov rose to his full height, almost as if he were ready to charge forward, and it was apparent that he was infuriated. No one raised any objection.

In the final analysis, the Puzyrev affair confirmed that in the first ten years after Stalin's death, Soviet society saw the beginnings of free thinking, the emergence of public opinion, and the recognition of responsibility for events.

While the institute was in an upheaval over the Puzyrev affair, yet another issue descended on it—the Nekrich affair. At precisely this time my manuscript of *June 22, 1941*, thoroughly laundered after passing through five censors, was finally registered for publication. Expecting major difficulties ahead of me, and not wishing to compromise the institute, I declined the proposal to give my book the institute imprimatur. That way I assumed full and sole responsibility for the contents. Here I turned out to be 100 percent right in my prediction.

At the same time, the tenth Volume of *World History*, on the history of the Second World War, which I had virtually edited myself, was also published. It was to be expected that there would be difficulties over this book as well, for volume ten contained the same ideas as those in *June 22, 1941*, although considerably watered down.

Fortunately, reviews of volume ten were favorable. The view of *June 22, 1941* among communists at the Institute of History was demonstrated by the new elections to the party committee in 1965: I was voted in by an overwhelming majority.

This time the elections brought into office people who had the reputation for being on the side of the progressive movement, highly qualified professionals. Eight doctors of science became party committee members. This had never happened before at the institute. The frightened director, V. M. Khvostov, did not want any part of a committee with such leanings and refused to accept nomination—an almost unprecedented situation, since the noninclusion of the director in a party committee meant, as a rule, a lack of trust in him either on the part of the staff or among higher bodies, and normally led to his replacement. Nor did the first deputy director, L. S. Gaponenko, wish to be part of the party committee. He also refused membership. From among the heads another deputy director was chosen to be a member of the committee—A. Shtrakhov.

From the very outset, the new party committee experienced difficulties. At the first organizational meeting we decided to elect as party committee secretary K. Tarnovsky, a talented scholar in Russian imperialism and a pupil of A. L. Sidorov. Not long before, Tarnovsky had on several occasions ventured to criticize strongly the situation in his field of historical study and had shown that chauvinistic considerations having nothing to do with Marxism had flourished in his field. The meeting of the party committee was also attended by the second secretary of the October District Committee of the Moscow party, Boris Nikolaevich Chaplin. He was a rather curious and not very typical figure in the party apparatus. The son of a secretary of the Komsomol Central Committee who had been executed in 1937, he was married to the daughter of another Central Committee secretary named Milchakov, who had been sent to the camps. Chaplin had graduated from the Moscow Aviation Institute and, after 1956, as a graduate student there, became a candidate of technical sciences. After his father's rehabilitation, it was suggested that he perform party work, and he agreed. Chaplin quickly advanced, first becoming a second secretary of the October District Committee, and then, after its split, became first secretary of the Cheremyshkinsky District Committee. A few years ago he was named ambassador to the Republic of Vietnam. Chaplin was a bright man, tactful and restrained. He was viewed with respect at the institutes, inasmuch as he belonged more or less to the academic world and, consequently, could not be a shameless Stalinist.

After beginning the meeting by extending compliments to the reelected members of the party committee, Chaplin, for no apparent reason, expressed opposition to Tarnovsky's candidacy, but he was met with a friendly rebuff. The first meeting was inconclusive, and we had to meet once again. This time Tarnovsky withdrew his name from consideration and, at Chaplin's suggestion, Viktor Petrovich Danilov was elected secretary. Khvostov, who had evidently been waging a campaign against Tarnovsky's candidacy behind the scenes, was finally forced to agree to the candidacy of Danilov in the hope of gaining influence over him. Danilov was a candidate of science, a specialist in the history of collectivization. Under his guidance a history of collectivization was being prepared which was finally supposed to give a scholarly analysis of an event which had turned upside down the entire way of life in the Soviet Union, had destroyed the productive forces in agriculture, and had been a cause of the chronic lack of agricultural productivity for forty-five years. Naturally the authors of the work, including Danilov himself, did not write about this directly and in so many words. On the basis of a study of source materials, they attempted to portray what they felt to be an objective picture of the collectivization of agriculture. Needless to say, the methodological basis for the study was Marxism-Leninism, for in fact historians of my generation and of Danilov's generation (he was ten years younger than myself) simply did not know any other methodology. As might be expected in such circumstances, this work was endlessly subjected to censorship, corrections, and redrafting, and the higher authorities were referred to for their reaction; but still the book did not come out. The main obstacle to its appearance was S. P. Trapeznikov, head of the science department of the party Central Committee, a confirmed Stalinist, and himself a specialist in the history of Soviet agriculture. For many years Trapeznikov held back the publication of the book. And then his own two-volume work appeared.

Danilov belonged to the progressive wing, to those who in political terms advocated the consistent implementation of the programs of the Twentieth and Twenty-Second Party Congresses and opposed dogmatism. In my view, in the final analysis a conscientious historian cannot fail to enter into conflict with the dead dogma of Marxism-Leninism. True, in recent decades there has appeared a way to include Marxism and declare as its inalienable advantage those changes in the social sciences which are not in contradiction with the overall conformist trend. Many historians who had long understood that there was nothing further to be accomplished through Marxism began to attribute to Marxism any bit of common sense they could come up with in the course of their studies. Normally they got away with it.

The new party committee secretary was a mild-mannered person and, unfortunately, one easily swayed by various influences. Because of this he sometimes involved the party in totally extraneous matters which only senselessly exacerbated tensions in the institute. Danilov made a point of strictly observing the formalities of democracy. At party committee meetings he would often blithely remark that the committee was under attack from the Stalinists, while giving them every opportunity to say whatever came into their heads. As a result, we wasted many long hours in fruitless debate. The oppositional wing of the institute, pro-Stalinist in its leanings and prepared to do everything necessary to advance its struggle against the party committee, was quick to make use of Danilov's weakness, and by extension that of the party committee itself, in order to fight it and to make unbridled attacks on the committee's individual members. Danilov's slightly neurotic character often lent an aspect of hypersensitivity to party committee business. Still, in other complex circumstances Danilov was commendably firm.

The overwhelming majority of party committee members felt that their task was to provide the best possible conditions for creativity among the staff at the institute. The freedom to defend one's scholarly views without fear of being slandered and accused of political crimes was the cornerstone of the party committee's policy. The committee held that the only safeguard for free expression was democratization of all academic institutions, and especially of our institute. I hasten to qualify that this meant democratization within the limits of Soviet ideology, not any of the "bourgeois" freedoms. We did believe, however, that even under such strictly limited and controlled circumstances, we did not enjoy legitimate opportunities for holding scholarly discussions. The party committee hoped to free the institute staff from the humiliating feeling of dependency on the will of its leadership. With this in view, the committee put forward a plan for democratization of all institute activities from top to bottom and proposed changes in electing the director of the institute, his deputies, the section heads, and senior and junior research staff members.

In accordance with the prevailing rules at the institute, the director was elected by a secret ballot among the appropriate subdivisions and then confirmed by the presidium of the Academy of Sciences. As a rule, such voting was purely a formality, since the director's candidacy had been approved beforehand and confirmed in the Communist party Central Committee, and only afterwards was it proposed for a secret vote in the Academy of Sciences.

Under the party committee's plan, the director, his deputies, and the section heads would be elected by secret ballot with the participation of the entire academic collective of the institute. In that way, the actions of the institute heads would be put under the direct control of staff, and the director would have to think not only about whether or not he would please the higher leadership but also about the extent to which his actions might further the academic activity of the staff. The party committee also wanted the senior researchers to be elected by secret ballot, not at a meeting of the academic council but by all senior research staff, while junior researchers would be elected by all junior research staff. Hence there would be constant two-way communication between staff groups and their individual members. These proposals were to be widely discussed on a preliminary basis not only by the academic council, but also by the lower party organizations, at section meetings, and so on. The party committee prepared a report to this effect but was unable to do anything more about it: new ideological heavy weather blew up, and the party committee's ship was caught in the stormy sea.

The committee came out strongly against the loafers who had been hanging around the institute for many years without showing any productive results. As a rule these were demagogues who intimidated the staff where they worked with accusations of a political nature. The party committee at the institute conducted a serious struggle against these people, who were especially comfortably ensconced in the division of the modern history of Western countries, which was headed by N. Samorukov. A discussion in the party committee of the situation in a most important area of work in the division—the history of the workers' movement—revealed serious trouble there. But the committee's decision to replace the section heads met with opposition from Khvostov, who kept in reserve a group of idlers in order to pit them against "recalcitrant" staff if necessary. The director followed an elementary principle, which he had expounded in a fit of candor to one of his closest associates when he was chief editor of the journal *Mezhdunarodnaya zhizn'*: "What you have to do," he said, "is divide the staff in two and then act as an arbiter with authority over them." Khvostov unswervingly applied this principle in his term as director of the Institute of History. The party committee was still trying to ensure equal working conditions and equal opportunities for all staff at the institute; beyond this, one's fate was up to the abilities of each and every researcher.

A serious conflict arose between Khvostov and the party committee which went on for two years, until conditions changed radically. Khvostov relied in this respect on the support of the science division of the Communist party Central Committee, on the presidium of the Academy of Sciences, and on the party district committee. The party committee, while not in direct conflict with any of these institutions, relied on the staff at the institute, and on the party organization there.

The authority of the 1965 party committee was considerable. The atmosphere at the institute changed before our very eyes. People began to talk more boldly, and to make more independent academic judgments, for they felt supported and knew they could count on the assistance of the party committee as long as they were in the right. These were surprising months. A year after Khrushchev's departure, the ideas set forth at the Twentieth and Twenty-Second Party Congresses had become an integral part of life at the institute.

Many institutes within the Academy of Sciences, as well as other higher educational institutions and bodies, carefully followed the events unfolding at the Institute of History. At one time the name Danilov meant progressiveness in the social sciences. On meeting an acquaintance from another institute, one could normally expect to hear the question: "Well, how is Danilov doing over there?" Everyone was concerned about how long the progressive party committee would last.

The committee's level of influence can be illustrated by the following incident. Moscow State University dismissed a Professor Duvakin for refusing to testify at the trial of Andrei Sinyavsky and Iuli Daniel. A petition was circulated demanding that Duvakin be reinstated. Two party members came to the committee to ask if they should sign the petition. I was in the party committee office at the time, discussing production plans with Danilov. We were astounded by the frankness of the question and the expectation of receiving an honest reply from the party committee. Earlier, in similar circumstances a person facing the dilemma of whether or not to sign such a document would primarily have tried to see to it that neither the party committee nor anyone else ever found out that such a proposal had been made to him. Now, people were coming freely to the committee for advice. Such was its authority.

There was one very important consideration in the strengthening of the committee's authority: none of the members attempted to derive any type of personal benefit from their membership. Normally, in due course the "pocket" secretaries in the party committee—that is, those scrupulously carrying out the will of the director, not to mention instructions from higher bodies—received a payoff: they were made deputy directors or section heads or the like, thereby being promoted to a higher-paying position. For example, one party committee member, Shtrakhov, was made deputy director as a reward for his servility to Khvostov. I have no doubts, however, that Shtrakhov, under obligation to Khvostov, in the depths of his soul really paid him back with unkindness.

Once, during a conversation with Chaplin at the party district committee, I said that the members of our committee were seeking nothing for themselves. Chaplin objected: "Well, that's not true. Do you think that just because you have been elected to the party committee, your wings are clipped?" Here was a different logic, more pragmatic, more modern, in keeping with the spirit of our fast-paced times.

Shtrakhov represented not only the director's office in the party committee, but the Stalinist wing of the party organization as well. In the party committee he was provocative and rude in his behavior, although it is true that he sometimes changed tactics (no doubt on Khvostov's advice) and tried to divide the committee. In so doing, he resorted to methods of outright blackmail. There was one especially memorable occasion when, during a discussion of a committee report on the status of historical scholarship he vehemently demanded the deletion from the report of a reference to Trotsky. The majority did not agree with him. Then, at another meeting, when clouds were already forming over the heads of the party committee members, he recalled this and said, "At that time I was supported by three people, you (he pointed a finger at one of the members), you (once again pointing), and a third person." He looked inquisitively at the remaining members of the party committee, as if to suggest that any one of them could still join him. But they all remained silent. I wound up in disputes with Shtrakhov more often than the others, and he hated me with a special intensity.

At the time, in order to map out means for a more effective development of historical study in the USSR, we set out to conduct a serious analysis of its status. Danilov decided that our party committee, which included highly qualified representatives of various branches in our field, should take on this task . The major portion of the work was done by Danilov and Tarnovsky. Later on, after they presented a draft of a report, "On the Status of Historical Study," other members of the committee became involved as well. The report was approved at a party meeting at the institute and, after many amendments by Khvostov, the majority of which were adopted in one way or other, recommended for publication. Moreover, the report was even sent to the "Nauka" publishing house and set in type. Then a halt was put to the printing. First in the Publications Committee and then in Glavlit there was an upheaval over the question of how permission had been given to print such "seditious" material.

The party committee sent a note on this subject to Mikhail Suslov, secretary of the Communist party Central Committee, but received no answer. More frequent requests by specific people to specific leaders were likewise unsuccessful. Nor was a second affirmation by the party committee of its approval the report of any help. At first we couldn't understand what the difficulty was, but gradually the situation became clear: there was under way a steady change in party political policy in the direction of conformism.

On January 30, 1966, an article appeared in *Pravda* signed by the secretary of the historical sciences division, Academician Ye. M. Zhukov, his deputy corresponding member of the USSR Academy of Sciences V. I. Shunkov, and the chief editor of the journal *Voprosy istorii*, corresponding member V. G. Trukhanovsky. The article clearly talked about the need to refrain from using the term *personality cult* and to reappraise Stalin's actions. But since that appraisal had been given at party congresses, the article virtually contained an appeal for revision of the decisions taken by the Twentieth to Twenty-Second Congresses of the Soviet Communist party. This is how it was interpreted by the public, and in the provinces it was simply interpreted as instructions for guidance. This was, apparently, the intention of those who were behind the article. The harm it did was enormous. Later on Zhukov and Shunkov confirmed that they had been drawn into this enterprise by Trukhanovsky. They said that the article had been the idea of S. P. Trapeznikov, which seems plausible, since Trapeznikov himself had repeatedly spoken at small meetings, and even, if I remember correctly, in one of his articles, along the same lines.

Among most historians the appearance of this article was met with indignation and with fear. The most reactionary among them greeted it with rejoicing. Some historians and philosophers decided to oppose the article and sent a letter to the Central Committee secretary, Suslov. The letter was signed by five people, including myself. We protested the clear attempt to rehabilitate Stalin. The letter said that references to the "period of the personality cult," against which the three academicians had argued, were completely justified, for they demonstrated that the entire era of the building of socialism was fraught with Stalin's mistakes and crimes. At the time only this kind of argument could repel the attack of the Stalinists.

A few days later, Suslov's assistant, V. V. Vorontsov, informed us that the Central Committee secretary agreed with the contents of the letter and that we would hear his ideas on the matter in his statement to the forthcoming Twenty-Third Party Congress. But, as is now known, neither Suslov nor most other members of the Central Committee Presidium, with the exception of three people, spoke at the congress. So we did not find out what Suslov thought of this matter. But it was apparent that Trapeznikov, who was the guiding force behind the article, had been too hasty. I am convinced that he first wanted to confront the party leadership with the "fact" that authoritative historians were opposed to the term *personality cult,* and that the term should be revised, followed by a revision of decisions made by the Twentieth Party Congress. No doubt someone from the Presidium had already promised his support. There were rumors circulating at the time to the effect that Stalin would be partially rehabilitated at the Twenty-Third Congress. But on the eve of the congress, agreement was reached among members of the Central Committee Presidium not to discuss this issue in general but to hold the congress under the slogan "massive party unity." Therefore the only people to speak were those who held the highest posts in the government—Brezhnev, Podgorny, and Kosygin—and primarily on practical matters at that.

I think that the party had come very close to some kind of rehabilitation of Stalin at the time: knowing Academician Zhukov as I do, I simply cannot imagine his taking such a risky step without being sure that the higher ups supported his point of view. And yet, as the Russian proverb goes, "every man has a fool up his sleeve."

In December 1966 a pitched battle took place between Stalinists and progressives at elections for the new membership of the Institute of History party committee. Long before the meeting the party district committee frequently summoned Danilov, Khvostov (who was a member of the district committee bureau), and others in order to agree on future candidates. There was especially stubborn opposition to my candidacy. Khvostov also insisted that Danilov be replaced as party committee secretary by the reliably subservient S. L. Utchenko. He, however, did not at all wish to be secretary. Danilov cautioned the district committee about an attack on me, predicting that my candidacy would be put forward and I would be elected.

By sheer coincidence, the day of the party election meeting was also the officially scheduled wedding day for Nadya and myself.

During the break between meetings, I went to the Civil Records Registration Office, where Nadya was waiting for me along with a few friends. We became man and wife, drank a glass of champagne, and then I hurried back to the party meeting. I didn't make it to my wedding reception until one in the morning, precisely the moment when my friend Zhora Fedorov was announcing with great fanfare that if I did not arrive within the next thirty minutes, he would exercise the rights of the wedding night on my behalf! The guests laughed, but Nadya was nervous. Finally I showed up, and the tense atmosphere changed to one of general fatigue. Nadya and her parents were kindhearted enough to forgive me. Furthermore, I was returning a hero, and victors, as is well known, are not judged. At the meeting there had taken place one of the fiercest battles in which I had ever participated. Buckets and buckets of mud had been slung at the party committee. What didn't they accuse the committee members of! Shtrakhov attacked me most violently of all. Incapable of accusing me of anything specific, he pounced on me with personal attacks. His statement sowed doubt among some in the audience and aroused indignation among others. Calmly, or as calmly as possible under the circumstances, I gave the necessary clarifications. When I tried to rebut Shtrakhov and show the purpose of his typically Stalinist methods, I was interrupted by the presiding officer, Volobuev, who in a far from dispassionate manner was discharging his duties as chairman.

The meeting concluded with the complete victory of the party committee. Almost the entire membership was reelected, along with some very worthy new members, including Yakubovskaya, Al'perovich and others. One hundred people voted against me, but two hundred voted for me. Shtrakhov had fallen greatly in the estimation of his colleagues at the institute. Later he expressed his feelings in a statement and made attempts at a reconciliation with me. But henceforth I stopped speaking to him, since in our disputes and disagreements he had overstepped the bounds of decency.

My book, *June 22, 1941*, came in for sharp attacks at the meeting, not only because of the internal situation but also because lengthy summaries of the book's contents as well as excerpts had been published in the socialist countries of Eastern and southeastern Europe. The press in the socialist countries had warmly welcomed the book's appearance. For many it was a sign that the struggle against Stalinism in the Soviet Union was still going on.

In the spring of 1967 a striking similarity, albeit on an incomparably smaller scale, could be recognized between what was happening in our institute and the quest for "socialism with a human face" in Prague. I think that this comparison is in keeping with reality, the only difference being that, apart from matters of scale, at our institute (and in the country as a whole) difficulties were subsiding, while in Czechoslovakia they were just getting under way. Some overlap in the process was natural. The outburst of emotions—indignation, grief, shame, repentance—caused by the widespread accounts of the crimes committed in the Soviet Union over decades had to, and indeed did, gain an outlet in the attempts to take some concrete measures to prevent the possibility that such crimes would be repeated in the future. Such a panacea could only be glasnost, only the Word. As it says in the Scriptures: "In the beginning there was the Word." Just as the walls of Jericho had collapsed from the sound of trumpets, the so-called socialist society began to crumble before our eyes in Prague because of the Word, because of glasnost. The quest for "socialism with a human face" spread, and the Western leftist intelligentsia took heart: finally, at last! There will still be socialism, but of another kind—not exactly the Soviet kind, but different, with "a human face"—without arbitrariness and violence, with democracy, respect for law, true equality, and freedom of expression. But we did not succeed in discovering at the time if a different socialism was possible, one without rivers of blood, "psychiatric" hospitals, prisons and labor camps, arbitrariness, the reign of the elite.

I felt keenly the relationship between what was going on in our country and events in Czechoslovakia. Although the sun rises in the East, does it, perhaps, reach its highest point in the West? At the request of a correspondent from Prague radio, I gave an interview on the events of 1941 and the lessons to be learned from them.

8

Expulsion

I do not fear judgment,
Perhaps I have long awaited it,
Let me not yet say the word,
Most of all to be said.
My word—from my heart—
is not said lightly
It stands ready to be uttered,
I lived, I was, and for all this
I shall answer on my head.
—A. Tvardovsky

All-Union Ideological Conference of 1966 — the attack — I repel the attack — article in *Der Spiegel* — party investigation — party Control Committee meeting — expulsion from CPSU — public condemnation — public reaction — Academician S. Strumilin's letter — General Pyotr Grigorenko's letter — friendship is indissoluble

A few days before my departure for Warsaw in late September 1966, I was told that a transcript of the February 16 discussion of my book, *June 22, 1941*, at the Institute of Marxism-Leninism had been confiscated from a Pole at the Polish-Soviet border. The party Central Committee was immediately informed of this. I was somewhat concerned. Why such a fuss? News of the discussion had long since crossed all borders: the summary record of the meeting had been circulating in Warsaw for half a year now; the same was true in Prague and, no doubt, the other socialist countries as well. A twofold explanation came to mind: first, that the authorities really did detain the Pole and confiscate the record. Those who held him probably were completely unaware of the institute discussion, but it is possible that the KGB or the Belorussian secret police were using this incident in their own interests to enhance their prestige. And second, that they were all the more glad to do this, in light of the mood prevailing "upstairs" in Moscow, for since the trial of Sinyavsky and Daniel, the neo-Stalinist grip had tightened.

I returned to Moscow in early October. Not a week had gone by when a friend, upset, phoned and asked to meet me somewhere in "neutral territory." We met in the street. He told me that an ideological conference was under way in the Central Committee and that D. Sturua, secretary of the Central Committee of the Georgian Communist party, had made vicious attacks on me there. That same day I learned the details of what had happened and even the precise text of Sturua's statement. This is what he said: "Nekrich's book is completely clear. Mr. Nekrich, if you please, slanders our party. Mr. Nekrich, if you please, slanders the foreign policy of the Soviet state and of the Communist party. Mr. Nekrich, if you please, asserts that the Soviet Union made far-reaching concessions to Nazi Germany."

In addition to Sturua, S. A. Pilotovich, secretary of the Central Committee of the Belorussian Communist party, spoke about the book at the conference, talked of the use made by bourgeois propaganda of the verbatim record of the discussion at the institute, and asked how the record had made its way abroad (later this issue would be discussed by the party Control Commission). V. E. Semichastny, chairman of the Committee for State Security, explained that the verbatim record was not the original but a falsification.

So it was that the book *June 22, 1941* became the focus of an ideological struggle. Hostilities had been declared. I had either to capitulate or to defend myself. I chose to fight.

On October 17, 1966, I sent out two letters. The first was addressed to the presidium of the All-Union Conference of Ideological Workers and the second to the secretary of the Central Committee of the Communist party, P. N. Demichev. In both letters I protested Sturua's statement and asked to be given the opportunity to reply at the conference.

After sending both these letters, I phoned Demichev's assistant I. T. Frolov (author's note: subsequently managing editor of the journal *Voprosy filosofii*, and by 1990 a member of the Politburo and editor in chief of *Pravda*). Frolov was very courteous and promised to inform the Central Committee secretary of my letter immediately. He then advised me to contact the deputy head of the propaganda and agitation department of the Central Committee, A. N. Yakovlev (author's note: in 1990 one of the most prominent supporters of perestroika, a member of the Presidential Council and the Politburo), who was responsible for the conduct of the ideological conference. Several times I tried in vain to reach Yakovlev by phone, but he was clearly avoiding a conversation with me. Meanwhile, the conference had ended. At the closing meeting Demichev spoke, and scolded Sturua for his rudeness. But even this mild reproach was very helpful to me, for Demichev's statement showed that the scales had not yet tipped the other way.

Three weeks later I received a phone call from Zaitsev, an official from the agitation and propaganda division, who informed me that Sturua had been corrected in Demichev's closing statement, that the matter was thus settled, and that the Central Committee had no claims against me regarding my book. Zaitsev's statement was extremely important, and I, after repeating back to him what he had told me, asked him to confirm that I had understood him correctly. This he did.

The following day I informed the members of the party committee at our institute of this phone call, and they heaved a sigh of relief.

Some role in halting the Nekrich affair had been played by my candidacy for corresponding membership in the Academy of Sciences. The elections were to take place that autumn, but the posting of my name in the general list of candidates throughout the Academy of Sciences (the list of all candidates is published in the central government organ, the newspaper *Izvestiya*) had some impact on the world of officialdom. My candidacy had been put forward by Academician I. M. Maisky and seconded by a number of other academicians. In the balloting I did not win enough votes for election, but I did well enough to emerge from the game with my honor intact. Needless to say, I had not seriously expected to be elected. But the results at least put a stop to the attack begun by the Stalinists for some time to come.

Two months later, at the beginning of 1967, after the Twenty-Third Communist Party Congress, the campaign was resumed with greater intensity.

Now it was being conducted gradually. Party opinion was being prepared step by step for the attack on my book. This letter, which I wrote to A. P. Shaposhnikova, secretary of the Moscow City Committee Communist party, gives some idea of the situation:

December 7, 1966

Distinguished Alla Petrovna:

I am obliged to write you in connection with a statement made by a senior official of the Moscow City Committee Communist party, Comrade Vladimirtsev, at a meeting of propagandists held in the Frunze district of Moscow on November 25 of this year.

Comrade Vladimirtsev claimed that at a discussion of A. M. Nekrich's book *June 22, 1941* in the Institute of Marxism-Leninism, the above-mentioned book *was condemned*.

Actually, at that discussion, convened by the Communist party Central Committee of the Institute of Marxism-Leninism at the initiative of the publications committee on February 16, 1966, the book was given a *positive* evaluation by all speakers without exception. Many of those who spoke suggested that the book be reissued and in this regard asked that the author take into account wishes and comments expressed during the course of the discussion.

This is what really happened [I enclosed the verbatim transcript of the discussion]. One wonders why Comrade Vladimirtsev deemed it necessary to state such an obvious untruth. The answer is clear: in order to support his own view of A. M. Nekrich's book as harmful with references to authoritative academic opinion. I strongly protest the unpartylike conduct of Comrade Vladimirtsev, which has misled the propagandists of an entire district of Moscow, and insist that his statement be rejected.

I received no reply to my letter.

The campaign became more violent. But life can be a rather strange and contradictory joke. At the very moment when clouds were gathering over my head, my application (and that of my institute) for permission to take an academic trip to England for work in the British archives was finally making progress after six years of deadlock. I filled out the visa forms and began to wait.

Later I learned that, with typical Russian good fortune, the right hand did not know what the left was doing; my request was simply proceeding in routine fashion from one office to another, being passed from desk to desk, but had not yet been submitted to the Central Committee's travel commission, which would make a final decision on the matter.

In March 1967 I was called in by the institute director, V. M. Khvostov. By that time passions had abated somewhat, and he wished to emphasize that he was loyal to me. Khvostov was a contradictory person: his ambition and his readiness to use the most primitive party methods for the sake of advancing his career contrasted with his intelligence and his education, his instinctive avoidance of open participation in pogroms, and a squeamish unwillingness to get his own hands dirty: when necessary, he sought and found, without special difficulty, people to do his dirty work for him.

Khvostov told me that he had been advised to take part in the devastating review of my book, but he had refused. Then he said to me:

"Aleksandr Moiseevich, a case has been initiated against you in the Central Committee. I advise you to write a statement to the Central Committee without delay."

"A statement to what effect?"

"There are faults and errors in your book, after all. You have said so yourself. So write about it, and express regret." Here Khvostov stopped, believing, no doubt, that he had told me enough.

I thanked him and promised to give the matter some thought. When we said good-bye, Khvostov added in a conciliatory tone, "I realize that there have been misunderstandings between us because you wished to assert your independence."

I said nothing.

This had been our first friendly meeting in a long time. It was also to be the last. Several times we would see each other from a distance and nod in greeting, but we were never to talk to each other again. Soon afterwards

Khvostov was made President of the USSR Academy of Pedagogical Sciences, and two years later he died unexpectedly.

I did give thought to what Khvostov had told me. In a few days I received yet another warning: I was given the draft of a devastating article under preparation at the Institute of Marxism-Leninism. The onslaught was clearly irreversible. But I had made my choice the moment I had written the first page of my manuscript. I did not intend to offer apologies, to make a confession. A new era had opened up before me in what would probably be the last part of my life, and there was no room for the conformism of our hypocritical society. I was withdrawing gradually from it, but portions of my past life like invisible threads still connected me, and I understood that this would always be the case.

However improbable it may seem, the last push, the thing that tipped the scales of my fate, was provided by the journal *Der Spiegel*, published in Hamburg. After this my fortunes plummeted—or perhaps they just began their ascent.

This is what happened.

In the issue for March 18, 1967, *Der Spiegel* published two lengthy articles on events in the USSR: one was devoted to Svetlana Alliluyeva, the other—to my book and myself.

One day, while I was sitting in the party committee office, a phone call came from the TASS photo archive. A correspondent informed me that he had been assigned to take a picture of me. I expressed surprise but decided that perhaps things were changing. This was not at all the case, however. The photographer-journalist who came to my home told me that a certain West German magazine had placed an order for my photograph, had paid in hard currency, and was now waiting for my picture. This was purely a business transaction, the TASS photo archive was simply filling a prepaid order.

Do not say that life in Russia is so bad. At least here you are never bored.

Der Spiegel included my photograph, duly taken by the TASS photographer, in a lengthy article about the book, including a discussion of the content and of the question of responsibility for the lack of preparedness for the war. The article was prefaced by an insert, the text of which was to serve as an impetus for the party's case against me. The insert stated, among other things, that at the Twenty-Third Party Congress party leader Brezhnev had wanted to rehabilitate Stalin. This was opposed by a group of progressive-minded intelligentsia, military, academics, and others. Their view was expressed in the book by the historian A. M. Nekrich, *June 22, 1941.*

I had long ago learned a rule of life: the most dangerous thing is to earn a personal enemy. The Stalinists were aware of this rule as well. The article in *Der Spiegel* was finally the pretext they needed for taking reprisals against me and teaching a lesson to all others, something they had been trying to do for more than a year and a half.

Soon Trapeznikov, deputy head of the Central Committee science department, showed the issue of *Der Spiegel* to a group of historians close to him. Then, I was told, he showed the magazine to Brezhnev, causing him to fly into a rage over the statement that he supposedly had wished to rehabilitate Stalin. Brezhnev gave the order for the party Control Committee to commence an investigation into my book, the circumstances under which the transcripts of the discussion at the Marxist-Leninist Institute had made their way abroad, and the use being made of the book abroad for bourgeois propaganda.

In late April I learned that at the Institute of Marxism-Leninism a devastating article was being prepared for *Pravda* by G. A. Deborin. With several of my friends present, I phoned Deborin at home and asked him if this were true. He attempted to avoid making a direct response, yet he tried to find out where I had heard this. I, too, was evasive, and joked that "rumors make the world go 'round." I took it from my conversation with Deborin that the information was accurate and that a case was being prepared against me, although at that moment I could not foresee what turn events would take. What concerned me most was that all this would have a harmful effect on our party committee. A very serious situation was developing, and a decision had to be made immediately. By coincidence, right after my talk with Deborin, the opportunity suddenly arose to make a direct request to Suslov, the secretary of the party Central Committee, for an appointment. Two days later I was informed of his reply: many people were dealing with this matter, and he, Suslov, could not interfere. Now all that was left was to await further developments. Two weeks later I received an official invitation to appear before the Control Committee of the Communist party Central Committee for an appointment with an official, party investigator S. I. Sdobnov. The investigation was being conducted by two party control officials: Sdobnov and I. N. Gladnev.

When I was invited before the Control Committee, I had no idea of party procedure, nor did Sdobnov see fit to inform me of it. Thus I was quite surprised to see the deputy director of the institute, Shtrakhov, there. My book, after all, had no direct relation to the institute. I could not understand why the party committee secretary, Danilov, had not been invited. It turned out that for the Control Committee it was important to have present a representative of the administration from the institution where the person under investigation worked. In this way the administration became virtually a participant in the investigation proceedings, assisting the Control Committee. I saw this for myself. Besides, Shtrakhov was hardly a silent witness, but, rather, actively assisted the investigators.

Fortunately, I still have in my possession notes which I made immediately following my meetings with the Control Committee, and documents which I wrote at the request of the party control officials. Therefore, I can be extremely accurate in describing everything that happened. It might be useful for the Western reader, and especially for specialists in history, politics and the social sciences, to know a few details. This will help them to gain a better understanding of the essence of the system in the Soviet Union.

My first talk with the party Control Commission took place on May 22, 1967, and lasted four hours. I was asked questions about my book—how I had conceived it and why I had written it. Afterwards I realized that the party investigators were trying to ascertain whether I had written it with malicious intent, in order to harm the interests of the Communist party and the Soviet state. Another group of questions pertained to my view of the book a year and a half after its appearance. The entire content, direction, and tone of the talk left no doubt that the party investigators felt an inner hostility toward me, although they were correct and polite. No notes were taken during the talk: there was no need for this, since a hidden microphone performed the duties of a secretary. Such a system eliminated the necessity of presenting the person under investigation with a record and deprived him of the opportunity to verify whether the answers he had given were correctly interpreted. In this regard a party investigation procedure is far worse than a normal judicial investigation.

Among the questions asked me by Sdobnov and Gladnev, two stood out as the most important. The first was, why did I not repudiate the statement made by Aleksei Vladimirovich Snegov at the Institute of Marxism-Leninism discussion? I replied that I did not refute anyone in general, no matter what nonsense had been spouted—for example, what was said by Deborin, which I did not repudiate either, and so on.

The second question, apparently, was the key one. Sdobnov asked me, "Which, in your view, is more important—political expediency or historical truth?" The investigator was letting me know indirectly that what was important was not whether my book was accurate or not—this was secondary—but rather how politically appropriate it was at that time to raise the issue of Soviet unpreparedness for the German attack and the question of responsibility for it. Sdobnov's query harked back to what had been said by the other investigator, Gladnev, when he saw me off after our first meeting: "Do not be mistaken. We are not your opponents, we are doing our work." That is, there is no point in wasting time trying to reason with us.

In answer to Sdobnov's question I said that political expediency and historical truth were not at all mutually exclusive. Historical experience had shown that in the final analysis, historical truth was in keeping with political expediency.

"Still, which for you is more important?" asked Sdobnov again. "Historical truth or political expediency?"

"Historical truth," I replied.

Shtrakhov zealously assisted the investigators. At one point I could stand it no longer and interrupted him abruptly, for which I received a sharp reprimand from Gladnev: "Comrade Nekrich, do not forget that you are at the Central Committee of the Communist party!"

I do recall one thing that was curious about the conduct of both of my interlocutors, if I may call them that. All the documents I showed them—letters from readers, reviews, my statements about the "once-over" received through administrative and propaganda channels—were carefully read by Gladnev and Sdobnov, who handed them to each other in silence, but without showing any emotion, just quick glances. Only once did Sdobnov explode, when he read my letter to Secretary Shaposhnikova about Vladimirtsev's statement.

At the end of our talk, it was suggested that I answer three questions in writing. Here are the questions and my answers to them:

Question: Give your view of the book *June 22, 1941.*

Answer: I consider the book *June 22, 1941* to be historically accurate, patriotic and in keeping with the decisions of the Twentieth, Twenty-Second, and Twenty-Third Congresses of our party, as well as with the Communist party Central Committee decree of June 30, 1956. The book was published as part of a general education series for "Nauka" publishers in the autumn of 1965. It had been approved by Glavlit, and then discussed by communist historians at the Communist party Central Committee Institute of Marxism-Leninism, where it was generally approved. There have been positive reactions and reviews from the press of the socialist countries and from the communist press of the Western European countries as well.

Question: Give your view of the discussion of the book at the Institute of Marxism-Leninism.

Answer: The discussion of my book on February 16, 1966, did not take place at my initiative. It was initiated by the publications committee and the Institute of Marxism-Leninism of the party Central Committee, which had direct responsibility for holding it. The academic discussion was open, inasmuch as it was about a book that had been published openly. The discussion was attended by approximately two hundred historians, both military and civilian, and about twenty-two people spoke, including the head of the department of the history of the Great Fatherland War, his deputy, and editors of all six volumes of *A History of the Great Fatherland War of the Soviet Union.* All those who spoke gave, overall, a positive evaluation of the book, while making a number of critical comments. All this can be seen from the verbatim records of the discussion.

*Question:*Give your view of the foreign reaction.

Answer: The foreign reactions were of two types. I was greatly gratified by the positive response from the communist press both in the socialist countries and in the capitalist countries of Western Europe. The communist press considered the book to be a weapon against the bourgeois reactionary press, which had claimed that a trend toward a restoration of the Stalin personality cult was under way in the USSR. I wrote an "open letter" in response to slanderous broadcasts by Deutsche Welle and gave it to the Novosti press agency. For reasons unknown to me, it was not published. In other publications of the bourgeois press, the discussion was not about my book but about the proceedings of the debate at the Institute of Marxism-Leninism.

I brought Sdobnov my replies on May 24. He read through them carefully, making no comment whatsoever. Then, when I took leave of him, he warned me that the talks would be continued. I shrugged my shoulders.

During the talks the investigators showed great annoyance at the facts I adduced, which obviously did not fit their prepared scenario. For example, everything I said about the artificial fuss raised over my book by chairman Mikhailov of the publications committee and his colleagues Makhov and Fomichev was violently rejected, and my indignation at the statement made at the ideological conference by the Georgian propaganda secretary Sturua came up against a wall of feigned indifference.

I asked Sdobnov the reason for these talks, and why the Control Committee was discussing matters of an academic nature. I was given the reply that on instructions from the leadership, an investigation was under way into an entire series of issues regarding *June 22, 1941* — namely, the book itself, the discussion of it, foreign reaction, and information leaks abroad.

"So what is this—a personal case?" I asked Sdobnov point-blank.

"The matter has not yet been settled," he replied evasively.

My written responses served as the main material for the charges against me. Realizing this, I also saw the importance of the American procedural rule whereby the accused is permitted not to answer questions on the grounds that they might be incriminating. But "socialist democracy" is very far from having a basic understanding of the protection of individual rights.

A month later, on July 24, II was once again called before the party Control Committee. This was just a few days after the Six-Day War in Israel, and the wave of anti-Semitism had not yet passed.

This time there were three investigators. A certain Senichkin from the press section had been called upon to assist the other two. This time we did not remain in Sdobnov's office but proceeded in silence along a long corridor up to the third floor. Evidently my face showed my bewilderment as to where I was being led, for Gladnev asked me, "Weren't you told where we are going?" I shook my head as if to say no. "We are going to see Comrade Melnikov, a party Control Committee member," Gladnev said to me in a half-whisper. I shook my head again. This name meant nothing to me.

Soon we entered a large office. Its occupant, a tall, thickset man of about sixty, rose to meet us, held out a broad hand in greeting, and asked us to take a seat. We sat down: Melnikov at the head of the table, the three investigators on his left, and me on his right. Looking at me with his enormous dark eyes, Roman Yefimovich Melnikov said that the committee was still not satisfied with my answers, and that on Wednesday, June 28, my case would be discussed at a meeting chaired by A. Ia. Pel'she. Pel'she was a member of the Politburo and chairman of the Control Committee. My case must have been thought to be one of special importance if it had been decided to bring it before such a high-level meeting. Melnikov then suggested that Sdobnov read out that part of the preparatory text for the meeting that referred to me. So, I had been invited to hear in advance the charges against me! I took a pencil and got ready to take notes, but at that point I realized that I would remember better if I listened closely.

In a low but distinct tone of voice, Sdobnov read out the indictment. Naturally this was not the document's formal title, but that is what it essentially was. I tried not to betray my distress, even though I was extremely upset. I saw that my fingers were shaking and rested the palm of my hand on the desk.

When Sdobnov read the most violent accusations, Melnikov glanced over at me as if to ask, "Well, what do you make of it?" and without turning his head checked my reaction, as if to see whether it would be easy to deal with me. At certain points I either sighed or winced, or, perhaps, simply looked straight ahead, pretending indifference. Finally, Sdobnov put the last page down on the desk. Melnikov suggested an exchange of views. I said that I could not immediately grasp an oral reading, and needed to go through the document with my own eyes, especially since—unlike the talks which had supposedly been about academic problems—this had raised serious political charges against me. All three investigators protested in a friendly manner. Oh, were they ever unwilling to let me take a look at that document! Sdobnov proposed reading the document aloud a second time, more slowly, even stopping at those parts I felt were especially important. I firmly protested and continued to stick to my position. Melnikov was hesitant. In the end he told Sdobnov to allow me to read the document and to take any necessary notes. Gladnev proposed that we should then return to see Melnikov in order to hear his views. Melnikov, either because he did not wish to define his own position or for some other reasons (it was near the end of the working day), proposed that the talks be continued without his participation. That seems reasonable, I thought to myself. First, he does not commit himself at all, and second, he can always listen to the tape recording.

I sat in Sdobnov's office for half an hour, reading and copying out the most important parts of the document. Soon the threesome appeared again (they must have gone to the refreshment stand for a snack). In spite of my protests, my notes were confiscated. Sdobnov explained that it was a secret document. I protested, but there was no one to complain to: Melnikov had had the foresight to step aside. The entire comedy began to come clear to me. Then Sdobnov suggested that we begin to talk about the substance of the charges. I refused, reiterating that I was not prepared for such a talk and needed time to think. The investigators insisted, and began to raise questions in an attempt to draw me into a conversation. I responded unwillingly, since I thought they wanted to drag arguments out of me with which they could later arm themselves in preparation for the forthcoming battle on Wednesday. "Well, it's clear he doesn't want to talk," exclaimed Gladnev in annoyance. He then got up and left, together with Senichkin. Sdobnov and I were left in the office. He put forward a final suggestion: if I came in the next day, I would be received by the first deputy committee chairman, K. N. Grishin. I promised to think about it, and we parted on that note. Since I suspected that the proposal was a trap, and I was feeling physically nauseated, knowing that I did not have enough time to prepare, I decided to go directly to the committee meeting instead and not ask for an appointment with Grishin. (Later on this would be used against me as proof of my disdain for the party.)

Only thirty-six hours remained before the meeting. Once again friends came to my rescue. My wife, Nadya, tried not to reveal her distress, although the dark circles around her eyes and the nervous twitching of her eyelids betrayed her. We went to bed late, and I got up at six o'clock the next morning.

On the eve of the meeting, I was informed that A. M. Rumyantsev vice president of the Academy of Sciences, had talked with Suslov about my case, and the latter had supposedly assured him that the matter would be limited to a reprimand. But I did not believe this, for why else was there such a hue and cry being raised over the matter? I realized that Rumyantsev sympathized with me and was trying to help improve my situation, but I still regarded the report as disinformation. Similar disinformation arrived from other sources as well. A trap was clearly being set for me.

I arrived at the committee meeting with Aleksandr Mikhailovich Samsonov, director of the "Nauka" publishing house, who had also been summoned for questioning. We lived across the street from each other and it was therefore quite natural that we go together.

I was standing in the corridor all alone, smoking, when an elegantly dressed old man in a gray suit walked by. He held his head high, and proceeded with the no-nonsense gait of a man aware of his own importance. Two or three meters behind him followed a thickset young man, dressed in the standard black suit. He was carrying a briefcase. The older man held in his hand a small bouquet of flowers neatly wrapped in paper. "Pel'she," I thought at once.

There was nowhere to go until a secretary came out and showed me to a room where those summoned to the committee waited to be received. This was a dark, windowless square with a constantly glowing electric light. A few pine tables and chairs stood around the room. It brought to mind a prison cell, the only difference being that here there were no guards, and it was still possible to get out, something I did on the spot. Everything here was calculated to affect the mood of the accused, to force him to feel depressed, hopeless, to break his will.

Soon the secretary came out into the corridor and said, "The person here for the Nekrich case is asked to come in." That meant a "case" really did exist.

Pel'she's office, where the meeting was being held, was a large, bright room. To the right of the door was a wall with several windows and balconies. Along the wall were placed soft leather chairs for visitors. On the same side, farther back in the room, stood a large desk of dark-yellow polished wood, and next to it a small table with multicolored telephone sets; along the rear wall there was shelving with books and wood paneling, and a door which evidently led to a room used for private purposes.

On the lefthand side stood a long, wide table covered with the customary green felt. At the far end of the table, facing the entrance, stood an armchair for the presiding officer. Along both sides of the table sat the members of the committee. They were of varying heights, tall and short, some bald and some with thick, wavy gray hair, some with and some without eyeglasses, some stout and some thin, but there was something inexplicably the same about all of them. The group included several women. One of them, a heavy, tall woman with thick graying hair pushed back from her forehead, turned and stared at me.

Closer to the doors the lesser ranks were seated around a second table: party investigator Gladnev, across from him Sdobnov, and next to him a light-haired woman in a white blouse and bright skirt. Next to her sat a person I knew well, the head of the agitation and propaganda department of the Moscow City party committee, Ivankovich, a short man with cold, evil eyes and artificial limbs in place of arms.

Among those invited I noticed P. N. Pospelov, director of the Institute of Marxism-Leninism, Generals Tel'pukhovsky and Grylev (the former from the Institute of Marxism-Leninism, the latter from the military history department of the General Staff), and the managing editor of the journal *Voprosy istorii KPSS* A. P. Kosul'nikov.

I also noticed an old acquaintance from my days of studying at the main library of the USSR Academy of Sciences, P. P. Sevastyanov, an historian and Far Eastern specialist who apparently represented the Ministry for Foreign Affairs. G. A. Deborin arrived, looked around, and took a seat next to Senichkin, a small, nondescript man who was trying to emphasize through his bearing the enormous importance of what was to happen here, as well as his own self-importance. The acting director of our institute, Luka Stepanovich Gaponenko, settled in across from him.

I sat down on a chair next to Samsonov, on the side nearer the window. The room was stuffy. Not far from me Lenya Petrovsky took a seat; he was a grandson of Grigory Ivanovich Petrovsky, a son of Pyotr Petrovsky, the Civil War hero and former leader of the Communist Youth International, who had been killed during the years of Stalinist terror, and a nephew of Corps Commander Petrovsky, who had been released from prison camp at the war's beginning and died heroically in battle. Lenya Petrovsky, who had gone through twenty-seven years of his life branded as the son of an enemy of the people, was accepted into the party after his father's rehabilitation and worked as a staff member of the V. I. Lenin Museum. He had once been close to the democratic movement and had taken part in the discussion of my book at the Institute of Marxism-Leninism, much to his misfortune. His speech was subsequently labeled antiparty, and now he was being called to task by the party in the Nekrich affair.

Pel'she called the meeting to order. Sdobnov then took the floor to give information. I began to take notes.

Sdobnov started by depicting all aspects of the circumstances surrounding the matter. Nekrich's book is flawed. He has given unsatisfactory explanations for this. The author's conclusions are not in accordance with Soviet historical concepts and resemble the concepts of bourgeois historians. He contrasts the total mobilization in Germany with the inertia of the Soviet government. He whitewashes the policy of England, France, and the United States. He falsifies the facts: warnings sent by Churchill to Stalin, Schulenburg's warnings. He includes as part of Germany itself lands it had occupied, thus playing into the hands of German revanchists. He blackens the reputation of Soviet industry, especially in defense. The Soviet-German pact is portrayed as being advantageous only to Germany. And it turns out that the Soviet government was hoodwinked. In this way he slanders the Soviet government.

The author will not repudiate the antiparty statements made during the discussion at the Institute of Marxism-Leninism. Some claimed at that discussion that there are two groups of historians: dogmatists and Marxists. Nekrich, said Sdobnov in an ironic tone of voice, was included in the second group. Nekrich writes about the deliberate annihilation of the military cadre: he claims that the main reason for Hitler's attack on the Soviet Union was fear of a coalition among the USSR, Britain, and the

United States, thereby justifying the Nazi thesis of a preventive war. He does talk about those truly responsible for the war—the monopolies. There are more quantitative references to foreign documents than there are to Soviet ones. (Here Senichkin intervened and quickly rattled off the figures for both.) Nekrich leads the reader to believe that the USSR's victory in the war defied logic.

Petrovsky, Sdobnov went on, made an anti-Soviet speech at the discussion. In talks at the party Control Committee he continued to insist on his brazen positions. He has not thus far submitted any written explanation to the Control Committee. [This, in fact, turned out to be precisely how Petrovsky saved himself from severe party punishment.] Petrovsky is the author of the summary record of the discussion at the Institute of Marxism-Leninism, which has made its way abroad.

Nekrich's book has been seized upon abroad by hostile propaganda: broadcasts of Deutsche Welle: publication of the verbatim records in the Italian Trotskyite journal *Sinistra*, in the *Nouvel observateur*, and in *Der Spiegel*, with a picture of the author and the caption: "Nekrich—a critic of Stalin."

Next, I was given the floor.

My statement had been prepared in advance and typewritten. I gave a copy to the Control Committee stenographer, but I made a few changes as I went along. Therefore, at the very outset I stated that even though the issue of the Stalin personality cult had not been raised at all in the document read out by Sdobnov, this was in fact what was involved; this was the subtext of the document.

On concluding my statement, I said that the book did, of course, contain faults and oversights. I acknowledged in particular Sdobnov's objection that I had included in the territory of Germany itself lands seized by the Reich.

I did not say before the committee, nor do I regret it, that I had noticed this error immediately after the book came out in print and had included it in a list of factual mistakes and misprints to be given to the Polish, Czechoslovak, and Hungarian publishers working on the translations of my book. I considered it humiliating to have to defend myself in this fashion.

I stated that there was a big difference between concrete comments and attempts to build up political accusations on the basis of them. I rejected all political accusations in full.

Furthermore, I exposed what was being camouflaged in the Control Committee document—an ex post facto attempt to relieve Stalin and the political leadership of responsibility for the difficult situation our country faced in June 1941. I recalled the basic facts from the history of that time and endeavored to demonstrate the groundlessness of the accusations made against me. I concluded as follows: "At the outset I have mentioned and wish to repeat once again that there is no doubt that the book does have its faults; it is far from perfect. But as regards the political accusations made against me, I firmly reject them. . . .

I thought it my duty as an historian and a communist to participate as much as I could in the party's struggle to overcome the mistakes of the personality cult period and help draw the necessary lessons from it."

While I was delivering my statement, hostile objections rang out every now and then, to which I did not react. After the conclusion of my statement the questions came one after another: many people asked me why I had not disassociated myself from Snegov's antiparty statement. I replied that the discussion was academic in nature and I responded only to statements of that kind.

"So, then," I was asked, "if antiparty things are said in your presence, it does not concern you? Where is your party spirit?" Pospelov burst out: You're the one who brought people with you to the Institute of Marxism-Leninism!"

I responded "I did not initiate the discussion. It was the institute that did so. Those who led the discussion bear responsibility for it. Announcements of the forthcoming discussion were posted. And this was totally natural. What is wrong if communist historians attended the discussion?"

While I replied, cries of indignation were heard. Only Pel'she remained completely calm. One could even say that he viewed this spectacle with disdainful indifference.

Samsonov, the "Nauka" publishing house director, himself an historian and author of books on the battle for Moscow and Stalingrad, spoke calmly, with dignity, acknowledging his error in allowing the editors to issue a book which should not have been published. At the same time, he stated that the book contained nothing that had not been published earlier in other Soviet editions. Samsonov's statement had a favorable effect on the committee members. His entire demeanor—he was a tall, stocky man with graying dark hair and large horn-rimmed glasses—his dignified yet unassuming bearing, and furthermore his admitting his error, were to the liking of the committee members. One of the members said thoughtfully, while turning the book over in his hands: "So, you see, Comrade Samsonov, had you been more careful about the book, it wouldn't have come out, and there would be no case."

Despite the seriousness of the situation, I had to control my facial muscles and hold back a grin. This is how simply matters are solved: if there's no book, there's no case, everything is fine, and everyone is satisfied. I remembered our famous comedian Arkady Raikin's portrayal of a Soviet petty bureaucrat: "Just to be left alone—that's what's most important." But on the whole, this was no laughing matter. Melnikov repeated several times, addressing Samsonov: "But Belokonev had told you not to print the book. He told you, yet you didn't listen to him." (Major General Belokonev had signed a negative review of my manuscript on behalf of the KGB.)

Then Petrovsky made a dramatic statement. He held forth with stern determination, firmly rejecting the accusation that his speech was anti-Soviet, as well as the blame attributed to him for composing the summary record. As regarded my book, he said that he thought it to be honest and in the party spirit. Then the committee members began to shout objections and go at him. The culmination of Petrovsky's statement was when he stated that party investigator Gladnev had shouted at him, pounded the table with his fists, and said: "I would be proud to have my name stand side by side with that of Comrade Stalin." There was a rustling in the room. Gladnev, flushed with rage, asked to be given the floor, but he did not refute Petrovsky's allegation. Gladnev was aware that there were many present who were advocates of rehabilitating Stalin. I am certain that several of those sitting in the room sympathized with Gladnev, and would have had no objection to having their portraits displayed next to one of Stalin.

"I said to Petrovsky," Gladnev explained, "that Lenin was hardly a little dove, and when necessary he could raise his voice and force someone to do as he ordered. This is how I banged on the table with my fist. But when I saw that Petrovsky had not understood me correctly, I apologized."

Here Melnikov, half-smiling, looked triumphantly around the room and nodded in approval, as if to say. "You see, Gladnev apologized."

In his statement Petrovsky recalled Molotov's speech at a session of the USSR Supreme Soviet in August 1939, when he spoke of the pointlessness of waging war under the false banner of "destroying Hitlerism." Molotov's words, as read out by Petrovsky, fell on dead silence, until finally Pel'she's deputy Grishin stated: "The Party has already settled the matter of Molotov."

Petrovsky replied: "He was expelled for taking part in an antiparty group. But the foreign policy he pursued was not condemned."

One of the committee members then said angrily: "We are not now discussing the question of Molotov but of you, Comrade Petrovsky."

Petrovsky suddenly began to talk about his family, of how they had given up "four wonderful lives," and that he, in spite of the injustices committed against his family, had entered the Communist party because he believed in the triumph of truth and the triumph of communism. The committee members sighed with relief.

After Petrovsky's statement a break was declared in the proceedings. The members of the committee, with Pel'she at their head, remained in his office, while the others filed into the secretary's room and into the corridor. I took note of a curious detail: all participants at the meeting were offered tea with lemon and sugar, but members of the committee were brought biscuits as well! Even in such minor details, everything goes according to rank, according to status, I thought to myself.

Before leaving the conference room, I went up to Pel'she and handed him a folder containing typewritten excerpts from documents and other materials supporting my point of view. "Fine," Pel'she answered, "give the materials to Sdobnov."

"But," I objected, "my case has already been concluded there. It is being decided here now," and I pointed to the end of the table where Pel'she sat.

"Fine," Pel'she repeated calmly, "leave the folder here." I laid down the folder and went out into the corridor. People were gathering there. I went up to the secretary and she poured me some tea.

"You didn't make it with your statement," Gaponenko said to me in sympathy. "That's right, you didn't make it," smiled Sevastyanov apologetically. Samsonov remained silent. Then Gaponenko, in order to cheer us up, began to tell us a funny story. I burst out laughing. At that moment Melnikov passed by. When the meeting resumed, he began his intervention with the following words: "Here we are criticizing Nekrich, and he thinks nothing of it; he just goes around laughing. "

Apparently during the tea break the members of the committee were being briefed in Pel'she's office on how to conduct themselves. Events were unfolding in a completely unexpected manner: so far no one had confessed, and only Samsonov had recognized his error, in a very dignified and calm manner.

After the break Pospelov was the first to take the floor. It would be impossible to recount everything he said. His testimony was a complete muddle made up of various and sundry memories from the war and a story of how a special steel had been poured for making antitank weaponry. All this was offered up in the best tradition of Stalinist oratory. On listening to Pospelov I felt, if not thirty years, then at least twenty years younger. He quite unabashedly turned upside down everything I had written in my book. And he did this with the knack of an expert who had devoted his entire life to this profession. Pospelov knew full well that he was talking to people the majority of whom had not read my book, and who saw in Pospelov a paragon of party spirit. Actually, this former Latin teacher was currently a member at large of the presidium of the Academy of Sciences, the eyes and ears of the party in that distinguished gathering of Soviet scholarship, and a member of the Communist party Central Committee. At various times in the past he had been a candidate member of the Central Committee Presidium, secretary of the Communist party Central Committee, managing editor of *Pravda*, and so on and so forth. Professor Pospelov, like Deborin, who was to speak after him, felt it important to show the Control Committee that he had realized not only the harmfulness of Nekrich's book but also the oversights that had been committed during the discussion at the Institute of Marxism-Leninism, of which he was still the director. He seemed to me to be completely dotty. My God, I thought, this senile old man was a Central Committee secretary!

Deborin, after first giving some "scientific" arguments, then looked from side to side and said, "I must tell you one curious fact." After waiting for complete silence to fall on the room, Deborin continued. "Nekrich, after learning that I had written a negative reaction to his book, phoned me at home and threatened me." Deborin's statement achieved the desired reaction: "So, he threatened him! See how low he has stooped!" I shouted from my seat: "That's a lie!" But, needless to say, no one paid any attention to what I had to say. Deborin, however, did not consider that one "curious fact" to be enough, for he continued: "Who is Nekrich depending on abroad? I can tell you. Recently I was at a conference in Berlin, and a Czechoslovak historian said to me there: 'Why do you always write books about your exploits? We need books about your failures, your mistakes, like Nekrich's book.'" The reaction to Deborin's words was predictable: an outburst of indignant exclamations. How they hate the Czechs, and probably not just them, I thought to myself.

Pel'she next gave the floor to yet another expert, Major General Grylev, head of the military history department of the General Staff, a man known for his firm pro-Stalinist views. Grylev, unlike Deborin, was outwardly calm, and spoke in a dry tone of voice, without emotion, but at the same time, like Pospelov and Deborin, he distorted my text without hesitation, dreaming up and concocting logical conclusions that were not to be found in the book.

At last the acting director of my institute, L. S. Gaponenko, was given the floor. He had a great deal of experience in handling such delicate situations. He immediately emphasized that my book had no relation to the institute, that it was an unscheduled work, that its publishers were responsible for it, and that I had been criticized at the institute in this regard, and he had taken personal offense. But then people "were found" who elected me to the party committee. (Yes, I chuckled to myself, only 280 people were found.) There was one amusing moment in his statement: he reproached me for not exposing in my book a book written by, of all people, the Menshevik Abramovich. The book in question was well known. It had nothing to do with the events of the Second World War, but was on the October Revolution. A few weeks later, when passions had abated, I asked Gaponenko what Abramovich's book had to do with mine, to which he replied in his usual half-friendly manner: "Well, you see, the situation was such that I had to think of *something* to say."

One after another, members of the committee began to speak: first Pel'she's deputies—K. N. Grishin, S. O. Postovolov—then Melnikov, then someone else. Their speeches were seething with hatred not only for me but for everything related to the departure from Stalin and his policies. Grishin referred maliciously to the rehabilitations, saying that they had stirred up trouble. As far as I was concerned, the main theme of all their statements without exception was: Nekrich has lost his party spirit. There is no place for him in the party. Someone proposed expelling Petrovsky from the party as well, someone else objected that they could confine themselves to a reprimand, and so on. And here a strange thing happened. Gradually the words being uttered began to lose any meaning for me. I was overwhelmed by this outburst of hatred. I suddenly came to the realization that my case was a desirable pretext for venting the anger accumulated over the past ten or twelve years, when these same people, brought up and promoted in Stalinist times, had been forced to participate in anti-Stalinist activities. They had done this against their will, often sabotaging or interpreting as they saw fit decisions adopted by the Central Committee and decrees made by Khrushchev, in an attempt to compromise him.

A vulgar farce was being played out in this room. I tuned out virtually everything else that was said, listening only to the buzzing of voices. Then suddenly someone tapped me on the shoulder. It seemed I was being given the floor at last. What could I say to these people who were so infinitely alien to me? What could I say to these people who were so brazen in defending Stalinism, formally condemned by the party, and who were doing this with the approval of the presiding officer, a member of the party Politburo? Should I refute one after another the facts they had cited? That would be senseless. And so I uttered only four sentences: "I am stunned by all that I have heard here. I have to take it all in. I did not enter the party by accident, I became a member at the front. I have written my book out of patriotic convictions."

I say these words and take my seat. A deadly silence reigns in the room. Pel'she sums up the discussion. There are two points of view: one is Nekrich's, the other is the party's. They are incompatible. Conclusion: I must be expelled from the Communist party of the Soviet Union. The grounds and actual wording are read out from a prepared and printed text. All I remember is this: the book is antiparty, is being used by reactionary propaganda, by enemies of the party—by the Trotskyites and somebody else as well—and Nekrich persists in his errors. Next I am told: "Hand in your party card." I stand up and go toward the door. A man, advanced in age, comes up to me and looks at me with a mixture of sympathy and apprehension, as if in fear that I might bite—but to what end? No, I won't.

I go down the stairs toward the building exit. All of a sudden I stop in bewilderment: How will I get out of the Central Committee building if my party card has been taken from me? The state security official who checks the documents of everyone entering and leaving looks at me inquisitively.

"My party card has been taken away from me."

"Your surname?"

I give my name.

"You may go."

It seems that is all. I go out into the street. It is still hot and humid. I unknot my tie and put it in my briefcase. I take a deep breath, and then breathe out. And then out of habit I begin to pronounce words in my mind:

Breathe in—go in.

Breathe out—go out.

Damn! So breathe out means go out, and go out means breathe out! For some reason I suddenly regain my calm and leave, moving farther and farther from the gray Communist party Central Committee building on Staraya Ploshchad'.

In spite of the fact that the Control Committee meeting had been carefully arranged, the entire basis for the charges was extremely shaky. Moreover, those who had prepared my case had to resort not only to misquotes and falsifications of the text of my book, but also to outright lies, to misleading the committee members. But this was more than likely the tried-and-true party practice over the years, in which the truth in general was of no significance.

I shall give one example. Sdobnov in his statement said that my book had received negative responses from marshals I. S. Konev, K. S. Moskalenko, and F. I. Golikov. This statement by Sdobnov was meant to have an effect on the committee members, despite the fact that not one of these supposed responses was read to them. I was not able to refute Sdobnov at the meeting. But a few days later I found out that Marshal Moskalenko had categorically stated that no one had approached him for a review of my book, and that therefore he had never written a reaction. As far as Golikov is concerned, he had indeed recorded his response. Here is what he wrote immediately after reading the book:

Karlovy Vary
November 24, 1965

The research borders on inquiry, if not investigation.

A good, accurate, useful, and extremely valuable book, no doubt a timely one.

The book contains a great many facts unknown not only to the mass reader but to the higher circles of society as well.

One discovers that many books we need by foreign authors are not published here, and this includes particularly necessary books by German authors.

As to my own reaction:

1. A great deal of what I read I did not know, and this includes the activities of the General Staff and the People's Commissariat for Defense, as well as of Stalin.
2. I will have to read many of the sources listed in the book, for the first time in fact.
3. Many of these sources are inaccessible to me, however, since they are not published here, and also because of my insufficient knowledge of German, English, and other languages.
4. While reading I recalled a great deal from my work in the intelligence directorate.
5. On the basis of what I have read, I could draw up a rather extensive list of questions for my own work on my memoirs of the intelligence directorate, and this includes the flagrant lack of coordination among agencies dealing in intelligence work, and the complete absence of contact among them.
6. On the military mission to Britain and the United States, I should refer to A. M. Nekrich for consultation and, perhaps, assistance.

It is a matter of interest that one of the main arguments supporting the claim that I had fallen under the influence of bourgeois ideology was the supposed number of references to foreign sources in comparison to Soviet ones. This count, conducted by Senichkin, Gladnev, and Sdobnov, demonstrated, or so they claimed, that I had referred to more foreign sources than Soviet ones. But what did that mean anyway? Nonetheless, this argument was advanced not only by them but also by one of the members of the Control Committee. What was amusing, however, was that even here the party investigators slipped up. Out of curiosity I once made a count of the references myself; it turned out that the Soviet sources actually outnumbered the foreign ones. This is the level at which we find our ideological elite! And yet, Sdobnov has a doctorate in economics, and is a professor at the Higher Party School.

At the end of July, I drew up a detailed analysis of the accusations leveled at me during the Control Committee meeting. This twenty-eight–page document began to make the rounds. Then the new party committee secretary, Pavel Volobuev (later director of the Institute of USSR History) called me in and asked me not to distribute it anymore.

A few hours after my expulsion from the party, I returned home and phoned my party committee secretary, V. P. Danilov, gave him a brief account of what had happened, and asked him to come over. He kept trying to make excuses, obviously he did not feel like coming. Finally, a few members of the party committee met at my home, and I reported to them in detail on what had occurred. I expressed the view that my expulsion from the party would be used against the committee as a whole and that it was probably better for them not to take up my defense. Knowing our party system as I did, I fully realized what course events might take. The committee members were confused, and indeed there were grounds for confusion. After a brief exchange of opinions they went home. This was my last meeting with the party committee.

All my subsequent steps were undertaken with the objective of sheltering my close colleagues in the committee from persecution by the vengeful Central Committee apparatus. It should not be forgotten that the science department of the Academy was headed by S. P. Trapeznikov, who deeply detested the Institute of History, and especially Danilov, whom he not only considered a historian on collectivization who had strayed from the correct party line, but whom he also personally held responsible for his own failure to gain election to corresponding membership in the Academy of Sciences—something about which he was, incidentally, mistaken.

I decided to act in accordance with party canons. Without waiting to receive my official notice of expulsion, on July 4, 1967, I sent a request to the Politburo appealing for reconsideration of the party Control Committee decision.

The Control Committee decree, as read out by Pel'she, consisted of five points: the first point referred to me, the second to Samsonov, who was given a reprimand to be recorded in his file; the third to Boltin and Tel'pukhovsky for their failures in conducting the discussion of my book. A fourth point proposed the establishment of a commission to verify the work of the Institute of History party organization and lend it assistance. And in a fifth it was proposed that an inquiry be conducted into the unpartylike conduct of individual communists who had spoken during the discussion at the Institute of Marxism-Leninism. This had one objective: to force all of them to repent and, thereby, wipe out the discussion at the Institute of Marxism-Leninism as if it had never taken place.

First and foremost, Kulish, Dashichev, and Anfilov—that is, all the military people—were called into the party Control Committee to see Sdobnov. I cannot say exactly what happened there, but the matter stopped with a severe reprimand. V. A. Anfilov, they say, wrote a confession.

Doctor of Historical Science Lev Yurevich Slezkin was summoned separately by the committee. He was one of the most honest people I had ever met in my life. The son of a once well-known but alas now forgotten Russian writer, Yury Slezkin, Lev was called up into army service as far back as the Finnish campaign of 1939, and served there right up until the end of the war in 1945. We were the same age, both having been born in 1920. Lev's mother was once an actress, and he inherited from his parents a highly nervous sensibility and an emotional disposition. During the war Lev Slezkin was a tank commander, and in the course of an attack lost an eye in a burning tank. From then on he went around with an eye patch, which was quite well suited to his refined image and slightly elongated face. His entire look was somewhat romantic, and he was, in fact, a romantic by nature. After the war he completed a degree in history at Moscow State University, did his graduate studies under the guidance of Professor A. S. Yerusalimsky, and then became a doctor of sciences, a specialist in U.S. and Latin American history. He wrote several very good books and was twice sent to Cuba. After returning to Moscow, he wrote a *History of the Republic of Cuba*.

After his return from Cuba, Lev Yurevich was called before the party Control Committee. No doubt the meeting was not a short one. He came out with a severe reprimand. Supposedly this was not a penalty, but when, in subsequent years, the question of foreign travel came up, Professor Slezkin's candidacy was inevitably rejected. For the last twelve years he has not been allowed to go abroad.

Fortunately Slezkin was creative by nature. In 1979 the first part of his marvelous study, to which he had devoted many years of his life, came out: *The Underlying Origins of American History*, on the early history of the United States. This book immediately became a best-seller.

When I think about the punishment inflicted on almost all those who participated in the discussion, I cannot help but feel that it was not only the book that was involved, but a general trend which had emerged in our country shortly after the Revolution. The unwritten party rule, never stated publicly or directly, was to create a new collective national memory, to sweep away all recollection of what had actually occurred, eliminate from history everything that did not correspond to the historical claims of the Communist party. A cleansing of the collective memory was carried out first of all through the physical annihilation of living witnesses to history. Systematic terror destroyed one stratum after another of the Russian intelligentsia, the crucible of national memory, including all the representatives of the bourgeois parties; then after them the socialist revolutionaries; then the Marxist Mensheviks, and, finally, the Marxist Bolsheviks. After this, regular purges began of the new generation of humanists. And each time the nation was deprived of a portion of its collective memory, of part of its history, and in its place there took hold a remembrance of something that had never actually happened—an artificial memory. And if someone suddenly threw up his hands and exclaimed, "Wait a minute, it didn't happen that way!" he was considered a very dangerous individual. The powers that be would demand renunciation and repentance, and if these were not forthcoming, they would take revenge.

The vindictiveness of power—I would say the *petty* vindictiveness of power—is an inherent characteristic of the Soviet regime.

After my expulsion from the party, almost all my friends suffered, not just Slezkin, but each one in his own way. None of them received further permission for travel abroad. One female colleague at the institute, with whom I was once on friendly terms, was dismissed from her post as academic secretary. Needless to say, no formal pretext was sought.

But the brainwashing was not the end of this affair. Dashichev, Kulish, and Anfilov went into retirement from military service. The well-known publicist Yevgeny Aleksandrovich Gnedin was dragged before the party Control Committee for a long session. (He had spent seventeen years in the Stalinist camps.) For two years the committee also attempted to nab Aleksei Vladimirovich Snegov, the old communist who had also served seventeen years in Kolyma and, after returning, had become an active champion of restoring historical truth. The order was given to expel Snegov from the party. Samsonov was deprived of his post as director of the "Nauka" publishing house, although some time later he was appointed senior editor of the institute publication *Istoricheskie zapiski*. Reprisals were directed not only against those who had taken part in the discussion of my book, but also against those for whom the Stalinists had long been sharpening their teeth.

The repression was directed, for example, at Viktor Ivanovich Zuyev, who had worked for many years at the "Nauka" publishers, first as an editor, then as head of history publications, and then as deputy senior editor. He had served for a long time as secretary of the publishers' party organization. A man of impeccable honesty, devoted to his work, he enjoyed enormous popularity not only among the staff at "Nauka" but also among many of the scholars who had worked in the Academy of Sciences system and among military circles as well. Zuyev was a veteran of the Fatherland War; he had been wounded, and his limp was to remain a permanent memory of his experience. Thanks to Zuyev's initiative and energy, a military history series was inaugurated at the "Nauka" publishing house. This series was, and continues to be, extremely popular. Zuyev's independent judgment, his authority, his outspokenness in expressing his views and evaluating manuscripts aroused the ire and dissatisfaction of the party idlers and ignoramuses, who attempted to force their own weak manuscripts into print. In an effort to conceal their incompetence, sometimes their abject illiteracy, these authors accused Zuyev of various political errors and slips (including, incidentally, "protecting Nekrich"). At last they succeeded after a fierce struggle in forcing him out of the publishing house. He was transferred to a job at the journal *Novaya i noveishaya istoriya.*

Two weeks after my expulsion from the party, I was called in to the October District Committee of the Communist party, where the department head, Knigin, showed me the party Control Committee decree. It had been decided: "To exclude CPSU member Nekrich, Aleksandr Moiseevich, a member of the CPSU since 1943, party card no. 00158709, for deliberate distortion in his book *June 22, 1941* on the policy of the CPSU and the Soviet government on the eve and at the beginning of the Great Fatherland War, which was used by foreign reactionary propaganda for anti-Soviet purposes."

When I read this decision, I was concerned over the phrase "deliberate distortion," for this expression corresponded to the legal formula "premeditation" and "with malice aforethought." It could—not necessarily, of course, but should the need arise—pave the way for criminal prosecution. Where did this wording come from? Here I recalled that the document prepared by the Control Committee contained the phrase "either unwittingly, or with malicious intent." I had been given the opportunity to repent before the committee, in which case it would have been considered that my "transgression" had been committed "unwittingly." My refusal to do penance automatically resulted in the alternative wording, which implied deliberate action. Such a decree could hang over my head like the sword of Damocles.

Therefore, on July 15 I sent out a second letter to Brezhnev, in which I strongly protested this wording and my expulsion from the CPSU.

Even before the meeting of the Control Committee, when I was first shown the indictment, I had drawn attention to the fact that I had seen only part of the document, the first ten pages. Later on, when the meeting was under way, I understood why this had been done: the officials did not want to show me the accusations made against the party committee of the Institute of History, of which I was a member. Nor was the party committee secretary, Danilov, allowed access to the Control Committee meeting, in spite of his request. Further on in one of the paragraphs of the Control Committee decree on the Nekrich case, provision was made for the establishment of a commission to verify the work of the Institute of History party organization.

I have already mentioned that I had long suspected that the attack launched against my book had actually been plotted on a wider scale, that it was designed to break up the democratic party committee at the Institute of History and put an end to criticism of Stalin. The activities of our committee had long been viewed with alarm at the top. Dozens of denunciations were sent to the Central Committee containing political accusations. Secretary Danilov did not succeed in answering all the inquiries and charges. It had not proved possible to replace the membership of the party committee through legitimate elections. The Nekrich affair was therefore used as a pretext to replace the party committee with another more compliant one. My expulsion from the party was meant to divide the party organization at the institute, enhance the position of the pro-Stalinist elements, instill hesitation and uncertainty in the staff of the party committee itself, and paralyze its will and its action. But in the early stages it was decided to proceed with caution. The Nekrich affair, after all, was based on very shaky grounds.

My expulsion from the Party had a stunning effect on the Institute of History; some of the party members phoned the Control Committee and met with Sdobnov and Gladnev, who gave some sort of vague explanation. In essence it boiled down to this: the road back to the party is not forbidden to Nekrich, but he must change his ways.

A few party members wrote a letter to the Politburo in which they expressed doubts concerning the fairness of the charges of deliberate distortion of party policy in my book and requested that my expulsion be reconsidered. Bearing in mind the mood that prevailed in the institute's party organization at the time, the Central Committee decided to convene an institute party meeting solely to inform members of the Control Committee decision, without opening a debate under any circumstances, and limiting itself to the customary resolution—"to take note" of the decision. The meeting was not a prolonged one. There were attempts by the Stalinists to introduce a resolution approving the Control Committee decision, but the district party representative reminded them that this was not required.

My situation was complicated. Normally, after expulsion from the party a humanist was dismissed from work or transferred somewhere out of sight, for example, to a library. In my case, it was decided to retain me at my job. Whose decision this was it is difficult to say. The decision of the Control Committee was affirmed either at a meeting of the Politburo or at a session of the Central Committee secretariat. It is said that Pel'she, in reporting my case, proposed that I be fired, but that this part of his proposal did not meet with support. The reactions of the communist parties of the socialist countries and of Western Europe were beginning to emerge at about that time. The result was that the book was getting a positive reaction everywhere, and was receiving many reviews in the press, some of which even pointed out that the publication of my book disproved rumors to the effect that a restoration of Stalinism was under way in the USSR. It was simply impossible to fly in the face of this type of reaction at the time. Moreover, not all Politburo members, apparently, were in agreement with the Control Committee decision. Several years afterwards, at a meeting of newspaper editors D. S. Polyansky took a copy of the book out of his desk and said, "I do not understand what is wrong with this book."

My behavior after being expelled would be of critical importance. I was determined to act in keeping with traditional considerations. Therefore, I submitted an appeal to the Communist party Central Committee and requested that my own party Committee support my appeal. But it was precisely here that quite a dramatic event occurred, which deserves to be recounted.

This was the statement I sent to the Party Committee of the institute:

September 1, 1967

On June 28 of this year I was expelled from party membership by a decision of the Communist party Central Committee Party Control Committee.

On July 4 and 15 I sent the CPSU Central Committee Politburo a request addressed to party General Secretary Comrade L. I. Brezhnev that this decision be reconsidered (copies of these statements were transmitted by me to the party committee). The reasons for my request have been set forth in detail in those statements.

In connection with the fact that for twenty-two years (since 1945) I have taken an active part in the work of the party organization of the Institute of History, and my scholarly activities have been performed in full view of institute staff officials, I ask that the party committee support my request for reconsideration of the decision to expel me from the CPSU.

A day later Danilov, with his deputy Ya. S. Drabkin present, told me that my statement would be considered at the next meeting of the party committee. Danilov assured me in this regard that he would support my action. Drabkin, too, promised me the same thing.

I had no doubt that my action would indeed find support in the Party Committee, where I had not been a member for so very long, although I did not believe that my Party membership would be restored.

It was a great blow to me when I learned a few days later that the Party Committee had decided to refrain from taking action. It was an even greater blow to me that neither Danilov nor Drabkin had supported my request. There were a few party committee members who insisted on action, but they turned out to be in the minority. I believe that this decision was in fact the beginning of the end for the party committee, in that many of its members lost their moral courage not only in the eyes of staff but also in their own eyes as well. As was to be expected in such cases, Danilov's reasoning was that "we cannot sacrifice the interests of institute staff for the sake of one individual." It was the same old song. No one had ever gained anything from such a position,and neither did Danilov gain anything by it.

Nothing, not even being expelled from the party, had the same effect on me as the 180–degree turn taken by the party committee leadership. I was terribly despondent. Naturally I was cheered by the fact that many of my comrades had condemned Danilov's stand, believing it to be misguided and shortsighted.

In the fall of 1967, regular elections to the party committee took place, and its membership was almost completely reelected.

Inasmuch as I had submitted an appeal to the Communist party Central Committee, the administration didn't touch me. They were waiting to see what the decision would be. I had my work set out according to plan, which was not scheduled to be completed until the fall of 1969. Part of it had already been discussed at a meeting of the section, and from an administrative standpoint there could be no claims made against me.

Meanwhile, the journal *Voprosy istorii KPSS* published a lengthy article about me written by Deborin and Tel'pukhovsky. The article was entitled "In Ideological Captivity to Bourgeois Falsifiers of History." It repeated and developed the main points in the statements made at the party Control Committee meeting. Now that everything had come out in the open, it quickly became clear that the accusations did not stand up to criticism. Deborin and Tel'pukhovsky did not stop here, though, at indulging in distortions and misquotes in full view of an indignant public.

Soon afterwards I sent a detailed analysis of the article to the journal's editors, going through each of the charges and showing them to be deliberate and false. I sent copies of the letter to Brezhnev and to the presidium of the Academy of Sciences.

Deborin and Tel'pukhovsky's article gave rise to an outburst of public indignation. The editors were deluged with individual and collective letters from historians, writers, old Bolsheviks, and readers in general. It would be impossible to quote them all, for this would require some several hundred pages. I shall point out only that among those who openly expressed their condemnation of the article were the academician-historians N. Druzhinin and M. V. Nechkina, the chairman of the National Committee of Soviet Historians A. A. Guber, the well-known economist Academician S. Strumilin, the writers V. Kaverin and V. Tendryakov and the poet B. Slutsky. I should like to ask all those whom I have failed to mention to forgive me and understand the reasons for this. I remember them all and thank them. I shall quote only one letter, the shortest but a very expressive one.

September 12, 1969

To the Editors of the journal *Voprosy istorii KPSS*

Distinguished Comrades:
    After reading your issue number 9 for this year, containing a scathing review by G. A. Deborin and V. S. Tel'pukhovsky of A. M. Nekrich's book, and comparing it with the real contents of this little book, I consider it my duty as a scholar and a communist to state the following:
    Nekrich's book can be given different evaluations, but even the sharpest criticism has its limits, beyond which it becomes barely tolerable slander. And I fear that the reviewers of Nekrich's book, whether they wished to or not, in distorting its contents beyond recognition have already slid down this slippery path. This would be only half the problem, if each of them were merely risking their own reputations as seekers of truth. It is all the worse that such a review does not at all enhance the journal on whose pages it appears without a worthy subsequent response, either from the editors themselves or from their readers. It is intolerable that readers of a journal that appears under the sponsorship of our party should, on referring to it in search of historical truth, feel that they have been misled in its pages even once.
    I hope that the editors of the journal will understand me.

Academician S. Strumilin

    One day I was sitting at home all alone when the doorbell rang. On my doorstep stood a middle-aged man with the look of an intellectual, almost smiling. I immediately took a liking to him and asked him in. We sat down. The stranger said to me:
    "General Grigorenko sends you his regards," and he took a package out of his briefcase. In the package was a letter from the general and his article on the beginning of the war, which later became world famous.
    I shall quote the text of Pyotr Grigorevich Grigorenko's letter in full.

Most Distinguished Aleksandr Moiseevich:

On reading the review of your book in the journal *Voprosy Istorii KPSS*, I could not get over it for a long time afterwards. The book, in both its contents and its presentation, does not give *any grounds whatsoever* for even a hundredth of the accusations made in the review. Therefore I regard the latter as an attempt to put a ban on the publication of your work.

No honest person could fail to be indignant about this. The vital importance of this topic *for our country* cannot be disputed. Work on it has not even really begun. In fact your book is more a statement of the topic than an analysis of it. Bearing this in mind, I have shown rather greater enthusiasm in my letter than one should in my position. But let this remain a matter for my own conscience. Only one thing disturbs me: that anything in this letter of mine should to be construed as disrespectful of you and of your work. Quite the contrary, I sincerely respect your civic courage and ability, in an accessible and tactful manner, to portray an extremely serious topic.

With sincere respect
P. Grigorenko.

Inc: a copy of my letter to the editors of the journal *Voprosy Istorii KPSS.*

P.S. If you do not agree with anything in this letter, I shall be pleased to receive your objections and comments in oral or written form, as you deem most appropriate for yourself. My address and phone number are at the end of my letter.
P. G.

Needless to say, I was extremely gratified by this letter. General Grigorenko was for me a symbol of honesty, daring, and integrity. The letter has been with me for ten years. Now I can publish it at last.

Sdobnov and others who had "commissioned" the article were somewhat disturbed by the public reaction, but here as well they did not lose their bearings and began to explain to high-ranking individuals in the Central Committee that all these reactions were inspired by Nekrich himself. The absurdity of this is obvious.

The deputy head of the Central Committee science department, Professor Chekharin, was extremely and unpleasantly surprised by such reactions and suggested that the journal's editors publish selected letters from readers and responses from some academics. A. P. Kosulnikov, the managing editor of the journal, did indeed, publish a few excerpts from letters—in which the article by Deborin and Tel'pukhovsky was applauded!

It had evidently been decided to play down the Nekrich affair, to keep me at my job but limit publication of my work, not allow me to go abroad, not entrust graduate students to me, and not include me in academic conferences.

Deborin was duly rewarded. He received the medal of the Red Banner of Labor on his sixtieth birthday.

But it had become impossible to hush up the Nekrich affair, for those who had organized it had given it maximum publicity. In the years to come, translations of *June 22, 1941* began to come out one by one, accompanied by commentaries, documents, prologues, and epilogues. The book was translated and published in Poland, Czechoslovakia, Hungary, Italy, Austria, France, Yugoslavia, and the United States.

In late November 1967 Sdobnov informed me by telephone that my appeal had been rejected. How could things have been otherwise? I had not shown any desire to repent, after all, and this violated all the unwritten rules of party conduct. The church is in need of sinners, but of sinners who repent. An unrepentant sinner is seen as an affront to the church. But in the dark days of the Inquisition a repentant heretic was still a heretic in the eyes of the church, and he was treated accordingly, and the same was true of the Soviet Communist party. Had I not been expelled from the party, for all my remaining days I would have been reminded of my "sins" and of the generosity shown by the party, which had forgiven me and taken me back to its bosom. This is how the moral destruction of the human being takes place.

After November 1967, not only did I not appeal further to the higher party organs for restoration of my Party membership, but I constantly rejected unofficial invitations to perform a formal act of repentance and thereby make it possible for the Control Commission to forgive me. I received many such hints and proposals over the course of the next nine years. The last time was during my talk with the director of the Institute of World History, Ye. M. Zhukov, in late February 1975. These proposals were transmitted to me by various people connected with the party and with the state security organs.

Immediately following my expulsion from the party, speakers at meetings of party propagandists began to explain the reasons for this treatment. And in actual fact my situation was rather a strange one: I had been expelled from the Communist party not for an underground publication, not for something published abroad, but for a book that had been thoroughly laundered by the censors and published by a Soviet academic publisher. Those making the explanations naturally had to squirm like eels in a frying pan.

It is interesting to note, however, what these speakers said. Here is a summary record of one statement made at the party office of the Moscow City Committee.

> Much that is malicious has been written about the Great Fatherland War. In Moscow, for example, a book has come out by Nekrich, a doctor of historical science and senior researcher at the Institute of History. The book essentially consists of criticism of Soviet policy at the beginning of the war. Nekrich tries, following the example of bourgeois propagandists, to show that if the USSR had not concluded a treaty with Nazi Germany, and had moved toward a rapprochement with Britain and America, the Second World War would never have taken place. Not to mention the fact that this is a slanderous treatment of the war, what is immediately evident is the clear convergence of views of reactionary English and German bourgeois propagandists with the views of a Soviet historian. The book contains assertions to the effect that the Soviet Union conducted itself treacherously and the Western powers honestly. These issues have been sufficiently dealt with in Soviet historical literature: Anglo-French diplomacy tried to thrust Nazi Germany against the USSR. We can see it all very clearly: one cannot fail to note that Nekrich's book is based on bourgeois sources and disregards Soviet data. Nekrich, in the final analysis, has accused the party and government of not sufficiently preparing the country for the attack, and for not rearming properly.

At a Moscow City Komsomol meeting in mid-July of 1967, the lecturer received two notes. The first question asked: What if Nekrich was simply mistaken and did not do this deliberately?

He could not have been mistaken, came the reply. He has a doctorate in history, after all.

The second asked: Why was the decision to expel him from the party not taken until two years after the book came out?

Because during that entire time we tried to explain his mistakes to him, but he did not want to listen.

Opinion was far from unanimous, however. At one closed meeting the speaker, a senior official, was asked whether he did not think that the Nekrich affair might do enormous harm to the reputation of the Soviet Union abroad, to which he replied quite honestly: "Yes. Something very stupid has been done, and he will have to be restored to membership."

Reports of the expulsion were immediately sent abroad by many foreign newspaper and radio correspondents. Commentators interpreted my expulsion as a sign of increasing pressure from the Stalinists and a strengthening of their position in the party leadership.

By a strange twist of fate, it was at precisely this time that a translation of my book came out in Czechoslovakia, followed by another in Hungary; the book had already appeared just a bit earlier in Poland.

A great deal had changed in our country since Stalin's death, and the changes that were carried out were irreversible, in spite of all the ups and downs of history. In Stalinist times I would have been arrested immediately and condemned as an enemy of the people. Perhaps some of my friends might have turned away from me, and acquaintances would have denied that they ever knew me, that they had ever laid eyes on me. This happened often and did not even cause much indignation, only a bitter aftertaste.

My expulsion from the party did not cool relations with my friends; indeed it had just the opposite effect. Each of them in his or her way tried to do something to make life more pleasant for me. One of my friends took me out for some fresh air to the places where the great Russian poet Aleksandr Pushkin had once lived, to the Pskov area, Mikhailovskoye and Trigorskoye. This was a wonderful trip which enabled me to regain my bearings quickly.

Many of my fellow workers at the institute were also very kind to me. Even the majority of those who were unfriendly exercised restraint in their hostility.

My friends never abandoned me in those most difficult, trying moments of my life. I am lucky to have such friendships. We formed an indissoluble whole, and I believe that neither distance nor the misunderstandings that can sometimes lead to unhappy consequences will, in the final analysis, dissolve our spiritual bonds.

And what about the book *June 22, 1941*?

On August 20, 1967, Glavlit, the official censor, ordered all libraries without special collections to remove the book, register it, and destroy it. The book was torn up and burned in many libraries across the country. And this was happening not in the Middle Ages, but in the second half of the twentieth century in the world's first socialist state.

9
Nine Lean Years

Be strong of spirit, do not give
in to misfortune.
And when a wind is blowing
by you at full force,
Trim back wisely, after gathering in
just a bit
the billowing sail.
—Goratsy Flakk

I am hounded — invasion of Czechoslovakia — reaction in the USSR — effect in the West — reorganization of the Institute of History — attempts to deprive me of my doctorate — I resist — my manuscript is blocked — in the historical institutes — the Volobuev incident — the world history congress in Moscow — they decide not to let me attend — a breakthrough

My expulsion from the Communist party changed my life drastically: I now had a lot more free time. No one asked me anymore to participate in public service work. I had my time all to myself, and I could use it as I saw fit.

I had long observed that scholars who were nonparty members, if they were at the proper professional level, lived better and more freely than party members. I once calculated that I spent no less than 30 to 40 per cent of my working hours in party meetings, public service, and related negotiations. If nonparty specialists are wise enough not to aspire to executive posts, then they have indisputable advantages, even in a totalitarian system.

Yes, I had time. I simply needed to put it to good use. My status was rather vague. I was not a nonparty member in the strictest sense. I was a former communist, expelled from the party for political reasons, and therefore I was somewhere in the middle, neither inside the party nor outside it. I now had to get used to my new situation. If I did not include my direct administrative obligations as a senior research staff member, I was much freer than I had been before 1967. But now a complication of another type had arisen: strange people began to come on the scene and then disappear, some of them very fine people indeed, but there were others who aroused my strongest suspicions. I had to expend a great deal of effort to get rid of the latter. Yet I still found it impossible to rid myself of all of them, just as it was impossible to make one of the most essential aspects of life under the Soviet system disappear as if by magic. I understood that henceforth I would become an object of observation everywhere by the state security organs. This, of course, did not mean that I would constantly be followed; but information about me, and about my conversations and meetings, would be gathered regularly. Soon I received warnings that a listening device had been placed in our entryway, but it was rather difficult to verify this. It was simpler to deal with the telephone, which could simply be unplugged. I figured out who among my acquaintances might have special instructions from state security to keep tabs on me, and I was not mistaken in my assumption. I had several such "tails," however, and here I grossly miscalculated, although I cannot blame myself entirely for this.

Approximately a month after my expulsion from the party, a very well known dissident phoned me (I do not even dare risk giving his initials, for this would be tantamount to naming him) and asked me whether I wished to meet with a lady who had occupied a very high-ranking position in the past and was friendly with some well-placed individuals who might exercise a favorable influence on my fate. He told me that this lady was prepared to meet me at the apartment of a friend by the name of Abram Isaakovich. I arrived at the appointed time, and our meeting took place. During the course of the next year and a half or so, I met periodically with Abram Isaakovich, either at his home or at his place of work in the permanent mission of the Azerbaijan SSR. We talked primarily about political topics. Abram Isaakovich was on friendly terms with Yakir, Gabay, and other democrats. I asked some of them about Abram Isaakovich and invariably received a most favorable response; he was considered a kind person who helped the democrats in their difficult situation. And this indeed was the case. But, furthermore, Abram Isaakovich was well informed about all events, and about many of the actions undertaken by the democrats. You could always find the newest samizdat literature at his place, learn the latest news, and so on. Once he even came to my home. My mother liked him very much, especially since, like my father, he had once worked in Azerbaijan, and, as he told us, he knew a lot of people there with whom my late father had been friendly. On the occasion of the fiftieth anniversary of the establishment of Soviet power in Azerbaijan, our family (and I am sure that Abram Isaakovich was the one who had included my father on the list) received a certificate of gratitude from the Azerbaijani government.

I later found out that it was to Abram Isaakovich's place that Yakir slipped out on August 25, 1968, when the famous protest demonstration against the invasion of Czechoslovakia by Soviet forces took place in Red Square. Pavel Litvinov, Vadim Delone, Natalya Gorbanevskaya, Viktor Feinberg, Vladimir Dremlyug, Konstantin Babitsky, and Larisa Bogoraz took part in that demonstration. Yakir was to participate in the demonstration as well, but, as he later claimed, he was supposedly detained by the militia. Actually he got cold feet at the last minute and went to Abram Isaakovich's place.

At any rate, in spite of our rather friendly relationship, I always felt somehow unsure about Abram Isaakovich. From the very first time I visited his apartment, I had the strange impression that all of his walls, ceilings, and doors were lined with bamboo matting. Then suddenly the decor changed; this time everything was covered in gray canvas. The thought occurred to me: might not microphones be hidden behind all this decoration? But I dismissed the idea. After all, Abram Isaakovich's wife was an artist, and I thought that perhaps she had her whims. Gradually, however, I developed further doubts for another reason. Once I visited Abram Isaakovich at work and unexpectedly found in his office a very elegantly dressed Azerbaijani about fifty years of age. I introduced myself, but the man did not give his name. The three of us sat together for about fifteen minutes. I got the clear impression that I was being shown off. Later on I was told that the democrats had heard from Abram Isaakovich that a friend of his from Azerbaijan worked for the KGB. I think that this must have been that same friend. Another interesting thing is that Abram Isaakovich's connections were long known.

Then Abram Isaakovich went on tour to Paris. This too gave me some doubt. Why was a person so closely linked to the democrats allowed to go to Paris? But what I found out after his return gave me even greater pause. It seemed that on his own initiative he had arranged for Ye. S. Ginsburg to receive royalties after her book on the repression of the 1930s, *Journey into the Whirlwind*, was published and became famous abroad. Yevgeniya Semyonova had not asked him to do this. Later on she cornered him and told him frankly that she had thought he worked for the KGB. But I parted company with Abram Isaakovich after all my suspicions were vindicated. This is how it happened. One time I went to visit him when he was ill with some heart problem. We talked about nothing in particular, and I left. The very next day he phoned me, asking me to come over quickly on some urgent matter, but when I arrived, he wanted to speak about something we had already discussed a long, long time before. I was very annoyed over this waste of time and was about to leave, but I could not restrain myself from asking him what the important matter was and why he had asked me to come. He hemmed and hawed a bit, and then he said: "What would you say if you were asked to apologize for your book and after that were restored to membership in the party?"

I must say that I am very skeptical when it comes to rumors that X, Y, or Z works for the KGB. You need facts, evidence; and even then, there were cases in which those who had cooperated with the KGB broke off all relations with them afterwards, although this put them at a great risk.

I answered: "I do not need to apologize. My case was trumped up by the Stalinists and will one day be declared null and void."

"Yes, yes, you're right," Abram Isaakovich replied hastily, and I left. We never sat down face to face with each other again. He phoned me several times and suggested that we get together, but I declined his offer. The last time I saw him was at Ilya Gabay's funeral.

One day I began to hear from my friends in secret that, according to A., who was working through the KGB, one high-ranking individual at the Committee for State Security had said: "Let Nekrich confess his mistakes, and he will be reinstated in the party." Finally, a third unofficial proposal of the same type came at approximately the same time from a certain official of the presidium of the Academy of Sciences.

Needless to say, my answers were always identical. My break with the party had been final. Once, when I met the famous dissident who had recommended that I meet Abram Isaakovich, I asked him outright: "Did you know that A. I. was linked to the KGB?" to which the latter, without batting an eye, replied: "Yes, I have known about it for a long time and do not maintain relations with him."

"So, why didn't you warn me then?"

"What do you mean? I thought you knew!"

There you have it—typical Russian carelessness. About two years ago Zhores Medvedev, in one of his articles published in England, flatly referred to Abram Isaakovich as a KGB agent.

Someone else was tailing me as well. I guessed this was happening, but since somebody had to be doing it anyway, I preferred that it be a person I knew. What can you do? That is a way of life in the Soviet Union.

At the end of July 1968, Nadya and I went to Yaremcha, a picturesque spot at the foot of the Carpathians. A rather large and boisterous group of our friends was already gathering there: physicists, artists, and just plain nice people. We vacationed and enjoyed ourselves as best we could. But convoys of military equipment, soldiers, and trucks were passing through Yaremcha at the time, on their way toward the Czechoslovak border, which was not far from there.

Newspapers were slow in arriving at Yaremcha from Moscow, and our major source of information was the radio, on which we could pick up foreign broadcasts: the BBC, Deutsche Welle, Voice of America, the Austrian and Czech radio stations.

We sighed with relief on learning of the meeting between Czechoslovak and Soviet leaders in Ciezna and decided that the danger of Soviet military intervention had been eliminated. We had previously had stormy arguments about whether the USSR would send its troops into Czechoslovakia or not. I had great misgivings, but I still hoped that the Soviet Union would not commit such a tremendous blunder as intervention. Several of my friends, as it turned out, took a more realistic view and argued that there was no blunder or crime that could not be committed by a state where constant violence was enshrined by law and tradition.

We sat for hours by the radio, which gave more and more details on the intervention in Czechoslovakia by troops from socialist countries. A radio station in Dresden spouted a stream of lies and slander against the Czechs. We fervently hoped with all our hearts that this time the Western powers would find the strength and opportunity through the United Nations at least to condemn the Soviet Union in moral terms. But just as in 1938, at the time of Munich, and afterwards in March 1939, during the dismemberment of Czechoslovakia by Nazi Germany, a good number of "realistic politicians" came forward in U.S. and Western European political circles and warned against the danger of confrontation with the Soviet Union. Among them were people who took pride in their liberal convictions.

During those days I was reminded of the policy of the Western powers toward Czechoslovakia in 1938–39, which I had studied in depth. There was, of course, a big difference in the historical situation, but much less so psychologically. I could feel in August 1968 an atmosphere of defeatism beginning to spread in the West. This feeling was different from that of the prewar period. A sense of defenselessness in the face of Soviet armies prepared at any time, if the order were given, to break through to the Rhine and the mouth of the Scheldt prevailed in the West. The idea was especially widespread that Czechoslovakia had already been turned over by the Western powers to the Soviet Union at the end of the Second World War and was part of its sphere of influence, and that there was thus no sense in getting involved in the matter.

When, soon after the events in Czechoslovakia, there began a period of reconciliation between the Soviet Union and West Germany, a country that Soviet propaganda had only recently accused of preparing an invasion of Czechoslovakia, the "realistic politicians" proudly repeated: "So, you see, we were right. The Soviet Union has calmed down now." But a few years later there was Angola. And this will not be the end of it. Incidentally, the so-called threat to Czechoslovakia from West Germany was one of the main arguments offered by the Soviet leaders for domestic consumption in explaining the "fraternal assistance" offered to the Czecho-slovak people. And this argument turned out to be extremely effective within the USSR. Two sentiments prevailed in the mood of the Soviet population at the time. The first: the Germans want war again. And the second: "We liberated the Czechs, and now those bastards want to live better than we do. We have to put them down." And so the Czechs were put down.

The overwhelming majority of Western politicians, with all their supposed wisdom, failed in August 1968, just as they had failed earlier, to understand the psychology and main motivation of the Soviet leadership, which reflected the essence of Soviet society and of the regime. The Soviet Union rejects in principle the possibility of maintaining the status quo for a lengthy period. Marxist ideology regards the world as being constantly in flux, in motion; and therefore one of the principles of Soviet foreign policy, to which—and due tribute should be paid here—the USSR adheres unswervingly, not only in theory but above all in practice, is to lend support to any force undermining the existing system in Western countries. This is stated by the Soviet leaders quite openly and is written about even more candidly in Soviet theoretical journals, essays on peaceful coexistence, and many of the books and pamphlets published in the Soviet Union. Gradually, it is thought, the West will become accustomed to this idea and will resign itself to it.

Let us return, however, to the events of the 1960s. The invasion of Czechoslovakia by Soviet troops aroused profound indignation among a segment of the Soviet intelligentsia. For the first time in the history of the Soviet state and in the many decades of its existence, a protest demonstration took place in Red Square. The demonstrators were very few in number, but on that day these courageous young people saved the honor of a nation of 210 million.

In our institute, as in other institutions, there were staff meetings to approve the Soviet government's action. But even at these official meetings there were people who, by their questions or abstention in the vote or, to a much lesser extent, their voting against, demonstrated that the spiritual revolution, whose origins went back to the end of the war against Nazi Germany, was under way. This spirit is developing and will continue to do so in spite of official Soviet conformism, repression, and persecution. This will be a drawn-out, tortuous process, but it is proceeding inexorably.

The invasion of Czechoslovakia in August 1968 was one of the turning points in the history of Soviet society. It laid the foundation for a rebirth of the intelligentsia in the Soviet Union and of its spirituality.

During the events in Czechoslovakia I began to gather material for a book about these events—the Czechoslovakian archive—but I had to destroy all the materials on my departure: it was impossible to take them out with me. The events in Czechoslovakia became for many a turning point in their world view. It is known that even the highest circles, including some members of the Politburo, were overcome by doubts as to whether it was right to send in Soviet troops. But once the leaders had made the decision, they were embarked on a most perilous path, one from which they could not stray. I know some very high-ranking people who, in the privacy of their homes, condemned this decision. Others, on learning of the intervention in Czechoslovakia, cried, parting company forever with their illusions. But what is interesting to note is that some of them became cynical careerists after this, ready to do anything for the sake of living a life of prominence and luxury, while still others cursed the system, a few of them openly joining forces with the dissidents. There were also those who unraveled all the spiritual threadas that still bound them to the Soviet system, although they did not openly leave the Communist party.

Before the invasion of Czechoslovakia, some of my friends had advised me to attempt to regain membership in the party. Once I had a painful discussion with a close friend, to whom I confided that I did not intend to try to regain my membership. He snapped at me in annoyance: "You can't be selfish. You have to think of other people." No, I was not being selfish, and everything I had done prior to my expulsion from the party and immediately afterwards (I had followed established tradition and submitted requests for reconsideration of the matter) I did in the general interest of the team to which I had belonged for many long years. But I had broken with conformism definitively and irrevocably. Sooner or later every person has to make a choice. Nevertheless, after the events of August 1968, many people envied me for no longer being in the party and thereby not being an accomplice to this latest crime.

After 1968 I came to the firm decision to do battle with conformism everywhere and always, not shrinking from confrontations, regardless of the consequences. I believe that I have kept this promise to myself.

After the intervention in Czechoslovakia, a period of some softening began. Periods of softening or of calming down have always accompanied unpopular actions by the Communist party and the Soviet state. This was almost a single process. A similar phenomenon occurs in nature: breathing in and breathing out. Such a system provides the opportunity for making balanced progress, or just for marking time.

Right after the invasion of Czechoslovakia, the USSR importunately called for peaceful, creative work, for a settlement of relations with the West, for fraternal friendships within the socialist system. The Soviet Union, an opponent in principle of maintaining the status quo, each time it committed yet another aggressive action or completed a successful operation in expanding its influence anywhere would appeal to the need for observing the rules of living together in human society, for supporting principles of peaceful coexistence and for maintaining strict legality in its own country. The same applied to the intervention in Czechoslovakia. Now, reasoned those liberal-minded government officials who believed themselves to be wise, the Soviet Union had stabilized the situation in its own sphere of influence, had calmed things down, and on this basis it was possible to go on. It is necessary to realize the inferiority complex of the Kremlin rulers, who are constantly obsessed by plots against the USSR. Such a "quasi-Munich" frame of mind was extremely typical of the governments of nearly all the major Western countries. For its part, the Soviet Union began an intensive diplomatic and propagandistic attack, closely tied with its requirements in the economic sphere.

Offering one enticement after another to foreign concerns and banks, placing or promising profitable orders, the Soviet Union began to receive enormous loans, soon making such countries as Italy somewhat economically dependent on the USSR, linking up with West German firms, and awakening business circles in the United States and Japan to the prospect of participating in the economic development of Siberia.

On the ideological front, the Communist party engaged in a number of maneuvers, making some concessions for show to the other communist parties, declaring (how many times!) that each party was independent, and that there could be different paths toward socialism. At the same time, the Soviet press maliciously derided those idealists who seriously believed that there could be socialism with a human face.

A more genuine manifestation of Soviet policy was to be found in the attempts to replace the leadership in the more "recalcitrant" communist parties, such as the Spanish party, for example, where the leadership, headed by Santiago Carrillo, was confronted with a fractious group headed by Enrice Lister, who attempted to establish among Spanish émigrés living in Moscow something akin to a new rival communist party. A similar situation prevailed in the communist party of Greece, where Soviet party support for the more pro-Stalinist faction of the divided leadership showed quite clearly how the principle of sovereignty for each communist party was observed. Attempts to sow discord in the Italian party were unsuccessful, although the pro-Soviet faction was strong and influential at the time.

Repercussions of the Czechoslovak drama even reached as far as the social sciences in the Soviet Union. Once again resounding appeals were made for merciless combat with the revisionists, "for the purity of Marxism-Leninism." It is rather curious to note how slogans in the ideological struggle changed at the time. After the Twentieth Party Congress in February 1956, the slogan was "Fight against dogmatism"; after the events in Hungary, it was "Fight against revisionists and dogmatists." This slogan took on different variations until the Twenty-Second Communist Party Congress. The removal of Stalin's remains from the mausoleum was the final apotheosis of the Khrushchev era. After Khrushchev's fall, the task of fighting revisionists was highlighted once again, and intensified as the "Prague spring" blossomed.

The events in Czechoslovakia caught the Institute of History at the height of its program of reorganization. The issue of reorganizing the institute had been pending for a number of years, and had been discussed at various meetings, conferences, and the like. It was felt that the institute had become too cumbersome and difficult to manage. In actual fact it had become difficult to manage not because it was cumbersome but because the academic leadership did not wish to heed the signs of the times, but rather preferred to work in the old-fashioned way. The activity of our party committee and the appearance of a number of books and articles by historians diverging from the "norm"—that is, from the official party line, itself not very clear-cut, by the way—were used by Trapeznikov to demonstrate to the right people "upstairs" that the institute had become unmanageable. Trapeznikov's failure to get himself elected to the Academy of Sciences in 1966 was of some significance here, and he chose this unique way of taking revenge. (He finally managed to get into the academy ten years later—when he was elected a corresponding member in 1976.) Trapeznikov made skillful use of the desire of some scholars to obtain appointments to high-ranking positions as institute directors or deputy directors, for which there was fierce competition. By decree of the Central Committee secretariat and the presidium of the Academy of Sciences, the Institute of History was divided in two: the Institute of USSR History and the Institute of World History.

The organization period lasted a year—a year of competition for appointment to posts and the like. The atmosphere in the Institute of World History, of which I was now a senior research staff member, became fairly calm. In the elections to the post of senior research staff member I received only one vote against. I was nevertheless perfectly aware of my vulnerability; my position was in fact far from stable and could change for the worse at any moment. It was also clear that, henceforth, I would be a convenient target for the neo-Stalinists in military and party propaganda circles. And indeed, more than just once or twice my name was bandied about at random on the pages of journals and newspapers, at lectures and orientations, and so on.

Yet, not only did I fight off attacks, but, when it was possible, I went on the offensive.

Thus, in my report to the institute on my work for 1967, I drew up a special section which I titled "On the Campaign Being Conducted against Me". I wrote:

> For almost two years now, a campaign has been under way, initiated in connection with my book *June 22, 1941*, which was issued by a Soviet publisher and given positive reviews both at a discussion at the Institute of Marxism-Leninism and in the Soviet and foreign communist and progressive press, especially in the communist countries of Europe, except for Romania,

where there was apparently no reaction. In 1967 the book was published in later editions in Poland, Czechoslovakia and Hungary.

In September of this year (that is, two years after the book came out in print) the journal *Voprosy istorii KPSS* (no. 9, 1967) published a slanderous article by G. A. Deborin and B. S. Tel'pukhovsky, entitled "In Ideological Captivity to Falsifiers of History."

On October 20 of this year I sent a reply to the editors of the journal, and on December 12 I was obliged to send yet another letter in connection with the fact that the editors have remained silent, do not answer my letters, and do not wish to publish my reply to the slander of G. A. Deborin and B. S. Tel'pukhovsky.

I am therefore being deprived of my unconditional right as a Soviet citizen and scholar to defend myself against press slander."

This was dated December 26, 1967, and signed Doctor of Historical Science A. M. Nekrich.

The institute management remained silent.

But at this point other events began to emerge, and interest in me, thank God, subsided for a time.

My tactic boiled down to not letting one single statement of any significance made in the press against me go unanswered, to giving a well-thought-out response, while distributing copies of my reply to the article by Deborin and Tel'pukhovsky which the journal *Voprosy istorii KPSS* had not dared to publish. That way, at least a certain number of people would find out the truth about the Nekrich affair, and the more people who knew about it, the better.

This is how I responded, for example, with regard to the publication in the Ministry of Defense newspaper *Krasnaya zvezda* of an article by a certain N. Matyushkin, who had once worked as deputy managing editor of the journal *Voprosy istorii*, deputy senior editor of Gospolitizdat, and so on, and had been fired from each and every job for his complete incompetence. I wrote to The Editors of *Krasnaya zvezda*,

Moscow
June 14, 1968

Distinguished Comrades:

On June 6 of this year an article by the candidate of historical science N. Matyushkin was published in your newspaper, entitled "A Powerful Force in the Struggle for Communism."

In this article, my book *June 22, 1941*, published by the "Nauka" publishing house three years ago in 1965, was subjected to crude attacks.

The accusations leveled against me by N. Matyushkin do not correspond to the true content of the book. For example, Matyushkin claims that I call the victory of the Soviet Union in the war against Nazi Germany unnatural, whereas the book states exactly the opposite. Other allegations made by Matyushkin are equally unreliable. Matyushkin's statement to the effect that the "Soviet people and our academic public opinion have strongly condemned Nekrich's book" is not in keeping with the truth either.

Three reviews were published in the Soviet press: two were positive and one was negative.

There was an academic discussion of the book on February 16, 1966, at the initiative of the Institute of Marxism-Leninism of the Communist party Central Committee. Two hundred and fifty historians participated, and twenty-two people spoke at the discussion. They all gave the book a generally positive appraisal. Naturally, critical remarks were made as well. Official speaker G. Deborin expressed the desire that the book be reissued.

This is how the book was received by Soviet academic opinion.

Communist and progressive public opinion abroad also responded positively to the book *June 22, 1941*.

In the socialist countries—in Poland, Hungary, Czechoslovakia, Yugoslavia, the GDR—there were many positive reactions and reviews. The same evaluation of the book was given in the communist press in Britain, Austria, Belgium, Italy, and Switzerland. Foreign communist press organs published more than twenty-five positive reviews of the book.

Last year the state publishers of political literature in Poland, Czechoslovakia, and Hungary translated and published the book *June 22, 1941* in large editions.

These are the facts, of which N. Matyushkin is obviously unaware.

A year and a half after the discussion of the book at the Institute of Marxism-Leninism, G. Deborin, together with another participant in the discussion, B. Tel'pukhovsky, who had also given a favorable reaction to the book at the time, published a carping review in the journal *Voprosy istorii KPSS* (no. 9, 1967).

Why G. Deborin and B. Tel'pukhovsky changed their opinion of the book and make a 180-degree turn is their own affair. But the methods they have resorted to in order to discredit the book and its author and conceal their own dishonesty are already a public matter.

Their methods are: distortion of the author's thinking, outright falsification of texts from the book and from documents, and outright slander. N. Matyushkin has also resorted to similar methods.

I resolutely protest the publication of slanderous fabrications by the candidate of historical science N. Matyushkin.

I am sending you a copy of my reply to the review by G. Deborin and B. Tel'pukhovsky, and ask that you give it your attention.

Doctor of Historical Science A. M. Nekrich

I received the following reply, dated June 19:

Distinguished Comrade Nekrich

We consider Comrade Matyushkin's criticism of your book to be correct. This criticism does not differ from the overall evaluation in principle given by party opinion recently.

Colonel V. Zmitrenko
Editor of Propaganda Section

Then there began a whole new set of problems as the Stalinists made an attempt to deprive me of my academic degree of doctor of historical science, which I had been granted in 1963.

One day in July 1969 (sometime around the twentieth, I believe) my wife, Nadya, after returning home in the evening from the historical library, where she was preparing for exams, told me that one of the staff members of the Institute of World History had come up to her in the library and told her that he wanted to introduce her to a friend. Nadya did not object. This friend introduced himself and said that he needed to see me about an extremely important matter, but that since she was present, he would tell her and she could pass the message on to me. What he told her was indeed very important for me and totally unexpected. It seemed that an order from the presidium of the Higher Qualifications Commission (it had been signed by the minister for higher education, Yeliutin) had come to reconsider the commission's decision made in 1963 to grant me a degree of doctor of historical science for my monograph "British Foreign Policy, 1939–1941." I had defended this work in manuscript form in the academic council of the Academy of Sciences in October 1962, and it had been approved by the commission in May 1963. Now, seven years later, the Higher Qualifications Commission had decided for some reason to reconsider this work.

The order given by Yeliutin was absolutely illegal, since the regulations governing the Higher Qualifications Commission indicate that the procedure for reviewing a decision can be initiated only by the academic council, which is required to consider the matter in the presence of the individual involved and decide on it in the same manner as with a dissertation defense, that is, by secret ballot. Nothing of the kind had taken place in this instance. Neither the academic councils of the institutes of USSR History and World

History, which had succeeded the Institute of History on its reorganization in 1968, nor, for that matter, the academic councils of the other institutes had raised the issue. Furthermore, the deadline for reviewing a decision was three months.

Experienced jurists to whom I turned for consultation unanimously replied that the only body that had the legal right to challenge Yeliutin's instructions was the Procurator's Review Office, which, as a rule, came out in defense of the institution rather than the private individual. And when an instruction from a minister was involved, the chances of reversing his decision through protest were nil. The jurists urged me not to address the procurator's office, but rather to try to proceed through administrative channels.

The man in the library also told my wife that the dissertation had been sent for review to F. D. Volkov of the Institute of International Relations of the Ministry for Foreign Affairs. On learning this, I realized that the matter was developing in an exceptionally unfavorable way for me, since Volkov had long dreamed of settling a score with me. The fact is that back in 1962 the Higher Qualifications Commission had asked me to verify an accusation that Volkov had committed plagiarism in his doctoral dissertation on Anglo-Soviet relations. In my reply to the commission, expressed in extremely mild terms, I made a comparative textual analysis of the dissertations of Volkov and of a certain Konontsev, which showed quite clearly that Volkov was a plagiarist. In spite of the incontrovertible evidence, Volkov was not only granted a degree as doctor of science but became an expert member of the commission several months later.

It soon emerged that as early as March 1969, Yeliutin had sent a letter to the Academy of Social Sciences requesting a review of my dissertation. The head of the history of international relations department was the director of our institute, Academician Ye. M. Zhukov. He replied, however, that he had no British specialists. After that, another letter was sent to the Institute of International Relations.

Zhukov expressed the view that the commission could hardly succeed in carrying out its intention, since there was no precedent for the case and a plenum of the commission would not sanction it. He advised me to exercise restraint and be patient, not to write letters or statements under any circumstances, including to Yeliutin, but calmly await further developments. The first part of his advice—not to write any letters or statements—I followed gladly, since this was fully in keeping with my own thoughts. But idly to await further developments was something I could not do, and, as it later turned out, by following my instincts I saved myself.

First of all, I decided not to keep the matter a secret, since only openness, if anything, could help defend me.

Soon, news of this story became widely known. Many historians, some of whom I knew and some of whom I did not, phoned me, expressing in various ways their indignation at this latest attack on me and conveying their sympathy. The members of the commission's group of experts were also upset by the matter, and many of them said that they would not allow such lawlessness to prevail. They knew that if they even began to discuss this matter, regardless of the eventual outcome, it would set a precedent which in the long run would be an unhealthy one for many scholars and, perhaps, in the final analysis, for the members of the commission themselves. After all, everyone has his enemies. The possibility of being deprived of one's academic degree, and thus one's salary, one's opportunity to publish, and other less obvious advantages, would become a threat constantly hanging over the heads of scholars, making them even more dependent on the will of management, and would limit their already heavily curtailed freedom of opinion. Such a precedent would sound the signal for denunciations, slander, and other vile acts, from which scholars in various fields would suffer. But, of course, the "recalcitrant" ones would be especially affected. Everyone understood this. It was all too clear. Many scholars with worldwide reputations, who had been indifferent to my expulsion from the party in 1967, feeling that it did not affect them, were in this case prepared to protest this illegal act. Some of them spoke with Yeliutin on the telephone, others with his deputy, N. N. Sofinsky.

For my part, I requested a meeting with the vice-president of the Academy of Sciences, A. M. Rumyantsev. I was not refused an appointment, but I was not received either. I did not insist, since I understood the awkwardness of the vice-president's situation, for he had been accused of liberalism, and his official reception of someone expelled from the party, in his capacity as a member of the Central Committee, according to the unwritten rules governing our lives might cost him dearly. Therefore, I confined myself to submitting a memorandum to him on the matter, which cited the paragraphs of the commission's charter flagrantly violated by Yeliutin.

My fears and suspicions turned out to be totally justified. At the very first meeting of the commission's panel of experts, which convened after the summer vacation on October 7, 1969, there was a proposal to consider the Nekrich affair.

The commission chairman P. Sobolev, the same person who had provoked the Burdzhalov affair, a man of staunch conservative views, a Stalinist by conviction and by his actions, had apparently not received additional instructions from the higher-ups. The commission members reviewed the affair, shrugged their shoulders, proposed that the chairman clarify the matter, and postponed consideration of it.

The next meeting was to take place in a week or two. Meanwhile, a rather strange situation had arisen. Just about everyone—the director of the institute, the presidium of the Academy of Sciences, the science department of the Central Committee—was against this affair and in favor of putting an end to it, but the matter kept on going forward, as if self-propelled. I also received a warning that it was possible for the case to be transmitted directly to a meeting of the Higher Qualifications Commission's humanitarian sciences section, which enjoyed the rights of a commission plenum; that is, its decision was considered final. (What was involved here was, in fact, a second decision, in that the first decision had been to grant me the degree).

The impact of this warning, in addition to the attitude of resigned anticipation, was tantamount to a death sentence. After some hesitation I decided to try to inform the president of the Academy of Sciences, Academician M. V. Keldysh, of the matter, and to do so in a private capacity, since it was highly unlikely that the president would see me officially. It was already completely unlikely that the leadership of the institute itself would appeal to the president. I shall omit a few details here, for understandable reasons. I shall say only that a decisive role was played by a certain young and talented scholar who was a pupil of Keldysh. The president intervened and did so energetically. When I told this story afterwards, Keldysh's intervention surprised many scholars, for this did not at all accord with the usual practice of addressing the president, or with his expected reaction.

Let me dwell for a moment on the overall viewpoint of the president. Keldysh understood perfectly well the significance for the academic world, and, first and foremost, for the Academy of Sciences, of rescinding an academic degree many years after it had been granted, especially in an unlawful manner and with regard to a person who has been done an injury in a completely unrelated matter. It was clear that this would look like an act of vengeance, and indeed this was exactly what it was. The president was apparently aware of the reaction that might result. I believe that just thinking about all the scholars who would be writing letters of protest and gathering signatures for a petition made him ill. The president's intervention, and his energetic and firm position, played a decisive role. At the next meeting of the commission, the folder concerning the Nekrich affair mysteriously disappeared. And, so I was told, the higher authorities (as they are called in the Central Committee apparatus) informed Yeliutin that the matter was to be "set aside" (but not canceled). Various rumors and conjectures sprang up. It was claimed, for example, that the president had talked with one of the Central Committee secretaries, who informed Keldysh that he knew nothing about the matter and that the Central Committee had not given its sanction. I am inclined to believe this—that is, that no formal decision was taken in this regard, but that it came about through the usual channels, so to speak.

It is obvious that the forces behind this initiative were rather influential individuals: Minister Yeliutin would not have set things in motion had he not felt obligated to these people, if not directly, then indirectly. Some hold the view that the initiative came from the military, in particular from the leadeership of Glavpur—that is, from Yepishev and his deputy, M. X. Kalashnik, who to this day never tire of finding some pretext for harassing me. There were also veiled allusions to KGB involvement, although there is no reliable information on that score. Anyway, we often tend to forget that the KGB acts on the basis of instructions from the Communist party Central Committee.

It was approximately half a year before this entire episode took place that Abram Isaakovich had sounded me out about the possibility of acknowledging my mistakes in connection with my book, after which I would supposedly be reinstated in the party.

The Ministry of Foreign Affairs leadership was dissatisfied with this entire matter, and especially with the fact that the rector of the Institute of International Relations, M. D. Yakovlev, had agreed to accept the dissertation for review. The reasons for this were rather clear. My examiners at the doctoral dissertation defense were Academician I. M. Maisky, Professor A. S. Yerusalimsky (he did not take part in the defense because of illness, but gave a written review), a corresponding member of the Estonian Academy of Sciences, V. A. Maamyagi, and Professor V. L. Izraelyan from the Ministry of Foreign Affairs Higher Diplomatic School, now head of the international organizations department of the Ministry of Foreign Affairs. The unofficial examiner was I. N. Zemskov, then head of the historical-diplomatic department of the Ministry of Foreign Affairs and now deputy minister for foreign affairs. The dissertation had been approved beforehand by the diplomatic history department of the Higher Diplomatic School. The work itself had been reviewed in the Ministry of Foreign Affairs and had been authorized for publication. After the book came out in print, the historical journal *Voprosy istorii* published a favorable review by Professor V. I. Popov, then assistant rector (and later rector) at the Higher Diplomatic School. Furthermore, the book came under attack by the BBC commentator Morris Lathy (quite unjustifiably, by the way, especially since Lathy himself, as it turned out, had not read the book). The well-known historian D. Melamid (Mel'nikov) gave a response in an ironic note published in the December 1963 issue of *Literaturnaya gazeta* entitled "Start Reading, Mr. Lathy."

I was told that when the Ministry of Foreign Affairs was questioned about my case, Minister Gromyko took a negative view of Yeliutin's "initiative."

One final curious detail. When I found out about the threat to deprive me of my degree, I naturally requested that all my former examiners give me written confirmation of their earlier views. Yerusalimsky, unfortunately, had died several years before. Izraelyan was the first to send his review. After him I received confirmation from Maisky. There was no response at all from Maamyagi, who became vice-president of the Estonian Academy of Sciences at about that time. We always used to send each other New Year's greetings, but after my request, Maamyagi stopped sending me cards.

I am consciously omitting the names of a number of people to whom I am eternally grateful, for they showed themselves to be selfless and noble in what was a difficult time for me. I hope that the day will come when I shall be able to rectify this necessary oversight.

During this period annoyance with me "upstairs" was intensifying because of my stubborn refusal to repent. I continued to feel pressure from various sources. Two months after the failed attempt to deprive me of my doctoral degree, in December 1969, I was invited in by the secretary of the historical sciences division, Academician Ye. M. Zhukov, the same man who had been director of my institute, and in his usual calm and courteous manner he explained to me that a number of my "friends" (here he ventured a chuckle) were annoyed that I was continuing to work at the institute, in spite of my expulsion from the party and my refusal, as he put it to "recognize my mistakes." They were particularly annoyed by the fact that not only had my book been published in the socialist countries of Eastern Europe, but it was beginning to be translated and published in the West as well. At one of the meetings of the board of the historical sciences division, the former director of the Institute of Marxism-Leninism, P. N. Pospelov, took out a copy of the Italian translation of my book, published under the extremely suspicious title *Did Stalin Open the Gates to Hitler?* and, pointing at the dust jacket (it showed a picture of the Kremlin tower with a star and a Fascist swastika) exclaimed: "This is what Nekrich has sunk to!" Needless to say, Pospelov was fully aware that no one had asked my permission to publish the book, since the Soviet Union was not a party to the international convention on copyrights at the time, but he made use of the Italian edition to raise once again the question of whether it was right for me still to be working in the Academy of Sciences. Zhukov asked that I write him a statement which he might show to those unfriendly to me in order to pacify them. He promised me that he would keep my letter in his safe. A few days later I brought him a statement concerning my overseas editions, after telling Zhukov again that my position on the events of 1941 was still firm. The letter was addressed to the director of the USSR Academy of Sciences Institute of World History, Academician Ye. M. Zhukov.

Moscow

December 15, 1969

Most distinguished Yevgeny Mikhailovich:
   Pursuant to our talk on December 8 of this year, I feel it necessary
to state the following:
   1.   Not one of the publishers in the capitalist countries has requested
        my permission to publish a translation of my book *June 22, 1941*,
        issued in Moscow in 1965 by the "Nauka" publishing house, nor
        have they informed me of their intentions or sent me any copies
        of the book.
   2.   I strongly condemn any attempts to distort the thrust or content
        of my book by way of tendentious changes in its title, through
        format, footnotes, distortion, or isolated quotation from the text.
   3.   A few years ago I sent to the Novosti press agency for pub-
        lication an open letter protesting the slanderous fabrications
        of the Deutsche Welle radio station (a copy of the letter is
        in the hands of party authorities). My position has also been
        expressed in a number of documents to be found in party bodies.
   4.   I bear sole responsibility for the Soviet and authorized editions
        of this book, as well as of any other work of mine.

Senior Research Staff Member
Doctor of Historical Science A. M. Nekrich

   At the Institute of World History itself I was more or less left alone.
No one prevented me from continuing work on my study *British Policy in
Europe, 1941–1945*, which was the culmination of many years' work on the
history of Britain and its policy before and during the Second World War.
But I was clearly conscious of the fact that I faced tremendous difficulties.
Since there was no longer any question whatsoever of my working in the
British archives, I had to rely only on those materials that were located in
Moscow, or those I could obtain from abroad on microfilm. Fortunately in
1966 I had brought back from Poland some very interesting documents from
the archives which enabled me to shed light on new aspects in the history
of the Polish question, which, as is known, played such an important role
in Anglo-Soviet relations.
   By accumulating those materials available to me little by little, toward
the end of 1969 I finished my manuscript (approximately seven hundred
pages) on schedule and submitted it for discussion in the section. This was
a year after the events in Czechoslovakia, and a sort of temporary calm
reigned. The discussion of the monograph went quite smoothly, and the

manuscript was recommended for publication. But the institute director, Ye. M. Zhukov, decided, just to be sure, to send the manuscript for review by the Institute of World Economy and International Relations. From there, too, came what was on the whole a favorable response. The academic council of our institute recommended the manuscript for publication. But at a meeting of the editorial publications council of the Academy of Sciences—the highest body in publishing—unexpected opposition to publication of the manuscript was voiced by the council's academic secretary, Ye. S. Likhtenshtein, who stated that without Central Committee instructions he would not publish a book by "that author." He raised no substantive objections to the manuscript. So began my fruitless struggle for publication which was to last five years, right up until my decision to leave my homeland.

First I wrote a letter to the president of the Academy of Sciences, Academician M. V. Keldysh:

Moscow
February 15, 1972

Most distinguished Mstislav Vsevolodovich:

I, Doctor of Historical Science A. M. Nekrich, am a senior research staff member at the USSR Academy of Sciences Institute of World History.

At the end of 1969 I completed my monograph *British Policy in Europe, 1941–1945*, written in accordance with the institute's 1965–1969 work schedule. This work is the culmination of a series of studies on the history of the foreign policy of Great Britain before and during the Second World War. (The first book from the series was *The Policy of British Imperialism in Europe, October 1938–September 1939,* USSR Academy of Sciences, 1955, 473 pp; the second was *British Foreign Policy, 1939–1941*, Moscow, "Nauka," 1963, 531 pp.).

The latest work was discussed at a meeting of the British history section in February 1970, approved, and recommended for publication. Views were expressed by eleven staff members, including outside reviewers invited from other academic institutions. Then the monograph was sent, on instructions from Institute Director Ye. M. Zhukov, for additional evaluation to the Institute of World Economy and International Relations of the USSR Academy of Sciences. In December 1970 a favorable response was received from that institute. Nine months later still, in September 1971, the monograph was discussed at a meeting of the Academic Council of the Institute of World History and recommended for publication.

Hence the monograph has received approval and authorization from specialists at two institutes of the Academy. In all twenty scholars have given their favorable judgment on the manuscript. There were, of course, critical comments, but there was no negative judgment whatsoever. In the autumn of 1971 the monograph was included in the 1972 schedule for editorial preparation at the Institute of World History as part of its allotment. The historical sciences division also included the work in its editorial preparation schedule.

It appeared as if everything was in order. In October 1971, however, at a meeting of the editorial commission of the USSR Academy of Sciences, the inclusion of my manuscript in the editorial preparation schedule was opposed by Academic Secretary Ye. S. Likhtenshtein, who not only had not read the manuscript but had never even laid eyes on it. The only reason given for opposing inclusion of the manuscript in the editorial schedule was Likhtenshtein's negative attitude toward the author as an individual. In spite of protests from representatives of the institute leadership and of the historical sciences division, who pointed out the absurdity of the arguments given by the editorial commission secretary, the latter arbitrarily failed to include the manuscript in the editorial preparation schedule. Now Ye. S. Likhtenshtein states that until there is a special instruction to publish A. M. Nekrich's monograph, he will not include it in the publication schedule. This is, therefore, in disregard of the decision of the academic council and the leadership of the Institute of World History, and of the historical sciences division, based on the opinions of a large community of scholars, and a flagrant violation of the academic publications procedure in the USSR Academy of Sciences. This is a case of high-handedness that leads one to believe that I have been placed "beyond the pale," and that the generally recognized rules do not apply to me. As a result an artificial atmosphere of discrimination is being created around me, with all its consequences.

Is this to be the finale of my five years of research work and two years spent in reviewing and discussing it?

I urgently request you to intervene and instruct the editorial commission to abide by the normal procedures with regard to my work as well.

Doctor of Historical Science A. M. Nekrich

Then I sent out additional letters—to president Keldysh, to vice-presidents Millionshchikov and Fedoseev—but I did not receive a single reply, even though Soviet law requires a response to letters from workers. But laws, as we know, are made to be broken. So it was in my case.

An unspoken quota was established for me: one article per year in a small academic publication, the annual yearly institute review such as *Problems of British History*. It was here that I managed to publish a few excerpts from my new work. During the years after my expulsion from the Communist party, I succeeded in getting a few more articles and reviews into print.

Once I tried to submit two articles simultaneously to institute publications—to *Problems of British History* and the *French Yearbook*. Zhukov proposed that one of my articles be withdrawn, on the grounds that "Nekrich is being published too much." As long as A. T. Tvardovsky was managing editor of *Novy mir*, I succeeded in publishing there occasionally, but then everything suddenly came to a halt. Over a long period of time I attempted to publish an article on the impact of stereotypical views on political decision making. The professional journals refrained from publishing my article not only because of my name, but also because the subject seemed too hot to handle. Finally in 1973 the journal *Znanie–Sila* published my article "Event, Evaluation, Decision." Three years later, in 1976, a Dr. Hecker published in the journal *Ost-Europa* a piece on my article, valuing it highly from the standpoint of historical theory. At the same time Hecker could not fail to point out that the article contained a covert criticism of Stalinism. At any rate, from time to time I succeeded in making it into print with one article or another.

But time would not wait for me. More radical decisions were required. At the institute life went on as usual. Soon after the intervention of Soviet troops in Czechoslovakia, the conformists and neo-Stalinists once again gained the upper hand. There was new talk of the need to politicize scholarship. This was the official viewpoint given by the vice-president of the Academy of Sciences, A. M. Rumyantsev. This meant essentially that political considerations of the moment must prevail over the interests of scholarship. But still, I repeat, irreversible changes had taken place. It was possible at discussions to talk about a certain historian's departure from the orthodox line. It was even possible to force him to repent for his sins. Such humiliation was inflicted, for example, on the historian Dunaevsky, who had written an article on a letter from Stalin to the journal *Proletarsakaya revolutsiya* in 1931 and had used information given him by the main victim of the Stalinist ideological purge of that time, the historian A. G. Slutsky.

Yet there were still books being written about more remote times, sometimes on local topics, sometimes broader in scope, and these were necessary, interesting books. By some miracle these books came out, and they were immediately snapped up by readers. I could name the books and articles of such marvelous historians of my generation and younger as A. Ya. Gurevich, V. M. Kholodkovsky, L. Batkin, L. Yu. Slezkin, and M. S. Al'perovich, the archaeologists A. L. Mongait and G. B. Fedorov, the Byzantinist A. P. Kazhdan, the historians of Soviet society Yu. Arutyunyan, S. I. Yakubovskaya, L. V. Danilova, and A. Grunt, the Russian historian A. A. Zimin—the list is not exhaustive.

Books published in the USSR are subjected to harsh censorship. But still the fate of a book depends to a great extent on how the book is written, for good studies are written in such a way that no matter how much the text is censored, no matter how many "suspicious" paragraphs, sentences, pages, and even whole chapters are taken out, the book remains in principle, conveying the meaning intended by the author. The entire issue boiled down to how talented the author is and how skillfully he writes. This is why from time to time the censor is not in a position to hold back a "harmful" book or article. Even when resorting to the all-encompassing and prohibitive formulation "unmonitored subtext," the censor is not in a position to put the author's ideas on the "right" track. There are many stories about how the censors in the Soviet Union have struggled with "unmonitored subtext." In one of the manuscripts about German Nazism there was the sentence "Hitler founded a party which one could enter but could never leave." The censor crossed out that sentence in determined fashion. One wonders why he did it. Maybe he saw in this an allusion to the Communist party of the Soviet Union, which one could enter voluntarily but which was impossible to leave voluntarily. One can get out of the Communist party only for reasons of mental deficiency and in that case, one needs to submit a medical excuse. The desire to leave the party is regarded as a challenge to the existing order, and in this connection various types of reprisals may be enacted—dismissal from work and even incarceration in a psychiatric hospital. There was such a case a few years ago involving the head of the radio and television personnel department, Vinokurov, who publicly proclaimed his withdrawal from the party. He was sent to a mental ward.

I have already mentioned that as a result of the activities of the progressive party committee at the Institute of History, the Nekrich affair, and the publication of a number of books and articles departing from the official party line, Trapeznikov decided that the institute had become "unmanageable," and that a major factor in his forming this opinion was his failure to gain election to the Academy. He managed to get the Central Committee secretariat to decide on a restructuring of the Institute of History, subdividing it into two institutes—the Institute of USSR History and the Institute of World History. The changes in the research staff of the institute were insignificant, even though there was a rather fierce struggle going on in the wings for cushy jobs as institute directors, deputies, and section heads. In the end, somebody got the job he hankered for while somebody else lost out. Under the watchful guidance of the instructor of the science department of the Central Committee and the curator of the institute, A. Kuznetsov, the settling of scores for old "sins" continued.

The events in Czechoslovakia caught the Institute of History at the height of its program of reorganization. In the spring and fall of 1968, the two institutes which emerged as a result of the division held a competition to fill the posts of senior and junior research staff members. The overwhelming majority of candidates conducted themselves calmly and modestly, so as not to get themselves thrown overboard in the reorganization. Yet there were still a few daredevils who voted against a resolution adopted at a staff meeting which approved the sending of Soviet troops into Czechoslovakia.

Afterwards life at the historical institutes returned to the usual routine, although things were somewhat smoother at the Institute of World History and bumpier at the Institute of USSR History.

The first director of the latter institute was Academician B. A. Rybakov, who held another post in addition. He had been director of the Institute of Archaeology for many years. A capable archaeologist in his youth, Rybakov gradually left genuine scholarship, for the life's goal he set for himself was to demonstrate the superiority of everything Russian. He was the creator of theories about the Slavic origin of a number of cities and trades in medieval Rus'. Rybakov was descended from a family of Old Believers. His father had owned a shop, which in the usual Soviet course of things would not have helped Rybakov's career prospects. Yet he still managed to forge vigorously ahead, since the ideology of Great Russian nationalism in combination with the Soviet Communist ideology had become as far back as the 1940s the best way to prove one's dedication to the ideals of the Party and loyalty to the Soviet regime.

It was natural, then, that the entire atmosphere in the Institute of USSR History became gradually more conservative. The Stalinists, some of them clearly anti-Semitic at heart, had triumphed. A planned attack was leveled against the liberal-minded scholars, who were responsible for the most important work at the institute. The attacks were especially violent against the historiography section, headed by Academician Militsa Vasilevna Nechkina, a leading scholar, well known for her work on the history of the Decembrists and on historiography. This campaign went on for a long time. In the end, Nechkina was forced to give up her post as section head. For many years the fifth volume of the history of historical study in the USSR, on the Soviet period, could not be issued. The managing editor of that volume was N. Ye. Gorodetsky. Just as in the "good old days"—Stalinist times—they "set the dogs" on him, accusing him of distortions, incorrect wording, and so on. The volume has not yet come out, even though it has been dummied, discussed, and approved for publication several times already.

Rybakov did not show any special interest in the activities of the institute. A year later he was elected academician-secretary of the historical sciences division and left the institute. After a lengthy struggle among the contenders, a comparatively young historian was elected to be the new director, Pavel Vasilevich Volobuev, a specialist in twentieth-century history and a pupil of Arkady Lavrovich Sidorov. Volobuev, after finishing Moscow State University and his graduate studies, worked for a number of years in the science department of the party Central Committee, was rather closely connected with the apparatus, and in the early stages enjoyed the support of the all-powerful Trapeznikov and Rybakov, who, in particular, had supported Volobuev's candidacy. A few years later, after a fierce struggle, Volobuev was elected corresponding member of the Academy of Sciences, consolidating his position considerably.

From a career standpoint, Volobuev's Achilles' heel was his professionalism. It was inevitable that, as a historian who had been schooled in sound academic training, Volobuev, in the course of his research, would come into conflict sooner or later with the official conformist viewpoint of a very influential group of party historians, concentrated in the Academy of Social Sciences, in the higher party schools, and in the IInstitute of Marxism-Leninism. It should be quickly pointed out that Volobuev did not at all strive to subvert the basis of Marxist-Leninist teachings or refute the accepted methods of research. It was simply that in the course of his studies, he made a number of observations and came to conclusions other than those that had been held for decades by an influential segment of Communist party historians. Volobuev was ambitious. And the position he occupied gave him a false sense of security. Apparently he thought that he could allow himself to fight seriously against both dogmatism and revisionism at the same time. In actual fact, perhaps even unconsciously, he had risen up against party conformism. On the one hand, Volobuev attempted to show his unswerving dedication to Marxism, but on the other, he considered it possible to subject to criticism the works of party historians who had long held sway over the social sciences. With Volobuev's silent approval a number of historians working at the Institute of USSR History began to build legends around him portraying him as virtually the sole defender of all historical scholarship from attacks by the Stalinists. Actually, he was far from playing the role they tried to ascribe to him.

Volobuev very soon aroused the hostility of such influential people as P. N. Pospelov, secretary of the Communist party Central Committee and formerly director of the Institute of Marxism-Leninism, and, at the time of these events, member of the presidium of the Academy of Sciences. The department head at the Academy of Social Sciences, Ivan Petrov, was also an enemy, among others. Open conflict arose during a discussion of a collection of essays, *The Russian Proletariat on the Eve of the February Revolution*, of which Volobuev was managing editor and author. At that discussion Volobuev ventured to say that party historians had "slept through" the events of the past thirty years. Petrov and others regarded his statement as a declaration of war, which Volobuev stood no chance of winning. In order to demonstrate that he was right, Volobuev read out at the discussion excerpts from the confidential verbatim record of a meeting of party historians in Leningrad, which testified to the complete ignorance of his opponents. Here he committed a fatal error: he maligned the party apparatus. This was especially inexcusable, since Volobuev himself had once belonged to that apparatus and was well aware of its unwritten rules. Volobuev had apparently gone too far: he had overestimated the support he might have received from two powerful people in the ideological sphere—Central Committee secretaries Suslov and Ponomarev. Soon afterwards criticism was leveled at Volobuev in the newspaper *Pravda*, and the usual brief note appeared: "The conclusions have been drawn." Translated, this meant that Volobuev was to be left alone, and was to remain in his position as Institute of History director.

But, to use a Russian expression, this was not the point. Volobuev decided to gain room for maneuver by sacrificing those people who had supported him in order to demonstrate that he did not belong to the "revisionists" who were supposedly guilty of error. He began administrative proceedings against Kiryanov, the chief editor of the essay collection, who bore full responsibility, and reprimanded the members of the editorial board, including the old Bolshevik Mark Volin and his own alter ego K. N. Tarnovsky. This was, incidentally, not the first time Volobuev had resorted to such tactics, having previously done so as director of the institute and before that as secretary of the party committee of the Institute of History (after Danilov's reelection). Volobuev, for example, had wrongly accused the editorial board of volume 8 of *A History of the USSR*, virtually slandering the chapters on the history of collectivization. As a result, the author of those chapters, Iu. S. Borisov, was forced to leave the institute.

But now the shoe was on the other foot. It was now Volobuev himself who was the object of attack. His own deputy, a certain Bavykin, accused him of aiding and abetting the revisionists, and so on. At the insistence of Academician Pospelov, the board of the historical sciences division adopted a decision on the errors committed in the collection of essays and on Volobuev's responsibility for them. After that everything proceeded as usual. Volobuev still tried to put up resistance, but now it was on an individual basis.

He wrote a disclaimer to the journal *Voprosy istorii KPSS*, which, needless to say, was not published. On instructions from the Central Committee science department, a special party meeting was called at the Institute of USSR History. At that time a vehement article on another collection in which the institute had taken part appeared in the newspaper *Sverdlovskii rabochii*. The focus of the article was primarily two talented historians, Tarnovsky and K. E. Shatsilo. The first was accused of nothing more or less than Trotskyism.

The Western reader might shrug his shoulders in confusion and ask, "So, what is going on here?" What was going on was that for fifty years an accusation of Trotskyism in the Soviet Union was the most serious political charge that could be made. In Stalinist days someone accused of this "crime" paid for it with his life. Times, of course, had changed, and everyone had forgotten, in fact, what exactly "Trotskyism" was. But the accusation cost Tarnovsky his doctoral dissertation, which the Higher Qualifications Commission refused to validate.

The Volobuev episode ended with his complete repentance at a meeting before the Central Committee. And not only repentance: Volobuev severely criticized Tarnovsky's views and, more mildly, those of his closest academic adviser, Aron Avrech. Next Volobuev submitted a statement asking to be relieved of his duties as director. He was sent to work as a senior researcher at the Academy of Sciences Institute of the History of Natural Sciences and Technology.

Some time later I met Volobuev not far from my home in Moscow on Dmitry Ulyanov Street, just an hour after I had submitted a statement to institute director Zhukov informing him of my intention to emigrate. The gist of what Volobuev told me was that he condemned my decision.

At the Institute of World History the main target of the neo-Stalinists' wrath, with the connivance, if you will, and even the cooperation of Ye. M. Zhukov, was M. Ya. Gefter. For several years, he was subjected to persistent discrimination. At first he was dismissed from his post as head of the historical methodology section; then the section was eliminated altogether; then he was completely deprived of the possibility of working on his chosen subject, twentieth-century Russian imperialism and historical methodology. His enemies created such a tense atmosphere for Gefter that it became totally intolerable for him to remain at the Institute of World History. These problems were compounded by the wounds Gefter had received during the Soviet-German war. All these conditions undermined his health, and he was forced to take early retirement before the usual age of sixty.

The neo-Stalinists tried to create a similar atmosphere of defamation around the talented medievalist A. Ya. Gurevich, whom the medieval history section categorically refused to hire. An historian of the Renaissance, Leonid Batkin, was unable to defend his dissertation for a doctorate in historical science, owing to the outright opposition of a reactionary group of medievalists from our institute and from the history department of Moscow State University. Meanwhile, the work of Gurevich and Batkin, their lectures and courses, enjoyed enormous popularity not only in the Soviet Union but abroad as well. The Institute of World History also went to considerable lengths to rid itself of the famous philosopher—I would call him a great thinker—Volodya Bibler, on the pretext that the subjects he dealt with were supposedly outside the purview of the academic research program set by the institute. In fact, Bibler would have done credit to any academic establishment, institute, or university that might have agreed to work with him.

I shall limit myself to these few examples, but actually there were many more. What always astounded and saddened me was the attempt by institute colleagues to blame those people under fire for bringing it on themselves. The typical argument went as follows: Why did X act that way? In doing so he has made it impossible for Y to defend him, whereas in fact Y wanted to, and so on and so forth. Alas, this rationale was nothing new. It is an integral part of the psychology of *Homo sovieticus* to whitewash the guilty party for victimizing the victim. How often I have had to witness this!

In the Soviet Union, especially in the humanities, scholars depend in their research work not only on the presence and availability of source materials, on favorable political circumstances, and on a degree of self-censorship, but also on the views of their colleagues, on recommendations for publication by an academic council, and on the will of the publishers and the arbitrariness of editors, not to mention the various types of official and unofficial censorship as well. While in recent years the views of censors and colleagues have not been binding on an author, at least not as categorically as in previous times, the author is nevertheless obliged not only to acknowledge valid observations, but also to appear as if he were taking outrageous comments fully into account as well so that it may not be said of him that he cannot accept criticism. That is seen as a very serious flaw. Sometimes the author is asked questions which are simply stupid from an academic standpoint but are very ticklish in terms of his ideological position.

Actually today there are very few people willing to support outright Stalinist diehards. The majority abide instinctively by the golden mean. At the Institute of USSR History, for example, there was a discussion in late June 1973 of a dissertation presented for a doctor of historical sciences degree by a certain V. S. Lel'chuk, a moderate conformist and a clever and gifted man. One of the Stalinist diehards by the name of Kovalenko felt that Lel'chuk's observations were suspect and since he was not in a position to analyze the problem, he asked Lel'chuk point-blank: "Are you for Stalin or against? Tell us frankly," to which Lel'chuk replied, to laughter and applause from the audience, "I am for our Soviet homeland and our Communist party."

Sometimes Stalinist methods are used for purposes of career advancement. At about the same time and in the same institute a woman named Alatortseva was defending her doctoral dissertation. Her academic adviser, Professor Ye. N. Gorodetsky, was not present at the defense. Alatortseva leveled crude, unbridled criticism at the *Handbook of USSR History*, which had just come out in a second edition. Now, the managing editor of that handbook was Gorodetsky. Alatortseva herself had helped to draft it. In reply to indignant questioning on the part of one of those present—"How can that be? You yourself are an author of the handbook and consequently bear responsibility!"—Alatortseva said, without batting an eye, "Ye. N. Gorodetsky bears full responsibility. He's the one who headed the work." Alatortseva was granted a degree of candidate of sciences unanimously, with one abstention.

Attempts to settle academic problems by administrative means are still being made, and I believe that they are simply inevitable, owing to the predominance of a single ideology and a single culture. For example, Aron Avrech, a senior research staff member of the Institute of USSR History, received a severe reprimand from the party bureau for his supposedly erroneous view of the role of the peasantry in Russia during the period of absolutism. After a three-and-a-half-hour inquiry, Avrech refused to acknowledge his "errors" and received a severe reprimand from the party bureau. In former times Avrech most certainly would have been accused of Trotskyism or some other infraction and he would have been thrown out of the party. Yet now he did not even receive punishment, merely a reprimand. Still, this case is fairly indicative of the atmosphere prevailing in the social sciences. In the field of history it is not as oppressive as in sociology or philosophy, where the moral destruction of thinking people goes on relentlessly.

While all these events were taking place and I was resisting one attack after another, my book *June 22, 1941* was leading a literary life of its own. Between 1968 and 1970 editions appeared in France, Britain, Yugoslavia, and the United States. I should like to discuss this in some further detail. Once—it was in 1968—a good acquaintance of mine, with whom I had long worked in the library of the Academy of Sciences, drew my attention to an advertisement in an issue of the *London Times Literary Supplement*. It announced the appearance in the United States of a book by a certain Vladimir Petrov, entitled *Soviet Historians and the German Invasion of June 22, 1941*, which included a complete translation of the well-known book *June 22, 1941* by the Soviet historian Nekrich. The advertisement commented that "nothing was known" about the fate of the book's author.

On reading this I laughed. For a long time I could not get hold of the book. Finally I received a copy of it as a gift from a Western colleague in August 1970 at the World Congress of Historians in Moscow. You can imagine my surprise and indignation when I saw that, although Vladimir Petrov was named as the author, almost the entire text belonged to me. Petrov had, in fact, translated the book into English and added a commentary on it. I was so far from the United States and in such a complex situation that the prospect of bringing suit was simply hopeless.

About two years later I heard reports to the effect that some foreign historians were angry about Petrov's action. This heartened me a bit, and in 1974 I sent two letters to the United States, one to the director of the Institute for Sino-Soviet Studies at George Washington University, the institute that had funded the publication of Petrov's book, and a second, similar in content, to the publications director of University of South Carolina Press, which had published the book. A reply came so quickly that I was simply astounded and even thought that perhaps censorship had been abolished in the Soviet Union! But the letter was neither from the director of the institute nor from the director of publications but from Petrov himself. This greatly surprised me, for I had not written to him. The reply was, from my point of view, totally unsatisfactory. I decided not to answer Petrov and to take no further action, for the speed with which the exchange of letters had taken place seemed suspicious to me: in eleven days my letter and the response to it had come full circle. It looked as if somebody was interested in creating an incident out of this affair and had something to gain from it. Not wishing to be drawn into a game for the sake of somebody else's interests, I decided to put aside the entire Petrov matter until a more appropriate time. And I turned out to be right. A few months later I was approached by one of the staff members of my institute, who I had always assumed to be connected with a Soviet institution clearly not academic in nature. He asked me if I was aware that Petrov had published my book under his own name and wondered what I intended to do about it. From what he said I concluded that my correspondence on this matter was no secret to him, and I replied that I had decided to leave things as they were for the time being. Incidentally, he told me that Petrov had done to the books of two other Soviet authors exactly what he had done with mine.

The World Congress of Historians in Moscow was for me a landmark, not only because it was there that I received the Petrov book, but, first and foremost, because the authorities had not wanted to let me attend the congress. The Western reader should not be surprised at this. Regardless of the charter of the congress, which stated that any professional historian was entitled to take part, the participation of Soviet historians was determined on an individual basis at the level of the historical sciences division and the National Committee of Soviet Scholars, while the list was drawn up by the science department of the Communist party Central Committee. On August 12, 1970, the head of the British history section, himself a very good historian and a decent man, Nikolai Aleksandrovich Yerofeev, transmitted to me instructions from the director of the institute, Zhukov, not to appear at the congress, since—he repeated Zhukov word for word—"this could distract the congress from its scheduled plan of work." I was furious, but at the same time I could not help laughing over the exaggerated importance the academic bosses attributed to my presence. At the same time I learned that some extremely well respected historians, including M. S. Al'perovich, M. Ya. Gefter, and others, had also been crossed off the list of delegates to the congress. I reacted swiftly and very decisively. On that same day I sent similar letters to Zhukov and to the chairman of the congress, Academician A. A. Guber.

August 12, 1970

Most distinguished Aleksandr Andreevich:

I have been officially informed today by the head of the British history section of the USSR Academy of Sciences Institute of World History N. A. Yerofeev, that I am not to be allowed to be present at the meeting of the Thirteenth World Congress of Historians.

I believe that it is useful for any professional historian to take part in the congress, since it gives him the opportunity of obtaining better guidance in dealing with problems which are of major interest to world historical study. This applies to me as well, since I have been engaged in research work for twenty years.

I consider the decision not to allow me access to the congress unfair, in violation of the status of the World Congress, and virtually an act of discrimination.

I urge you to reconsider this decision and make it possible for me to participate in the work of the congress on an equal footing with hundreds of other Soviet historians.

I am sending a letter of similar contents to the director of the USSR Academy of Sciences Institute of World History, Ye. M. Zhukov.

Doctor of Historical Sciences A. M. Nekrich

At the same time, I informed some of my Western colleagues of what had happened, and at the traditional cocktail party preceding the congress one of them asked Guber whether it was true that Nekrich had been prohibited from appearing. Guber vehemently denied this.

Two days later Guber invited me into his office at the division and handed me an invitation. It was not a delegate's invitation, but merely a guest pass. Thus, this was still a violation of the congress charter. But I decided that there was no point in trying to take the matter any further, since the congress was due to start the next day. On handing over the guest pass, Guber said in his usual friendly manner: "Sasha, there has been a misunderstanding, but I would never have expected such a letter from you."

"What did you find strange about it?"

"Well, some of the wording," said Guber haltingly.

Of course Guber found my references to the congress charter strange. We are all so accustomed to asking meekly even for what we are entitled to.

Al'perovich and Gefter also received passes to attend the Conference.

During the congress, at all times, no matter where I appeared, I was kept under constant observation (and not only I). The system of observation itself was a primitive one: downstairs, between the entrance to Moscow State University building in the Lenin Hills, where the meetings took place, and the stairwell which led to the conference hall stood several officials from the state security organs, dressed in civilian clothes. Upstairs, in all the halls, corridors and other areas stood monitors, officials of the Institute of USSR History and the Institute of World History. Since I knew all or most of the officials, they could easily observe me and, especially, my contacts with foreign scholars.

One day at the congress I went to a section meeting where Professor Richard Pipes of Harvard was delivering a paper. During the break a certain person came up to me and demanded to know from me why I was present at a meeting of a section which did not directly relate to the problems on which I was working. "Because I find it interesting," I answered sharply. This person went away. But whenever I began a conversation with one of the foreigners, a familiar face would pop up nearby.

Once I was approached by the press chief of the congress, Dr. I. R. Grigulevich, the author of books on Vatican history well known for his many articles on the history of the Jesuits in Latin America, where at one time Grigulevich had been a Soviet agent. This was written about openly in a book published in the USSR. He was a cheerful man, clever, they say, broad, and very shifty, believing neither in God nor in the devil. Grigulevich came up to me and asked whether it was true that I had given an interview to a correspondent from a Western newspaper. It must be said that granting an interview to a correspondent without prior agreement from the authorities, without permission from as high a body as a Central Committee department, was considered a most serious blunder for a Soviet citizen, and it could entail dismissal from work. I let myself blow up and began to tell Grigulevich off, saying that I did not intend to answer his provocative questions. The confrontation had occurred near a book display. Beside us there appeared a very frightened deputy to Guber at the congress, A. L. Narochnitsky, and Central Committee science department instructor Kuznetsov. True, they did not venture to come over to us but rather listened from afar.

"I'm fed up with your questions, and I'm fed up with your discrimination," I said to Grigulevich's face, raising my voice. Somewhat taken aback, he tried to switch to a more conciliatory tone: "What do you mean, old man," and so on. Later it became clear that one of the informers had denounced me, claiming that I had been chatting with a foreign correspondent. He even provided a name—a correspondent from the English newspaper *The Observer*. Actually my Italian friend, the late Professor Ernesto Raggioneri, had introduced me to a correspondent named Benedetti from the communist newspaper *Unità*, and the reporter asked me my impression of the congress. The denunciation was made immediately.

The congress was for me an extremely interesting and even pleasant experience. Many delegates, in an attempt to convey their sympathy and their solidarity, offered me books which they had brought to the congress, firmly shaking my hand and taking an interest in my life. I was not alone. One evening I invited to my home historians from different countries, both socialist and capitalist. This was a genuine "International"! We drank Armenian brandy, discussed serious historical problems, and told political jokes in total disregard of the fact that, as I had alerted my guests, my apartment was probably bugged by a listening device.

10
The Parting

*The times have such a longing desire
to find a break in the chain among us all . . .
Oh, let us join our hands, my friends
so that, one by one, we do not fall*
—*Bulat Okudzhava*

The parting — my friend Donald Maclean — Pasternak's and Tvardovsky's funerals — the passing of Khrushchev — Ilya Gabay's suicide — my speech at A. L. Mongait's funeral — more on historians and history — on the dissidents — they tear up the photograph — friends from the West — the final attempt — my choice — they declare me a traitor — in defense of Mustafa Dzhemilev — forsake fear.

There were many tragic events during those years. Relatives and loved ones, friends, comrades and simply those whom I had known and for whom I felt affection and respect all passed away.

And every time, when it came time to part company, I felt as if some of me went with them. So it must be, and so it was. Or perhaps it was not a fragment of my being but the simple and trivial sensation that the circle of life was gradually growing smaller around me, and I was being left all alone.

And there was to be yet another parting: from familiar surroundings, from a materially comfortable and secure life, from Moscow, from those streets, sidewalks, and embankments along which I had wandered thousands and thousands of times, and from the cemetery where my loved ones were buried.

And there was a parting from the living, too: from friends who had been my most reliable and lasting shelter in the good and bad times of my life, from relatives in the warmth of whose glow I had basked, from hundreds of people known only by sight whom I smiled at when we met.

Parting: with tears, kisses, and hugs, with firm handshakes, with the usual, "Well, take care," and with the prophetic send-off: "May God grant you shelter and food."

And that final brief moment when we realize that it is for good.

Donald Maclean and I were bound together by many years of friendship. This is how it all began. One day I arrived at the offices of the journal *Mezhdunarodnaya zhizn'* in order to give its editor, Boris Izakov, a copy of my first book, on British policy before the Second World War, which had just recently come out. At the editorial offices I ran into my wartime friend Sasha Galkin. He introduced me to a man who was as thin as a rail, with the profile of a Greek warrior and bright pale blue eyes. "A Roman centurion," I thought to myself for some inexplicable reason upon seeing him. The lanky fellow's name was Mark Petrovich Madzoyevsky. We exchanged a friendly handshake, and, as it turned out much later, we grew to like each other. I was writing reviews of books and memoirs on the history of the Second World War for *Mezhdunarodnaya zhizn'* at the time.

Naturally in the beginning I did not at all think that the amiable "Mark Petrovich Madzoyevsky," in fact a certain Fraser by name, was really the famous Donald Maclean, the British diplomat who had been in the service of the Soviet intelligence agency NKVD since the 1930s. I need not describe the history of that spy organization whose leader was the deputy head of the British intelligence service's USSR section, Kim Philby, and whose intellectual dynamo was Guy Burgess. It arose at Cambridge University among leftwing thinkers. A great deal has been written about it in revelatory articles and, to a lesser extent, in books. In all truthfulness, what impressed me most was the comment made by the British prime minister Harold Macmillan before the House of Commons in connection with Philby's escape to the Soviet Union. He explained to the members of Parliament that the origins of the English intellectuals' treason and of their spying activity should be sought in events of the 1930s—when anti-Fascist feeling was at its height because of the Nazis' coming to power in Germany. Leftwing intellectuals in the West looked to the Soviet Union as a force to counter fascism. The illusions of that time were so great that a dedication to communism completely blinded the Cambridge intellectual elite. I recall a letter by the English poet John Cornford to his beloved, in which he wrote: "I love you with all my strength and all my will and my whole body . . . The Party is my only other love." Cornford was killed in Spain in 1937. The illusions of that time were shattered for many leftists—and not for very long at that—only in August of 1939, when the Soviet-Nazi pact was signed. But for some of them it was already too late: they were locked into the Soviet spy network, an organization unprecedented in scope. Involved here as well was Donald Maclean, a product of the highest ranks of the British intelligentsia (his father had been minister of education in Ramsay MacDonald's cabinet) and a graduate of Cambridge University.

Later on Donald said to me: "You know how it began? I was lying about in my room at Cambridge. It was 1934. Suddenly a friend of mine runs in and shouts: 'The Fascists are beating our people!' I jumped up and rushed out to lend a hand. I had made my choice in that fight. It all began with that." It must be said that I never questioned Donald about anything myself, believing it would have been indiscreet. That is probably why our friendship continued right up until the moment I left Moscow forever. For example, I still do not know today under what circumstances Donald was recruited, but it was, no doubt, Guy Burgess who was responsible.

Once Donald invited me to his home. Melinda, his wife, and the children were absent, having gone off to their dacha somewhere. This was not the best of times for him: he was in the midst of a drinking bout. He lived in a large building on Dorogomilovskaya Street; one of the building's wings looked out on the Moscow River. Donald's apartment was on the fourth floor, and, following his instructions, I found it without much difficulty. When I went up to the door, however, and reached out to ring the doorbell, I noticed a note attached to the door, poorly scrawled in Russian, saying: "Wait for me ten minutes. Have gone to the store." Indeed, he soon returned bringing a couple of bottles of red wine, on which he would periodically get drunk. Finally, he landed in the hospital, and came out almost completely cured. I say "almost" because he sometimes had lapses (who has not?). But he was quite capable of drinking socially, in moderation, without any consequences, and he went on in this way for years.

Maclean and Burgess, with the threat of exposure hanging over them, fled to the USSR during the grimmest period of Stalin's final years. I think they were very fortunate: Maclean was kept in Kuybyshev, far removed from the bloody drama being played out in the capital. In Kuybyshev he spent a total of four and a half years. It was only in 1955 that he moved to Moscow. Two years earlier, his family had arrived to join him: his wife, two boys—Fergus and Donald—and a daughter, also named Melinda. Apparently Maclean had some difficulties in teaching English at the Kuybyshev Pedagogical Institute, and they were not just linguistic. Maclean was stubbornly persevering in mastering the language of the country he had chosen in exchange for his homeland, but the move had taken place under critical and desperate circumstances.

After Kuybyshev, of course, Moscow was for him, and for the whole family as well, the promised land. Although by Western standards the apartment was not at all large for five people—three rooms, one of which was a good-sized living room with a sort of skylight—it was relatively spacious. There his life underwent a radical change.

The time came when a great deal depended on "Mark Petrovich" himself. He could live decently on his adequate lifelong pension, equal to the earnings of a doctor of sciences, but the life of a pensioner, and in a foreign country at that, was not for him. It so happened that he was invited to work at the journal *Mezhdunarodnaya zhizn'*, and soon articles and reviews began to appear with the signature "Madzoyevsky." The journal came under the authority of the Ministry of Foreign Affairs. In fact, "Mark Petrovich Fraser" was himself nominally considered to be an adviser to the ministry, even though, as he once pointed out to me in jest, they had never once called him in for consultation.

The only reminder of his connection with the Ministry of Foreign Affairs was the rental of a small house with a tiny plot of land at the Ministry of Foreign Affairs dacha compound located in Chkalovskaya, not far from Moscow.

The years went by. Maclean left *Mezhdunarodnaya zhizn'* and went to work at the Institute of World Economy and International Relations, whose director at the time was N. N. Inozemtsev, a capable, career-oriented man from the A. M. Rumyantsev clique, the latter having once been a member of the Communist party Central Committee Presidium, and later vice president of the Academy of Sciences. Eventually Inozemtsev himself became a Central Committee member and vice president of the Academy.

Work at the institute brought Maclean some satisfaction for the first time in all his years in the USSR. It forced him out of his usual circle of retired intelligence agents and gave him new opportunities. He had been only thirty-eight years old when he arrived in the USSR. His career at the Foreign Office was on the rise, although I believe that deep down he could not help thinking that at any moment the building would come tumbling down, burying him in the debris. He did not possess the cynicism of Guy Burgess, an effete, refined intellectual, of whom a certain American woman once remarked to me with great conviction, "He was the devil incarnate." (Others called him a fallen angel.) Apparently Burgess had that rare ability to seduce even the far-from-naive minds of English intellectuals. I have been told, and repeatedly so, that a significant role was played here by the homosexual tendencies among some of the members of the Cambridge circle, turning it into a sort of closed elite society. Perhaps. But Maclean, at any rate, whatever might be said of him, was not a homosexual. All such rumors—and they recurred from time to time—were something he dismissed.

I believe that Donald more than once sought justification for his past. And he found it, at first in Khrushchev's reforms, then in the Suez crisis, and then in the war in Vietnam. This last event especially seemed to serve as a moral bulwark for what he had done, a kind of moral justification, for this proved to him beyond a doubt that American imperialism was in any case no better than Soviet power.

For many years Maclean was involved in the foreign policy of Great Britain as a career diplomat. His last position in the Foreign Office had been as head of the American desk. At the Institute of World Economy he became the main expert on British policy. In 1970 he wrote a book on the foreign policy of Great Britain after the Suez crisis. It was published in Moscow in Russian, and then in England in the original English. The appearance of his book compelled the British press once again to recall Philby, Maclean, and Burgess. Yet by this time Burgess was dead. He had committed suicide, Donald told me several years after the event. "You see, that happens to homosexuals owing to the fact that they can't find a long-term partner." With Maclean's other companion, Philby, relations had been cut short. I met Philby once at a dacha in Chkalovskaya. He impressed me as a man who was charming but with a very strong character.

Once Donald asked me to come see him at a specific time. At his home I met a pleasant Englishman about fifty years of age. He greeted me with the greatest of courtesy and, it seemed to me, with some surprise, apparently not expecting anyone else to be present. For a while the two of us were left alone, exchanging pleasantries, while Donald went into another room. The stranger gave me his calling card: it turned out that he had arrived from London with instructions from a medical relief fund providing assistance to Vietnam. Donald then appeared, holding a check in his hand. He had signed over all of his royalties from the British edition of the book on the foreign policy of Great Britain (and the royalties were considerable—some five thousand pounds, I believe) to the fund. "You see," Donald said later on, apologetically, "I called you because I wanted a witness when the check was handed over."

They say that the Scots are miserly. No doubt Donald was not a typical Scotsman. He did not squander his money, of course, but he was not seduced by it either. On several occasions he was offered a substantial advance to write a book about his espionage activities (once he even mentioned the amount of one hundred thousand dollars), but each and every time he declined the offer. Occasionally books and articles about him would appear. He never entered into polemics with their authors, even though, as he claimed, they contained quite a few fantasies.

At my home or at his we would talk completely freely, except that we tried not to mention names. Once during an argument I attempted to draw his attention, without speaking, to a suspicious ventilation duct between the wall and the ceiling. He waved his hand in disdain and said, "If you had to think about that, too, then life would simply be impossible." He understood perfectly well that one way or another, he was constantly under observation. Sometimes he would say to me, half-smiling, "N. phoned again, for no apparent reason. Before this he did the same thing exactly one month ago. Thank God it's only once a month. What can you do, he's got his reports to write."

Maclean read a great deal: the Russian classics, some books by contemporary authors, and later on, at the height of the dissident movement, unpublished manuscripts which Russian friends would bring to him at his home. His cultural heritage, however, was obviously Western. He came from the highest intellectual circles, and, I am certain, he took pride in this. Maclean needed to be surrounded by people who shared the same culture. I soon came to understand this, since I often met at his home various types of people from the West, in addition to his close friends, such as those who worked for the British communist newspaper *Morning Star*, but also people such as, for example, the prominent English leftwing Labourite and longtime member of Parliament D. N. Pritt, who was the author of a well-publicized book in the 1930s entitled *Light over Moscow*, in which he defended the Moscow trials of that decade. Maclean played host to a good number of foreigners with communist leanings or just with favorable feelings toward the Soviet Union—and not only Englishmen. I often wondered why they were so eager to visit him at his home. It was probably due not only to some degree of ideological sympathy but also to his intellect and his natural charm. I would put it this way: Maclean won people over with his intelligence, simplicity, and straightforwardness. It was very rare indeed—during heated debates on political issues, when passions sometimes ran high—for him to yield to emotional pressure; he did not waive his convictions, but they did change.

He was, when I met him, a confirmed communist and, I would add, an educated Marxist. Once, in a fit of anger, I called him the "communist's communist," and he took it not as a touch of irony but altogether seriously, even though he had a fairly good sense of humor. Here he remained inflexible. One time when he was in the hospital he met a certain young doctor, and they became friends. Their relationship gradually became more trusting, and finally the doctor began to tell Maclean of his rather unflattering opinion of the regime and of the very idea of socialism. They quarreled, parting for good. Maclean could not forget this for a long time, and once, without naming names, he even recounted the essence of the quarrel to a rather large gathering of Russians and foreigners. The doctor had claimed that there was nothing worse in the world than the Soviet regime and that therefore sooner or later it had to disappear.

"Mark Petrovich" attempted to lead the same life-style as that of his colleagues at the Institute of World Economy and International Relations: he spent his days in the institute library, primarily in the special reserved section, where the British periodicals and books he needed were kept, and many of his evenings were spent in editing manuscripts. In summer he would vacation, as a rule, at his dacha in Chkalovskaya, and in winter he would travel to a recreation center near Moscow for skiing. He learned to ski rather quickly, by the way, but I always found it a bit frightening when he skied down a snowy slope: what if he, with his enormous height, were suddenly to come down with a crash?

At his institute, in which he was, incidentally, not the only visitor from another world, Maclean enjoyed the complete respect and possibly even the love of his colleagues. He attracted people with his patience, a quality so rarely found in the average Soviet person, his sharp mind, and his total dedication to his work. He was elected a member of the institute party committee. (For services rendered in this nonacademic calling, he was awarded the Order of the Red Banner.) Maclean attached great importance to precise thinking and well-defined positions. And he was a good judge of character, although he took a rather condescending view of other people's weaknesses.

The years went by, and hopes for turning Soviet society into "socialism with a human face" were not realized. Maclean could not avoid the painful process of reappraising his values. Here he was not alone. He did, however, hold his doubts against himself. As the years progressed his views became less and less orthodox, and his concessions even greater. Disappointment increased. It became deeper especially after the Pasternak affair and grew worse when persecution of the dissidents began. This was a harsh blow for him, in light of what were, from a Soviet standpoint, his absurd concepts as a civilized Westerner. He could consider the accusations of treason made against General A. A. Vlasov to be valid, but he refused to join with those who declared writers to be criminals simply for publishing their works abroad.

But worse times were to come. Zhores Medvedev was packed off to a psychiatric hospital, and this was where the inexhaustible patience of the "communist's communist" came to an end. Maclean sent a letter to the head of the international department and secretary of the Communist party Central Committee Boris Ponomarev, in which he explained politely and calmly the great harm this action had done to the prestige of the Soviet Union and to the international communist movement. I believe that Maclean's intervention helped strengthen the pressure brought to bear by Tvardovsky, Sakharov, and others. Zhores Medvedev was released soon afterward.

Donald never took part in the dissident movement, and in the beginning he obviously disapproved of the small group of dissidents, who progressed from criticism of the Soviet regime to a rejection of the socialist system in general. Once he began to criticize individual actions taken by the regime, however, he tried in his own way to combat its excesses. I believe he increasingly came to feel that the communism for which he had sacrificed everything had turned out to be altogether different in practice from what he used to imagine back in the British Isles. At one time the victory over fascism in the Second World War confirmed for him, or so it seemed, that he had made the right choice. Atomic bomb secrets, in the transfer of which he had apparently been instrumental, were, as he saw it, something the Soviet Union needed in order to even the balance of military power with the United States. Had not President Truman, in fact, threatened to use the atom bomb during the Korean War? Maclean's work for the Soviet Union was, in his view, also a response to McCarthyism. In short, there was more than enough justification for his actions. But gradually the rationalizations ceased to satisfy him. And his response to the concrete questions posed by life was to take concrete action. There came the arrest and then the internment in a psychiatric ward of General Pyotr Grigorenko. Maclean decided to protest, and, in his usual manner, he preferred to act individually, independently. It so happened that the regular elections to the Supreme Soviet were about to take place. Maclean, on receiving his election ballot, went into the booth and there he wrote on the ballot more or less the following: "While I am voting in favor of the proposed candidate, I hereby express my protest against the arrest of General Grigorenko." And he put down his name and address. This was his way of dissenting.

Quite naturally, the bosses dragged Maclean over the coals. As he told me later, there was a sharp exchange of words. The concrete result for him was a suspension of his pension payments for several months. But Maclean remained faithful to his position.

Shortly before my departure for the West, I told Donald about the serious physical condition of Vladimir Bukovsky, who had been kept imprisoned, and I drew up a brief report on this situation for Maclean at his own request. I believe that the letter Maclean sent to Boris Ponomarev had some influence on the final decision to exchange the Soviet dissident for Luis Corvalan, for Ponomarev's office was directly involved in this deal.

The it was discovered that Maclean had cancer of the bladder. At first an operation was performed on him and it was successful. I shall never forget how I came to visit Donald in Kuntsevo, in a ward of the Kremlin hospital, and how he then saw me off, and we stood there on either side of the fence talking, joking, and laughing. But never before had I come away from seeing someone with such an uneasy feeling. The clock was ticking away the minutes of his life.

Donald constantly reproached himself for the fact that, once having made the important decision that was to change his life completely, he had forced his family to live in the Soviet Union as well, and in so doing had unwittingly deprived his wife and children of the right to choose. This was incalculably hard for him to bear. And so he decided to undo this situation in his own way. He managed, in spite of the obstacles, to obtain permission for his children to travel abroad. The idea was to give them the opportunity to experience life in the West and then make their own choice. And they made that choice after returning to Moscow. One by one his children left the Soviet Union. His elder son, Fergus, settled in England, Donald Junior and Mimsy in the United States, which is where Maclean's wife, Melinda, an American by birth, also went. They all left legally; they did not defect. So it was that Donald Maclean fulfilled his duty to his family but ended up alone.

I never saw him again after I left the Soviet Union. Once I phoned him from the United States, and later simply sent my regards through friends. It should be said that Maclean was aware of my plans to leave and approved of them. We discussed them on more than one occasion, as we strolled along the Dorogomilovskaya Embankment of the Moscow River. Donald wanted me to settle in his country, in Britain. He loved his homeland. But he died in Moscow. His ashes were sent to the Scottish island of Tiree, from where his family had come. There Donald Maclean found his final refuge.

In Russia, both old and new, funerals have always been an occasion for people of a certain time to express their feelings. I need only refer here to the funerals of Lev Nikolaevich Tolstoy, V. I. Lenin, and I. V. Stalin.

A public demonstration was the natural outcome for the funeral of the writer A. E. Kosterin, a well-known public figure who had defended the unjustly excluded small nationalities of our country

At these funerals the conscience of the people, who remained silent under ordinary circumstances, rose to the surface. I can recall the funeral for Boris Pasternak. That was in 1960. In the final years of Pasternak's life, after he had written *Doctor Zhivago*, he had been harassed and even threatened with expulsion from the Soviet Union. Many well-known Soviet writers and people prominent in the arts took part in that shameful campaign. Soon afterwards Pasternak died. His funeral was turned into a demonstration of public condemnation for the harassment he had suffered. I remember the surprising statement made at his funeral by a young man dressed in dark blue, perhaps a naval uniform, and the statement made by B. P. Asmus, most heartfelt, and dangerous for Asmus himself. I arrived at Peredelkino, where the poet was being buried, together with the archaeologist Aleksandr Mongait, Naum Korzhavin, Bulat Okudzhava, and the actress Zhanna Prokhorenko. Pasternak was buried on a hillside under some trees, and hundreds of people, spilling out over the fields, slowly made their way in a snakelike procession as they lined up to pass the place of burial. This was an expression of genuine, sincere grief for a poet persecuted by the authorities and an expression of sympathy for him more as a sufferer than as a writer.

Nothing of the kind occurred at the funeral for Tvardovsky, although this funeral, unlike that of Boris Pasternak, was an official, solemn one, with the changing of an honor guard and with a statement made by the secretary of the Writers' Union. But only one person said a few human words—Konstantin Simonov. Those who spoke carefully avoided any reference to what was the most important aspect in Tvardovsky's life and activity—the years in which he headed *Novy mir*, the finest literary and sociopolitical journal in the country. This was disgraceful, not only for those who spoke but for all those present at the meeting of remembrance held at the Writers' Union as well, for they were virtually being spat on by those who pretended that Tvardovsky had never existed as editor in chief of *Novy mir*, that there had never been reprisals taken against the editors of the journal and against Tvardovsky himself, who was forced to step down from the helm. Still, a miracle occurred: just as the meeting was about to adjourn, but while the speakers were still on the platform and the people in the hall had barely risen from their seats, a woman shouted out in a terrifying voice, the voice of a person bringing word of some terrible misfortune: "Why do you remain silent? Why won't you say that Tvardovsky was taken off *Novy mir*, that they hastened his death?" The crowd fell silent. Then a sort humming began, and suddenly everyone was moving toward the exit. Yet all the same, this wailing had been the voice of future hope, which would forever hover over the ceremonial hall.

Now, at Novodevichy Cemetery, here was Aleksandr Isaevich Solzhenitsyn, on whose arm leaned Tvardovsky's widow—Solzhenitsyn, who had made his way into the hall at the Writers' Union in spite of the special patrols set up in order to stop him.

On September 11, 1971, Nikita Sergeevich Khrushchev ended his days. That evening, radio stations abroad broadcast to the world news of the death of one of the most surprising statesmen ever to spring from Russian soil. It was not until the thirteenth that the newspaper *Pravda* published an official announcement. It stated:

> The Central Committee of the Communist party of the Soviet Union and the USSR Council of Ministers announce the death on September 11, 1971, after a prolonged serious illness, of former First Secretary of the CPSU Central Committee and Chairman of the USSR Council of Ministers, private pensioner Nikita Sergeevich Khrushchev.

No reference was made to the day and place set for the funeral. Radio Moscow spoke of everything imaginable, except this one event of such tremendous importance.

Nevertheless, in spite of the fact that the time and place for the funeral had not been given, rumors had already spread throughout Moscow on the evening of September 11 that the ceremony would be held on Monday, September 13, at noon in the Novodevichy Cemetery.

I agreed to go to the funeral with an artist friend of mine and his wife. At the appointed time, 10:45 A.M., we met not far from the entrance to the cemetery at 20 October Square.

I arrived a bit earlier than the agreed time. Alongside Novodevichy, by the entrance to the church, military posts had already been set up, and small groups of state secret police officials in civilian clothes had appeared. But in addition to them, here and there, there began to gather small groups of citizens who had somehow heard about the funeral. At the corner of Pirogov Street and the square were a few officers, cadets at the nearby Frunze Military Academy. Officers from the armed forces, in most cases standing alone, I noticed later on.

Soon my friends came up to me. On seeing that barriers had already been set up and that it was impossible to get through the main gates of the cemetery, we attempted to enter through the monastery courtyard, but we immediately discovered that "Operation Funeral" had been planned extremely carefully: militia patrols had already been positioned, and KGB officials milled about the courtyard. All the openings along the monastery wall had also been put under guard. Militia cars stood parked by the blocked driveways.

On the right side of the church a wall was being repaired. We went up to an elderly man in a shapeless, mud-stained cap, apparently a work foreman, and asked him how to get through, or rather how to sneak into the cemetery. "You'll never get in through here, there are guards everywhere," he replied, and with a nod of his head he pointed at a gap in the wall where the faces of two militiamen had suddenly appeared. "But what's so interesting, anyway?" continued the foreman, laughing. "Funerals are funerals." For some reason he pronounced the first letter of the Russian word for funeral, *pokhorony*, with a *k*, and this made his words sound somehow special, almost mystical. "They'll bury him, and they'll bury you. They'll outlive all of us."

Sent off on our way with these philosophical words of wisdom, we left the outer monastery courtyard in pursuit of our quest. After much wandering along the street opposite the cemetery wall, soaking wet from a driving rain, we finally came upon the most advantageous spot for observation—the intersection of an alley and a street at the very end of the avenue, across from the cemetery gates.

During the course of our wanderings we discovered that all the entrances and driveways were blocked by militia and secret police officials, and, perhaps, by activists brought in for that purpose as well. Some distance away inside the courtyard stood tarpaulin–covered military trucks, in which soldiers from the internal troops, young, strapping men neatly dressed and freshly shaven, were huddled. An officer sat in the driver's seat in each of the trucks. Near each group of cars of what was evidently a military company there stood a communications man with a portable radio set, who was constantly in touch with his superiors.

As I walked by one of the cars, I stared at the soldiers sitting inside. One of them met my glance with an embarrassed, seemingly apologetic smile, as if he were saying: "What do you expect? We have nothing to do with this." And suddenly a song by Bulat Okudzhava came to mind: "So what if something is amiss! As they say, the Homeland ordered this." That is how I recalled the soldier with the slight, apologetic smile. "No, not everything is lost yet, no, not yet," I would repeat to myself more than once, on remembering the soldier. Still an uneasy feeling over the presence of such a large number of soldiers, ready to obey any orders on command, stayed with me for a long time.

We were lucky. The militiamen who were guarding access to the cemetery turned out to be courteous and calm. From time to time they would ask us to move back from the driveway onto the sidewalk, but there was no rude shouting, nor, especially, was there any physical abuse. A few journalists, both foreign and Soviet, passed by our station and were politely let in on presentation of their credentials. Permission to go up to the cemetery gates was given to a few old people, primarily women, after they exchanged a couple of quiet words with the militia. These were former political prisoners who had returned and been rehabilitated during the years of Khrushchev's rule.

At first it was pouring rain. Then it began to snow. Then suddenly it came back to me: yes, of course, I recalled joyfully, *then* it began to snow . . . It is on Christmas Eve, December 24, 1942, near Stalingrad, on the outer rim of the Stalingrad "cauldron," the encirclement of the German troops. "Nekrich, quick!" someone calls. In the doorway appears my superior officer, Captain Arkady Kvasov. Buttoning my overcoat as I go, I nearly run together with Kvasov to an outlying house. There is to be an interrogation of the Germans from Manstein's army. Tyul'panov, head of the Stalingrad front political command department for enemy activity had proposed an operation to throw the enemy forces into the "cauldron." There are several people in the spacious room, and the cleverest of all is Sergei Ivanovich Tyul'panov. I look around the room. Everyone is talking in a low tone of voice. They sometimes glance toward the door, evidently expecting the higher-ups to arrive. The door swings open wide, and in a blast of chilly December wind the outline of a thickset man appears and then seems to fade for a second in the doorway. Someone else is behind him. Khrushchev! I recognize him. It is member of the front military council, Nikita Sergeevich Khrushchev in person. "Damn it," I think to myself, "this is going to be serious." Khrushchev greets everyone in turn. I am the most junior in rank, and therefore I am the last to be introduced. "Lieutenant Nekrich," I say distinctly. Khrushchev, smiling, shakes my hand.

So Khrushchev himself will be speaking with the prisoners of war. He suggests to them that they go into the "cauldron," where Paulus' army sits surrounded, and themselves serve as living witnesses to the defeat suffered by General Manstein as he hurried to Paulus' rescue. My role is, without attracting attention, to sit behind a curtain and take down a record of Khrushchev's words, but in such a way that none of the Germans might suspect my presence. The curtain that separates one part of the hut from another is too short. I sit on a high stool with my legs slightly crossed, and am overcome by terror. What if I don't understand the Germans correctly? What if I suddenly fall off the stool? My God! Then I regain my composure and almost automatically take down what Khrushchev says.

He speaks in a friendly manner, and tells the captured Germans, almost mockingly, how the surrounded army of three hundred thousand men will perish. "This is senseless!" he exclaims. And he explains to the Germans that they can help avoid unnecessary bloodshed and save their compatriots simply by telling them the truth, which is that Manstein will never come to Paulus' rescue: he is beaten. The prisoners of war celebrate Christmas, and afterwards they go off into the "cauldron," taking upon themselves the mission proposed by Khrushchev.

This was my only meeting with Khrushchev. And I remembered it, standing in the pouring rain on the sidewalk near the Novodevichy Cemetery. Then I remembered it once again when I read about this episode in Khrushchev's memoirs and was overwhelmed by his excellent memory.

At Novodevichy the rain kept coming down in buckets. At approximately a quarter to twelve, microphones blared a command: "March!" I shuddered. Just like during the war!

On the opposite side of the street motorcycles streamed by, and behind them at great speed a truck bearing floral wreaths, and just behind it, also at breakneck speed, an ordinary hearse. Then came a file of cars. Acquainted as I was with the principles of Soviet hierarchy, I could see right away that no one from the highest ranks was present, for there was nothing but black Volgas here: only second– or third-rank officials ride in those.

Musicians entered the gates of the cemetery one by one, holding silvery instruments in their hands or under their arms.

Twelve noon: the sounds of a funeral march could be heard from the cemetery. The ceremony had begun. The tension diminished somewhat. Our militiamen began to talk with the public. "When will we be let in?" we asked them. "In an hour," came the reply. Soon we were approached by a youthful-looking and only slightly gray-haired major general from the internal troops, apparently the officer in charge. He was accompanied by a colonel. The general had just come up to us when an elderly woman with a dried-out, yellowish-brown face went over to him. Cancer, I thought to myself for a moment. The woman was explaining something to the general in a soft tone of voice. Yes, she has cancer, I thought once again. "Fine, go on," answered the general. The woman made her way slowly toward the cemetery gates. Those who had been standing next to her—I was among them—began to ask that we be let in as well. "Why you?" asked the general, nearly laughing. "To pay my last respects to the deceased," I replied. "No, it is not allowed," and off the general went. After a few minutes three elderly people, a man and two women, came up to our station. One of the women must have been the man's wife, the other his sister. The man excitedly explained something to the head of our station, a militia captain. The latter heard them out, and then gestured with his hand to let them through. The three quickly made for the gates. "Allow me in as well," I said to the captain. He looked me up and down. Apparently I made a favorable impression on him: "Fine, go ahead." A few more people were waved in behind me.

We went up to the gates of the cemetery. I looked at my watch: it was half-past twelve. But then at the gate itself (it was closed) something went wrong; we were not allowed in. One of the older women began banging insistently on the gate. The guard standing on the other side peered through the peephole and opened the gate just a bit. "Let us in," a few voices said. "Rita," said a short man, all excited. He had a lively, expressive face. "Doesn't that peephole remind you of something?" "What do you mean, of course it reminds me," she answered with a strange sort of laugh. Another conversation: "How did you find out that the funeral was at twelve? Did they really announce it on the radio?" And the reply: "They announced it from 'over there'"—that is, on a foreign radio station.

The rain came down even harder. I put up the collar of my raincoat. I stood and I listened. People were getting annoyed, and becoming more and more excited. The secret police officials, taking refuge in the doorway of a flower stall, stood silently, occasionally smiling slightly. The rain poured down.

Out of nowhere a junior militia colonel appeared. "Let us in!" the soaking wet crowd demanded almost in chorus.

"The cemetery is closed" was his curt response.

"How can it be closed? There's a funeral going on in there!" shouted angry voices.

"The cemetery is closed," the junior colonel repeated and disappeared behind the gate.

By this time about twenty people had gathered by the cemetery gates. The secret police officials, dressed in civilian clothes or in militia uniform, observed the crowd carefully. But they did not make a single hostile gesture or enter into conversation, obviously following strict instructions. The crowd was becoming more and more upset. "You don't need to make noise. Let's stand in silence at the locked gate," a tall middle-aged man addressed the crowd. But very few seemed to understand the deeper meaning of what he had said.

The crowd was becoming increasingly excited and more insistent in their demands that they be let through the cemetery gates. Finally, a man in civilian clothes appeared. He looked to be somewhere between the ages of thirty and forty.

"What is the matter?" he asked.

Cries came in response: "Why aren't we being allowed into the funeral?"

"Don't you see that the cemetery isn't open today? It is a cleaning day," and he pointed to the announcement posted on the gates, written by hand in red pencil: "On September 13 the cemetery will be closed. Cleaning day."

An outburst of ironic comments came in response: "Cleaning day! The day for a cleaning treatment!" "What about those who were let into the funeral? Did they go through a cleaning treatment? And do you have a note saying that you've been put through a cleaning treatment for delousing?"

The tall man, without a tremble, put his oar in. "Funerals are for relatives and friends."

"And you, no doubt, are a relative?" someone asked ironically.

"Yes, I am a relative." Laughter broke out in response. But the laughter was hollow, for this was the son of the deceased, Sergei. Thanks to his intervention, the gate was finally opened for us. I hurried over to where the funeral was taking place. At that moment the coffin with Khrushchev's body was being lowered into the grave. The orchestra had begun to play a hymn. Four strapping gravediggers began to throw in the earth, filling up the grave. I looked around me. On all sides cameras were clicking and the correspondents' news cameras were humming. There were quite a few reporters—probably several dozen. Wreaths were laid, and earth scattered over the grave. Then the gravediggers set a white-colored marble marker on top. It bore a rather banal inscription in gold letters: Nikita Sergeevich Khrushchev, 1894–1971. Above it a portrait of the deceased in a glass-enclosed frame, the same sort of photograph as on the neighboring gravestone, that of a people's artist from the Sadovsky dynasty who had died in April of that same year.

Throughout the ceremony a man stood in front of the gravestone holding a panel draped in red silk on which were embossed the gold stars and medals that had belonged to the deceased. All the requisite honors were there: wreaths from the Communist party Central Committee and the USSR Council of Ministers, from A. I. Mikoyan, from family members, from friends, and a few more besides.

Khrushchev's relatives gathered around the tombstone. There were many of them. One could just glimpse the tortured, tear-stained face of Nina Petrovna, Rada Nikitichna's face crumpled into a ball, a beautiful, stately young woman held up by an equally young air force colonel, the broad figure of Adzhubey.

The photographers clicked away; the movie cameras keep on rolling. Behind me some American correspondents were speaking in a low tone of voice: "Exceptional event... the whole word press and world radio..."

I caught sight of a friend of mine and made my way toward him. He was standing there looking tall and sad. Pensioner Khrushchev had once invited him for a visit, but he ended up not going. Now he regretted it, no doubt. I tapped him on the shoulder. There were many secret police officials all around us, all in civilian dress. From the way they behaved and the cut of their suits I could distinguish the higher-ranking ones from the rest. But why were there so many of them? Why so many militiamen and soldiers from the internal troops, hidden under tarpaulin-covered military trucks? Why the "cleaning day"? Why the Novodevichy Cemetery and not the Kremlin wall?

What an ironic twist of fate! Nikita Khrushchev laid to rest among artists, poets, academicians, in short, among the intellectuals to whom he was so often unfair; but it is only they who have a kind word for him now in remembrance. As for the "other one," even in death he finds himself among his companions along the Kremlin walls.

There were only a few—a very few—average citizens, simple Soviet people, who wished to say farewell to Khrushchev. Indeed, there were only the intellectuals. And it wasn't just because there had been no public announcement of the funeral. The reason was altogether different: forgotten was the return of the prisoners, the posthumous rehabilitations, the massive housing construction which had taken place during the years of Khrushchev's rule. What the people remembered was the end to advantageous loan conditions, even though they forgot the loans had been canceled altogether. They remembered the increase in prices, the costly junkets abroad, the long, flowing speeches of the deceased.

The sparse crowd gathered around the fresh gravesite slowly thinned out. My friend and I walked up to Rada Nikitichna. I said a few brief words of sympathy, introduced myself, and shook hands firmly. We moved toward the exit and out the gates. On the sidewalk opposite, a good number of people had gathered. A line of militiamen stood in front of them. No one else was being allowed through the cemetery gates. I looked back. The announcement written by hand in red pencil was still hanging there: "On September 13 the cemetery will be closed. Cleaning day."

In the autumn of 1973 Ilya Gabay committed suicide. I had met him at the home of Zhora Fedorov in the mid-sixties, and I took an immediate liking to him because of his intelligence, his wit, and his good nature. Moreover, Gabay was a courageous man. He was among the first to initiate the democratic movement in the USSR, which came about after the Twentieth Party Congress. Shocked by his death, I wrote a short notice. Regretfully, through an unfortunate set of circumstances at the time, this notice never made its way into samizdat. The first page is all that I have left in my possession. Here it is:

The Demise of Ilya Gabay

On Saturday, October 20, 1973, at about ten o'clock in the morning, Ilya Gabay committed suicide. He jumped from the balcony of his eleventh-floor apartment on Novolesnaya Street in Moscow.

Gabay took off his glasses and put them neatly on the kitchen table. Before this he had written a note in which he asked everyone to forgive him. He wrote that he had become a burden to his family. Then he went out on to the balcony . . .

His body fell onto the concrete roof of a beauty parlor adjacent to the apartment tower in which he lived. Gabay fell face down. And that is how he lay until a neighbor saw a man's body spread out on the roof and phoned the militia.

Gabay's wife, Galya, discovered that her husband had disappeared at about eleven o'clock, when she got up out of bed. She went through the entire apartment in search of him and ventured into the kitchen. The door to the balcony had been left ajar. She stepped out and saw below a crowd of people and an ambulance. The horrifying truth was revealed to her in an instant.

At the entryway, in the stairwell, and in the apartment itself were officials from the secret police and the militia. No one was allowed into the apartment. Friends of Gabay's who arrived had their documents carefully checked. Gabay's wife was allowed to view the body of her husband just before it was sent to the morgue. The note Gabay left behind was found beside the telephone by a militia official.

That same evening, radio stations (not Soviet ones, needless to say) broadcast a brief report on the suicide of the dissident, teacher of literature, and poet Ilya Gabay. One radio station reported that the reason for his suicide was supposedly his remorse over the harm he had caused the Soviet authorities. It is easy to imagine who was behind the spreading of this false report.

The rest I must reconstruct from memory:

After being released from three years' imprisonment in the camps, Gabay returned to Moscow a physically broken man, but still he retained his spiritual strength. He did not compromise his principles or betray anyone, but he was tired. The first thing he did with the first money he earned was to go to the Moscow bookstores and buy books. This act sums up Gabay entirely, an intelligent, refined, bookish type, a person with an extremely fragile spirit.

The state secret police did not leave Gabay in peace even when he was given his freedom. On more than just one occasion they called him in for talks "to save his soul," and they continually demanded that he either renounce his beliefs or give information. But Gabay remained firm. At that time the KGB was preparing for the trial of Yakir and Krasin, and Gabay suffered deeply over the wavering of his close friend Pyotr Yakir. He liked Yakir, and Yakir's behavior during the investigation was a terrible shock for him. And then, Gabay didn't have any job either. He could not obtain any sort of employment in his field—the teaching of Russian literature—for which he not only felt a passionate love but also had a profound knowledge and appreciation. He could have obtained such work, had he satisfied the demands of the KGB. But for him this was impossible.

So all the sad circumstances in the last years of his life became one tangled knot, and he did not have the strength to unravel it. He preferred to chop it to pieces. And this he did—he did it frighteningly and without mercy: he killed himself.

Russia! Your son Ilya Gabay has left you, has left you forever. Weep, Russia!

While still a student during the prewar years, I used to go on archaeological expeditions. In 1939, during excavations in Novgorod, I became friendly with many archaeologists, and we remained friends for life. Shura (Aleksandr L'vovich) Mongait was one of them. We were friends—Shura and his wife, Valya, with whom I was a bit in love, as well as his entire family—for a period of three and a half decades. For the last eighteen years we lived in the same Academy of Sciences cooperative apartment building at number 4 Dmitry Ulyanov Street, off Lenin Prospekt in Moscow. That building and the people who have lived and still live in it could, no doubt, be the subject of more than one story. But what I have to say now is not about them.

In 1974 a great misfortune occurred: Shura became ill with cancer of the pancreas, an incurable and very painful disease. The last years of his life were ruined by harassment from the director of the Institute of Archaeology, Academician Rybakov. Academician Rybakov forced Mongait, Fedorov, and the paleontologist V. D. Tsalkin, three outstanding scholars, off the Academic Council. No one at the Institute of Archaeology dared raise his voice in protest. But Rybakov did not stop there. He removed Fedorov from an expedition which he had set up in Moldavia and had been running for twenty years, simply because Rybakov did not like Fedorov's independent thinking. He also created obstacles for both Fedorov and Mongait in the publication of their manuscripts.

Rybakov managed the entire staff at the institute with an iron fist. The slightest sign of criticism was nipped in the bud. Both the party bureau and the trade union organization were under Rybakov's thumb. This is, briefly, what the atmosphere at the Institute of Archaeology was like around the time of Mongait's death.

Dozens of people filed into the conference hall to say farewell to Mongait. He had been a friend to many scholars, composers, artists, and writers. Among those who came to pay their last respects to Shura was Andrei Dmitrievich Sakharov. Mongait's children, Borya and Dima, asked me to say a few words. I did. But they were not just words about Shura. I spoke about our conformist society and about how hard things were for a true scholar in a time of rampant conformism. I recalled the reprisals enacted by Academician Rybakov, the expulsion from the academic council of three outstanding scholars. I recalled Shura's life, but I had in mind all of those who were present at the funeral. I spoke for the living, for the staff at the Institute of Archaeology, as if to urge them to renounce their fear of Rybakov, to feel like real human beings and rise to the level of ordinary human dignity. My words fell on a cold silence. Later I saw how surprised was Rybakov, who had come to the funeral. In fact he had been asked not to attend, as this would make things unpleasant for Mongait's family. But he still came—came to get his due.

It was later said in party circles that I used Mongait's funeral in order to make a political statement. The statement did not have any visible consequences for me, however. Yet I did not fear the consequences. I had already made my decision not to compromise with our conformist society.

For thirty years I had worked in the same institute, and for many years the institute was the center of my life. It represented not only the work for which I received a salary but also the center for historical study in the USSR, and I was a historian by vocation. I will not hide the fact that I was and remain proud of this. My entering the field of history has been and remains for me a source of enjoyment, and yet of sorrow as well.

Dealing with history in the Soviet Union is extremely complex from a psychological perspective. History, like all other fields of study in the USSR, is the preserve of the Communist party and the state. The state, virtually the only employer in the country, subsidizes such study. Therefore, every scholar is, at the same time, a state official: he must constantly keep this in mind and construct his work in such a way as to render useful service to the state. The party takes upon itself concern for ideological policy in the social sciences. It directs this policy based not only on its strategic plans but also, first and foremost, on tactical plans calculated for the short term. And scholars in the social sciences are forced to adapt their academic interests to the interests of current party considerations. Yesterday Marshal Tito was a traitor to the cause of socialism, a CIA agent, a Trotskyite, and a tool of imperialism. And in the Soviet Union dozens of dissertations were written in which future candidates and doctors of science attempted, in scholarly fashion, to demonstrate this. Then it was admitted that a slight mistake had been made and that Tito was not a spy but a communist. Some people say that the poor dissertation writers went to the Lenin Library and furtively ripped out those pages that bore witness not so much against Tito as against themselves. And this was not a matter related to a specific campaign "for" or "against" but a routine, everyday affair. In short social scientists in the Soviet Union were and remain prisoners of changing political circumstances.

For seven years the manuscript of G. B. Fedorov's book *The Archaeology of Romania* lay in the "Nauka" publications office because of the disorder in Soviet-Romanian relations. But it was not only the social sciences that were involved. Scholars in the field of the physical, technical, and natural sciences are also dependent to varying degrees on concerns of the moment and pay tribute in their own way through quotations in their books from the classics of Marxism-Leninism. These quotations actually have nothing to do with, say, the theory of light or with biophysics, but they are evidence of the loyalty and political maturity of the individual scientist.

And I too had paid this tribute all my life. At first I paid dearly, and then less so, until I rebelled. And when I rebelled, my life began to change quickly. The institute kept its distance from me and soon ceased to be a second home for me. The idea that year after year was going by for nothing had long troubled me, even when I was not being subjected to systematic persecution. Gradually I began to tire of the need for self-censorship of my books and articles, and for constant political self-control in my conversations and talks. A strange metamorphosis was taking place: the easier it became to breathe in our country, the more harshly I felt the daily oppression of the Soviet totalitarian regime. But once having rebelled, I began to feel more and more the practical consequences of my rebellion: limiting the publication of my major work, forbidding me to travel abroad, not allowing me to attend international meetings of scholars in my own country, and so on. Not only had my life changed, but I consciously began to make changes in it myself in accordance with my moral convictions. My views on many things had changed thoroughly.

I, who had once imagined myself a soldier in the world revolution, began to hate violence in any form. The reorganization of society by force appeared to me to be a most serious crime against humanity: killing, annihilating, starving to death tens of millions of people in the name of building an ideal society? But a society built by such methods can never be moral, can never be successful, for the crimes committed in its name will not only constantly haunt it but will become an integral part of its psychology, morality, and ethics. Conformism in such a society is the be all and end all. Do not be misled: whatever artistic work is created, whatever scientific discussion takes place, it belongs first and foremost to the society and the state and only secondarily to mankind.

I do not have, nor have I ever had, any program for reorganizing society. As for myself, I have always felt it absolutely necessary to help people who are in difficulty because of their political convictions, and particularly their break with the rampant conformism of Soviet society. While I was living in the Soviet Union, I was close to many dissidents of various stripes and various political persuasions, helped them as well as I could, and sometimes took part in their actions. I did not, however, belong to any of the movements but always remained under my own banner. I did this not so much out of individualism, since I could be counted, in fact, more among the collectivists, but because I did not find among the dissidents any positive program that inspired me. Once I asked Pyotr Yakir, with whom I used to meet and talk frequently: "What is it that you want?" and I received from him a rather vague reply: that everything in society be just. This was a noble desire, but not at all a program.

Nor did I find plausible the program of Roy Medvedev, who believed, or pretended to believe, in our young leaders, who, it was said, would replace the elderly Soviet leadership and gradually change the face of our society while abiding by the precepts of Marxism and socialism. This program could not elicit any enthusiasm from me, since, first, I do not believe in the leaders in general, and second, I do not believe in the so-called younger leaders. With the existing system of selecting the leadership, those who reach the pinnacle of power are already far from young by then; as they crawl higher and higher up the power pyramid, and the pyramid, in accordance with the law of geometric progression, gets smaller and smaller toward the top, they are forced at each level to cast off their opponents in order to stay aloft, making use in the process of all their resources, letting loose, figuratively speaking, their claws and fangs. By the time one of them finally manages to reach the top, it turns out that not only is he past his youth, but he has already become jaded, has lost all his ideals and creative energies and now thinks only of power—how to hold on to it and how to enjoy it as long as possible. Third, I do not believe in the possibility of major change within the scale of values established by the Soviet regime and in the prospect that the existing system could grow into something more humane. There is another, different prospect: the transformation of this system into an imitation of a just society. It is possible, of course, to try to make the Soviet way of life more cosmetically attractive, for example, to nominate for election two or even three candidates instead of one (and indeed I can only express surprise that this is not done, since all these candidates would still be approved by the Communist party Central Committee). It would be possible to close one's eyes to the books published abroad by members of the "loyal opposition" and even to the publication of a critical journal, especially if its basic goal is to campaign against people and ideas even more dangerous and more hostile to the existing regime.

I am not drawn to dissidents who uphold narrow nationalist ideas, although I do understand and sympathize with the idea of defending one's own people, their cultural and moral values, but not to the detriment or denigration of other nationalities and peoples. Chauvinism, apartheid, anti-Semitism, the idea of being chosen or having a special mission are alien to me, and just as inimical as Nazism and fascism.

I identify most closely of all with the ideas set forth by Academician Andrei Dmitrievich Sakharov, since these ideas are based on the interests of human society as a whole, even though they are first and foremost in keeping with the vital interests of my country. I would venture here to point out that by virtue not only of his entire way of thinking but also of his noble way of life, Andrei Dmitrievich Sakharov is truly the father of our country. Here is an awe-inspiring historical figure, a man for all seasons, one of the few whose stay on earth will enrich mankind and justify the existence of the human race.

It is claimed that only a small handful of dissidents are waging a struggle in the Soviet Union for human rights. This is only half true. Let us take, for example, the problem of freedom of national self-expression. It affects the interests of probably millions of people whose national feelings are violated or suppressed by the regime. Or let us take a look at such a pan-national problem as freedom of expression. The struggle for this is being waged, at times even subconsciously, by thousands of people: scientists, writers, artists. All of them, either actively or passively, depending on their specific circumstances, are defending their rights from pressure by the authorities. They are all part of the overall democratic movement which is in its initial stages, but which has a certain degree of potential for the future.

The dissidents in fact represent that part of this overall democratic movement which is the most aware, determined, and prepared for self-sacrifice. They are the essence of its avant-garde and therefore relatively small in number.

Close to them are the liberal nondissidents, who, according to their degree of courage or fear, are still consciously or instinctively in opposition to the existing regime, although they often are inclined to compromise and give in to it. Yet still many of them are involved somehow. For example, in order to clear their conscience, they help to collect money and supplies for political prisoners and their families, or they read samizdat literature and lend it out to their friends, and so on. They do very little? Yes, very little indeed. But that is still better than nothing.

I myself had occasion more than once to collect money for political prisoners and for dissidents, and this money was often given by people who would not want to meet or get to know such individuals. But they gave money and clothing willingly, asked for and took samizdat literature to read. These liberal-minded people were capable of suddenly turning their backs and even of raising their hand at a meeting to condemn Sakharov or Solzhenitsyn or even their own colleagues at work, of putting their signature on some disgraceful resolution. But another time, in a milder political and moral climate the liberals might do something useful, say, come to the defense of someone threatened with dismissal from work. We saw examples of this repeatedly, even after Khrushchev's departure, in 1965-66 and afterwards. I can recall, for instance, the petitions written, signatures gathered, and statements made against the election of extremely reactionary figures to the Academy of Sciences.

The liberals can be a part of the general democratic movement, but they can also be a wellspring for the forces of reaction. It is hardly worthwhile to disdain them in either case.

One incident forced me once again to contemplate the possibility of a resurgence of Stalinism. I was among those who thought that a return to Stalinism was hardly likely in our country, since the psychological atmosphere had changed radically. But, then, consider what happened in our Institute of World History just a few years ago. We were commemorating the seventieth birthday of Professor V. M. Dalin, whose return after many years in a labor camp I have already mentioned. Viktor Moiseevich was liked by all at the institute, and the hall in which the ceremony took place was full. The speakers said many nice things about the guest of honor, all of which he unquestionably deserved. But then Dalin was given the floor. He spoke rather wittily of his life, but he was almost entirely silent about the time he had spent in the camp, which had taken up at least a third of his adult life. Toward the end he became very emotional, and suddenly, in a broken voice, he exclaimed: "Comrades, let us sing our party anthem, 'The International'!" And everyone stood up and sang. Everyone, that is, except me. I stood and remained silent and thought of how the River of Blood flows and how even those who managed miraculously to escape it lost their memory and forgot about the past. Is it not true that he who forgets the past is condemned to relive it? Is it that easy, then, to whip up such a hysterical psychological atmosphere? Is it impossible to distinguish between an atmosphere in which one feels inspired to sing the party anthem and an atmosphere of offering sacrifices to the tune of that anthem?

As everyone was leaving the hall, I was approached by a woman I knew and with whom I was friendly. She said to me softly, smiling just a bit, "I know who wasn't singing 'The International'."

In our institute there is a stand on which are displayed the photographs of those who took part in the Great Fatherland War. My photograph was there as well. Once—it was in 1975—I was told that something was wrong with my picture. I went up and took a look: someone had defaced the eyes. Soon afterwards another photograph of me took its place. Someone made the suggestion that the picture had been defaced by some children who had come to see the New Year's tree at the institute, while others joked that it had been done by some woman out of jealousy. The matter was settled on that note. But I quickly realized what was going on. There had never been such an incident at the institute before.

A few months later the new photograph was simply torn off the stand. This time I was told that it was vandalism, but no one seemed intent on searching out the vandals. It was at precisely that time that it became known that I was planning to leave the country. There can be no doubt that in both cases this vandalism was done on purpose, and there were even suggestions that it had been done by a certain B., the local informer. It was typical that in this, as well as in other instances, no one from the administration or from the public organizations of the institute deemed it necessary to express to me even the slightest regret. I myself interpreted the first action as a warning from the authorities, and the second as revenge and a declaration of war.

But the tearing of the photograph was far from the only episode in recent years which had indicated to me that my position had become more difficult and would probably worsen. Here, for example, is another incident.

Donald Maclean invited me to the dissertation defense for his degree as doctor of historical sciences. Quite a few people were present—primarily officials from the Institute of World Economy and International Relations. There were only a few outsiders, and I was among them. The meeting was chaired by the institute director, Academician N. N. Inozemtsev, who was at that time a candidate member of the Communist party Central Committee.

A few minutes before the start of the meeting the academic secretary of the institute, Litvin, made a brief announcement to the audience, to the effect that the presence of noninstitute officials and even of people not directly involved in the subject under discussion was not obligatory. I regarded this as an invitation to leave the meeting hall, but I pretended not to have caught the hint and remained in my seat. Some confusion followed. But it was time to convene the meeting. Neither Inozemtsev nor Litvin wanted to ask me directly to leave the conference hall. Inozemtsev is not a stupid man, and during the break, when I walked by him, he stood and extended his hand. We exchanged a handshake. But I was distressed. Once again it had been affirmed that I was, so to speak, persona non grata, an object of hostility. Inozemtsev was an excellent barometer of the party authorities' attitude toward me.

I gained new friends during those years. They were of various nationalities: Germans, Frenchmen, Italians, Englishmen, Scandinavians, Czechs, Hungarians, Poles and even New Zealanders.

I became particularly friendly with the historian and journalist Nils Morton Udgaard, a correspondent for the Norwegian newspaper *Aftenposten*. I read his very fine book *Norway and the Great Powers during the Second*

World War, and I liked it very much. He soon left Moscow, but he managed to do me an enormous favor. I met with him in Oslo in the summer of 1976. Then fate brought me into contact with the wonderful Mario Corti and his wife, Lena. Mario worked as a translator at the Italian embassy in Moscow. His kindheartedness, as well as his excellent knowledge of the Russian language, opened the doors to the homes of many Moscow intellectuals. We became friends—I hope for life. In 1978 Mario and Lena translated my book *Punished Peoples* into Italian. Once, too, I invited guests from New Zealand to my home, and we fixed a marvelous dinner of New Zealand lamb, Muscovite vodka, and Russian hors d'oeuvres. Then we watched films about New Zealand.

That year I invited the Cortis to my home for the Christmas holidays. They had four children: a little boy, Alessio, and three girls, Olga, Alexandra, and Ilari. We made elaborate preparations for a Christmas celebration with several close friends: after all, there were going to be four children there. We brought gifts. The Cortis finally arrived. The occasion was unusually cheerful: Christmas crackers exploded, the floor was strewn with confetti. And then the children gathered in a circle and began to sing in Russian to the tune of "Frère Jacques," imitating the ring of Christmas bells:

> Artichokes and almonds
> Artichokes and almonds
> But alas
> But alas
> Do not grow
> Do not grow
> On your ass
> On your ass

I laughed so hard that I almost fell off my chair. The same went for all the other adults, and the children laughed joyfully, pleased with the effect they had made.

The Italian Ministry of Foreign Affairs did not renew its contract with Mario, apparently at the urging of the Soviet authorities. He left Moscow, but Lena stayed behind for a while with the children. We continued to meet. Once Lena left my place late, and I accompanied her through our dark courtyard. Suddenly, from behind the trees, a figure appeared in our path. I squeezed my friend's hand and whispered to her: "Keep calm. He's just trying to scare us." But she was calm anyway. We had hardly emerged from under the archway when someone else began to follow us. We stepped out onto Lenin Prospekt, where her car was parked near the Cinemaphile shop. Across the avenue, on a bench, three people were sitting. My friend got into her car and drove off. I made my way home. Suddenly someone shouted behind me, "Hey, Pops, wait a minute!" Without turning my head or losing a step, I continued along the street. Once again came the shouting: "Hey, wait a minute!" I returned home upset, wondering how Lena was. Finally, she phoned. I went to bed relieved. A few days later I heard that somebody had smashed the windshield of Lena's car. When she returned to Italy I learned that, as she was on her way from the Soviet Union to Poland, driving at top speed, one of her tires blew out, and she survived only by some miracle.

So the months passed. Only contact with the outside world made my life bearable.

Time went by, and my concerns, my uneasy feelings about my professional degradation, took ever-greater hold on me. A historian, like a writer, needs to have his reading public. If he doesn't have it, then he gradually fades, and he loses his professional skills. I worked, I wrote, and then I put away in a desk drawer whatever I had written. Things could not go on that way forever.

In January 1975 I decided to clarify my situation radically. First of all, I tried to gain the support of my trade union organization, of which I had been a member since 1937. Naturally, I had no illusions about the role played by trade union organizations in our country, especially in our institute, but I felt the need to exhaust all legal possibilities before deciding on extreme action. My talk with the chairman of our local committee Z. G. Samodurova, was calm, unhurried, and quite frank. Samodurova asked me not to rush her for a response, to give her a month in which to air my grievances. I agreed. My request was clear and simple: that the authorities stop the discrimination, evaluate my work on the basis of its quality, and treat me like any other research scholar. I cautioned Samodurova that if I did not receive a satisfactory response, I would have to think about changing my life.

A month later Samodurova came up to me and with obvious relief told me: "I spoke with Yevgeny Mikhailovich"—that is, with Zhukov, the institute director—"and he told me that the higher authorities are dealing with you, and that it is not for the trade union to handle this matter. He also said, 'If Nekrich has any further questions, he should come to me.'"

So a few days later I went to Zhukov and explained to him quite frankly my view of the situation as it existed. I gave many examples of how I was being discriminated against. Naturally Zhukov was fully aware of what had been going on. His response was extremely simple: "Everything depends on you yourself. If you were to show..." He stopped short here for a moment, searching for the proper words, and then went on, "great loyalty, or whatever, toward the party Control Committee, then your situation would change immediately."

"I would not wish to link the question of my party membership with my status as senior research staff member at the institute and with my civil rights. Let us draw a distinction between these two issues. As far as my being in the party is concerned, in the seven years since my expulsion from the party, there have been no new documents or materials which might have shaken my point of view on the events of 1941."

"So, you see," said Zhukov, making a helpless gesture with his hands.

"Quite the contrary," I went on. "All the materials published since 1967 strengthen my point of view."

"Which ones, for example?"

"A compilation of documents entitled *USSR Border Troops, 1939-1941*, Khrushchev's memoirs . . . "

"What memoirs are you talking about? They are a very unreliable source."

"I found in Khrushchev's memoirs a description of two episodes in one of which I myself had participated, and the other one of which I knew all about."

Zhukov became interested. I told him about the talk Khrushchev had had with the German prisoners of war from Manstein's army, which had rushed to Paulus' rescue just before Christmas 1942. "I was present at that talk and even compiled a record of the proceedings. The second episode involved the suicide of a member of the military council of General Larin's Second Guards' Army in that same month of December. Khrushchev, apparently, had an excellent memory." I concluded, "I have no doubts that the memoirs are genuine."

Zhukov remained silent. Then I summarized my requests in five points: (1) publication of the monograph *British Policy in Europe, 1941-1945*, which I had written in accordance with the work program and which had been approved for publication by the institute's academic council; (2) an end to the discrimination against my other work and a lifting of the ban on my articles in professional periodical journals; (3) assignment of graduate students to me; (4) participation in academic conferences; and (5) a lifting of the ban on travel abroad. I asked Zhukov to take my request very seriously and warned him that a refusal to halt the discrimination would compel me to think about redirecting my entire life, so that "the final years remaining to me for creative work would not be for nothing, as have been the past seven years."

Zhukov promised to negotiate with the proper authorities, and on that note our talk ended. A month later I found out that in Leningrad, at the beginning of April, there was to be a symposium of Soviet and foreign historians on problems in German-Soviet relations before Hitler's rise to power. This issue was of great interest to me, and it was closely connected with my research on the origins of the Soviet-German pact of August 23, 1939, on which I had been working for many years.

I went to see the deputy director, Ivan Ivanovich Zhigalov, who was responsible for our section. Zhigalov at first took a negative view of my request, putting forward all kinds of senseless arguments, including the question of payment for travel and living expenses in Leningrad. But after I told him that I was prepared to go at my own expense, he promised that he would speak to the chairman of the organizational committee for the symposium, the director of the Institute of USSR History, Academician A. L. Narochnitsky. He said he would give me a reply soon. Actually he did call me back shortly and told me that Narochnitsky had taken a sharply negative stand, saying, "I shall categorically protest Aleksandr Moiseevich's participation in the symposium." Whether that really was the case or not I do not know, but that is not the main point. The main point is that the denial of my right to be present at the symposium was virtually an answer to my request to Zhukov during our last meeting. At least, that was how I interpreted it. I should add that in the months to follow, Zhukov did not express any intention of giving me a formal reply to the request I had made. It became obvious to me that I could expect no change whatsoever in my situation, except for the worse—such as being dismissed during a regular cutback in staff or perhaps just giving in.

So, I had my back up against the wall. After the refusal to let me go to a seminar in Leningrad—not London, not Paris, not even Sofia, but Leningrad!—I felt that I no longer wanted to put up with this anymore. I decided to move away, to leave my country.

Did I have any other options? Yes, I did. For example, I could have chosen not to care one bit about anything, just work at my profession enough to continue receiving my salary, which was rather high by Soviet standards, and at the age of sixty be put on a retirement pension—also a decent pension by Soviet standards. Live a little, if possible, to my own satisfaction, and then go on to a better world. That, in fact, is how the majority of Soviets live. My life in Moscow had been mapped out for the remainder of my days. I could even imagine how one of my well-wishers, on hearing about my passing, might ask the Institute of World History to organize my funeral, how the telephones would be buzzing at the Central Committee science department, how they would advise that a commemoration not be held in the institute building but, at most, that representatives of the trade union organization be sent to my funeral. Quite frankly, such an enchanting prospect I found to be neither joyful nor attractive.

There was another option. I could remain in my own country and wage a struggle for human rights, a path I had embarked on practically before there was any dissident movement. My commitment began, as the reader will recall, back in Stalinist times, when I was a graduate student. In recent years I had taken step after step toward the dissident movement, growing increasingly close to them. My statements at the funerals of academicians A. M. Deborin (1963) and A. L. Mongait (1974) were in open defiance of conformism. And then of course there was my book *June 22, 1941*, and the events pertaining to it.

I also believe that the activities of the party committee of the Institute of History from 1964 to 1966 objectively helped prevent a widespread onslaught of neo-Stalinism in historical scholarship and to some extent deprived that attack of momentum in the social sciences in general. I would also like to think that I did something to help a few people free themselves from the ideological influence of conformism. I shall not exaggerate the numbers—there were only a few of them—but I did at least this much.

All the while I understood more and more clearly that most people were indifferent to the events taking place around them. I was not at all certain that the population in general was intent on gaining and safeguarding human rights. The familiarity of conformism, requiring no special thinking or decision making, suited the people much more than slogans proclaiming a struggle for human rights. For in any struggle the participants face the prospect of having to be prepared to shoulder responsibility for some goal or for the fate of some other person. But it was precisely the habit of making their own individual decisions that the Soviet people were made unaccustomed to during the years of Soviet power. This turned out to be extremely convenient and totally in conformity with certain established attitudes: "I am not me and this is not my hut", or " Our affair is raising calves—piss off, and off to the barn with you," and so on.

The dissidents were harassed and persecuted, sent into forced labor camps, to prisons, and to psychiatric hospitals. Others, in accordance with the subtle designs of the authorities, were not only left free but were somehow acknowledged as a kind of "loyal opposition." I was acquainted with and even friendly with some of the dissidents, and I used to help them as much as I could, but I still tried not to be included totally in that movement. I preferred, as I have said, to march under my own banner.

Still, one way out would be to participate actively in the dissident movement. And I thought about this possiblity on many occasions. I was not frightened of the consequences, although I fully realized that I could not be a hundred percent sure that I would not be subject to physical torture in a labor camp or in prison. What worried me was something altogether different: Did the people need *me* to defend them? It has been a common occurrence throughout history that prophets or false prophets have spoken out on behalf of the people without ever being authorized by the people to do so. No doubt only a spontaneous outbreak of national feeling, expressed in terms of violent action, might reflect for the briefest moment an entire people's way of thinking, and these aspirations might likewise be expressed in folk songs and folk tales.

It is true that one may enter the dissident movement not only for the sake of defending people's rights but also for the sake of self-expression. Here, in this movement, joined in the search for truth and threatened by danger, people may find themselves. Their action, their alienation, imbues them with self-respect and gives them a goal in life. But once in the movement, one must possess a profound mind, a talent for self-criticism, and the ability to take a hard look at oneself in order not to harden into a revolutionary dogmatist or a reverse conformist. History has seen so many examples.

I also thought that I could make my contribution to the democratic movement most successfully within my profession, in the field of history. This is why, in the final years of my life in Moscow, I wrote a short book entitled *Punished Peoples*, about the deportation of the peoples of the Caucasus, the Crimean Tatars, and the Kalmyks and their subsequent fate. At the same time, I began to write this book, a book of remembrances, tentatively entitled *Forsake Fear*. That was in 1972, when I was still far from making a final decision as to whether I should remain in my native country or leave it. My decision took shape gradually under the influence of both the overall political situation in the country and my personal position. I had gained internal freedom, but I was in need of external freedom as well.

The institute director's refusal to grant me a recommendation for a trip to Hungary reflected, naturally, not so much his personal attitude toward me as the instructions given him from above with regard to my personal status. My index card in the file of the party Central Committee must have stipulated clearly what was allowed for me and what was forbidden. I suspect that a notation could be found there to this effect (I cannot swear by the accuracy of the wording, but I can swear to its contents): "publications limited," "books not to be published," "travel abroad prohibited," and so on.

My attempts to get my book published did not meet with success. The authorities expected capitulation, repentance, but for me this was absolutely out of the question. And so, the line was clearly drawn. I decided to leave my country and go into voluntary (if it can be called that) exile. In the summer of 1975 I managed to enter into contact with my cousin Vera, who had left Latvia for Palestine, where she had been living since 1932 and was by now, as I soon learned, a mother and a grandmother with numerous offspring.

Our relationship had its own history. In 1932, when I learned of her intention to leave for Palestine, I wrote her a horrible letter, of which I was ashamed for the rest of my life. I accused her of betraying the international proletariat and so on. Her mother, my dearly beloved Aunt Ioanna, once said many years later that Vera cried after she received my letter. When I wrote this letter I was twelve years old, but somehow that did not console me.

Therefore, first of all, I sent my cousin a letter in which I simply asked forgiveness for my disgusting action. In reply I received from her a very wise message which was also very important to me. Vera cautioned me not to make a hasty decision, and she described quite precisely and objectively the difficulties I would have to face in my new situation. After a year of living in the West, I must admit that she foresaw a great deal. Then, in October, Vera sent me a formal invitation to settle in Israel.

Before that, in August 1975, my mother had died. This was a matter of chance, foolish and tragic. I had gone to Donald's dacha for three days, and when I returned, I did not find my mother at home. It turned out that on going out into the courtyard of our building, she had fallen and had broken her hip. Two weeks later she was gone. We were very close spiritually, and her death was one of the harshest blows I have ever suffered. My father had died earlier, in 1965, and I had said farewell to Nadya in 1973.

After my mother's death, I felt as if loneliness had caught me by the throat with an iron grip. For several weeks I did not have the strength to remain long in my mother's room. I had friends who had been with me for many years, and together we had had our share of joy and sorrow. And yet, when I returned home, I felt alone—alone with my thoughts and with the absence of certain people—and this was not easy. I felt that I needed to leave Moscow at least for a while.

For a long time, over the course of many years, some of my university friends had been trying to get me to make a trip to visit them in Tashkent in Central Asia, where I had never been. So, in September 1975, I joined them there. Our travels began in Tashkent. We visited Samarkand, Khiva, Bukhara, and Nukus, the capital of the Kara-Kalpak autonomous region, where there is a remarkable art museum established by an artist and collector. You won't find another like it, not only in the Soviet Union but outside it either. We traveled from Frunze, the capital of Kirghizia, along the shore of the mountain lake Issyk Kul, and found ourselves in Przheval'sk, a charming little town in the foothills of the Tien Shan Mountains. There stands a monument to the great Russian explorer Przheval'skii. Rumor has it that he was Stalin's real father. At any rate, the portraits and sculptures of him really do remind one of Stalin's features. From Przheval'sk we flew to Alma-Ata, the capital of Kazakhstan. To make a long story short, in one month we covered all of Central Asia except for Turkmenia and Tadzhikistan. There just wasn't enough time.

These travels will undoubtedly remain among the most vivid impressions of my life. And this was so thanks to the concern of my dear friends in Tashkent.

When I returned to Moscow, I opened the door to my apartment and discovered on the floor a pile of letters. Among them was the one I had been waiting for with such impatience—a formal invitation to emigrate from Vera.

My talk with Zhukov was extremely brief.

"You're firmly decided?"

"Yes, of course. I did warn you of such a possibility nine months in advance. Since that time you have not given me any answer."

Zhukov remained silent as I took leave of him. I received my background report in ten days. Two weeks later, after gathering the necessary documents, I submitted a request for an exit visa.

At first the institute accepted my decision quite calmly. But in mid-January 1976 the attitude toward me changed drastically. On someone's orders the director, Zhukov, convened the most reliable staff members of the institute, some forty people who made up the so-called active group. At that meeting he made an announcement about my intention to leave. He did not conceal the fact that I had been to see him the previous February and had made demands, which in his words "the institute could not meet," and had warned him of the possibility of my moving away. They say that there is no retreating for those who wish to speak out. Especially clamorous in their response were a number of young people, quite reminiscent of that infamous year of 1937. But it was not their statements that saddened me, especially since it was no real secret that some of them were working not just for the institute. I was saddened by the statements made by members of the older generation, people such as S. L. Utchenko and V. M. Dalin. Especially the last. Dalin had spent twenty years in a labor camp and remained psychologically just where he had been at the time of his arrest. And yet Dalin was a genuine scholar, an impartial thinker. Someone who spoke at the meeting shouted hysterically: "Nekrich has betrayed the ideals for which he has shed his blood!" Patently false statements were made as well. The staff meeting adopted a resolution condemning my act of "treason" and recommended holding similar meetings in the party section organizations.

The condemnation procedure went on for a month and a half, ending only as February drew to a close.

I myself was not present at any of the meetings. I had been invited to the staff meeting, but in a rather strange manner: I received a phone call telling me that I was being called in by the director, and was given a specific time. The cowardice of this final vile act was obvious: the director of the institute was afraid of telling me openly why I was being summoned. I understood this ploy and did not go to the meeting, assuming reasonably that I might lose my temper or be provoked to harsh words by someone. Furthermore, what these people wanted to do was to get on my nerves, something which they had been trying to achieve in various ways over the past seven years. Did they really think I would break down at this final moment? Our interests were diametrically opposed. If they wanted me to attend, then I would not go. And so I stayed away.

Soon after the meeting held in our party section organization, at which someone claimed that I was all but connected with Bonn, the overwhelming majority of my section colleagues stopped speaking to me.

I felt no anger deep down. Instead, I felt sorry for these people, with whom I had worked side by side for so many years, I felt sorry that they had agreed voluntarily to endure such humiliation.

I continued to carry out my responsibilities, completing my scheduled work on a collective study of the history of the British working class. The volume was entitled *The British Working Class and the Second World War*. I submitted it on schedule and waited for a discussion which never took place.

Sometime later I was called in by the institute's academic secretary, N. Kalmykov, who informed me that at all the meetings a resolution had been unanimously adopted condemning my decision to leave the Soviet Union, and that the view had been expressed that I should leave the institute after submitting a statement requesting to be released from my position.

I asked Kalmykov to show me the records of the proceedings, but he replied that the records were with the director and that I could not see them until they had been corrected. This never did happen. My reply to Kalmykov was crystal clear: emigration was officially permitted by the Soviet government. I had submitted documents for travel and was awaiting a response in accordance with the law. This matter was to be decided on by agencies specifically authorized to do so by the government. Any meetings, condemnations, and so on were an amateur performance and were in flagrant violation of the law. Therefore, I firmly rejected any resolutions adopted at such meetings and would calmly await the decisions of the appropriate bodies. I intended to continue my work at the institute until such time as I received permission for travel. Of course, if the institute wished me to leave as soon as possible, then why did it not address the proper agencies and ask them to speed up the visa procedure? Our talk ended on that note and was never resumed.

Although I had been condemned by the overwhelming majority of the staff, there were to be found among them a few courageous people who refused to support the proposed resolution, saying that the issue of emigration was a personal matter and not a subject for public inquiry. Several staff members simply did not appear at the meetings where I was condemned on various pretexts. Yes, much had changed since the time of Stalin's death. The feeling of self-respect had grown immeasurably, and it will continue to grow, destroying the roots of conformism. This process can be stopped only by a resumption of mass terror, and I believe the time for that is past.

Sometime in mid-April of that year I turned on the radio and heard a BBC report on the Omsk ttrial of Mustafa Dzhemilev, leader of the Crimean

Tatar movement for the restoration of their rights and the return to their homeland. He was to leave prison, having served out his sentence, but the hangmen did not wish to let this courageous man go free, for they had not succeeded in breaking his will. At the time of the trial clashes had occurred during which the guards had raised their hand against Academician Sakharov and his wife. When I heard that, I was suddenly overcome by such anger that I could not control myself. I sat down and wrote an appeal to my fellow historians to protest. After calming down somewhat, I phoned Sakharov but found out that he had not yet returned from Omsk. I decided to wait for him to arrive, in order to obtain reliable information about what had happened. We met after he had been interviewed by foreign correspondents about the trial. When I expressed my sympathy to Sakharov and his wife, he replied, "I'm not the one who needs an expression of sympathy, Dzhemilev is." He was right, of course.

Around this time I phoned Reuters and agreed to meet with a correspondent from the agency. We met near the Obraztsov puppet theater on the Sadovoye Kol'tso. As I walked up to him, a black KGB Volga sedan pulled away from the theater. Due note had been taken of our meeting. But that was the least of my worries. I decided that it would be a mistake on my part if I were to give my statement only to representatives of the bourgeois press. I thought it wrong as a matter of principle for dissidents to ignore the communist press in the West, for they thus deprived themselves of the opportunity of appealing to all currents of public opinion abroad. And I had often said as much to the dissidents. I did not find the correspondents for *Humanité* and *Unità* at home, but I did transmit my statement to a correspondent from the British communist newspaper, the *Morning Star*. It must be said that the London *Morning Star* was the first Western newspaper to publish my statement in full (for a text of the statement, see my book *The Punished Peoples*, W. W. Norton, 1979). The April 21 edition of the newspaper was taken off the stands in Moscow. And so it happened that I involuntarily caused the newspaper some financial harm.

My statement was greeted by the public with understanding. This was not the case with others of my colleagues, to whom the appeal had been addressed in particular. Some of them reproached me for putting them in a difficult moral situation, in that I was planning to leave the country. The view that my statement was inappropriate because of my forthcoming departure was expressed by several other people as well. I did not then nor do I now consider these reproaches to be just, since I had made this statement before receiving permission for travel abroad, while I still continued to live in Moscow and work at the Academy of Sciences. This is what I believed then and I have not changed my opinion: one must be free to express one's agreement or disagreement publicly at any time, regardless of one's life plans. I knew that many of my friends shared this conviction.

Permission for travel came five and a half months after I had submitted the request—on May 24, 1976. I wasn't even sent the usual notice from OVIR, the visa registry, but instead I received a telephone call warning me that I had two weeks to prepare for departure. But the deadline for leaving was June 1, only six days away! In response to my confused question, the OVIR inspector asked me in a concerned tone of voice, "What do you mean, six days?"

"Count them yourself," I told her.

She counted, and then she said that the deadline would be set for June 7. I had only twelve days left—not a very long time for a fifty-six-year-old scholar who had lived his entire life in the USSR. But there was nothing I could do about it. True, I could ask for a postponement, but I knew from other people's experience that this would result in meetings with officials who would make counter proposals and suggestions. I did not want to face that. So I began to make preparations for my departure.

The day after receiving permission for travel, on May 25, 1976, I went to an appeals hearing for Mustafa Dzhemilev at the RSFSR Supreme Court, which is located on Kuybyshev Street. I expected to meet a large crowd of dissidents and of the accused's relatives, but when I got to the third floor, where the hearing was to take place, I found only a few people: Andrei Dmitrievich Sakharov, Pyotr Grigorevich Grigorenko and his wife, Nina Ivanovna Bukovskaya; then Ada Naidenovich came up and joined us. There were a few other people, but I did not know all their names. No one was allowed into the meeting hall except for Dzhemilev's sister, so we all cooled our heels in a small cubbyhole of a room next door to the typing pool. At least there was a window, so it was bright in there. From time to time we went out to the stairwell, where militiamen and officials were standing guard. They looked at me with interest, but apparently did not recognize my face; then a few more agents appeared, evidently called in to help establish my identity. They soon figured out who I was; this was easy, since my name was mentioned several times as I was introduced to people.

In the cubbyhole with us there sat a pregnant woman whom none of us knew, apparently a KGB official, who listened carefully to our conversations. Ada began to seethe at this, and we managed to calm her down only with great difficulty. I was surprised when, about an hour and a half later, this pregnant woman was replaced by another female official, also pregnant! This amused me considerably, for at least it meant that the employment security laws were being strictly observed in some agencies, where pregnant officials were being sent out for "light" work such as overt observation and eavesdropping. I was amazed at the significant number of women among the officials present there. It had never occurred to me before that so many women were doing operations work.

Finally, the court proceedings were adjourned. Through the door of the conference hall came Dzhemilev's sister, a small, fragile figure with a very pleasant face and a mild manner. I was introduced to her, and we exchanged kisses in greeting. We were both touched. Dzhemilev's sister told us that the trial, as usual, had been nothing but a farce, that all the convincing evidence for the defense had been rejected, and the denial by the main witness for the prosecution, Vladimir Dvoryansky, of testimony made under pressure during the pretrial investigation had not been taken into account. The severe sentence handed down by the court in Omsk had been confirmed. We went out on to the street and said good-bye to one another. Andrei Dmitrievich and I went to the Metro station. Two meters from us on the curbside, two officials in militia uniform were walking down the sidewalk. One of them unabashedly held a listening device in his hands. As I approached the entryway to my building, these two got into a car parked by the entrance. Evidently they had wondered where I would go after leaving the courthouse.

Parting. Friends come to visit, and they wind up packing my suitcases for me. From time to time I go over to them and joke a bit, but my heart aches. Here are the kind hands of my friends sending me on my way: that small, fragile, courageous woman and her husband—I jokingly call a jealous man—and another woman who, possibly, is still in love with me. Still other partings from my closest friends. One of them has the strong profile of a Roman centurion and bright blue eyes. Friends come and go. Precious minutes in a life to be left behind forever. My God, is it really true that I shall never see them again?

Never? I hate that word. *Never*: it means nothingness, death, oblivion. I try to reassure myself that of course I will see them again. It will happen, it will happen—I inspire them with this belief, and so, no doubt, we will meet again. But for now we must part for a time, until we meet again.

And another parting with those who stay behind in this country, in order to continue the struggle for human rights. They remain, these courageous people: Sakharov, Grigorenko, Orlov, and others. Last meetings, handshakes, good wishes to send me on my way. On the eve of my departure I learn that a group has been established to monitor compliance with the Helsinki agreement.

There is a final gathering at my home with my friends. I have given away all my belongings to friends and relatives, but I have asked them not to touch anything before my departure. I want to leave my home in a state of order, as if I were leaving not for good but for a short while, to leave my home as it has always been.

Then I am being seen off at the airport. We say good-bye: embraces, kisses, tears, wishes for a safe trip. I climb the stairs to the upper level, leaving my friends standing below. I motion farewell with a wave of the hand and shout out gaily, like a slogan, "Penga-Penga!" (I would say to my friends as a joke that I was going to a desert island in the Pacific called Penga-Penga.) I call out cheerfully. Down below they are smiling, laughing, waving their hands. I pass behind the enclosure. Tears well up my throat, and I burst into sobs. But I take hold of myself. I regain my composure. I once said to someone who left Moscow before me, as if by way of consolation: "Remember, the world is an enormous and wonderful place. You only need to forsake fear." And now I suddenly remember my own words.

April 1972 – September 1977
Moscow – Cambridge, Massachusetts

Index